Table of Conte

Frontmatter 1
Dedication 3
Preface 5
Foreword 7
1. Introduction 9
2. Prerequisites 11
    2.1. Who this book is for 11
    2.2. What you need for this book 11
    2.3. Conventions 11
    2.4. Reader feedback 12
    2.5. Getting the Code 13
    2.6. Building the Code 13
    2.7. Running the Code 13
    2.8. Some Foundational Java 14
    2.9. Next Steps 17
3. Bootstrap 19
    3.1. A Big ol' Bag o' Beans 25
    3.2. The `CustomerService` 25
    3.3. An Inflexible Implementation 28
    3.4. A Parameterized Implementation 33
    3.5. Templates 35
    3.6. A Context For Your Application 39
    3.7. Component Scanning 48
    3.8. Declarative Container Services with `@Enable*` Annotations .. 51
    3.9. A "Bootiful" Application 54
    3.10. But What If... 64
    3.11. Deployment 66
    3.12. Next Steps 67
4. IO, IO, It's Off to Work We Go 69

  4.1. A Natural Limit 71
  4.2. The Missing Metaphor 75
  4.3. The Reactive Streams Initiative 77
  4.4. Are We There Yet? 79
  4.5. Towards a More Functional, Reactive Spring 81
  4.6. Next Steps 82
5. Reactor 83
  5.1. The Reactive Streams Specification 84
  5.2. Project Reactor 88
  5.3. Creating New Reactive Streams 90
  5.4. Processors 96
  5.5. Operators 100
  5.6. Operator Fusion 114
  5.7. Schedulers and Threads 115
  5.8. Hot and Cold Streams 122
  5.9. Context 128
  5.10. Control Flow 130
  5.11. Debugging 142
  5.12. Next Steps 149
6. Data Access 151
  6.1. Why Should You Go Reactive? 151
  6.2. What About Transactions? 152
  6.3. Reactive SQL Data Access 156
  6.4. More Efficient, Reactive Data Access in NoSQL Pastures 175
  6.5. Review 195
  6.6. Next Steps 195
7. HTTP 197
  7.1. HTTP Works 197
  7.2. HTTP Scales 199
  7.3. REST 201
  7.4. Spring WebFlux: a Net-New Reactive Web Runtime 202
  7.5. Long-Lived Client Connections 230

- 7.6. Server-Sent Events (SSE) 232
- 7.7. Websockets 235
- 7.8. Reactive Views with Thymeleaf 248
- 7.9. A Reactive Servlet Container 256
- 7.10. The Reactive Client 258
- 7.11. Security 269
- 7.12. Next Steps 277
- 8. Testing 279
  - 8.1. How I Stopped Worrying and Learned to Love Testing 279
  - 8.2. Test-Driven Development 282
  - 8.3. Inside-Out or Outside-In 283
  - 8.4. The `Customer` Object is Always Right (Right?) 284
  - 8.5. A Repository of (Untested) Knowledge 287
  - 8.6. On The Web, No One Knows You're a Reactive Stream 292
  - 8.7. The `Customer` is Always Right! 296
  - 8.8. The `Customer` Is Not Always Right 303
  - 8.9. Next Steps 314
- 9. RSocket 315
  - 9.1. Motivations for RSocket 315
  - 9.2. Common Infrastructure for Raw RSocket 319
  - 9.3. Raw RSocket 323
  - 9.4. Bootiful RSocket 348
  - 9.5. Security 384
  - 9.6. Spring Integration 391
  - 9.7. Next Steps 398
- 10. Service Orchestration and Composition 401
  - 10.1. Service Registration and Discovery 402
  - 10.2. Some Simple Sample Services 404
  - 10.3. Client Side Loadbalancing in the `WebClient` 418
  - 10.4. Resilient Streams with Reactor Operators 421
  - 10.5. Resilient Streams with Resilience4J 426
  - 10.6. Hedging 436

10.7. Reactive Scatter/Gather	442
10.8. API Gateways with Spring Cloud Gateway	449
10.9. Next Steps	467
11. Action!	469
11.1. Websites to Bookmark	469
11.2. Additional reading	469
11.3. Next Steps	470
About the Author	471
Acknowledgements	473
Colophon for *Reactive Spring*	475

Frontmatter

Reactive Spring by Josh Long

© 2020 Josh Long. All rights reserved.

ISBN: 978-1-7329104-1-6 Version 1.0.

Reactive Spring logo (as used in the cover design and elsewhere) is used with license and permission.

While the author has used reasonable faith efforts to ensure that the information and instructions in this work are accurate, the author disclaims all responsibility for errors or omissions, including without limitation, responsibility for damages resulting from the use of or reliance on this work. The use of the information and instructions contained in this work is at your own risk. If any code samples or other technology this work contains or describes is subject to open source licenses or the intellectual property rights of others, it is your responsibility to ensure that your use thereof complies with such licenses and/or rights.

Reactive Spring

Dedication

To my "bears:" my partner Tammie and her daughter Kimly, who have become my family, and with whom I dare to dream of a better tomorrow: I love you both so much.

To my late father, Clark Long, who passed away in December 2019: we miss you and love you. Rest in peace, dad.

To Dr. Fauci and the men and women of the world who labor (hopefully by the time you're reading this, we'll be able to use the past tense: *labored*) tirelessly to save lives during the COVID-19 pandemic: thank you.

Reactive Spring

Preface

I am terrible at writing books. I am good at iterating on books. But, getting them done? So that they're in the past? In the rearview mirror? That's a different thing altogether. I'm terrible at writing books.

I wrote this book thinking I could take a reasonably large 70+ page, multipart article that I had co-authored by with my buddy and Java industry legend Matt Raible, flesh it out, and turn it into a book. That was mid-2018, and here we finally are! It's been *years*. I've traveled more than a million miles since 2018. I've been to every continent and dozens of countries many times since then. And it's only 2020 as I write this. I knew writing something would be difficult with my commitments to work and my growing family, but I still wanted to try.

There was one more problem: Spring. You see, Spring grows and evolves and does more and more exciting things day by day. It's a whirlwind! I wish that I could write fast enough to capture the state of the art, and then publish, but I just can't.

This book represents my best attempt at keeping up. It's filled with focused analyses on the various things you'll need to understand when building reactive services and systems with Spring.

I wrote this because this is the book I wish I could have read when I first started with reactive programming. It's not easy, but here I am on the other side of the conceptual chasm, and it was worth the effort.

Reality informs architecture, and reactive programming is a sea-tide change in architecture representing the changing, cloudy realities of production. Reactive programming emerged in its current form in research in academia and then in the industry at organizations like Microsoft, Netflix, VMware, and Lightbend. As you read this, we're more than a decade into the evolution of those applied practices. It's no accident than reactive programming emerged in the industry around the same time as microservices.

While I know what production looks like without reactive programming, I don't like to think about it. I can't imagine what the architecture of production looks like without reactive programming. By the time you finish this book, dear reader, you too will be able to and want to build production-optimized software and services. Production is the happiest place on Earth. You'll love it there.

Josh Long
Summer, 2020

Foreword

Dear Reader,

Welcome to the Reactive Revolution! It's been a few years since the concept of Reactive Systems was first floated as an answer to all sorts of scalability and resiliency problems. With the maturity of the ecosystem, standards, and practices around Reactive, there has never been a better time to start learning about it.

During the last decade, I dedicated most of my energy to exploring and crafting "non-blocking" solutions, including Project Reactor. It allowed me to meet with many engineers from different horizons.

One thing I've learned is that writing more efficient software is rarely the focus of engineering groups. One possible cause is the endless race to market new features faster than our competition to improve our productivity.

But what if you could both have efficiency and productivity? Here you have it in a nutshell: the mission of the Spring Reactive stack.

I can't think of a better mentor than Josh to guide you, and I hope you will enjoy reading him as much as I did! In this book, Josh has depicted pragmatic use cases and code samples to demonstrate Reactive Programming's value.

You will learn everything about the game-changing aspect of "flow control," something your container resources will never stop loving. You will start transforming your blocking services into non-blocking ones and understanding its ramifications. You will get more vertical as you start diving into the web layer and the data layer. In the process, you will accumulate more and more knowledge of Project Reactor, the reactive library of choice for building Spring applications.

Finally, once you have mastered designing Reactive microservices, the book will invite you to its penultimate software design lesson: Distributed Reactive Systems with RSocket.

My friend has worked extra hard to make this journey fun and rewarding for the curious mind. I am incredibly proud that someone as talented as Josh took the time to introduce to the world the collective effort I had the chance to be part of. You will soon understand he is one of those humans who love sharing their in-depth knowledge whenever you need it. He will do so in a concise way because he respects your time.

Dear Reader, I must warn you. Do not devour the book too quickly, or you might feel as overwhelmed as I do, and you will eagerly wait for your next chance to learn from Josh Long.

Stephane Maldini
Project Reactor co-founder
Senior Software Engineer | Productivity Engineering - Runtime Java Platform
Netflix Los Gatos

Chapter 1. Introduction

Welcome to the reactive revolution! You hold in your hands a guided tour to the wide and wonderful reactive world of Spring.

Reactive programming intends to help you build more efficient, more resilient services to respond to cloud-native, distributed, microservices realities. Today's architectures are different. They must contend with several demands that are more exacerbated than ever, if not entirely novel. Today's architectures must support agility, so they are typically decomposed into smaller, singly focused, bounded-contexts, or *microservices*, to better align with team sizes. Microservices enable continuous delivery. Microservices also imply more network communication as services are distributed. That decomposition also implies more risk, more volatility. Services may change more readily. They may disappear; they may suffer outages, etc.

Reactive programming is a way to address these demands. It gives you a pattern and paradigm that embraces the volatile nature of distributed systems. It introduces a new way to think about building services keeping in mind that computers have finite resources, even in the cloud. Reactive programming changes how we think about interactions between actors in a system, moving from push-based to a pull-based approach.

I love reactive programming, and I've tried over and over to embrace it over the years. I was there when we released the first versions of Reactor back in 2011. I was there when we shipped WebSocket-support infrastructure based on Reactor in Spring Framework 4 in 2013. I saw the potential, but it just didn't seem sufficiently ready. I couldn't see a way to mesh the reactive programming paradigm with Spring's component model. Then came Spring Framework 5, which promoted reactive programming as a core part of the abstraction. That release changed my perspective. Suddenly it was possible to write end-to-end reactive applications. Suddenly, I could do a comprehensive demo! And so I did. I've been doing talks, blogs, articles, podcasts, and now a book on reactive programming for *years*, buoyed in part by my natural enthusiasm for the topic and in part to the considerable community feedback I get due to my visibility in the ecosystem.

I love reactive programming. It helps me complete the cloud-native arc, going from monoliths, to microservices, to resilient, cloud-native systems. It yields more functional, safer, more resilient, scalable software. But I didn't invent it. I didn't even jump on to the bandwagon at the outset. I wasn't even a first-mover. I waited for others to pave the way. And pave they did. If you've been paying attention, you'll know that Netflix, one of the largest-scale services on the planet (with tons of services built on Spring), embraced reactive programming nearly a decade ago. And you'll know that Alibaba (with tons of services built on Spring) has also embraced reactive programming. You'll see that some of the largest sites on the planet choose to embrace reactive programming because it allows them to build better, more production-ready software.

You can enjoy the same benefits if you build reactive services on Spring, friends. It's not a hypothetical; it has already been demonstrated by some of the largest organizations on the planet. Join me on this adventure, and together, we'll build reactive Spring-powered applications and services.

Nows a great time to get started. I release this book confident than many (if not every) use-case that most applications will have are now supported. It's the best time to embrace the paradigm shift; you'll be joining the critical mass of people also making a move, and you'll be there to help pave the path for the stragglers who leap later.

Don't get left behind. Turn the next page, and we'll begin our journey to production with *Reactive Spring*.

Chapter 2. Prerequisites

Ah ah! Not so fast, friend! I know you want to skip ahead, and I don't blame you! But let's take a few minutes to establish some conventions before we get too far down the path.

2.1. Who this book is for

This book assumes you've got some familiarity with writing and running Java, but that's about it. The main goal is to help people get to production and build better, more reactive services. Perhaps you've heard about reactive programming and want it explained, and you want those explanations married to practical applications. If so, I am happy to confirm that you're reading the right book!

2.2. What you need for this book

To try code samples in this book, you will need a computer running an up-to-date operating system (Windows, Linux, or Mac OS X). You'll need Java 8 or better, and Maven 3.3 or later. We'll introduce additional dependencies, like, for example, a database like MongoDB, as they come up on an as-needed basis.

2.3. Conventions

We use several typographical conventions within this book that distinguish between different kinds of information.

Code in the text, including commands, variables, file names, CSS class names, and property names are shown as follows:

> Spring Boot uses a `public static void main` entry-point that launches an embedded web server for you.

A block of code is set out as follows. It may be colored, depending on the format in which you're reading this book. If I want to call your attention to specific lines of code, the lines will be annotated using numbers accompanied by brief descriptions.

```
@Service ①
class SimpleService {
}
```

① this is a Spring stereotype annotation

> Tips are shown using callouts like this.

> Warnings are shown using callouts like this.

> **Sidebar**
>
> Additional information about a particular topic may be displayed in a sidebar like this one.

Finally, this text shows what a quote looks like:

> Spring Boot lets you pair-program with the Spring team.
>
> — Me

2.4. Reader feedback

I'm always happy to have your feedback.

To send feedback (questions, comments, or anything else), please e-mail me at ReactiveSpring@joshlong.com [mailto:ReactiveSpring@joshlong.com] or send a tweet to @ReactiveSpring [http://twitter.com/ReactiveSpring].

2.5. Getting the Code

The code for everything in this book (including the publication pipeline I used to build the book itself!) is available at github.com/Reactive-Spring-Book [http://github.com/Reactive-Spring-Book]. It's all Apache 2 licensed, and I encourage you to use it and - if you're feeling so inclined and happen something to motivate it - to file issues or send pull requests! I'd be happy to help, either way.

2.6. Building the Code

You'll need Java 11 or later and Apache Maven 3 or later to build and work with this code. You should be able to go to each of the modules' root directory and run `mvn clean install` to get a working build of the code. If there are any variances in the procedure, I'll document those variances in a `README` file in each module.

2.7. Running the Code

Any IDE will run the code as they are all nothing more than `public static void main` methods and some classes. Nothing too interesting. You might be able to run them using the Spring Boot Maven plugin `mvn spring-boot:run`, but keep in mind that many modules have more than one `main` method, which defeats the Maven plugin's ability to detect the unique class that should be run as the main class.

Also, some of the code can be quite demanding on your system! Remember, the goal is to write code that does as much as possible, so you will perhaps get plenty of occasions to see your CPU working to keep up for the first time in a long time. This is a *wonderful* problem to have! It means you're getting the full run of your systems thank to the incredible efficiency you get from building reactive services. Gone are the days of idle CPUs for services that somehow can't accept any more requests!

I also noticed that some things tend to give up the ghost much less quickly than others. In particular, I found the RSocket services would sometimes terminate slowly when canceled from within the IDE. Check top on your

UNIX-like operating system or the Windows Task Manager to ensure no runaway java processes clinging to life. I had some RSocket services that I thought I'd killed (I clicked the red button in IntelliJ! Surely, that means they're done and dusted, right?), and they were still running, hogging memory and power. I only realized the problem when I noticed my MacBook Pro 2019 could not keep a charge, even while plugged in! The CPU was so taxed that the charge from the current was enough, so it was drawing from the battery, and quickly too! `pkill <PROCESS_ID>` or `sudo kill -9 <PROCESS_ID>` and Windows Task Manager (`CTRL + ALT + DELETE`, find `java` in the resulting task list, and then choose `End Task`) are your friends here.

2.8. Some Foundational Java

There's not a whole heckuva lot of stuff that should trip you up, but if you haven't used some of the new features in Java 8 or later, then you may appreciate the following refreshers.

2.8.1. Type Inference

Java 11 and later support a new form of type inference where types can be inferred, given sufficient information on the right side of an assignment, and then dropped from the left definition.

Basically:

```
Customer customer = new Customer(1L, "Jane");
```

is easily defined as:

```
var customer = new Customer(1L, "Jane");
```

2.8.2. Function Interfaces, Lambdas and Method References

Java 8 and later support lambdas. A lambda is to method definitions of what anonymous classes are to class definitions. They let us treat functions as first-class citizens. Well, almost. In Java, lambdas are slightly limited; they're *not* first-class citizens. But, close enough! They *must* have return values and input parameters compatible with the sole abstract method's signature on an interface. This is called a *functional interface*. (Interfaces may have *default*, non-abstract methods where the implementation is provided in the interface.)

There are some very convenient and oft-used functional interfaces in the JDK itself. Here are some of my favorites.

- java.util.function.Function<I, O>: an instance of this interface accepts a type I and returns a type O. This is useful as a general-purpose function. Every other function could, in theory, be generalized from this. Thankfully, there's no need for that as there are several other handy functional interfaces.
- java.util.function.Predicate<T>: an instance of this interface accepts a type T and returns a boolean. This is useful to model filters that visit a series and - based on the logic in this predicate - c
- java.util.function.Supplier<T>: A supplier accepts no input and returns an output.
- java.util.function.Consumer<T>: A consumer is the mirror image of a Supplier<T>; it takes an input and returns no output.

You can also create and use your custom functional interfaces.

Let's suppose you had the following functional interface:

```
@FunctionalInterface
interface MyHandler {

  String handle(int one, java.util.Date two);
}
```

This can be expressed in Java as:

```
MyHandler handler = (one, two) -> "Hello";
```

15

Any parameter in any method of type `MyHandler` can be given as a lambda, as well.

```
void process(MyHandler mh) { ... }

...

process((one, two) -> "Hello");
```

If you've already got a method you'd like to use that takes an `int` and returns a `String`, it would seem pointless to express a lambda that then forwards its input parameters to that method. You can cut out the intermediate lambda and point at that method using a method reference. All modern JVM languages (even Java) support method references.

```
class Delegate {

 String pleaseHandle(int one, Date two) {
   return one + ":" + two;
 }
}

...
Delegate delegate = new Delegate();
process(delegate::pleaseHandle);
```

2.8.3. Lombok

A lot of the code in this book uses Lombok [http://lombok.org], a compile-time annotation processor, to augment the Java code. Lombok isn't so valuable when using other JVM languages, like Kotlin, but it can save reams of typing - not to mention printed page space! - in Java. Lombok provides annotations like `@Data`, to create an `equals()` and `hashCode()` and `toString()` method for our objects. It provides annotations like `@NoArgsConstructor` and `@AllArgsConstructor` to create new constructors. It provides annotations like `@Log4j` or `@Log`, which create fields - named `log` - using a logging framework in the classes on which the annotations are parked.

Lombok does this with a Java annotation processor. You don't need to worry about this if you're using Maven to compile the code. It will become momentarily problematic if you intend to edit code using an IDE like IntelliJ or Eclipse. Make sure you've installed the relevant plugin for your IDE.

2.9. Next Steps

See? That wasn't so bad! I bet you already knew most of it. You can never be *too sure* though… All that's left to do is apply it.

Reactive Spring

Chapter 3. Bootstrap

To appreciate reactive programming in the broader ecosystem's context, we'll need to learn about Spring. What is Spring? What is dependency injection? Why do we use Spring Boot over (or in addition to?) Spring Framework? This chapter is a primer on the basics. We don't talk about reactive programming in this chapter at all. If you already know the fundamentals of dependency injection, inversion-of-control, Java configuration, Spring application contexts, aspect-oriented programming (AOP), and Spring Boot auto-configuration, skip this chapter!

For the rest of us, we're going to demonstrate some key concepts by building something. We'll begin our journey, as usual, at my *second* favorite place on the internet, the Spring Initializr - Start dot Spring dot IO [http://start.Spring.io]. Our goal is to build a trivial application. I specified `rsb` in the `Group` field and `bootstrap` in the `Artifact` field, though please feel free to select whatever you'd like. Select the following dependencies using the combo box text field on the bottom right of the page where it says `Search for dependencies`: `DevTools`, `Web`, `H2`, `JDBC`, `Actuator` and `Lombok`.

Devtools lets us restart the application by running our IDE's build command. No need to restart the entire JVM process. This lets us iterate quicker and see changes in the compiled code quicker. It also starts up a Livereload-protocol server. Some excellent browser plugins out there can listen for messages on this server and force the browser page to refresh, giving you a seamless what-you-see-is-what-you-get experience.

> If you're using the Spring Tool Suite, you need only save your code, and you'll see changes here. IntelliJ has no built-in notion of a "save," and so no hook off of which to hang this event. You'll need to instead "build" the code. Go to `Build > Build the project`. On a Mac, you could use Cmd + F9.

Web brings in everything you'd need today to build an application based on the Servlet specification and traditional Spring MVC. It brings in form validation, JSON and XML marshaling, WebSocket support, REST- and HTTP-controller support, etc. H2 is an embedded SQL database that will lose its state on every restart. This is ideal for our first steps since we won't have to install a database (or reset it).

JDBC brings in support, like the `JdbcTemplate`, for working with SQL-based databases.

Lombok is a compile-time annotation processor that synthesizes things like getters, setters, `toString()` methods, `equals()` methods, and so much more with but a few annotations. Most of these annotations are self-explanatory in describing what they contribute to the class on which they're placed.

Actuator contributes HTTP endpoints, under `/actuator/\*`, that give visibility into the application's state.

There are some other choices if we're so inclined. What version of the JVM do you want to target? (I'd recommend using the version corresponding to the latest OpenJDK build.) What language do you want? We'll explore Kotlin later, but let's use Java for now. Groovy is... well, *groovy*! It's a recommended choice, too. You can leave all the other values at their defaults for this simple application.

For all that we *did* specify, we *didn't* specify Spring itself. Or a logging library. Or any of a dozen sort of ceremonial framework-y bits that we'll need to do the job. Those are implied in the other dependencies when using Spring Boot, so we don't need to worry about them.

Now, I hear you cry, "what about reactive?" Good point! We'll get there, I promise, but nothing we're introducing in this section is reactive simply because we need to have a baseline. These days, it's fair game to assume you've some familiarity with things like JDBC (the Java Database Connectivity API) and the Servlet specification (there's traditionally been very little to be done on the web tier in Java that doesn't involve the Servlet specification).

Scroll to the bottom and select `Generate Project`.

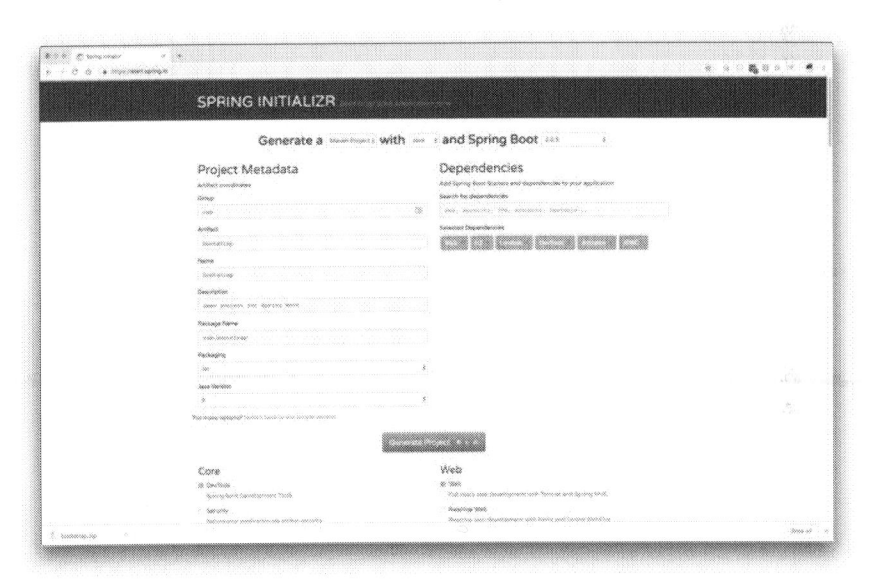

Figure 1. This shows us the selections on the Spring Initializr for a new, reactive application.

This will generate and start downloading a new project in a `.zip` archive, in whatever folder your browser stores downloaded files. Unzip the archive, and you'll see the following layout:

The generated project structure.

```
.
├── mvnw
├── mvnw.cmd
├── pom.xml
└── src
    ├── main
    │   ├── java
    │   │   └── com
    │   │       └── example
    │   │           └── bootstrap
    │   │               └── BootstrapApplication.java
    │   └── resources
    │       └── application.properties
    └── test
        └── java
            └── com
                └── example
                    └── bootstrap
                        └── BootstrapApplicationTests.java

12 directories, 6 files
```

This is a stock-standard Maven project. The only thing that might not be familiar is the Maven wrapper [https://github.com/takari/maven-wrapper] - those files starting with mvnw. The Maven wrapper provides shell scripts, for different operating systems, that download the Apache Maven distribution required to run this project's build. This is particularly handy when you want to get the build to run as you'd expect it to run in a continuous integration environment. If you're on a UNIX-like environment (macOS, any Linux flavor), you will run mvnw. On Windows, you would run mvnw.cmd.

Your Maven build pom.xml *should look something like this:*

```
<?xml version="1.0" encoding="UTF-8"?>
<project xmlns="http://maven.apache.org/POM/4.0.0"
         xmlns:xsi="http://www.w3.org/2001/XMLSchema-instance"
         xsi:schemaLocation="http://maven.apache.org/POM/4.0.0 http://maven.apache.org/xsd/maven-4.0.0.xsd">
    <modelVersion>4.0.0</modelVersion>

    <groupId>rsb</groupId>
```

```xml
<artifactId>bootstrap</artifactId>
<version>0.0.1-SNAPSHOT</version>
<packaging>jar</packaging>

<name>bootstrap</name>
<description>Demo project for Spring Boot</description>

<parent>
    <groupId>org.springframework.boot</groupId>
    <artifactId>spring-boot-starter-parent</artifactId>
    <version>2.1.0.RELEASE</version>
    <relativePath/> <!-- lookup parent from repository -->
</parent>

<properties>
    <project.build.sourceEncoding>UTF-8</project.build.sourceEncoding>
    <project.reporting.outputEncoding>UTF-8
    </project.reporting.outputEncoding>
    <java.version>1.8</java.version>
</properties>

<dependencies>
    <dependency>
        <groupId>org.springframework.boot</groupId>
        <artifactId>spring-boot-starter-actuator</artifactId>
    </dependency>
    <dependency>
        <groupId>org.springframework.boot</groupId>
        <artifactId>spring-boot-starter-web</artifactId>
    </dependency>
    <dependency>
        <groupId>org.springframework.boot</groupId>
        <artifactId>spring-boot-starter-jdbc</artifactId>
    </dependency>
    <dependency>
        <groupId>org.springframework.boot</groupId>
        <artifactId>spring-boot-devtools</artifactId>
        <scope>runtime</scope>
    </dependency>
    <dependency>
        <groupId>com.h2database</groupId>
        <artifactId>h2</artifactId>
        <scope>runtime</scope>
    </dependency>
    <dependency>
        <groupId>org.projectlombok</groupId>
        <artifactId>lombok</artifactId>
```

```xml
            <optional>true</optional>
        </dependency>
        <dependency>
            <groupId>org.springframework.boot</groupId>
            <artifactId>spring-boot-starter-test</artifactId>
            <scope>test</scope>
        </dependency>
    </dependencies>

    <build>
        <plugins>
            <plugin>
                <groupId>org.springframework.boot</groupId>
                <artifactId>spring-boot-maven-plugin</artifactId>
            </plugin>
        </plugins>
    </build>

</project>
```

Our Maven build file, `pom.xml`, is pretty plain. Each checkbox selected on the Spring Initializr is represented as a dependency in the `pom.xml` build file. Most of them will have the `groupId` `org.springframework.boot`. We selected Web, and that corresponds to a dependency for building web applications with `artifactId` `spring-boot-starter-web`, for example. That explains where at least three of our dependencies came from. But that doesn't explain all of them. Testing is important, and we're in the future, and in the future, everybody tests. (Right!!...?) You'll see at least `spring-boot-starter-test` among the dependencies added to your Maven build. The Spring Initializr often adds other testing libraries where appropriate based on the libraries you've added. There's no "opt-in" for it. The Spring Initializr generates new projects with test dependencies automatically. (You're welcome!)

There's also an empty property file, `src/main/resources/application.properties`. Later, we'll see that we can specify properties to configure the application. Spring can read both `.properties` files and `.yaml` files.

This is a stock-standard Spring Boot application with a `public static void main(String[] args)` entry-point class, `BootstrapApplication.java`. It is an empty class with a `main` method and an annotation, and it is *glorious*! While I'd love to stay here in the land of little, to jump right into bombastic Spring Boot, this wouldn't be much of a *bootstrap* lesson without some background! So, delete `BootstrapApplication.java`. We'll get there. But first, some basics.

3.1. A Big ol' Bag o' Beans

Spring Framework, the first project to bear the Spring moniker, is at its core a dependency injection framework. Dependency injection frameworks are simple things with very profound possibilities. The idea is simple: applications change a lot. Decoupling, broadly, helps to reduce the cost of changing our application code and system architecture. So we write code in such a way that it is ignorant of where dependencies - collaborating objects - originate.

3.2. The `CustomerService`

Suppose we've written an interface, `CustomerService`, for which we need to provide an implementation.

```java
package rsb.bootstrap;

import java.util.Collection;

public interface CustomerService {

    Collection<Customer> save(String... names);

    Customer findById(Long id);

    Collection<Customer> findAll();

}
```

The work of the `CustomerService` implementation itself isn't so interesting as how it's ultimately wired together. The wiring of the implementation - which objects are used to satisfy its dependencies - has an impact on how easy it is to change the implementation later on. This cost grows as you add more types to a system. The long tail of software project costs is in maintenance, so it is *always* cheaper to write maintainable code upfront.

The `JdbcTemplate`, in Spring's core JDBC support, is for many the first thing in the grab bag of utilities that led people to use Spring. It's been around for most of Spring's life. It supports common JDBC operations as expressive one-liners, alleviating most boilerplate (creating and destroying sessions or transactions, mapping results to objects, parameter binding, etc.) involved in working with JDBC.

To keep things simple and distracting discussions around object-relational mappers (ORMs) and the like - a paradigm well supported in Spring itself one way or another - we'll stick to the `JdbcTemplate` in our implementations. Let's look at a base implementation, BaseCustomerService, that requires a DataSource to do its work and instantiate a new JdbcTemplate instance.

```
package rsb.bootstrap;

import org.springframework.jdbc.core.JdbcTemplate;
import org.springframework.jdbc.core.RowMapper;
import org.springframework.jdbc.support.GeneratedKeyHolder;
import org.springframework.jdbc.support.KeyHolder;
import org.springframework.util.Assert;

import javax.sql.DataSource;
import java.sql.PreparedStatement;
import java.sql.Statement;
import java.util.ArrayList;
import java.util.Collection;
import java.util.List;
import java.util.Objects;

①
public class BaseCustomerService implements CustomerService {

    private final RowMapper<Customer> rowMapper = (rs,
            i) -> new Customer(rs.getLong("id"), rs.getString("NAME"));

    ②
    private final JdbcTemplate jdbcTemplate;
```

```
    ③
    protected BaseCustomerService(DataSource ds) {
        this.jdbcTemplate = new JdbcTemplate(ds);
    }

    @Override
    public Collection<Customer> save(String... names) {

        List<Customer> customerList = new ArrayList<>();
        for (String name : names) {
            KeyHolder keyHolder = new GeneratedKeyHolder();
            this.jdbcTemplate.update(connection -> {
                PreparedStatement ps = connection.prepareStatement(
                        "insert into CUSTOMERS (name) values(?)",
                        Statement.RETURN_GENERATED_KEYS);
                ps.setString(1, name);
                return ps;
            }, keyHolder);
            Long keyHolderKey = Objects.requireNonNull(keyHolder.getKey())
.longValue();
            Customer customer = this.findById(keyHolderKey);
            Assert.notNull(name, "the name given must not be null");
            customerList.add(customer);
        }
        return customerList;
    }

    @Override
    public Customer findById(Long id) {
        String sql = "select * from CUSTOMERS where id = ?";
        return this.jdbcTemplate.queryForObject(sql, this.rowMapper, id);
    }

    @Override
    public Collection<Customer> findAll() {
        return this.jdbcTemplate.query("select * from CUSTOMERS", rowMapper);
    }

}
```

① This is a public class because we'll have several different implementations, in different packages, in this chapter. Normally you wouldn't have multiple implementations in different packages, and you should strive to assign a type the least visible modifier. A great majority of my code is package-private (no modifier at all).

② The `JdbcTemplate` reference to talk to our `DataSource`

③ For this implementation to do its work, it needs a `DataSource`

3.3. An Inflexible Implementation

The first cut at that implementation might depend on a `java.sql.DataSource` instance that allows it to talk to an RDBMS. It needs that object to be able to transact with the database, the store of record. This database is sure to change locations depending on the environment. It would therefore be a mistake to hard code credentials for the development database in the Java code. More broadly, it would be a mistake to bury the creation of the `DataSource` object in the `CustomerService` implementation itself. It's a terrible idea for a whole host of reasons, not least because of its bad security practice. It's also a bad idea because it couples the code to the data source running on the local machine. I can't switch out the URL to which my database driver should connect.

> It's a seriously bad code smell if your development database, testing, and integration testing database, and production database are all the same database instance!

A naive implementation of `CustomerService.java` - *don't do this!*

```
package rsb.bootstrap.hardcoded;

import org.springframework.jdbc.datasource.embedded.EmbeddedDatabaseBuilder;
import org.springframework.jdbc.datasource.embedded.EmbeddedDatabaseType;
import rsb.bootstrap.BaseCustomerService;
import rsb.bootstrap.CustomerService;
import rsb.bootstrap.DataSourceUtils;

import javax.sql.DataSource;

class DevelopmentOnlyCustomerService extends BaseCustomerService {

    DevelopmentOnlyCustomerService() {
        super(buildDataSource());
    }

    private static DataSource buildDataSource() { ①
        DataSource dataSource = new EmbeddedDatabaseBuilder()
                .setType(EmbeddedDatabaseType.H2).build();
        return DataSourceUtils.initializeDdl(dataSource);
    }

}
```

① This is brittle. It hardcodes the creation recipe for the `DataSource`, here using an embedded H2 in-memory SQL database, in the `CustomerService` implementation itself.

The biggest pity is that this implementation doesn't do anything except pass in the hardcoded `DataSource` to the base implementation's super constructor. The `BaseCustomerService` is parameterized. It preserves optionality. This subclass almost goes out of its way to remove that optionality by hardcoding this `DataSource`. What a waste. The `DataSource` *needs* to be created *somewhere*, but hopefully, we can agree it shouldn't be implemented. The `DataSource` represents a live connection to a network service whose location may change as we promote the application from one environment (development, QA, staging, etc.) to another. In this silly example, we're using an in-memory and embedded SQL database, but that's not going to the be the common case; you'll typically have a `DataSource` requiring environment-specific URIs, locators, credentials, etc.

The `DataSource` requires some initialization before any consumers can use it. This example collocates that creation and initialization logic in the `CustomerService` implementation itself. If you're curious, here's the initialization logic itself. We'll use this method - `DataSourceUtils#initializeDdl(DataSource)` - in subsequent examples.

```java
package rsb.bootstrap;

import org.springframework.core.io.ClassPathResource;
import org.springframework.jdbc.datasource.init.DatabasePopulatorUtils;
import org.springframework.jdbc.datasource.init.ResourceDatabasePopulator;

import javax.sql.DataSource;

public abstract class DataSourceUtils {

    public static DataSource initializeDdl(DataSource dataSource) {
        ①
        ResourceDatabasePopulator populator = new ResourceDatabasePopulator(
                new ClassPathResource("/schema.sql"));  ②
        DatabasePopulatorUtils.execute(populator, dataSource);
        return dataSource;
    }
}
```

① the `ResourceDatabasePopulator` comes from the Spring Framework. It supports executing SQL statements against a `DataSource` given one or more SQL files. It even has options around whether to fail the initialization if, for example, a database table already exists when trying to run a `CREATE TABLE` operation or whether to continue.

② Spring provides an abstraction, `Resource`, that represents some sort of resource with which we might want to perform input and output. The `ClassPathResource` represents resources found in the classpath of an application.

Here's an example demonstrating how we might wire up such an implementation.

Chapter 3. Bootstrap

```
package rsb.bootstrap.hardcoded;

import rsb.bootstrap.Demo;

public class Application {

    public static void main(String[] args) {
        DevelopmentOnlyCustomerService customerService = new DevelopmentOnlyCustomerService();
        Demo.workWithCustomerService(Application.class, customerService);
    }

}
```

We exercise the resulting implementation with `Demo#workWithCustomerService(CustomerService)`. We'll use this method in subsequent examples, so let's look at it.

```java
package rsb.bootstrap;

import lombok.extern.log4j.Log4j2;
import org.springframework.util.Assert;

import java.util.stream.Stream;

@Log4j2
public class Demo {

    public static void workWithCustomerService(Class<?> label,
            CustomerService customerService) {
        ①
        log.info("====================================");
        log.info(label.getName());
        log.info("====================================");

        ②
        Stream.of("A", "B", "C").map(customerService::save)
                .forEach(customer -> log.info("saved " + customer.toString()
));

        ③
        customerService.findAll().forEach(customer -> {
            Long customerId = customer.getId();
            ④
            Customer byId = customerService.findById(customerId);
            log.info("found " + byId.toString());
            Assert.notNull(byId, "the resulting customer should not be null"
);
            Assert.isTrue(byId.equals(customer),
                    "we should be able to query for " + "this result");
        });
    }

}
```

① announce generally what we're doing

② write some data to the database using our implementation

③ find all records in the database

④ confirm that we can find each record by its ID

If that code looks suspiciously like a test... it is! Each example even has a

JUnit unit test that exercises the same code path. We'll focus on how to stand up each example in the context of a `public static void main` application, and leave the tests. Suffice it to say, both the test and our demos exercise the same code.

`DataSource` instances are expensive and typically shared across services. It makes little sense to recreate them everywhere they're used. Instead, let's centralize their creation recipe and write our code so that it doesn't care what reference it's been given.

3.4. A Parameterized Implementation

The simplest thing we can do to improve our example, and restore optionality, is to parameterize the `DataSource` through the constructor.

```
package rsb.bootstrap.basicdi;

import rsb.bootstrap.BaseCustomerService;
import rsb.bootstrap.CustomerService;

import javax.sql.DataSource;

class DataSourceCustomerService extends BaseCustomerService {

    ①
    DataSourceCustomerService(DataSource ds) {
        super(ds);
    }

}
```

① Not much to it! It's a class with a constructor that invokes the super constructor.

Here's the refactored `main` method.

```
package rsb.bootstrap.basicdi;

import org.springframework.jdbc.datasource.embedded.EmbeddedDatabaseBuilder;
import org.springframework.jdbc.datasource.embedded.EmbeddedDatabaseType;
import rsb.bootstrap.CustomerService;
import rsb.bootstrap.DataSourceUtils;
import rsb.bootstrap.Demo;

import javax.sql.DataSource;

public class Application {

    public static void main(String[] args) {
        ①
        DataSource dataSource = new EmbeddedDatabaseBuilder()
                .setType(EmbeddedDatabaseType.H2).build();
        ②
        DataSource initializedDataSource = DataSourceUtils.initializeDdl
(dataSource);
        CustomerService cs = new DataSourceCustomerService
(initializedDataSource);
        Demo.workWithCustomerService(Application.class, cs);
    }

}
```

① Our `CustomerService` depends only on a pointer to a `DataSource`. So, if we decide to change this reference tomorrow, we can!

② Much better! Our `CustomerService` only cares that it has a fully-formed `DataSource` reference. It doesn't need to know about initialization logic.

Much better. This implementation supports basic parameterization through generic base types. In this case, our code is ignorant of where the `DataSource` reference comes from. It could be a mock instance in a test or a production-grade connection pooled data source in a production environment.

One thing you'll note is that the code is a little naive with respect to transaction management in that it doesn't handle transactions at all. Our base implementation is, let's say, *optimisitic*! It's all written in such a way that we assume nothing could go wrong. To be fair, the `findById` and `findAll` methods are queries. So, either the query returns the results we've asked for, or it doesn't.

3.5. Templates

You're *probably* fine ignoring discussions of atomicity and transactions for those methods that read data since there's only one query. Things get sticky when you look at the save(String ⋯ names) method that loops through all of the input parameters and writes them to the database one by one. Sure, we probably should've used SQL batching, but this gives us the ability to have a thought experiment: what happens if there's an exception in processing midway through processing all the String ⋯ names arguments? By that point, we'll have written one or more records to the database, but not all of them. Is that acceptable? In this case, it might be. Some are better than none, sometimes! It could be a more sophisticated example, though. You could be trying to write several related pieces of information to the database. Those related pieces of information would be inconsistent if they weren't all written to the database simultaneously; if their integrity wasn't maintained.

Some middleware, including SQL datastores, support a concept of a transaction. You can enclose multiple correlated things into a unit of work and then commit all those correlated things simultaneously. Either everything in the transaction is written, or everything is rolled back, and the results are as-if you hadn't written anything at all. It's much easier to reason about the system this way. You don't have to guess at what parts of the write succeeded and what didn't.

While we're looking at the concept of a transaction in the context of a SQL-based datastore and the JdbcTemplate, they're by no means unique to them. MongoDB supports transactions. So do many of your favorite message queues like RabbitMQ or those supporting the JMS specification. So does Neo4J. This basic workflow of working with a transaction is represented in Spring with the PlatformTransactionManager, of which *many* implementations support many different technologies. You can explicitly start some work, commit it or roll it back using a PlatformTransactionManager. This is simple enough, but it can be fairly tedious to write the try/catch handler that attempts the unit of work and commits it if there are no exceptions or rolls it back if there, even with a `PlatformTransactionManager`.

So, Spring provides the `TransactionTemplate`, which reduces this to a one-liner. You provide a callback that gets executed in the context of an open transaction. If you throw any exceptions, those result in a rollback. Otherwise, the transaction is committed. Let's revisit our example, this time incorporating transactions.

```
package rsb.bootstrap.templates;

import org.springframework.transaction.support.TransactionTemplate;
import rsb.bootstrap.BaseCustomerService;
import rsb.bootstrap.Customer;

import javax.sql.DataSource;
import java.util.Collection;

public class TransactionTemplateCustomerService extends BaseCustomerService {

    private final TransactionTemplate transactionTemplate; ①

    public TransactionTemplateCustomerService(DataSource dataSource,
            TransactionTemplate tt) {
        super(dataSource);
        this.transactionTemplate = tt;
    }

    @Override
    public Collection<Customer> save(String... names) {
        return this.transactionTemplate.execute(s -> super.save(names));
    }

    @Override
    public Customer findById(Long id) {
        return this.transactionTemplate.execute(s -> super.findById(id));
    }

    @Override
    public Collection<Customer> findAll() {
        return this.transactionTemplate.execute(s -> super.findAll());
    }

}
```

① this class depends on having a `TransactionTemplate` in addition to a `DataSource`

Much better! We only even bother to catch the exception so that we can return a sane result, not because we need to clean up the database. It isn't so difficult to get this all working. Let's look at an application that wires the requisite objects together.

```
package rsb.bootstrap.templates;

import org.springframework.jdbc.datasource.DataSourceTransactionManager;
import org.springframework.jdbc.datasource.embedded.EmbeddedDatabaseBuilder;
import org.springframework.jdbc.datasource.embedded.EmbeddedDatabaseType;
import org.springframework.transaction.PlatformTransactionManager;
import org.springframework.transaction.support.TransactionTemplate;
import rsb.bootstrap.DataSourceUtils;
import rsb.bootstrap.Demo;

import javax.sql.DataSource;

public class Application {

    public static void main(String args[]) {

        DataSource dataSource = new EmbeddedDatabaseBuilder()
                .setType(EmbeddedDatabaseType.H2).build();
        DataSource initializedDataSource = DataSourceUtils.initializeDdl
(dataSource); ①
        PlatformTransactionManager dsTxManager = new
DataSourceTransactionManager(
                initializedDataSource);②
        TransactionTemplate tt = new TransactionTemplate(dsTxManager); ③
        ④
        TransactionTemplateCustomerService customerService = new
TransactionTemplateCustomerService(
                initializedDataSource, tt);
        Demo.workWithCustomerService(Application.class, customerService);
    }

}
```

① initialize a `DataSource`, just as before…

② create an instance of `PlatformTransactionManager` called `DataSourceTransactionManager`.

③ wrap the `PlatformTransactionManager` in a `TransactionTemplate` object.

④ …and the rest is just as before.

Much better! We only even bother to catch the exception so that we can return a sane result, not because we need to clean up the database. The `TransactionTemplate` is just one of many *Template objects - like the

`JdbcTemplate` - that we've been using thus far that is designed to encapsulate boilerplate code like transaction management. A template method handles and hides otherwise boilerplate code and lets the user provide the little bit of variable behavior from one run to another. In this case, what we are doing with the database - queries, extraction, and transformation of results, etc. - is unique and so we need to provide that logic. Still, everything else related to using the `PlatformTransactionManager` implementation is not.

You will find that Spring provides a good many *Template objects. The `JmsTemplate` makes working with JMS easier. The `AmqpTemplate` makes working with AMQP easier. The `MongoTemplate` and `ReactiveMongoTemplate` objects make working with MongoDB in a synchronous, blocking fashion and in an asynchronous, non-blocking fashion, respectively, easier. The `JdbcTemplate` makes working with JDBC easier. The `RedisTemplate` makes working with Redis easier. The `RestTemplate` makes creating HTTP client requests easier. There's another dozen or so you'll encounter in day-to-day work and a dozen more that are obscure but nice to have if you need them. One of my favorite, more obscure, examples is the `org.springframework.jca.cci.core.CciTemplate`, which makes working with the client-side of a Java Connector Architecture (JCA) connector through the Common Connector Interface (CCI) easier.

> Will you ever need to use this? Statistically? No. Hopefully, never! It's an API that you'll need to integrate enterprise integration systems to your J2EE / Java EE application servers. We won't be anywhere near one of those in this book!

3.6. A Context For Your Application

This last example had more moving parts than any previous example. We had to create and configure four different objects to get to the point where we could do anything. Did I say "do"? I meant to exercise the API by passing the resulting, fully configured `CustomerService` as a method invocation parameter. We're still a long way from providing value to a business outcome, though. To do that, we'd need to connect actual clients to this functionality. We'd need to deploy this somewhere. We'd need to create more such services, too. And maybe change out our in-memory embedded SQL databases for a real one whose data endures across restarts. We're going to need to capture and componentize the recipes for these various objects. Right now, everything's buried in our `main(String[] args)` method. We have to copy and paste the code into our tests to confirm that things work as expected.

This isn't going to scale. Let's look at an example that uses Spring to describe the wiring of objects in your application. We'll see that it supports the flexibility we've worked so hard to obtain, thus simplifying our production code and our test code. This won't require a rewrite of the `CustomerService` - virtually everything is identical to before. It is only the wiring that changes.

Spring is ultimately a big bag of beans. It manages the beans and their lifecycles, but we need to tell it what objects are involved. One way to do that is to define objects (called "beans"). In this example, we'll define "beans" in our application class.

```
package rsb.bootstrap.context;

import org.springframework.context.ApplicationContext;
import org.springframework.context.annotation.Bean;
import org.springframework.context.annotation.Configuration;
import org.springframework.context.annotation.Import;
import org.springframework.jdbc.datasource.DataSourceTransactionManager;
import org.springframework.transaction.PlatformTransactionManager;
import org.springframework.transaction.support.TransactionTemplate;
import rsb.bootstrap.CustomerService;
import rsb.bootstrap.DataSourceConfiguration;
import rsb.bootstrap.Demo;
import rsb.bootstrap.SpringUtils;
import rsb.bootstrap.templates.TransactionTemplateCustomerService;

import javax.sql.DataSource;

①
```

```java
@Configuration
@Import(DataSourceConfiguration.class) ②
public class Application {

    ③
    @Bean
    PlatformTransactionManager transactionManager(DataSource ds) {
        return new DataSourceTransactionManager(ds);
    }

    @Bean
    TransactionTemplateCustomerService customerService(DataSource ds,
            TransactionTemplate tt) {
        return new TransactionTemplateCustomerService(ds, tt);
    }

    @Bean
    TransactionTemplate transactionTemplate(PlatformTransactionManager tm) {
        return new TransactionTemplate(tm);
    }

    public static void main(String args[]) {
        ④
        ApplicationContext ac = SpringUtils.run(Application.class, "prod");

        ⑤
        CustomerService cs = ac.getBean(CustomerService.class);
        Demo.workWithCustomerService(Application.class, cs);
    }

}
```

① the Application class is *also* a @Configuration class. It is a class that has methods annotated with @Bean whose return values are objects to be stored and made available for other objects in the application context

② The definition of our DataSource changes depending on whether we're running the application in a development context or production. We have stored those definitions in another configuration class, which we import here. We'll review those definitions momentarily.

③ Each method in a @Configuration-annotated class annotated with @Bean is a *bean provider method*.

④ I've hidden the complexity of creating a Spring ApplicationContext in this method, `SpringUtils.run`. There are a half dozen interesting implementations of the `ApplicationContext` interface. Usually, we won't need to care which and when we use what because the creation of that object in Spring Boot, which we'll use later, is hidden from us. To arrive at a working instance of the Spring `ApplicationContext`, we need to furnish both the configuration class and a *profile*, a label, `prod`. We'll come back to labels momentarily.

⑤ The `ApplicationContext` is the heart of a Spring application. It's the thing that stores all our configured objects. We can ask it for references to any bean, by the beans class type (as shown here) or its bean name.

Those `@Bean` provider methods are important. This is how we define objects and their relationships for Spring. Spring starts up, invokes the methods, and stores the resulting objects to be made available for other objects that need those references as collaborating objects. When Spring provides a reference to the dependency, we say it has "injected" the dependency. If any other code anywhere in the application needs an object of the type (or types, if interfaces are expressed on the resulting type) returned from the method, they'll be given a reference to the single instance returned from this method the first time it was invoked.

If a bean needs a reference to another to do its work, it expresses that *dependency* as a parameter in the bean provider method. Spring will look up any beans of the appropriate definition, and it will provide them as parameters when it invokes our method.

We can recreate the entire application by recreating the `ApplicationContext`.. In this first example, we're using plain ol' Spring Framework. Nothing special about it. Let's look at how we create our `ApplicationContext` instance, but keep in mind that we'll not need this boilerplate code later.

Chapter 3. Bootstrap

```
package rsb.bootstrap;

import org.springframework.context.ConfigurableApplicationContext;
import org.springframework.context.annotation.AnnotationConfigApplicationContext;
import org.springframework.util.StringUtils;

public abstract class SpringUtils {

    public static ConfigurableApplicationContext run(Class<?> sources, String profile) {
        ①
        AnnotationConfigApplicationContext applicationContext = new AnnotationConfigApplicationContext();

        ②
        if (StringUtils.hasText(profile)) {
            applicationContext.getEnvironment().setActiveProfiles(profile);
        }

        ③
        applicationContext.register(sources);
        applicationContext.refresh();

        ④
        applicationContext.start();
        return applicationContext;
    }
}
```

① we're using an `ApplicationContext` instance that can handle annotation-centric configuration, also known as "Java configuration".

② You can tell Spring to create, or not create, objects based on various conditions. One condition is, "does this bean have a profile associated with it?" A profile is a label, or a tag, attached to an object's definition. We haven't seen one yet, but we will. By setting an active profile, we're saying: "create all objects that have no profile associated with them, *and* create all objects associated with the specific profiles that we make active."

③ In this case, we're registering a configuration class. In other contexts, the "sources" might be other kinds of input artifacts.

④ finally, we launch Spring, and it, in turn, goes about triggering the creation of all the objects contained therein.

Let's look at how the `DataSource` definitions are handled in a separate class, `DataSourceConfiguration`. I've extracted these definitions out into a separate class to more readily reuse their definition in subsequent examples. I want to centralize all the complexity of constructing the `DataSource` into a single place in the codebase. We're going to take advantage of profiles to create two `DataSource` definitions. One that results in an in-memory H2 `DataSource` and another configuration that produces a `DataSource` when given a driver class name, a username, a password, and a JDBC URL. These parameters are variable and may change from one developer's machine to another and one environment to another.

Spring has an `Environment` object that you can inject anywhere you want it, that acts like a dictionary for configuration values - just keys and values associated with those keys. Values may originate anywhere - property files, YAML files, environment variables, databases, etc. You can teach the `Environment` about new sources for configuration values by contributing an object of type `PropertySource` to the `Environment`. Spring has a convenient annotation, `@PropertySource`, that takes any configuration values from a file and adds them to the `Environment`. Once in the `Environment`, you can have those values injected into configuration parameters in your bean provider methods with the `@Value` annotation.

```
package rsb.bootstrap;

import org.h2.Driver;
import org.springframework.beans.BeansException;
import org.springframework.beans.factory.annotation.Value;
import org.springframework.beans.factory.config.BeanPostProcessor;
import org.springframework.context.annotation.Bean;
import org.springframework.context.annotation.Configuration;
import org.springframework.context.annotation.Profile;
import org.springframework.context.annotation.PropertySource;
import org.springframework.jdbc.datasource.DriverManagerDataSource;
import org.springframework.jdbc.datasource.embedded.EmbeddedDatabaseBuilder;
import org.springframework.jdbc.datasource.embedded.EmbeddedDatabaseType;

import javax.sql.DataSource;
```

```
@Configuration
public class DataSourceConfiguration {

    ①
    @Configuration
    @Profile("prod")  ②
    @PropertySource("application-prod.properties")  ③
    public static class ProductionConfiguration {

        @Bean
        DataSource productionDataSource(@Value("${spring.datasource.url}")
String url,  ④
                @Value("${spring.datasource.username}") String username,
                @Value("${spring.datasource.password}") String password,
                @Value("${spring.datasource.driver-class-name}") Class<
Driver> driverClass  ⑤
        ) {
            DriverManagerDataSource dataSource = new DriverManagerDataSource
(url,
                    username, password);
            dataSource.setDriverClassName(driverClass.getName());
            return dataSource;
        }

    }

    @Configuration
    @Profile("default")  ⑥
    @PropertySource("application-default.properties")
    public static class DevelopmentConfiguration {

        @Bean
        DataSource developmentDataSource() {
            return new EmbeddedDatabaseBuilder().setType(
EmbeddedDatabaseType.H2).build();
        }

    }

    @Bean
    DataSourcePostProcessor dataSourcePostProcessor() {
        return new DataSourcePostProcessor();
    }

    ⑦
    private static class DataSourcePostProcessor implements BeanPostProcessor
```

```
{

        @Override
        public Object postProcessAfterInitialization(Object bean, String beanName)
                throws BeansException {

            if (bean instanceof DataSource) {
                DataSourceUtils.initializeDdl(DataSource.class.cast(bean));
            }
            return bean;
        }

    }

}
```

① `@Configuration` classes can act as a container for other configuration classes. When we import the `DataSourceConfiguration` class, Spring also resolves any nested configuration classes.

② This configuration class is only meant to be active when the `prod` profile is active.

③ Tell Spring that we want configuration values from the `application-prod.properties` property file, located at src/main/resources/application-prod.properties, to be loaded into the `Environment`.

④ inject values from the configuration file by their key using the `@Value` annotation

⑤ Spring can convert string values in property files to more complex types, like `Class<T>` literals, because it delegates to another subsystem in Spring called the `ConversionService`. You can customize this object, too!

⑥ the `default` profile is a special profile. It is active *only* when no other profile is active. So, if you specifically activate the `prod` profile, then `default` won't be active. If you don't activate any profile, then `default` will kick in. Thus, all objects in this `default` profile will be contributed by default. Here, we contribute an in-memory H2 embedded SQL database.

⑦ In previous examples, we used our initializer,

`DataSourceUtils.initializeDdl`, to ensure that the `DataSource` had the required DDL run against it before it was put into service. Now, we have two places where we define a `DataSource`. We could simply duplicate that logic across both locations, but that violates the DRY (Don't Repeat Yourself) principle. Instead, we will configure an object of type `BeanPostProcessor`. `BeanPostProcessor` is a callback interface. It provides two (default) methods. Here, our class overrides `postProcessAfterInitialization` which is invoked for every object in the Spring application. We interrogate the type of the object, confirm it is a `DataSource` of some sort, and then initialize it. This way, it doesn't matter how or where the `DataSource` is created. The `BeanPostProcessor` ensures it is properly initialized. Spring has other lifecycle events and associated callback interfaces that might be interesting that you'll see from time to time. `BeanPostProcessor` is one of the more common.

In the `Application` class, we explicitly pass in the profile, `prod`. This is not the only way to configure the profile, though. It's a limiting approach, too. Consider that the profile, so specified, is hardcoded into the application logic. In a normal workflow, you would promote the application binary from the environment to another without recompiling to not risk inviting variables into the builds. So, you'd want some way to change the profile without recompilation. Spring supports a command-line argument, `--spring.profiles.active=prod`, when running java to start the application. You could also specify the property in your main class's `main` method - say `System.setProperty("spring.profiles.active", "prod")` right before the `SpringApplication.run` call. The `prod` profile consults properties in its property file, `application-prod.properties`.

```
spring.datasource.url=jdbc:h2:mem:rsb;DB_CLOSE_DELAY=-1;DB_CLOSE_ON_EXIT=false
spring.datasource.username=sa
spring.datasource.password=
spring.datasource.driver-class-name=org.h2.Driver
```

Naturally, you could change any of these property values. If you were using PostgreSQL or MySQL or Oracle, or whatever, it'd be a simple matter to update these values accordingly.

3.7. Component Scanning

The configuration class approach has the advantage of being explicit; we need only to inspect the class to see every object in the application and its wiring. It's also another artifact we need to evolve as we move forward in time, as we add new objects to the application. Each time we add a new service, we need to configure it in this configuration class. Spring supports a ton of different types of objects - components are the simplest of the hierarchy. It also supports controllers, services, repositories, and any of several other types of objects. For each object you add to a Spring application, you need to have a corresponding entry in the configuration class. Is that, in its way, a violation of DRY, as well?

Spring can *implicitly* learn the wiring of objects in the application graph if we let it perform component scanning when the application starts up. If we added the `@ComponentScan` annotation to our application, Spring would discover any objects in the current package, or beneath it, that had identifying marker - or "stereotype" - annotations. This would complement the use of Java configuration nicely. In this scenario, Spring's component scanning would discover all Spring objects that we, the developer define, things like our services and HTTP controllers. At the same time, we'd leave things like the `DataSource` and the `TransactionTemplate` to the Java configuration. Put another way; if you have access to the source code and can annotate it with Spring annotations, then you might consider letting Spring discover that object through component scanning.

When Spring finds such an annotated object, it'll inspect the constructor(s). If it finds no constructor, it'll instantiate an instance of the application using the default constructor. If it finds a single constructor with no arguments, it'll instantiate that. Suppose it finds a constructor argument whose values may be satisfied by other objects in the Spring application (the same way that they might for our bean definition provider methods). In that case, Spring will provide those collaborating objects. If it finds multiple, ambiguous constructors, you can tell Spring which constructor to use by annotating that constructor with the `@Autowired` annotation to disambiguate it from other constructors.

Chapter 3. Bootstrap

Let's rework our application, ever so slightly, in the light of component scanning.

```java
package rsb.bootstrap.scan;

import org.springframework.context.ConfigurableApplicationContext;
import org.springframework.context.annotation.Bean;
import org.springframework.context.annotation.ComponentScan;
import org.springframework.context.annotation.Configuration;
import org.springframework.context.annotation.Import;
import org.springframework.jdbc.datasource.DataSourceTransactionManager;
import org.springframework.transaction.PlatformTransactionManager;
import org.springframework.transaction.support.TransactionTemplate;
import rsb.bootstrap.CustomerService;
import rsb.bootstrap.DataSourceConfiguration;
import rsb.bootstrap.Demo;
import rsb.bootstrap.SpringUtils;

import javax.sql.DataSource;

@Configuration
@ComponentScan ①
@Import(DataSourceConfiguration.class)
public class Application {

    @Bean
    PlatformTransactionManager transactionManager(DataSource ds) {
        return new DataSourceTransactionManager(ds);
    }

    @Bean
    TransactionTemplate transactionTemplate(PlatformTransactionManager tm) {
        return new TransactionTemplate(tm);
    }

    public static void main(String args[]) {
        ConfigurableApplicationContext applicationContext = SpringUtils
                .run(Application.class, "prod");
        CustomerService customerService = applicationContext
                .getBean(CustomerService.class);
        Demo.workWithCustomerService(Application.class, customerService);
    }

}
```

① The only thing of note here is that we've enabled component scanning using the `@ComponentScan` annotation and that we don't have a bean provider method for the `CustomerService` type since Spring will now automatically detect that type in the component scan.

It will discover the `CustomerService` type in the component scan, *if*, that is, we annotate it to be discovered. Let's create a new type that does nothing but host a stereotype annotation, `@Service`.

```java
package rsb.bootstrap.scan;

import org.springframework.stereotype.Service;
import org.springframework.transaction.support.TransactionTemplate;
import rsb.bootstrap.CustomerService;
import rsb.bootstrap.templates.TransactionTemplateCustomerService;

import javax.sql.DataSource;

①
@Service
class DiscoveredCustomerService extends TransactionTemplateCustomerService {

    ②
    DiscoveredCustomerService(DataSource dataSource, TransactionTemplate tt) {
        super(dataSource, tt);
    }

}
```

① the `@Service` annotation is a stereotype annotation. This class exists in the same package as `Application.java`, only to allow us to annotate it so that it can be discovered. Most codebases will have much shallower hierarchies. The stereotype annotation will live on the class with the business logic's implementation, not just a subclass of some other thing extracted into another package just for improvement as in this book!

② the `Application` class defines instances of these types, so we know that Spring can satisfy these dependencies.

3.8. Declarative Container Services with `@Enable*` Annotations

We introduced Spring and added a class to support our configuration. We extricated the objects' wiring from the `main(String[])` method and into this new configuration class. Our code has more moving parts, not less. It's not hard to see Spring could make things simpler - particularly when using component scanning - as we add even more objects to our application. The configuration, amortized over the cost of more objects in the application, is almost nothing at all. That's a win in the near term but doesn't apply to us right now. What can we do to simplify the code right now? Our service now uses the `TransactionTemplate` to manage transactions. We use the `TransactionTemplate` to demarcate transactional boundaries for our core functionality. For every method we add, we need to wrap the transaction demarcation logic in the same way. This cross-cutting concern - transaction demarcation - is one thing with which we'll have to often contend, even though its a fairly straightforward requirement. It shouldn't require constant code to support it, either. Let's look at how we can simplify the code with declarative transaction demarcation.

```
package rsb.bootstrap.enable;

import org.springframework.context.ConfigurableApplicationContext;
import org.springframework.context.annotation.Bean;
import org.springframework.context.annotation.ComponentScan;
import org.springframework.context.annotation.Configuration;
import org.springframework.context.annotation.Import;
import org.springframework.jdbc.datasource.DataSourceTransactionManager;
import org.springframework.transaction.PlatformTransactionManager;
import
org.springframework.transaction.annotation.EnableTransactionManagement;
import org.springframework.transaction.support.TransactionTemplate;
import rsb.bootstrap.CustomerService;
import rsb.bootstrap.DataSourceConfiguration;
import rsb.bootstrap.Demo;
import rsb.bootstrap.SpringUtils;
import rsb.bootstrap.templates.TransactionTemplateCustomerService;

import javax.sql.DataSource;

@Configuration
@EnableTransactionManagement ①
@ComponentScan
@Import(DataSourceConfiguration.class)
public class Application {

    @Bean
    PlatformTransactionManager transactionManager(DataSource ds) {
        return new DataSourceTransactionManager(ds);
    }

    @Bean
    TransactionTemplate transactionTemplate(PlatformTransactionManager tm) {
        return new TransactionTemplate(tm);
    }

    public static void main(String args[]) {
        ConfigurableApplicationContext applicationContext = SpringUtils
                .run(Application.class, "prod");
        CustomerService customerService = applicationContext
                .getBean(CustomerService.class);
        Demo.workWithCustomerService(Application.class, customerService);
    }

}
```

① the *only* difference now is that we're enabling declarative transaction management.

This is otherwise the same as any other example, except that we have the one extra annotation. Now, we can reimplement the `CustomerService` implementation. Well, we don't have to reimplement it. Simply declare it and annotate it with `@Transactional`. All `public` methods in the implementation class then have transactions demarcated automatically.

```java
package rsb.bootstrap.enable;

import org.springframework.stereotype.Service;
import org.springframework.transaction.annotation.Transactional;
import rsb.bootstrap.BaseCustomerService;
import rsb.bootstrap.Customer;

import javax.sql.DataSource;
import java.util.Collection;

@Service
@Transactional ①
public class TransactionalCustomerService extends BaseCustomerService {

    public TransactionalCustomerService(DataSource dataSource) {
        super(dataSource);
    }

    @Override
    public Collection<Customer> save(String... names) {
        return super.save(names);
    }

    @Override
    public Customer findById(Long id) {
        return super.findById(id);
    }

    @Override
    public Collection<Customer> findAll() {
        return super.findAll();
    }

}
```

① this is the only thing that we have to do - decorate the Spring bean with `@Transactional`.

That's it! The `@Transactional` annotation has attributes that we can use that give us some of the flexibility that we have in explicitly managing the transactions with the `TransactionTemplate`. Not all, but most. As written, we get default transaction demarcation for all public methods. We could explicitly configure transaction demarcation per-method by annotating each method with the `@Transactional` annotation and overriding the class-level configuration there.

3.9. A "Bootiful" Application

So far, we've built a working application that talks to a database, manages declarative transactions, and we've streamlined the code as much as possible. The code is svelter because Spring can handle a lot of boilerplate code for you. So far, though, we've focused *only* on creating a service that talks to a database. We're nowhere near ready for production! There's a ton of things to sort out before we have a working REST API to which clients might connect. And we have considerably more still to do before we have a client of any sort - HTML 5, Android, iOS, whatever - to connect to our REST API. We've come a long way! And yet... we're still nowhere. We need to stand up a web server, configure a web framework, set up security, etc.

Spring has us covered here. Indeed, Spring has us covered... anywhere! We could use Spring MVC for Servlet-based web applications. We could use Spring Data and its numerous modules supporting data access across SQL and NoSQL datastores. We could use Spring Security to integrate authentication and authorization in our application. We could use Spring Integration to build out messaging-centric integration flows, talking to technologies like Apache Kafka, RabbitMQ, FTP, IMAP, JMS, etc. We could use Spring Batch to support batch processing for large, sequential data access jobs. And microservices? Yah, there is a *lot* to absorb for that, too!

We also need to care about observability - something needs to articulate the application's health so that we can run it with confidence in production and so that it can be effectively monitored. Monitoring is critical; monitoring gives us the ability to measure and, with those measurements, advance. Let's see if we can kick things up a notch.

3.9.1. The Rise of the Convention over Configuration Web Frameworks

We need to be more productive; there's (a lot) more to do, and it would be nice if we could exert less energy to do it. This isn't a new problem. There have been many efforts in the Java community, and in other communities, to support more productive application development.

Ruby on Rails, a web framework that debuted in 2004 and became white-hot popular in the early 2000s, is owed a large credit here. It was the first project to support what it called "convention over configuration," wherein the framework was optimized for common sense scenarios that it made trivial. In those days, there was a lot of discussion of web applications "babysitting databases." What else do you need? An HTML-based frontend that talked behind the scenes to a SQL database described 80% of the applications at the time. Ruby on Rails optimized for this particular outcome, but it was *really* optimized! The Rails team had the famous 5-minute demo. In the space of five actual minutes, they initialized a new application and integrated data access and a user interface that supported manipulating that data. It was a *really* quick way to build user interfaces that talked to SQL databases. Ruby on Rails was driven by code generation and buoyed by the Ruby language's dynamic nature. It coupled the representation of database state to the HTML forms and views with which users would interact. It made heavy use of code generation to get there; users interact with the command-line shell to generate new entities mapped to state in the SQL database; they used the shell to generate "scaffolding" with the views and entities. The approach is a considerable improvement over the then prolific technologies of the day.

Ruby on Rails critics would say that it was very difficult to unwind the underlying assumptions. As most of a Ruby on Rails application is generated code and highly opinionated runtime code, it is very difficult to unwind the choices made by the framework without having to rewrite entire verticals of the framework. Either the code it generated for you worked the way you wanted it to, or you'd have to scrap everything. The use cases average web developers face evolved, too. If you wanted to have a user interface that, in turn, manipulated two different database entities, then things got difficult. If you wanted to build an HTTP-based REST API, then you were out of luck. If you wanted to integrate a NoSQL datastore, then you were on your own. All of these things were ultimately added to Ruby on Rails; it's evolved, certainly. But the criticisms linger. Now, closer to 2020 than 2000, Ruby on Rails is optimized for the wrong thing. Most applications are not web applications babysitting a database anymore. They're client-service based architectures. The clients run in different logical tiers and different physical tiers, in Android runtimes, on iOS, and in rich and capable HTML 5 browsers like Google Chrome and Mozilla Firefox.

The Spring team has had an interesting history here, too. There were two efforts of note with which the Spring team was involved. The first, Spring Roo, is a code-generation approach to Java development. The premise behind Spring Roo is that there were a ton of moving parts in a working Java application circa 2008 that weren't Java code. XML deployment descriptors. .JSP-based views. Hibernate mapping configuration XML files. Just a ton of things! Spring Roo took a very Ruby on Rails-centric approach to code generation, with the same fatal flaws. Assumptions were too difficult to unwind. It was optimized for one type of application.

Grails leaned more heavily on runtime configuration. It had code generation, but most of its dynamic nature came from the Groovy. Both Spring Roo and Grails built on Spring. Spring Roo generated a whole bunch of Spring-based code that could be changed if needed, but the effort could be an uphill battle. Grails instead supported metaprogramming and hooks to override runtime assumptions. Grails is far and away from the most successful of the two options. I'd even argue it was the most successful of all the convention-over-configuration web frameworks after Ruby on Rails itself!

What's missing? Grails is a Groovy-centric approach to building applications. If you didn't want to use the Groovy programming language (why wouldn't you? It's *fantastic*!), then Grails is probably not the solution for you. Grails was for most of its life optimized for the web applications babysitting database use case. And, finally, while Java and regular Spring could never hope to support the kind of metaprogramming that is uniquely possible in the Groovy language, they were both pretty dynamic and could offer more.

3.9.2. Cloud Native Applications and Services

The shape of modern software has changed with architecture changes. No longer do we build web applications babysitting databases. Instead, clients talk to services. *Lots* of services. Small, singly focused, independently deployable, autonomously updatable, reusable, bounded contexts. *Microservices*. Microservices are the software manifestation of a new paradigm, called *continuous delivery*, where organizations optimize for continuous feedback loops by embracing software that can be easily, continuously, and incrementally updated. The goal is to shorten feedback loops to learn from iterations in production. Kenny Bastani and I look at this paradigm in O'Reilly's epic tome *Cloud Native Java* [http://cloudNativeJava.io]. One knock-on effect of this architectural paradigm is that software is constantly being moved from development to production; that change is constant. The things that you only worry about when you're close to production become things you need to worry about when you're just starting. In a continuous delivery pipeline, you could see software pushed to production due to every single git push! How will you handle load-balancing? Security? Monitoring and observability? DNS? HTTPS certificates? Failover? Racked-and-stacked servers? VMs? Container security?

Our frameworks need to be optimized for production. They must simplify as much of this undifferentiated heavy lifting as possible.

3.9.3. Spring Boot

In 2013, we released Spring Boot to the world. Spring Boot is a different approach to building Java applications. It offers strong opinions, loosely held. Spring Boot integrates the best-of-breed components from the Spring and larger Java ecosystems into one cohesive whole. It provides default configurations for any of some scenarios but, and this part is key; it provides a built-in mechanism to undo or override those default configurations. There is *no* code generation required. A working Spring application is primarily Java code and a build artifact (a `build.gradle` or a `pom.xml`). Whatever dynamic behavior is needed can be provided at runtime using Java and metaprogramming.

Let's revisit our example, this time with Spring Boot. Spring Boot is just Spring. It's Spring configuration for all the stuff that you *could* write, but that you don't need to. I like to say that Spring Boot is your chance to pair-program with the Spring team.

First, let's look a the `Application` class.

```
package rsb.bootstrap.bootiful;

import org.springframework.boot.SpringApplication;
import org.springframework.boot.autoconfigure.SpringBootApplication;
import org.springframework.boot.context.event.ApplicationReadyEvent;
import org.springframework.context.annotation.Profile;
import org.springframework.context.event.EventListener;
import org.springframework.stereotype.Component;
import rsb.bootstrap.CustomerService;
import rsb.bootstrap.Demo;

①
@SpringBootApplication
public class Application {

    public static void main(String args[]) {
        ②
        System.setProperty("spring.profiles.active", "prod");
        ③
        SpringApplication.run(Application.class, args);
    }

}

④
@Profile("dev")
@Component
class DemoListener {

    private final CustomerService customerService;

    DemoListener(CustomerService customerService) {
        this.customerService = customerService;
    }

    ⑤
    @EventListener(ApplicationReadyEvent.class)
    public void exercise() {
        Demo.workWithCustomerService(getClass(), this.customerService);
    }

}
```

① @SpringBootApplication is an annotation that itself is meta-annotated with a few other annotations including @Configuration, @ComponentScan and `@EnableAutoConfiguration`. The first two should be familiar, but we'll come back to the last one in a moment.

② This application has code that runs under different profiles. Spring can take a hint from the environment as to which profile should be active in several different ways, including environment variables or Java `System` properties. I'd *normally* stick with just using the environment variables.

③ `SpringApplication.run(⋯)` is standard Spring Boot. This is part of every single application. It comes provided with the framework and does everything that our trivial `SpringUtils.run` method did (and considerably more).

④ In previous examples, constructing the application in production was different from the recipe for testing it. So we had to duplicate code. Here, Spring Boot behaves the same in both a test and in the production code, so we keep the call to `Demo.workWithCustomerService(CustomerService)` in a bean that is only active if the `dev` Spring profile is active.

⑤ Spring is a big bag of beans. Components can talk to each other through the use of `ApplicationEvent` instances. In this case, our bean listens for the `ApplicationReadyEvent` that tells us when the application is just about ready to start processing requests. This event gets called as late as possible in the startup sequence as possible.

The event listener mechanism is nice because it means we no longer have to muddy our `main(String [] args)` method; it is the same from one application to another.

The `@EnableAutoConfiguration` annotation, though not seen, is arguably the most important part of the code we just looked at. It activates Spring Boot's auto-configuration. Auto-configuration classes are run by the framework at startup time and given a chance to contribute objects to the resulting object graph. Specifically, when Spring Boot starts up it inspects the text file, `META-INF/spring.factories`, in all `.jar` artifacts on the CLASSPATH. Spring Boot itself provides one, but your code could as well. The `spring.factories` text file enumerates keys and values associated with those keys.

Therein, Spring Boot inspects a line that begins with

org.springframework.boot.autoconfigure.EnableAutoConfiguration. This line has as its value a *yuuuuge* list of fully-qualified class names. These class names are Java configuration classes. They're classes that, in turn, contribute objects to the Spring object graph. Objects that do the things we'd much rather not do. Like, configure a web server. Or a DataSource. Or a PlatformTransactionManager and TransactionTemplate. Did you notice that we didn't import the rsb.bootstrap.DataSourceConfiguration class as we did in previous examples? That we didn't define anything, really, except the bean required to exercise our CustomerService implementation.

```
package rsb.bootstrap.bootiful;

import org.springframework.stereotype.Service;
import rsb.bootstrap.BaseCustomerService;
import rsb.bootstrap.CustomerService;
import rsb.bootstrap.enable.TransactionalCustomerService;

import javax.sql.DataSource;

①
@Service
class BootifulCustomerService extends TransactionalCustomerService {

    BootifulCustomerService(DataSource dataSource) {
        super(dataSource);
    }

}
```

① This implementation simply extends the existing @Transactional-annotated example. We could've defined that bean using a @Bean provider method, too, I suppose.

Thus far, the properties we've been using - from application.properties - are automatically read in when the application starts up. We've been using keys that start with spring.datasource all this time because those are the keys that Spring Boot is expecting. It'll even load the right property file based on which Spring profile is active!

This auto-configuration is helpful already, but we can do a whole lot more. Let's build a REST API.

```
package rsb.bootstrap.bootiful;

import org.springframework.web.bind.annotation.GetMapping;
import org.springframework.web.bind.annotation.RestController;
import rsb.bootstrap.Customer;
import rsb.bootstrap.CustomerService;

import java.util.Collection;

①
@RestController
public class BootifulRestController {

    private final CustomerService customerService;

    public BootifulRestController(CustomerService customerService) {
        this.customerService = customerService;
    }

    ②
    @GetMapping("/customers")
    Collection<Customer> get() {
        return this.customerService.findAll();
    }

}
```

① This is another stereotype annotation, quite like @Component and @Service. It is itself meta-annotated with @Component. It tells Spring that this class is also a @Component but that it is specialized; it exposes handlers that it expects Spring MVC, the web framework in play here, to map to incoming HTTP requests

② Spring MVC knows which HTTP requests to match to which handler based on the handler methods' mapping annotations. Here, this handler method is mapped to HTTP GET requests for the URL /customers.

Run the application and inspect the logs. It will have announced Tomcat started on port(s): ⋯. Note the port. I'm just going to assume it's 8080. You should replace it with the noted port. Then visit http://localhost:8080/customers in your browser to see the resulting JSON output! You could also request that resource using curl. Spring Boot not only configured a working web framework for us, it also configured a webserver! Not just any webserver. It auto-configured Apache Tomcat, the world's leading Java web server, that powers the very large majority of all Java web applications.

Spring Boot will run the application, by default, on port 8080. However, we can easily customize that and so many other things about Spring Boot applications' running behavior by specifying the relevant properties in a `application.properties` or `application.yml` file. Let's look at the configuration file.

```
①
spring.jmx.enabled = false
②
server.port=0
③
management.endpoints.web.exposure.include=*
management.endpoint.health.show-details=always
```

① Do we want Spring Boot to export information about the application over the JMX protocol?

② On what port do we want the web application run? `server.port=0` tells Spring Boot to run the application on any unused port. This is doubly convenient

③ These last two properties tell Spring Boot to expose all the Actuator endpoints and expose the Actuator Health endpoint's details.

What is the Actuator? Glad you asked! Our application is intended for production, and in production, no one can hear your application scream... unless it is visible from an HTTP JSON endpoint that your monitoring systems can inspect. The Spring Boot Actuator library, which is on your CLASSPATH, auto-configures a standard set of HTTP endpoints that articulate the application's state to support observability and operations. Want to know what the application's health is? Visit `http://localhost:8080/actuator/health`. Want to see metrics? Visit `http://localhost:8080/actuator/metrics`. There are many other endpoints, all of which are accessible at the root endpoint, `http://localhost:8080/actuator`.

"Hold on a tick!" I hear you exclaim. "Where did these Actuator endpoints, and the web server that serves them up, come from?" Recall that, way back at the beginning of this journey, we visited the Spring Initializr [http://start.Spring.io], where we selected some dependencies, including `Web` and `Actuator`. This resulted in build artifacts `spring-boot-starter-web` and `spring-boot-starter-actuator` being added to the resulting project's build file. Those artifacts, in turn, contained code that our Spring Boot auto-configuration picks up and configures. It detects the classpath classes and, because those classes are on the classpath, it configures the objects required.

Pretty *bootiful*, right?

3.10. But What If...

You know, I wasn't sure how long this chapter was going to take or if it was even worth doing. I halfway thought that I could take for granted that many people already knew Spring and Spring Boot basics. I wasn't going to do it. I wasn't going to do it until one day; a student approached me with a fairly trivial question in one of my classes. She had used Spring Boot for a couple of years. She'd come to the Spring Boot ecosystem from the Node.js ecosystem and had no other Java background. She had joined a team, and they'd been successful in building a monolithic application with Spring Boot because the happy path cases were friction-free and worked as advertised. Her team had built a pretty sophisticated application and took it to production, entirely by adhering to the happy-paths. She was stuck, however, and wondered if I could help. We spent ten minutes answering the wrong questions when it dawned on me she had no familiarity with Spring Framework itself! She'd never had to use it before Spring Boot. Here was this very competent engineer (she had successfully built React-based applications! She was more sophisticated than I am...) who was stuck because she lacked a foundational understanding of the technologies behind Spring Boot! That is our fault. We on the Spring Boot team are always trying to do better here. I hope that this chapter is a straight line from basics to "bootiful" and that you have an idea of, roughly, what's supposed to happen in a Spring Boot application. Hopefully, this clears up a few things. Hopefully, you've got a clear picture of what to do next.

Sometimes you won't, though! Sometimes things break, and it's hard to be sure why. It can be daunting to debug an application if you don't know where to start, so let's talk about some first-line-of-defense tricks for understanding Spring Boot applications.

- **Use the Debug Switch**: Spring Boot will log all the auto-configuration classes that were evaluated, and in what way, if you flip the debug switch. The easiest way might be to set an environment variable, `export DEBUG=true`, before running the application. You can also run the Java program using `--debug=true`. Your IDE, like IntelliJ IDEA Ultimate edition or Spring Tool Suite, might have a checkbox you can use when running the application to switch the debug flag on

- **Use the Actuator**: the Actuator, as configured in our example, will have many useful endpoints that will aid you. `/actuator/beans` will show you all the objects and how they are wired together. `/actuator/configprops` will show you the properties that you could put in the `application.(yml|properties)` file that can be used to configure the running application. `/actuator/conditions` shows you the same information as you saw printed to the console when the application started. `/actuator/threaddump` and `/actuator/heapdump` will give you thread dumps and heap dumps. Very useful if you're trying to profile or debug race conditions.

- **@Enable Annotations Usually Import Configuration Classes**: You can command or ctrl-click on a `@Enable-` annotation in your IDE, and you'll be shown the source code for the annotation. You'll very commonly see that the annotation has `@Import(…)` and brings in a configuration class that might explain how a given thing is coming to life.

These are some first-cut approaches to problems you might encounter, but they're by no means your only recourse. If you're still stuck, you can depend on the largest community in the Java ecosystem to help you out! We're always happy to help. There is, of course, the chatrooms - `spring-projects`[http://Gitter.im/spring-projects] and `spring-cloud`[http://gitter.im/Spring-Cloud] - where you need only your Github ID to post questions and to chat with the folks behind the projects. The Spring team frequent those chat rooms, so drop on in and say hi! Also, we monitor several different tags on Stackoverflow so be sure to try that, too [http://spring.io/questions]!

3.11. Deployment

We've got an application up and running, and we've even got Actuator in there. At this point, it's time to figure out how to deploy it. The first thing to keep in mind is that Spring Boot is deployed as a so-called "fat" `.jar` artifact. Examine the `pom.xml` file, and you'll find that the `spring-boot-maven-plugin` has been configured. When you go to the root of the project and run `mvn clean package`, the plugin will attempt to bundle up your application code and all the relevant dependencies into a single artifact you can run using `java -jar ...`. In our particular case, it will fail because it won't be able to unambiguously resolve the single class with the `main(String ... args)` method to run. To get it to run, configure the Maven plugin's `mainClass` configuration element, pointing it to the last `Application` instance we created.

```
<plugin>
    <groupId>org.springframework.boot</groupId>
    <artifactId>spring-boot-maven-plugin</artifactId>
    <configuration>
        <mainClass>rsb.bootstrap.bootiful.Application</mainClass>
    </configuration>
</plugin>
```

Now, when you run `mvn clean package`, you'll get a working `.jar` in the `target` directory. You can do any of some things with it from there. You might deploy it to a cloud platform, like Cloud Foundry.

Deploying the application to a Cloud Foundry foundation

```
cf push -p target/my-jar.jar my-new-app
```

This will upload the artifact to the platform, which will assign it a `PORT` and a load-balanced URI to announce on the shell.

You could also containerize the application [https://spring.io/guides/gs/spring-boot-docker/] and deploy that to Cloud Foundry, or a Kubernetes distribution like PKS [https://pivotal.io/platform/pivotal-container-service].

3.12. Next Steps

In this chapter, we've examined the logical evolution of an application from basic to "bootiful." We've hopefully established that Spring Boot is a force multiplier. Hopefully, you're clear on how it could be used to build an application that's destined for production. Hopefully, you're clear on the basic workflow. You start at the Spring Initializr [http://start.spring.io], you add the relevant "starter" dependencies to activate desired functionality, and then configure the application, if necessary, by changing properties and contributing objects. From here, the world is your oyster! There are dozens of Pivotal-sponsored projects supporting Spring and far more besides maintained by third parties. Want to work with Microsoft Azure? Use their Spring Boot support. Want to work with Alibaba's Cloud? Use Spring Cloud Alibaba. Want to work with Google Cloud Platform? Check out Spring Cloud GCP. Want to work on Amazon Web Services? Check out Spring Cloud AWS! The list of interesting third party APIs goes on and on.

Thus far, we've focused entirely on synchronous and blocking, input and output because I presume that this is a model with which you're already familiar, and we could focus in this chapter on Spring itself. The general workflow of building reactive, non-blocking, asynchronous Spring Boot applications is the same as introduced in this chapter. We've just left those specifics for later.

So, let's get to it!

Reactive Spring

Chapter 4. IO, IO, It's Off to Work We Go…

Reactive programming is an approach to writing software that embraces asynchronous input and output (IO). Asynchronous IO is a small idea that portends big changes for software. The idea is simple: alleviate inefficient resource utilization by reclaiming resources that would otherwise be idle as they waited for IO activity. Asynchronous IO inverts the familiar design of IO processing: a client of a stream of data is notified of new data instead of asking for it; this frees the client to do other things while waiting for new notifications. Let's look at an example that compares and contrasts asynchronous IO to synchronous IO.

Let's build a simple program that reads data from a source (a `java.io.File` reference, precisely). First up, an implementation that uses the trusty `java.io.InputStream` implementation:

Read data from a file, synchronously

```
package rsb.io;

import lombok.extern.log4j.Log4j2;
import org.springframework.util.FileCopyUtils;

import java.io.File;
import java.io.FileInputStream;
import java.io.IOException;
import java.util.function.Consumer;

@Log4j2
class Synchronous implements Reader {

    @Override
    public void read(File file, Consumer<Bytes> consumer, Runnable f) throws
IOException {
        try (FileInputStream in = new FileInputStream(file)) { ①
            byte[] data = new byte[FileCopyUtils.BUFFER_SIZE];
            int res;
            while ((res = in.read(data, 0, data.length)) != -1) { ②
                consumer.accept(Bytes.from(data, res)); ③
            }
            f.run();
        }
    }
}
```

① source the file using a regular `java.io.File`

② *pull* the results out of the source one line at a time..

③ I've written this code to accept a `Consumer<BytesPayload>` that gets called when there's new data

Pretty straightforward, eh? The logger will note the current thread for any logged messages towards the beginning of the line. So, if you run this, you'll see in the log output that all input and output is happening on a single thread.

We're *pulling* bytes out of a source of data (in this case, a `java.io.InputStream` subclass, `java.io.FileInputStream`). What's wrong with this example? Well, probably nothing! In this case, we're using an InputStream pointing to data on the local file system. If the file is there, and the hard drive is working, then this code will work as we expect.

What if, instead of reading data from a File, we read data from a network socket and used a different implementation of an InputStream? Nothing to worry about! Well, nothing to worry about *if* the network is infinitely fast, at least. And *if* the network link between this node and another never fails. If those things are correct, then there's certainly nothing to worry about! This code will work just fine..

4.1. A Natural Limit

What happens if the network is slow or down? That would certainly prolong the time it takes to read from the InputStream. Indeed, the read operation may *never* return! A stuck read operation would be a problem if we were planning on doing anything else with the thread on which we're reading data. Sure, we can spin up another thread and read from that one instead. We could keep doing this, up to a point, but eventually, we'll run into a limit where adding threads doesn't increase our ability to scale. We can't have true concurrency beyond the number of cores on our machine. We're stuck! We can't handle more I/O, reads in this case, without adding threads, and our ability to scale up with more threads is, ultimately, limited.

Why is our ability to scale up using threads limited? Natural limitations constrain it in the way Java creates threads using operating system threads. Threads in Java, .NET, and other popular runtimes like Python and Ruby, are backed by operating system threads that the operating system schedules. They have context associated with each one of them. By default, it's 1MB of stack space on the JVM. This space configuration can be changed up and down a little, but ultimately we're not going to add a ton more threads because we're constrained by, if nothing else, RAM. Assuming RAM wasn't a limitation, we'd then be constrained by how quickly the JVM can call into the operating system to switch from one thread to another. What's the point of more threads if we can't reasonably engage all of them to get more work done at the same time? Context switching is expensive.

It's worth mentioning that platforms like the JVM, .NET, and others take a natural middle-of-the-road approach to concurrency. Delegating to the operating system is a safe bet that leads to predictable results and requires minimal concessions from the programmer. Throw your code on a new `java.lang.Thread`, call `Thread#start()`, and you're done! You're officially writing concurrent code. The programmer doesn't have to rethink their approach to coordination between concurrent actors in a system. It can be as straightforward or as complicated as it needs to be.

Other languages take different approaches.

In that example, the bulk of the work is in the reading - there's not much else going on anywhere. We are *IO bound*. We're not, notably, CPU/GPU bound. We're not doing cryptography, or password encoding, or bitcoin mining, for example. Our constraint isn't RAM or disk space, either. We're IO-bound, and if you have to choose a thing to be constrained on in 2018, you could do *much* worse than to be IO bound.

Let's see how an asynchronous IO-centric solution can help us alleviate the monopolization of our threads.

Read data from a file asynchronously

```
package rsb.io;

import lombok.extern.log4j.Log4j2;
import org.springframework.util.FileCopyUtils;

import java.io.File;
import java.io.IOException;
import java.nio.ByteBuffer;
import java.nio.channels.AsynchronousFileChannel;
import java.nio.channels.CompletionHandler;
import java.nio.file.Path;
import java.nio.file.StandardOpenOption;
import java.util.Collections;
import java.util.concurrent.ExecutorService;
import java.util.concurrent.Executors;
import java.util.function.Consumer;

@Log4j2
class Asynchronous implements Reader, CompletionHandler<Integer, ByteBuffer>
```

Chapter 4. IO, IO, It's Off to Work We Go...

```
{
    private final ExecutorService executorService = Executors
.newFixedThreadPool(10);

    private int bytesRead;

    private long position;

    private AsynchronousFileChannel fileChannel;

    private Consumer<Bytes> consumer;

    private Runnable finished;

    public void read(File file, Consumer<Bytes> c, Runnable finished) throws
IOException {
        this.consumer = c;
        this.finished = finished;
        Path path = file.toPath(); ①
        this.fileChannel = AsynchronousFileChannel.open(path,
                Collections.singleton(StandardOpenOption.READ), this
.executorService); ②
        ByteBuffer buffer = ByteBuffer.allocate(FileCopyUtils.BUFFER_SIZE);
        this.fileChannel.read(buffer, position, buffer, this); ③
        while (this.bytesRead > 0) {
            this.position = this.position + this.bytesRead;
            this.fileChannel.read(buffer, this.position, buffer, this);
        }
    }

    @Override
    public void completed(Integer result, ByteBuffer buffer) {

        this.bytesRead = result; ④

        if (this.bytesRead < 0) {
            this.finished.run();
            return;
        }

        buffer.flip();

        byte[] data = new byte[buffer.limit()];
        buffer.get(data);

        ⑤
```

```
        consumer.accept(Bytes.from(data, data.length));

        buffer.clear();

        this.position = this.position + this.bytesRead;
        this.fileChannel.read(buffer, this.position, buffer, this);
    }

    @Override
    public void failed(Throwable exc, ByteBuffer attachment) {
        log.error(exc);
    }

}
```

① this time, we adapt the `java.io.File` into a Java NIO `java.nio.file.Path`

② when we create the `Channel`, we specify, among other things, a `java.util.concurrent.ExecutorService`, that will be used to invoke our `CompletionHandler` when there's data available.

③ start reading, passing in a reference to a `CompletionHandler<Integer, ByteBuffer>` (this).

④ in the callback, we read the bytes out of a `ByteBuffer` into a `byte[]` holder.

⑤ As in the `Synchronous` example, the `byte[]` data is passed to a consumer.

This code's far more complicated. There's a ton of things going on here, and it can seem overwhelming. This code reads data from a Java NIO `Channel` and processes that data, asynchronously, on a separate thread in a callback handler. The thread on which the read was started is free to return to the thread pool where something else will be able to use it. We return virtually instantly after we call `.read(..)`, and when there is finally data available, our callback is invoked, and on a different thread. If there is latency between `.read()` calls, then we can move on and do other things with our thread. The duration of the asynchronous read, from the first byte to the last, is at best as short as the synchronous read duration. It's likely a tiny bit longer. But, for that complexity, we can be more efficient with our threads. We can handle more work, handling more IO across a finite thread pool.

Why does this matter? Why should we be more frugal with our threads so that we can better reuse them? That's a good question! For a start: I work for a cloud computing company. We'd *love* it if, instead of moving beyond synchronous IO, you solved your scale-out problems by buying more application instances! (I kid. I kid.) Jokes aside, you really can buy yourself some more scale if you've built your architecture to be as stateless as possible and to depend on as horizontally-scalable a datastore as possible.

And who says you *do* have a scale problem, anyway? That's also a good point! Suppose the web service you've built (with traditionally synchronous IO) can produce responses to the people's incoming requests faster than when people are arriving and making requests. In that case, you don't need to bother! Indeed, if you feel like you can do that consistently, now and in the future, then your problem's solved, and you don't need this book!

It is worth mentioning that you often can scale out your application instances to handle more users concurrently. Indeed, asynchronous IO *does* make things a bit more complicated, too. That's a reasonable complaint, I'd say. Suppose we agree on nothing else, though. In that case, hopefully, this example highlights the ultimate benefit of reactive code: we can handle more requests and do more work, using asynchronous I/O on the same hardware *if* our work is IO-bound. If it's CPU-bound (e.g., the Fibonacci series, bitcoin mining, or cryptography), then reactive programming won't buy us anything.

4.2. The Missing Metaphor

Most of us don't work with `Channel` *or* `InputStream` implementations for our day-to-day work. We think about things in terms of abstractions. Things like arrays, or, perhaps more likely, the `java.util.Collection` hierarchy. A `java.util.Collection` maps very nicely to an `InputStream`: they both assume that you'll work with all the data, near instantly. You expect to be able to finish reading from most `InputStreams` sooner rather than later. Collection types start to become a bit awkward when you move to larger sums of data; what happens when you're dealing with something potentially infinite - unbounded - like WebSockets or server-sent events? What happens when there's a latency between records? One record arrives now and another not for another minute or hour, such as with a chat, or when the network suffers a failure?

We need a better way to describe different kinds of data. We're describing something asynchronous - something that will *eventually* happen. This might seem a good fit for a `Future<T>` or a `CompletableFuture<T>`, but that only describes *one* eventual thing. Not a whole stream of potentially unlimited things. Java hasn't offered an appropriate metaphor by which to describe this kind of data.

	Synchronous	**Asynchronous**
Single Value	`String read();`	`CompletableFuture<String> read();`
Multiple Values	`Collection<String> read();`	?

Both the `Iterator<T>` and Java 8 `Stream<T>` types can be unbounded, but they are both pull-centric; you ask for the next record instead of having the thing tell you. One assumes that if they did support push-based processing, which lets you do more with your threads, that the APIs would also expose threading and scheduling control. `Iterator` implementations say nothing about threading and Java 8 streams *all* share the same, global, fork-join pool.

If `Iterator` and `Stream` did support push-based processing, then we'd run into another problem that only becomes an issue in IO: we'd need some way to *push back*! As a consumer of data being produced asynchronously, we have no idea when or how much data might be in the pipeline. We don't know if one byte will be produced in the next callback or if a terabyte will be produced! When you pull data off of an `InputStream`, you read as much data as you're prepared to handle, and no more. In the examples above, we read into a `byte[]` buffer of a fixed and known length. In an asynchronous world, we need to communicate to the producer how much data we're prepared to handle.

Yep. We're *definitely* missing something.

4.3. The Reactive Streams Initiative

What we want is something that maps nicely to asynchronous I/O, and that supports a push-back mechanism, or *flow control*, in distributed systems. In reactive programming, the client's ability to signal how much work it can manage is called *backpressure*. There is an excellent deal many projects - Vert.x [https://vertx.io/], Akka Streams [https://doc.akka.io/docs/akka/2.5/stream/], and RxJava 2 [http://reactivex.io/] - that support reactive programming. The Spring team has a project called Reactor [http://projectreactor.io]. There's enough common ground across these different approaches. In cooperation with the community, the people behind these four projects worked to extract from their projects a de-facto standard, the Reactive Streams initiative [http://www.reactive-streams.org]. The Reactive Streams initiative defines four (yep! Just four) types:

The Publisher<T> is a producer of values that may eventually arrive. A Publisher<T> produces values of type T to a Subscriber<T>.

the Reactive Streams Publisher<T>.

```
package org.reactivestreams;

public interface Publisher<T> {

    void subscribe(Subscriber<? super T> s);
}
```

The Subscriber<T> subscribes to a Publisher<T>, receiving notifications on any new values of type T through its onNext(T) method. If there are any errors, its onError(Throwable) method is called. When processing has been completed normally, the subscriber's onComplete method is called.

the Reactive Streams Subscriber<T>.

```
package org.reactivestreams;

public interface Subscriber<T> {

    public void onSubscribe(Subscription s);

    public void onNext(T t);

    public void onError(Throwable t);

    public void onComplete();
}
```

When a Subscriber first connects to a Publisher, it is given a Subscription in the Subscriber#onSubscribe method. The Subscription is arguably the essential part of the whole specification: it enables backpressure. The Subscriber uses the Subscription#request method to request more data (long n more records, or Long.MAX_VALUE, which is virtually unlimited) or the Subscription#cancel method to halt processing.

The Reactive Streams Subscription<T>.

```
package org.reactivestreams;

public interface Subscription {

    public void request(long n);

    public void cancel();
}
```

The Reactive Streams specification provides *one* more useful, albeit obvious, type: A Processor<A, B> that extends both Subscriber<A> and Publisher<B>.

The Reactive Streams `Processor<T>`.

```
package org.reactivestreams;

public interface Processor<T, R> extends Subscriber<T>, Publisher<R> {
}
```

4.4. Are We There Yet?

The specification is not meant to be a prescription for the implementations. Instead, it defines types for interoperability. The Reactive Streams types are so obviously useful that they *eventually* found their way into the recent Java 9 release as one-to-one semantically equivalent interfaces in the `java.util.concurrent.Flow` class, e.g.: `java.util.concurrent.Flow.Publisher<T>`. These are just interfaces at the moment. As of this writing, the JDK doesn't offer any implementations of these types, but you can build implementations of reactive types using other projects and then adapt them to and from the JDK 9 types. So, *clearly*, we'll need an implementation to use either the reactive streams types or the JDK types.

Look at those types and imagine trying to write asynchronous code in terms of the interactions between `Publisher<T>` and `Subscriber<T>`. Imagine being able to describe *all* asynchronous operations in terms of these new, succinct, types. That's what got me hooked. I wanted a "grand unified theory" for incorporating asynchronicity into my code. I wouldn't say I liked that this fundamental pattern needed to be re-implemented for each implementation. I've got a lot of experience working in messaging and enterprise-application integration. I know that systems are more robust when they're better decoupled, and asynchronicity is a form of temporal decoupling. It means that the consumer doesn't need to be there when the producer is. Spring Integration makes it easy to address integration because many of the enterprise systems with which Spring Integration integrates are asynchronous.

I love Spring Integration and the projects that build upon it, including Spring Cloud Stream. They simplify the abstraction of messaging for intra-process communication. It's nice to know I can think about distributed things that way with no friction. The core of the Spring Integration abstractions, a `Message<T>` and `MessageChannel`, have been in Spring Framework itself since 4.0.

It's *almost* painless to string together two services asynchronously. This approach to integration works, but there is no built-in notion of backpressure (for the simple reason that not all systems with which Spring Integration integrates) support it. So it's a case-by-case thing. This approach doesn't *quite* feel right when thinking about IO. It's close! It's just *not quite* there! I want types that support backpressure, and I want that same sense of ubiquitous purpose that the Spring Integration types gave me. The Reactive Streams types, paired with an implementation like Reactor [http://ProjectReactor.io], give me that.

Big things happen when big ideas become small. Realistically, asynchronicity isn't such a big deal once you get used to it. Several languages (Erlang, Go, to name but a few) have surfaced this asynchronicity as a first-class construct. Programmers of those languages wield asynchronicity with ease. The tooling (the language and the runtime) are purpose-built to support asynchronous idioms. It becomes commonplace and cheap to achieve. This gives rise to abstraction and higher-order systems. If *everything* is a reactive streams `Publisher<T>`, we can think about bigger things more freely. We can take the asynchronous interaction for granted.

We're not done, though, are we? Those types are useful, but they do one thing and one thing only, really well: move data from producer to consumer. They're sort of like the equivalent of reactive `Object[]` arrays. Want to process the data in-flight? Want to filter it? Transform it? We can do that sort of thing in the Java `Collection` and `Stream` APIs, why not here? This is where there's room for implementation differentiation, and so these sorts of operations are instead supported by projects like the Reactor project [http://projectreactor.io/].

Is Reactor enough? Are we *there* yet? Not quite! Imagine if, for the last however many years, the popular projects powered your stack (including Spring and Hibernate) *didn't* support things like the `java.util.Collection` hierarchy. I mean, imagine if they *really* hated those types. Imagine that, beyond merely throwing an `Exception`, those types also caused those projects to send an impolite email to your boss and then segfault your machine! They really, *really* hated those types! Would you still use them? The technologies that you use in your day to day work don't support these types, but you've got work to be done and a way to get it done. You'd make sure to steer well clear of the `java.util.Collection<T>` types and instead use whatever was recommended. You can't just *not* get work done, after all!

4.5. Towards a More Functional, Reactive Spring

The same situation applies here. The Reactive Streams types, and Reactor itself, are only as useful as their possible applications. It is with this insight that we on the Spring team began our reactive journey years ago. It is a journey that reached its first significant landmark with the generally available Spring Framework 5 in September 2017. That release was the first to ship a net-new reactive web runtime called Spring WebFlux. Spring Data Kay and Spring Security 5 both followed a few months later; both provide reactive integrations and build on Spring Framework 5. In March of 2018, we released Spring Boot 2, and a handful of months later, we released Spring Cloud Finchley, a framework supporting (reactive) distributed systems and microservices.

Those releases all assume a Java 8 baseline. Java 8 brings with it lambdas and a ton of other niceties that are compelling features for application developers and, us, the framework developers! The Spring team has created new APIs that assume the presence of lambdas. These APIs are more functional; they benefit from Java 8's strengths in building DSLs.

But Java 8 isn't the only language to support DSLs! The furthest thing from it. Groovy, Scala, and Kotlin all work nicely with existing Java APIs. We've been quite taken with Kotlin on the Spring team. It's an excellent language with a ton of features. It's got, by some measures, the largest community on the JVM after Java itself, and the team behind it seem keen on making it the right choice for Spring developers. Its popularity on Android doesn't hurt things, either. Kotlin would've been a fine choice for Spring developers, even if we did nothing else. We wanted to go further, to build more elegant integrations. We've shipped Kotlin-first APIs that live collocated alongside Java APIs, often in the same `.jar`. You won't even really encounter these extension APIs unless you're consuming these libraries from Kotlin. Kotlin makes it possible for us to create even nicer DSLs than is currently possible with Java. We'll cover Kotlin, too.

4.6. Next Steps

With those releases behind us, you and I, we, have an opportunity to look forward to a horizon where our applications are end-to-end reactive, where applications are both as efficient as can be for the common cases *and* as straightforward as possible.

Chapter 5. Reactor

In this chapter, we'll look at the foundational types from the Reactive Streams specification and from Pivotal's project Reactor that you'll use for virtually everything else in the rest of the book. Arguably, this is the most important chapter. Almost everything else in this book just builds these types into Spring.

If you already know Spring, then this is the missing piece, the delta. For you, those familiar with Spring, the rest of this book will just be about exploring the possibilities made possible with the integration of reactive programming. How cool is that? Here we are, folks. I don't want to diminish the rest of the book. They introduce the details that make clear how to follow through. But this is where I'd start. If you *don't* know Spring, well, I've got an introductory chapter you can read that doesn't assume reactive programming at all. It introduces core Spring concepts. Read that first. Then this. Voilá.

You don't need Spring to write Reactor-based applications any more than you need Reactor to write Spring-based applications. It's their synergy, that's so exciting. But plenty of people do amazing things with just Reactor. The Microsoft Azure SDK team, for example, uses it in the implementation of their Java SDK clients. They even encourage its use, in some cases over other options, in the Microsoft Azure SDK guidelines for Java [https://azure.github.io/azure-sdk/java_design.html#async-api].

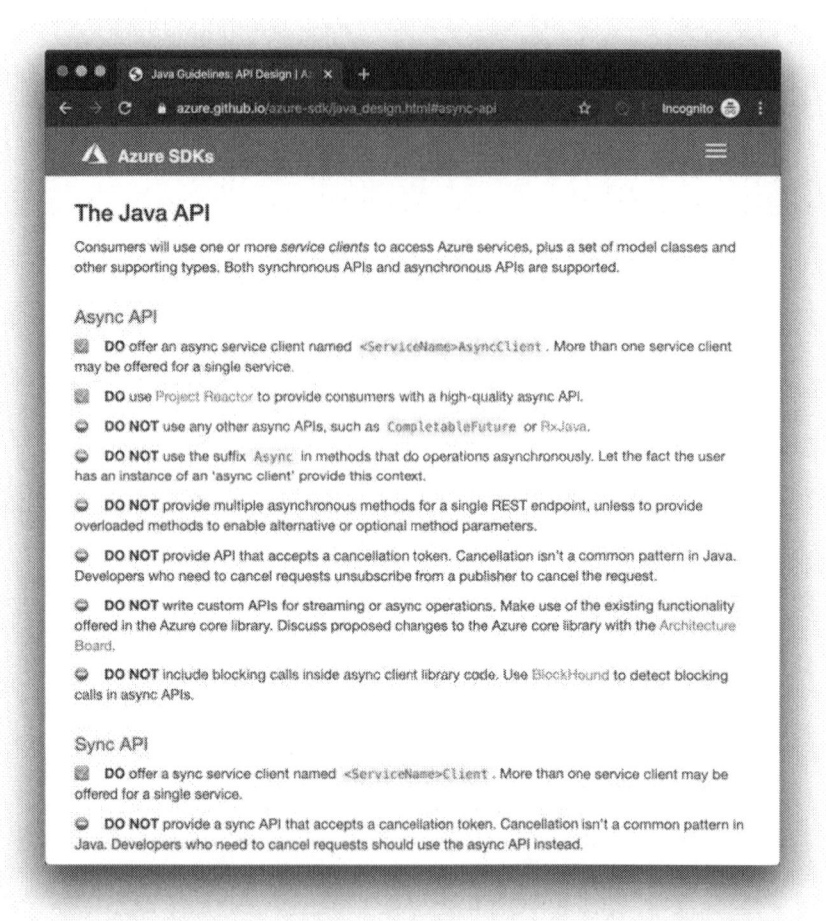

Figure 2. The Microsoft Azure SDK guidelines for Java

The CloudFoundry team also built their Java client using just Reactor [https://www.infoq.com/articles/Designing-Implementing-Using-Reactive-APIs/].

5.1. The Reactive Streams Specification

Reactive programming offers a solution to a reasonably old problem: how do we handle more users? How do we scale? How do we make more efficient use of our threads? Reactive programming supports cooperative multithreading. If we are willing to change the way we write code, so that we can give the runtime better insight into when we're not using a given thread, then the runtime can more responsibly schedule work on threads. This efficiency is a good thing, so long as threads are a precious resource on the JVM.

Reactive programming requires that we rewrite our code to signal to the runtime when we're using or not using a given thread. We need to change the way we describe asynchronous processing. Suppose you wanted to make a network call to another node. In a traditional blocking IO, your code would sit on a thread, blocking, waiting for the new data arrives. During this time, nobody else in the system could reuse the thread on which you were working.

In 2015 a few organizations, including Pivotal, Netflix, Lightbend (né "Typesafe"), and the Eclipse Foundation, worked together to extract some common-ground interfaces to represent asynchronous, latent, possibly unbounded streams of data.

The Reactive Streams specification consists of four interfaces and a single class. Let's look at the four interfaces.

The Reactive Streams Publisher<T> *interface.*

```
package org.reactivestreams;

public interface Publisher<T> {
    public void subscribe(Subscriber<? super T> s);
}
```

The first interface, Publisher<T>, *publishes* - broadcasts! - data (of type T) to a Subscriber<T>.

The Reactive Streams Subscriber<T> *interface.*

```
package org.reactivestreams;

public interface Subscriber<T> {

    public void onSubscribe(Subscription s);

    public void onNext(T t);

    public void onError(Throwable t);

    public void onComplete();
}
```

As soon as a Subscriber<T> subscribes, it receives a Subscription, which is arguably the most crucial class from the whole Reactive Streams specification, and we'll return to it in a moment.

The onError method processes any errors encountered in the stream. Errors - or Exception instances - are just another kind of data in the Reactive Streams specification. There's nothing special about them. They're conducted, in the same way, as regular data. Remember, Reactor moves the flow of execution from one thread to another in the course of its work. It's a scheduler. You can't rely on the standard control-flow mechanisms like try-catch. It's a simplifying matter then to have a uniform channel for processing errors.

The Reactive Streams Subscription *interface.*

```
package org.reactivestreams;

public interface Subscription {

    public void request(long n);

    public void cancel();
}
```

The Subscription, which the Subscriber<T> receives in the onSubscribe method, is unique for each Subscription. New Subscriber<T> instances create new `Subscription` instances. The subscribers will have three distinct subscriptions. A subscription is a link between the producer and the consumer, the `Publisher<T>` and the `Subscriber<T>`. The `Subscriber<T>` uses the `Subscription` to request more data with the `request(int)` data. This last point is critical: the subscriber controls the flow of data, the *rate* of processing. The publisher will not produce more data than the amount for which the subscriber has asked. The subscriber can't be overwhelmed (and if it is ever overwhelmed, it has only itself to blame).

Have you ever used a message queue, like Apache Kafka or RabbitMQ? Message queues are a critical component of a distributed system. They ensure that decoupled components remain alive by buffering the messages, allowing the consumers of those messages to consume the messages as they can, and no faster. This regulated consumption of data is flow control.

Have you ever written a network protocol using TCP/IP or UDP? When you design network protocols, you'll need to think about creating message frames (the structure of a message sent over the wire), and you'll need to think about what happens when one side in a network exchange moves faster than the other. Then you get into discussions of buffering and so on. This regulated consumption of data is flow control.

The `Subscription` allows the subscriber to request more data when it's ready to process that data. This regulated consumption of data is flow control.

In the world of reactive programming, sometimes flow control is - as a matter of marketing perhaps as much as anything else - called *backpressure*.

The Reactive Streams `Processor<T,R>` *interface.*

```
public interface Processor<T, R> extends Subscriber<T>, Publisher<R> {
}
```

`Processor<T>` is the last interface in the Reactive Streams specification. It is just a bridge, implementing both `Publisher<T>` and `Subscriber<T>`. It is a producer *and* a consumer, a source *and* a sink. That's it.

These types are useful. They plug a significant gap in our working vocabulary. They're so helpful that they've since been incorporated into the JDK, starting with version 9, as part of the `java.util.concurrent.Flow` top-level type. The types are otherwise identical.

The last type in the Reactive Streams library, `org.reactivestreams.FlowAdapters`, is a concrete class that helps you adapt the Reactive Streams types interchangeably to and from the Java 9 `Flow`. analogs.

5.2. Project Reactor

The Reactive Streams types are not enough, ultimately. You'll need higher-order implementations to support operations like filtering and transformations. Pivotal's Reactor project [http://ProjectReactor.io] is the right choice here; it builds on top of the Reactive Streams specification and fleshes out the API to support everyday processing tasks.

The Reactor project is an opensource project that's sponsored principally by Pivotal and, if you'll indulge me in a little horn-tooting: it's become quite popular. Facebook uses it in its reactive network protocol, RSocket Java [https://github.com/rsocket/rsocket-java] client. Salesforce uses it in its reactive gRPC implementation [https://github.com/salesforce/reactive-grpc]. It implements the Reactive Streams types specification and can interoperate with other technologies that support Reactive Streams, like Netflix's RxJava 2 [https://github.com/ReactiveX/RxJava/blob/2.x/src/main/java/io/reactivex/Flowable.java], Lightbend's Akka Streams [https://doc.akka.io/docs/akka/current/stream/operators/Sink/asPublisher.html#aspublisher], and the Eclipse Foundation's Vert.x project [https://vertx.io/docs/vertx-reactive-streams/java/].

Reactor is a wise choice. The iteration shipped in Spring Framework 5 was co-developed in tandem with RxJava 2, and with the direct support of RxJava's lead, David Karnok. Even before it's debut in Spring Framework 5 as a top-level component model, Reactor was part of Spring Framework 4, shipped in 2014, to support the WebSocket integration first shipped in that release. It was there, but not surfaced as a top-level abstraction. In Spring Framework 5, Reactor is front-and-center. Its APIs permeate Spring

Webflux, the net-new reactive web runtime developed from the ground up on top od Reactor.

You could use RxJava 2, of course. Any technology that can produce a `Publisher<T>` will work just fine with Spring. I wouldn't since it'd be an extra classpath dependency for Spring Webflux applications. But you could. RxJava is a pleasant environment. It offers a lot of the same, productive operators, uniformly named, that Reactor does while also working on older versions of Java. Reactor has a Java 8 baseline version. RxJava is popular on Android, among other places, where it is harder to ensure that your programs will run on newer versions of the JVM.

Reactor provides two specializations of `Publisher<T>`. The first, `Flux<T>`, is a `Publisher<T>` that produces zero or more values. It's unbounded. The second, `Mono<T>`, is a `Publisher<T>` that emits zero or one value.

They're both publishers, and you can treat them that way, but they go much further than the Reactive Streams specification. They both provide operators, ways to process a stream of values. Reactor types compose nicely - the output of one thing can be the input to another, and if a type needs to work with other streams of data, they rely upon `Publisher<T>` instances.

Both `Mono<T>` and `Flux<T>` implement `Publisher<T>`; we recommend that your methods accept `Publisher<T>` instances but return `Flux<T>` or `Mono<T>` to help the client distinguish the kind of data given. Suppose a method returns a `Publisher<T>`, and you need to render a user-interface for that `Publisher<T>`. Should you deliver a detail page for one record, as you might, given a `CompletableFuture<T>`? Or should you render an overview page, with a list or grid displaying *all* the records in a pageable fashion? It's hard to know. `Flux<T>` and `Mono<T>`, on the other hand, are clear. You know to render an overview page when dealing with a `Flux<T>`, and a detail page for one (or no) record when dealing with a `Mono<T>`. The specializations have distinct semantics.

In the Reactor world, we say that a stream emits *signal*. Each time it emits a new message, that's a signal. Each time a subscriber gets a new subscription, that's a signal. Each time a stream aborts abnormally, that's a signal. A `Signal` is a concept and a part of the interface for these types, and we'll see later that we can listen for these signals.

5.3. Creating New Reactive Streams

You can create a new `Publisher<T>` in several ways. The *worst* way to do it is to implement `Publisher<T>` yourself. Whatever your result, it'll be half-baked, insufficiently specified, and buggy version of the types in Reactor. Not to mention, it'll be a huge time waste! So don't do it.

You can create a `Flux<T>` that emits multiple elements, synchronously or asynchronously, through the API.

```
package rsb.reactor;

import org.junit.Test;
import org.reactivestreams.Publisher;
import reactor.core.publisher.Flux;
import reactor.core.publisher.Mono;
import reactor.test.StepVerifier;

import java.util.Arrays;
import java.util.Date;
import java.util.concurrent.atomic.AtomicInteger;
import java.util.function.Supplier;
import java.util.stream.Stream;

public class SimpleFluxFactoriesTest {

    @Test
    public void simple() {

        ①
        Publisher<Integer> rangeOfIntegers = Flux.range(0, 10);
        StepVerifier.create(rangeOfIntegers).expectNextCount(10)
.verifyComplete();

        ②
        Flux<String> letters = Flux.just("A", "B", "C");
        StepVerifier.create(letters).expectNext("A", "B", "C").
verifyComplete();

        ③
        long now = System.currentTimeMillis();
```

```
        Mono<Date> greetingMono = Mono.just(new Date(now));
        StepVerifier.create(greetingMono).expectNext(new Date(now))
.verifyComplete();

        ④
        Mono<Object> empty = Mono.empty();
        StepVerifier.create(empty).verifyComplete();

        ⑤
        Flux<Integer> fromArray = Flux.fromArray(new Integer[] { 1, 2, 3 });
        StepVerifier.create(fromArray).expectNext(1, 2, 3).verifyComplete();

        ⑥
        Flux<Integer> fromIterable = Flux.fromIterable(Arrays.asList(1, 2, 3
));
        StepVerifier.create(fromIterable).expectNext(1, 2, 3).verifyComplete
();

        ⑦
        AtomicInteger integer = new AtomicInteger();
        Supplier<Integer> supplier = integer::incrementAndGet;
        Flux<Integer> integerFlux = Flux.fromStream(Stream.generate(supplier
));
        StepVerifier.create(integerFlux.take(3)).expectNext(1).expectNext(2)
.expectNext(3)
                .verifyComplete();
    }

}
```

① Create a new Flux whose values are in a (finite) range

② Create a new Flux whose values are the literal strings A, B, and C

③ Create a new Mono whose single value is a java.util.Date

④ Create an empty Mono

⑤ Create a Flux whose elements come from a Java Array

⑥ Create a Flux whose elements come from a Java Iterable, which describes among other things all java.util.Collection subclasses like List, Set, etc.

⑦ Create a new Flux from a Java 8 Stream

There are also various factory methods that you can use to adapt Reactive

Streams types from those of java.util.concurrent.Flow.*. If you have a Java 9 Flow.Publisher, you can use the Reactor-specific reactor.adapter.JdkFlowAdapter to create Flux<T> and Mono<T> instances from a Flow.Publisher instance. There's also a Reactive Streams type called FlowAdapters, which converts generic Reactive Streams types to and from the various Java 9 types. Here's an example that demonstrates how to convert to and from Flow.* types and Reactive Streams types.

Chapter 5. Reactor

```
package rsb.reactor;

import org.junit.Test;
import org.reactivestreams.FlowAdapters;
import org.reactivestreams.Publisher;
import reactor.adapter.JdkFlowAdapter;
import reactor.core.publisher.Flux;
import reactor.test.StepVerifier;

import java.util.concurrent.Flow;

public class FlowAndReactiveStreamsTest {

    @Test
    public void convert() {
        ①
        Flux<Integer> original = Flux.range(0, 10);

        Flow.Publisher<Integer> rangeOfIntegersAsJdk9Flow = FlowAdapters
                .toFlowPublisher(original);
        Publisher<Integer> rangeOfIntegersAsReactiveStream = FlowAdapters
                .toPublisher(rangeOfIntegersAsJdk9Flow);

        StepVerifier.create(original).expectNextCount(10).verifyComplete();

        StepVerifier.create(rangeOfIntegersAsReactiveStream).expectNextCount(10)
                .verifyComplete();

        ②
        Flux<Integer> rangeOfIntegersAsReactorFluxAgain = JdkFlowAdapter
                .flowPublisherToFlux(rangeOfIntegersAsJdk9Flow);
        StepVerifier.create(rangeOfIntegersAsReactorFluxAgain)
.expectNextCount(10)
                .verifyComplete();

    }

}
```

① The first few lines demonstrate converting to and from Reactive Streams types with the Reactive Streams conversions

② The second few lines demonstrate converting to and from Reactor Flux<T> and Mono<T> types using the Reactor conversions

The best part of reactive programming is that it gives you one kinda "stuff" - a uniform interface for dealing with asynchronous streams in an asynchronous world. The only trouble is that for Reactor to do its magic and support your use cases, you need to adapt the real world's asynchronous events into the requisite `Publisher<T>` interface. How do you take events from a Spring Integration inbound adapter and turn it into a stream? How do you take events from a JMS broker and turn those into a stream? How do you take data emitted from an existing threaded application and process them as a reactive stream?

Let's look at an example using the `Flux.create` factory method. The factory method takes a consumer as a parameter. The consumer contains a reference to an emitter of data, a thing of type `FluxSink<T>`. Let's see what that looks like to create a stream for data published in a raw background thread. The `Flux.create` factory method is a great way to adapt non-reactive code, piece by piece, to the reactive world.

The following example launches a thread when the stream initializes. The new thread stashes a reference to the `FluxSink<Integer>`, using it to emit random value at random times up until five values have been emitted. Then, the stream completes. This example shows how to adapt asynchronous things in the world to a Reactive Stream type using some convenient factory methods.

```
package rsb.reactor;

import lombok.extern.log4j.Log4j2;
import org.junit.Assert;
import org.junit.Test;
import reactor.core.publisher.Flux;
import reactor.core.publisher.FluxSink;
import reactor.test.StepVerifier;

import java.util.concurrent.ExecutorService;
import java.util.concurrent.Executors;
import java.util.concurrent.atomic.AtomicInteger;

@Log4j2
public class AsyncApiIntegrationTest {

    private final ExecutorService executorService = Executors
```

```
    .newFixedThreadPool(1);

    @Test
    public void async() {
        ①
        Flux<Integer> integers = Flux.create(emitter -> this.launch(emitter, 5));
        ②
        StepVerifier
                .create(integers.doFinally(signalType -> this.executorService.shutdown()))
                .expectNextCount(5)//
                .verifyComplete();
    }

    ③
    private void launch(FluxSink<Integer> integerFluxSink, int count) {
        this.executorService.submit(() -> {
            var integer = new AtomicInteger();
            Assert.assertNotNull(integerFluxSink);
            while (integer.get() < count) {
                double random = Math.random();
                integerFluxSink.next(integer.incrementAndGet());④
                this.sleep((long) (random * 1_000));
            }
            integerFluxSink.complete(); ⑤
        });
    }

    private void sleep(long s) {
        try {
            Thread.sleep(s);
        }
        catch (Exception e) {
            log.error(e);
        }
    }
}
```

① The Flux.create factory passes a reference to a FluxSink<T> in a Consumer<FluxSink<T>>. We will use the FluxSink<T> to emit new elements as they become available. It is important that we stash this reference for later.

② It's important to tear down any resources once the Flux has finished its work.

③ The `launch` method spins up a background thread using the `ExecutorService`. Setup whatever connections with an external API only after execution inside the callback has begun.

④ Each time there's a new element, use the `FluxSink<T>` to emit a new element

⑤ Finally, once we've finished emitting elements, we tell the `Subscriber<T>` instances.

5.4. Processors

Thus far, we've looked at how to create new `Flux` and `Mono` instances and how to adapt them to an from the java 9 `Flow.` variants. All of these things are, ultimately, just `Publisher<T>`. They produce data that a Subscriber eventually consumes. Whenever you have a `Publisher<T>`, there's bound to be a `Subscriber<T>` somewhere. They're a package deal. A `Publisher<T>` produces data, and a `Subscriber<T>` consumes data. Sometimes, you will want something that acts as a bridge, performing double duty and satisfying the contract for both `Publisher<T>` and `Subscriber<T>` - useful if you need to adapt from one type to the other, for example. `Processor<T>` is fit for purpose here.

Project Reactor supports several handy `Processor<T>` implementations. Let's look at some of them.

The first one up is the `EmitterProceessor`, which acts like a `java.util.Queue<T>`, allowing one end to pump data into it and the other to consume that data.

Chapter 5. Reactor

```
package rsb.reactor;

import org.junit.Test;
import reactor.core.publisher.EmitterProcessor;
import reactor.core.publisher.Flux;
import reactor.core.publisher.FluxSink;
import reactor.test.StepVerifier;

public class EmitterProcessorTest {

    @Test
    public void emitterProcessor() {
        EmitterProcessor<String> processor = EmitterProcessor.create();①
        produce(processor.sink());
        consume(processor);
    }

    ②
    private void produce(FluxSink<String> sink) {
        sink.next("1");
        sink.next("2");
        sink.next("3");
        sink.complete();
    }

    ③
    private void consume(Flux<String> publisher) {
        StepVerifier //
                .create(publisher)//
                .expectNext("1")//
                .expectNext("2")//
                .expectNext("3")//
                .verifyComplete();
    }
}
```

① The EmitterProcessor.create factory method creates a new EmitterProcessor that acts as a sort of queue.

② The produce method publishes three strings, 1,2, and 3 with the EmitterProcessor.

③ The consume method confirms the publication of the three elements.

Another quite useful `Processor<I,O>` is the `ReplayProcessor` that replays either unbounded items or a limited number of items to any late `Subscriber<T>`. In the example below, we configure a `ReplayProcessor` that will replay the last two items observed for as many `Subscriber<T>` instances as want to subscribe.

```
package rsb.reactor;

import org.junit.Test;
import reactor.core.publisher.Flux;
import reactor.core.publisher.FluxSink;
import reactor.core.publisher.ReplayProcessor;
import reactor.test.StepVerifier;

public class ReplayProcessorTest {

    @Test
    public void replayProcessor() {
        int historySize = 2;
        boolean unbounded = false;
        ReplayProcessor<String> processor = ReplayProcessor.create(historySize,
                unbounded); ①
        produce(processor.sink());
        consume(processor);
    }

    ②
    private void produce(FluxSink<String> sink) {
        sink.next("1");
        sink.next("2");
        sink.next("3");
        sink.complete();
    }

    ③
    private void consume(Flux<String> publisher) {
        for (int i = 0; i < 5; i++)
            StepVerifier//
                    .create(publisher)//
                    .expectNext("2")//
                    .expectNext("3")//
                    .verifyComplete();
    }

}
```

① The ReplayProcessor.create factory method creates a processor that will retain the last 2 elements (its history) and that will only do so for a limited (bounded) number of subscribers.

② The `produce` method publishes three elements.

③ The `consume` method then confirms the last two elements' publication for five different subscriptions.

5.5. Operators

Once you've got a working `Publisher<T>`, you can use operators on it. There are tons of operators. We'll review them shortly, but what you need to remember is that they don't affect the publisher on which they operate. They create new `Publishers`. Each `Publisher<T>` is immutable.

In this chapter, we're going to look at a *lot* of different examples, and we're going to do so in terms of small, usually in-memory, reactive streams. I would encourage you to imagine that each of these streams has data that *could* be coming from a database or another microservice. A `Flux<Integer>` is the same regardless of whether those `int` values come from a network call or a hardcoded literal values in code.

5.5.1. Transform

I did just say that a stream is immutable. But, what if you want to operate on an existing publisher? Use the `transform` operator. It gives you a reference to the current Publisher in which you can customize it. It's convenient as a way to generically modify a `Publisher<T>`. It gives you a chance to change the Publisher at assembly time, on initialization.

```java
package rsb.reactor;

import org.junit.Assert;
import org.junit.Test;
import reactor.core.publisher.Flux;
import reactor.test.StepVerifier;

import java.util.concurrent.atomic.AtomicBoolean;

public class TransformTest {

    @Test
    public void transform() {
        var finished = new AtomicBoolean();
        var letters = Flux//
                .just("A", "B", "C").transform(
                        stringFlux -> stringFlux.doFinally(signal -> finished.set(true)));①
        StepVerifier.create(letters).expectNextCount(3).verifyComplete();
        Assert.assertTrue("the finished Boolean must be true.", finished.get());
    }

}
```

① The `transform` operator gives us a chance to act on a Flux<T>, customizing it. This can be quite useful if you want to avoid extra intermediate variables.

There are several operators that you need to know to be productive. The Reactor team talks about some of these as the "reactive starter pack." Let's look at some of those.

5.5.2. Do This and Then That

In typical, non-asynchronous programming, network requests issued on line one finish before those on the next line. This deterministic behavior is critical in reasoning about the application. In the asynchronous and reactive world, we have fewer guarantees. If you want to string together the resolution of data in a stream, use the thenMany operator variants.

```java
package rsb.reactor;

import org.junit.Assert;
import org.junit.Test;
import reactor.core.publisher.Flux;
import reactor.test.StepVerifier;

import java.util.concurrent.atomic.AtomicInteger;

public class ThenManyTest {

    @Test
    public void thenMany() {
        var letters = new AtomicInteger();
        var numbers = new AtomicInteger();
        Flux<String> lettersPublisher = Flux.just("a", "b", "c")
                .doOnNext(value -> letters.incrementAndGet());
        Flux<Integer> numbersPublisher = Flux.just(1, 2, 3)
                .doOnNext(number -> numbers.incrementAndGet());
        Flux<Integer> thisBeforeThat = lettersPublisher.thenMany(numbersPublisher);
        StepVerifier.create(thisBeforeThat).expectNext(1, 2, 3).verifyComplete();
        Assert.assertEquals(letters.get(), 3);
        Assert.assertEquals(numbers.get(), 3);
    }

}
```

There's another variant, then, that accepts a Mono<T> instead of a Flux<T> but whose usage is otherwise the same.

5.5.3. Map

The first is map, which applies a function to each item emitted in the stream. This function modifies each item by the source Publisher<T> and emits the modified item. The source stream gets replaced with another stream whose values are the output of the function applied to each item in the source stream.

```
package rsb.reactor;

import org.junit.Test;
import reactor.core.publisher.Flux;
import reactor.test.StepVerifier;

public class MapTest {

    @Test
    public void maps() {
        var data = Flux.just("a", "b", "c").map(String::toUpperCase);
        StepVerifier.create(data).expectNext("A", "B", "C").verifyComplete();
    }

}
```

5.5.4. FlatMap and ConcatMap

The question then is, what happens if I have a Publisher of items, and for each item, I call into another service that returns a `Publisher<T>`? Then, if you only had map, you'd have `Publisher<Publisher<T>>`, which is harder to work with. We have an outer stream made up of inner streams.

There are several operators, `flatMap`, `concatMap`, and `switchMap`, that flatten inner streams, merging them into the outer stream.

Two operators, `flatMap` and `concatMap`, work pretty much the same. They both merge items emitted by inner streams into the outer stream. The difference between `flatMap` and `concatMap` is that the order in which the items arrive is different. `flatMap` interleaves items from the inner streams; the order may be different.

Suppose you had an outer stream with values 1, 2, and 3. Let's suppose you needed to send those values to some network service that returns a `Flux<String>`. You could `flatMap` over the outer stream, launching network calls as you go. Some network calls might take 10 ms, others 100ms. You don't know. And in this case, the order doesn't matter. So we might see the results from 2 emitted before the result for 1.

Here's a simple example that artificially delays each inner stream. So the first item is the most delayed, the second item is less delayed, and the third item is least delayed. The result is that the items in the outer stream emit backward, 3, 2, 1. Whichever items from the inner stream finish publishing data, then merge into the outer stream. As the data in the inner stream finishes emitting, it merges into the outer stream.

```
package rsb.reactor;

import lombok.AllArgsConstructor;
import lombok.extern.log4j.Log4j2;
import org.junit.Test;
import reactor.core.publisher.Flux;
import reactor.test.StepVerifier;

import java.time.Duration;

@Log4j2
public class FlatMapTest {

    @Test
    public void flatMap() {

        Flux<Integer> data = Flux
                .just(new Pair(1, 300), new Pair(2, 200), new Pair(3, 100))①
                .flatMap(id -> this.delayReplyFor(id.id, id.delay));
        StepVerifier//
                .create(data)//
                .expectNext(3, 2, 1)//
                .verifyComplete();
    }

    private Flux<Integer> delayReplyFor(Integer i, long delay) {
        return Flux.just(i).delayElements(Duration.ofMillis(delay));
    }

    @AllArgsConstructor
    static class Pair {

        private int id;

        private long delay;

    }
}
```

The concatMap operator, on the other hand, preserves the order of items. The main disadvantage of concatMap is that it has to wait for each Publisher<T> to complete its work. You lose asynchronicity on the emitted items. It does its work one-by-one, so you can guarantee the ordering of the results.

Reactor team member Sergei Egorov has often talked about the great example of event processing. In such a scenario, each message corresponds to a mutation of some state, The following events, in the following order, mutate the state in a customer record: "read," "update," "read," "delete," and "read." These commands should be processed in the same order; you don't want those updates processed in parallel. Use `concatMap` to ensure that ordering.

In this test, we repeat the same test as last time but verify that the results come out in the same order as they arrived.

```java
package rsb.reactor;

import lombok.AllArgsConstructor;
import lombok.extern.log4j.Log4j2;
import org.junit.Test;
import reactor.core.publisher.Flux;
import reactor.test.StepVerifier;

import java.time.Duration;

@Log4j2
public class ConcatMapTest {

    @Test
    public void concatMap() {
        Flux<Integer> data = Flux
                .just(new Pair(1, 300), new Pair(2, 200), new Pair(3, 100))//
                .concatMap(id -> this.delayReplyFor(id.id, id.delay));
        StepVerifier//
                .create(data)//
                .expectNext(1, 2, 3)//
                .verifyComplete();
    }

    private Flux<Integer> delayReplyFor(Integer i, long delay) {
        return Flux.just(i).delayElements(Duration.ofMillis(delay));
    }

    @AllArgsConstructor
    static class Pair {

        private int id;

        private long delay;

    }

}
```

5.5.5. SwitchMap

Both `flatMap` and `concatMap` eventually process every inner stream so long as they all finally complete.

`switchMap` is different; it cancels any outstanding inner publishers as soon as a new value arrives.

Imagine a network service offering predictions based on input characters - the quintessential lookahead service.

You type "re" in a textbox, triggering a network request, and predictions for possible completions return. You type "rea" and trigger another network request.

You type "reac" and trigger yet another request.

You might type faster than the network service can provide predications, which means you might type "react" before the predictions for "reac" are available. Use `switchMap` to cancel the previous as-yet incomplete network calls, preserving only the latest outstanding network call for "react" and, eventually, "reactive."

In the example, characters are *typed* faster than the network service call delivering predictions, so there's continuously an outstanding request. In this example, we use `delayElements(long)` to artificially delay the publication of elements in the streams. So, the outer stream (the words typed) emits new values every 100 ms. The inner stram (the network call) emits values every 500 ms. The outer stream only ever sees the final results for the last word, "reactive."

```
package rsb.reactor;

import org.junit.Test;
import reactor.core.publisher.Flux;
import reactor.test.StepVerifier;

import java.time.Duration;

public class SwitchMapTest {

    @Test
    public void switchMapWithLookaheads() {
        Flux<String> source = Flux //
                .just("re", "rea", "reac", "react", "reactive") //
                .delayElements(Duration.ofMillis(100))//
                .switchMap(this::lookup);
        StepVerifier.create(source).expectNext("reactive -> reactive")
.verifyComplete();
    }

    private Flux<String> lookup(String word) {
        return Flux.just(word + " -> reactive")//
                .delayElements(Duration.ofMillis(500));
    }

}
```

5.5.6. Take and Filter

A `Publisher<T>` might emit an infinite number of records, and you may not be interested in everything, so you can use `take(long)` to limit the number of elements.

If you want to apply some predicate and stop consuming messages when that predicate matches, use `takeUntil(Predicate)`. There are other take variants. One that might be particularly useful in a networked microservice context is `take(Duration)`.

```
package rsb.reactor;

import org.junit.Test;
import reactor.core.publisher.Flux;
import reactor.test.StepVerifier;

public class TakeTest {

    @Test
    public void take() {
        var count = 10;
        Flux<Integer> take = range().take(count);
        StepVerifier.create(take).expectNextCount(count).verifyComplete();
    }

    @Test
    public void takeUntil() {
        var count = 50;
        Flux<Integer> take = range().takeUntil(i -> i == (count - 1));
        StepVerifier.create(take).expectNextCount(count).verifyComplete();
    }

    private Flux<Integer> range() {
        return Flux.range(0, 1000);
    }

}
```

As you work your way through a stream, you might want to selectively filter out some values, which you can do with `filter`. The `filter` operator applies a predicate to a stream of values, discarding those that don't match the predicate.

```
package rsb.reactor;

import lombok.extern.log4j.Log4j2;
import org.junit.Test;
import reactor.core.publisher.Flux;
import reactor.test.StepVerifier;

@Log4j2
public class FilterTest {

    @Test
    public void filter() {
        Flux<Integer> range = Flux.range(0, 1000).take(5);
        Flux<Integer> filter = range.filter(i -> i % 2 == 0);
        StepVerifier.create(filter).expectNext(0, 2, 4).verifyComplete();
    }

}
```

5.5.7. The DoOn* Callbacks

The two specializations in Reactor - `Flux` and `Mono` - implement `Publisher<T>` and handle all the work of buffering, emitting, handling errors, etc.

```
package rsb.reactor;

import lombok.extern.log4j.Log4j2;
import org.junit.Assert;
import org.junit.Test;
import org.reactivestreams.Subscription;
import reactor.core.publisher.Flux;
import reactor.core.publisher.Signal;
import reactor.core.publisher.SignalType;
import reactor.test.StepVerifier;

import java.util.ArrayList;
import java.util.Arrays;

@Log4j2
public class DoOnTest {

    @Test
    public void doOn() {
```

```java
        var signals = new ArrayList<Signal<Integer>>();
        var nextValues = new ArrayList<Integer>();
        var subscriptions = new ArrayList<Subscription>();
        var exceptions = new ArrayList<Throwable>();
        var finallySignals = new ArrayList<SignalType>();

        Flux<Integer> on = Flux//
                .<Integer>create(sink -> {
                    sink.next(1);
                    sink.next(2);
                    sink.next(3);
                    sink.error(new IllegalArgumentException("oops!"));
                    sink.complete();
                })//
                .doOnNext(nextValues::add) //
                .doOnEach(signals::add)//
                .doOnSubscribe(subscriptions::add)//
                .doOnError(IllegalArgumentException.class, exceptions::add)//
                .doFinally(finallySignals::add);

        StepVerifier//
                .create(on)//
                .expectNext(1, 2, 3)//
                .expectError(IllegalArgumentException.class)//
                .verify();

        signals.forEach(log::info);
        Assert.assertEquals(4, signals.size());

        finallySignals.forEach(log::info);
        Assert.assertEquals(finallySignals.size(), 1);

        subscriptions.forEach(log::info);
        Assert.assertEquals(subscriptions.size(), 1);

        exceptions.forEach(log::info);
        Assert.assertEquals(exceptions.size(), 1);
        Assert.assertTrue(exceptions.get(0) instanceof
IllegalArgumentException);

        nextValues.forEach(log::info);
        Assert.assertEquals(Arrays.asList(1, 2, 3), nextValues);
    }

}
```

5.5.8. Taking Control of Your Streams' Destiny

So far, we've looked at a lot of different operators that give you the ability to control flow - the control what value arrives and when, to control how values arrive, to control *if* they arrive. Sometimes, however, you may want a little more control. You might have some complex logic, and you want to see all the pieces in one place. In this case, you use `Flux#handle` or `Mono#handle`.

Let's look at an example that analyzes values in the stream and emits them as long as they're less than an upper bound max. If processing completes, then the stream emits a completion signal.

If a value in the stream equals the error parameter, then an error arrives.

The following example creates two streams. The first emits an exception, and so the stream completes exceptionally, and never emits a completion signal.

The second stream never emits an error signal and so completes and emits a completion signal.

```
package rsb.reactor;

import lombok.extern.log4j.Log4j2;
import org.junit.Test;
import reactor.core.publisher.Flux;
import reactor.test.StepVerifier;

import java.util.stream.Collectors;
import java.util.stream.Stream;

@Log4j2
public class HandleTest {

    @Test
    public void handle() {

        StepVerifier//
                .create(this.handle(5, 4))//
                .expectNext(0, 1, 2, 3)//
                .expectError(IllegalArgumentException.class)//
```

```
                .verify();
        StepVerifier//
                .create(this.handle(3, 3))//
                .expectNext(0, 1, 2)//
                .verifyComplete();
    }

    Flux<Integer> handle(int max, int numberToError) {
        return Flux//
                .range(0, max) ①
                .handle((value, sink) -> {
                    var upTo = Stream.iterate(0, i -> i < numberToError, i ->
 i + 1)
                            .collect(Collectors.toList());
                    if (upTo.contains(value)) {
                        sink.next(value);
                        return;
                    }
                    if (value == numberToError) {
                        sink.error(new IllegalArgumentException("No 4 for
 you!"));
                        return;
                    }
                    sink.complete();
                });
    }
}
```

① The `Publisher<T>` publishes `max` elements which are then passed to the handle method where we can veto its emission, emit an error, or anything else we'd like to do.

5.6. Operator Fusion

We've just introduced a ton of new operators. They're useful because they give us ways to work with different streams - to compose them, to process them, etc. The programming model provides a very convenient way to work with data; I hope you'll agree. Keep in mind, however, that they're not general-purpose Java 8 Streams replacements or `Array[]` replacements. If you're just looping through records, then those are going to be faster. Reactor is still very efficient, mind you. It's just not as efficient as primitives not designed to support all the things that Reactor supports.

When you change a stream using an operator, there's an internal queue that stages the changes from the previous stream operator to the next one.

One of the things that makes Reactor so efficient is what it calls "operator fusion." RxJava lead David Karnok worked with Project Reactor lead Stéphane Maldini and implemented the concepts, along with standard operators, in a shared foundational library, `reactive-streams-commons`. RxJava 2+ lead David Karnok does a great job describing operator fusion in this blog post [https://akarnokd.blogspot.com/2016/03/operator-fusion-part-1.html], from which I'll borrow in this example.

The idea is simple: identify operators that could share implementation details like the internal queues, atomic variables, etc., so to cut down on inefficient allocation and garbage collection. Reactor does this sort of thing behind the scenes, without you needing to ask it.

There are two types of operator fusion: micro and macro.

Micro fusion happens when two or more operators share their resources or internal structures, bypassing some of the typical overhead. Micro-fusion happens mostly at subscription time. The original idea of micro-fusion was the recognition that operators that end in an output queue and operators starting with a front-queue could share the same `Queue` instance, saving on allocation and saving on the drain-loop work-in-progress serialization atomics.

Macro fusion refers to the collapsing of similar, compatible operators into one operation. So, `a.then(b).then(c).then(d)` could be fused into `a.then(b,c,d)`, for example.

5.7. Schedulers and Threads

Thus far, you've seen me introduce a lot of asynchronicity using `delayElements(Duration)`. It delays the emission of data in a stream. It's a great way to simulate the latency or asynchronicity in real-life events- and events-processing scenarios. Everything else we've seen so far is more or less like a Java 8 stream: containers holding data with operators to operate on the data. What's the missing piece that handles time? How'd time get mixed into all of this?

Behind the scenes, Reactor has a `Scheduler`. In Reactor, the runtime effortlessly moves the thread of execution for your streams - your streams - from one thread to another. You don't have to worry bout this, but it is critical to how it works. Reactor is an event loop: it spins up a `Scheduler` (sort of like a thread pool) to move work on and off of the CPU as quickly as possible.

By default, all code runs on a non-blocking `Scheduler`. This global, default `Scheduler` creates one thread per core on your machine. So, if you have four cores, then you'll have four threads. This arrangement is perfectly acceptable, assuming you don't block on any of those threads. If you do something that blocks, remember that you wouldn't be blocking only one request, you could be preventing a quarter of your users from getting responses! We'll discuss later how to identify blocking code, so you never make that mistake. If you didn't do it by mistake - if you genuinely have something that can only scale-out by adding threads - you must offload that work to another `Scheduler`, one designed to scale up and down to accommodate extra work.

Remember though that if you introduce code into the stream that requires threads, you'll limit your scalability to your system's ability to create new threads, effectively putting you back at square one. Hopefully, your blocking interactions are few and far between and easily isolated.

You can control which Scheduler you're using, and you can manipulate the defaults as well. The centerpiece for all schedulers in a Reactor-based application is `Schedulers`.

The `Schedulers` class offers static factory methods that support creating different kinds of schedulers supporting synchronous execution, scalable thread pools, and custom `Schedulers` backed by custom `java.util.concurrent.Executor` instances.

```
package rsb.reactor;
```

```java
import lombok.extern.log4j.Log4j2;
import org.aopalliance.intercept.MethodInterceptor;
import org.junit.After;
import org.junit.Assert;
import org.junit.Before;
import org.junit.Test;
import org.springframework.aop.framework.ProxyFactoryBean;
import reactor.core.publisher.Flux;
import reactor.core.scheduler.Schedulers;
import reactor.test.StepVerifier;

import java.time.Duration;
import java.util.concurrent.ScheduledExecutorService;
import java.util.concurrent.atomic.AtomicInteger;

@Log4j2
public class SchedulersExecutorServiceDecoratorsTest {

    private final AtomicInteger methodInvocationCounts = new AtomicInteger();

    private String rsb = "rsb";

    @Before
    public void before() {
        ①
        Schedulers.resetFactory();
        ②
        Schedulers.addExecutorServiceDecorator(this.rsb, (scheduler,
                scheduledExecutorService) -> this.decorate
(scheduledExecutorService));
    }

    @Test
    public void changeDefaultDecorator() {
        Flux<Integer> integerFlux = Flux.just(1).delayElements(Duration
.ofMillis(1));
        StepVerifier.create(integerFlux).thenAwait(Duration.ofMillis(10))
                .expectNextCount(1).verifyComplete();
        Assert.assertEquals(1, this.methodInvocationCounts.get());
    }

    @After
    public void after() {
        Schedulers.resetFactory();
        Schedulers.removeExecutorServiceDecorator(this.rsb);
    }
```

```java
    private ScheduledExecutorService decorate(ScheduledExecutorService executorService) {
        try {
            var pfb = new ProxyFactoryBean();
            pfb.setProxyInterfaces(new Class[] { ScheduledExecutorService.class });
            pfb.addAdvice((MethodInterceptor) methodInvocation -> {
                var methodName = methodInvocation.getMethod().getName().toLowerCase();
                this.methodInvocationCounts.incrementAndGet();
                log.info("methodName: (" + methodName + ") incrementing...");
                return methodInvocation.proceed();
            });
            pfb.setSingleton(true);
            pfb.setTarget(executorService);
            return (ScheduledExecutorService) pfb.getObject();
        }
        catch (Exception e) {
            log.error(e);
        }
        return null;
    }

}
```

① We will customize the defaults for all `Schedulers` in this test, so it's important to reset the changes between runs

② `Schedulers.addExecutorServiceDecorator` lets you decorate the newly minted `Scheduler` instances in some fashion. Our decorator is a fairly tame proxy that logs out any method invocations

You can also tap into the scheduled execution of a given stream using `Schedulers.onScheduleHook`. It lets you modify the `Runnable` that ultimately gets executed by the Reactor Scheduler. You can see it in action here.

Chapter 5. Reactor

```
package rsb.reactor;

import lombok.extern.log4j.Log4j2;
import org.junit.Assert;
import org.junit.Test;
import reactor.core.publisher.Flux;
import reactor.core.scheduler.Schedulers;
import reactor.test.StepVerifier;

import java.time.Duration;
import java.util.concurrent.atomic.AtomicInteger;

@Log4j2
public class SchedulersHookTest {

    @Test
    public void onScheduleHook() {
        var counter = new AtomicInteger();
        Schedulers.onScheduleHook("my hook", runnable -> () -> {
            var threadName = Thread.currentThread().getName();
            counter.incrementAndGet();
            log.info("before execution: " + threadName);
            runnable.run();
            log.info("after execution: " + threadName);
        });
        Flux<Integer> integerFlux = Flux.just(1, 2, 3).delayElements(
Duration.ofMillis(1))
                .subscribeOn(Schedulers.immediate());
        StepVerifier.create(integerFlux).expectNext(1, 2, 3).verifyComplete(
);
        Assert.assertEquals("count should be 3", 3, counter.get());
    }

}
```

You don't need to change the global Scheduler to influence how (and where) a single stream is executed. You can specify the Scheduler on which to publish or subscribe to messages in a stream.

Use subscribeOn(Scheduler) on either Mono or Flux to specify on which Scheduler the runtime should run subscribe, onSubscribe, and request. Placing this operator anywhere in the chain will also impact the execution context of onNext, onError, and onComplete signals from the beginning of the chain up to the next occurrence of a `publishOn(Scheduler)`.

Use `publishOn(Scheduler)` on either `Mono` or `Flux` to specify on which `Scheduler` the runtime should run `onNext`, `onComplete`, and `onError`. This operator influences the threading context where the rest of the operators in the chain below it will execute, up to the next occurrence of `publishOn(Scheduler)`. This operator is typically used to serialize or slow down fast publishers that have slow consumers.

```java
package rsb.reactor;

import lombok.extern.log4j.Log4j2;
import org.junit.Assert;
import org.junit.Test;
import reactor.core.publisher.Mono;
import reactor.core.scheduler.Scheduler;
import reactor.core.scheduler.Schedulers;
import reactor.test.StepVerifier;

import java.util.concurrent.ConcurrentHashMap;
import java.util.concurrent.Executors;
import java.util.concurrent.atomic.AtomicInteger;

@Log4j2
public class SchedulersSubscribeOnTest {

    @Test
    public void subscribeOn() {
        var rsbThreadName = SchedulersSubscribeOnTest.class.getName();
        var map = new ConcurrentHashMap<String, AtomicInteger>();
        var executor = Executors.newFixedThreadPool(5, runnable -> {
            Runnable wrapper = () -> {
                var key = Thread.currentThread().getName();
                var result = map.computeIfAbsent(key, s -> new AtomicInteger());
                result.incrementAndGet();
                runnable.run();
            };
            return new Thread(wrapper, rsbThreadName);
        });
        Scheduler scheduler = Schedulers.fromExecutor(executor); ①
        Mono<Integer> integerFlux = Mono.just(1).subscribeOn(scheduler)
                .doFinally(signal -> map.forEach((k, v) -> log.info(k + '=' + v)));②
        StepVerifier.create(integerFlux).expectNextCount(1).verifyComplete();
        var atomicInteger = map.get(rsbThreadName);
        Assert.assertEquals(atomicInteger.get(), 1);
    }

}
```

① We create our own Scheduler using a custom Executor. Each thread created in our custom Executor ends up wrapped in a custom Runnable that notes the name of the current thread and increments the reference count

② Use the `subscribeOn` method to move the subscription to our custom `Scheduler`

Many different static factory methods supporting the creation of new `Scheduler` instances hang off the `Schedulers` class. You can use `Schedulers.immediate()` to obtain a `Scheduler` that runs code on the current, caller thread. `Schedulers.parallel()` is optimized for running fast, non-blocking executions. `Schedulers.single()` is optimized for low-latency one-off executions. `Schedulers.elastic()` is optimized for longer executions, and is an alternative for blocking tasks where the number of active tasks and threads grow indefinitely. This is an unbounded thread pool. `Schedulers.boundedElastic()` is optimized for longer executions, and is an alternative for blocking tasks where the number of active tasks (and threads) is capped. If none of these suit your use case, you can always factory a new `Scheduler` using `Schedulers.fromExecutorService(ExecutorService)`.

5.8. Hot and Cold Streams

So far, most of the streams that we've looked at are what we would call *codl streams* - they represent a sequence of data that materialized when we started subscribing to the data. We could subscribe again and get the same data back. The source of data is produced by the act of subscription. The producer of the data is created by the consumer, in this case.

A stream is said to be *hot* when the consumer of the data does not create the producer of the data. This is a natural scenario, such as when the data stream exists independent of any particular subscriber. A stream of stock ticker updates, presence status change events, time, etc. These are all things that re the same for any subscriber, no matter when the subscriber subscribes to it. A consumer that subscribes to the current price of a stock isn't going to get the first price that the stock has ever had; it'll get the current price, whatever and whenever that is. A hot stream is more like our notion of a real stream of water: each time you step foot (or, in this case, subscribe to it) into it, you're stepping into a different stream.

This example shows how to use an `EmitterProcessor` (which are like synchronous Queue<T>s) to publish three items of data. The first subscriber sees the first two elements. The second subscriber subscribes. Then a third item is published, and both the first and the second subscribers see it. The fact that the producer is *hot* means that the second subscriber observes only the last element, not the first two.

```java
package rsb.reactor;

import org.junit.Assert;
import org.junit.Test;
import reactor.core.publisher.EmitterProcessor;
import reactor.core.publisher.FluxSink;

import java.util.ArrayList;
import java.util.List;
import java.util.function.Consumer;

public class HotStreamTest1 {

    @Test
    public void hot() throws Exception {

        var first = new ArrayList<Integer>();
        var second = new ArrayList<Integer>();

        EmitterProcessor<Integer> emitter = EmitterProcessor.create(2);
        FluxSink<Integer> sink = emitter.sink();

        emitter.subscribe(collect(first));
        sink.next(1);
        sink.next(2);

        emitter.subscribe(collect(second));
        sink.next(3);
        sink.complete();

        Assert.assertTrue(first.size() > second.size());①
    }

    Consumer<Integer> collect(List<Integer> collection) {
        return collection::add;
    }

}
```

① There should be more elements captured in the first subscriber's collection than in the second one since the second one only observed one element.

This example is a little more involved. It uses an actual asynchronous

Consumer to subscribe two times to a hot stream. The first subscriber sees all the elements since it subscribed at the outset. The example publishes ten integers into the stream, each item delayed by ten milliseconds. The first subscriber subscribers immediately and sees all the values. A bit of time passes. A second subscriber subscribes and observes only the values published since it subscribed.

This example is a little more involved since it forces convergence of both asynchronous subscribers with a CountDownLatch and then evaluates whether the first stash of observed elements from the first subscriber is more massive than the second stash of items from the second subscriber.

```java
package rsb.reactor;

import lombok.extern.log4j.Log4j2;
import org.junit.Assert;
import org.junit.Test;
import reactor.core.publisher.Flux;
import reactor.core.publisher.SignalType;

import java.time.Duration;
import java.util.ArrayList;
import java.util.List;
import java.util.concurrent.CountDownLatch;
import java.util.concurrent.TimeUnit;
import java.util.function.Consumer;

@Log4j2
public class HotStreamTest2 {

    @Test
    public void hot() throws Exception {
        int factor = 10;
        log.info("start");
        var cdl = new CountDownLatch(2);
        Flux<Integer> live = Flux.range(0, 10).delayElements(Duration
.ofMillis(factor))
                .share();
        var one = new ArrayList<Integer>();
        var two = new ArrayList<Integer>();
        live.doFinally(signalTypeConsumer(cdl)).subscribe(collect(one));
        Thread.sleep(factor * 2);
        live.doFinally(signalTypeConsumer(cdl)).subscribe(collect(two));
```

```
            cdl.await(5, TimeUnit.SECONDS);
            Assert.assertTrue(one.size() > two.size());
            log.info("stop");
        }

        private Consumer<SignalType> signalTypeConsumer(CountDownLatch cdl) {
            return signal -> {
                if (signal.equals(SignalType.ON_COMPLETE)) {
                    try {
                        cdl.countDown();
                        log.info("await()...");
                    }
                    catch (Exception e) {
                        throw new RuntimeException(e);
                    }
                }
            };
        }

        private Consumer<Integer> collect(List<Integer> ints) {
            return ints::add;
        }

}
```

This shows how to use the `publish` operator to create a `Publisher<T>` that lets you "pile on" subscribers until a limit is reached. Then, all subscribers may observe the results.

```java
package rsb.reactor;

import org.junit.Assert;
import org.junit.Test;
import reactor.core.publisher.Flux;
import reactor.core.scheduler.Schedulers;

import java.util.ArrayList;
import java.util.List;
import java.util.function.Consumer;

public class HotStreamTest3 {

    private List<Integer> one = new ArrayList<Integer>();

    private List<Integer> two = new ArrayList<Integer>();

    private List<Integer> three = new ArrayList<Integer>();

    private Consumer<Integer> subscribe(List<Integer> list) {
        return list::add;
    }

    @Test
    public void publish() throws Exception {

        Flux<Integer> pileOn = Flux.just(1, 2, 3).publish().autoConnect(3)
                .subscribeOn(Schedulers.immediate()); ①

        pileOn.subscribe(subscribe(one));
        Assert.assertEquals(this.one.size(), 0);

        pileOn.subscribe(subscribe(two));
        Assert.assertEquals(this.two.size(), 0);

        pileOn.subscribe(subscribe(three));
        Assert.assertEquals(this.three.size(), 3);
        Assert.assertEquals(this.two.size(), 3);
        Assert.assertEquals(this.three.size(), 3);
    }

}
```

① Force the subscription on the same thread so we can observe the interactions.

5.9. Context

Reactor provides operators that support the construction of streams that operate on your data, and it moves work effortlessly across threads as it needs to support efficient processing. This is part and parcel of the goals of reactive programming: efficient multithreaded processing. It is our contention that most things you might do in an application will look-and-feel the same with this new multithreaded arrangement.

There are some exceptions. Where does the venerable `ThreadLocal` live in this new seamlessly multithreaded world? A `ThreadLocal` is like a map that has as its key the name of the current client thread and as a value a thread-specific (or "local") value. `ThreadLocal`s are great in the old, non-reactive world for stashing values that are visible to everything in the current thread. This is useful for all sorts of things like storage for the present, ongoing transaction, storage for the currently authenticated user; logging contexts; the request graph trace information associated with the current request, etc. Spring uses them heavily to support the resolution of important values. Typically there's a well known static field of type `ThreadLocal`, a value unique to the current request on a given thread is stashed in the `ThreadLocal`, and framework code that can find that, no matter what tier of the processing chain you are in, to make available for injection.

This arrangement does not work in the brave new reactive world.

Reactor provides a solution called the `Context`. It is a map, as well, supporting any number of keys and values that are tied to the current `Publisher`. The values in the context are unique to the current `Publisher`, *not* the current thread.

Here's an example of a simple reactive `Publisher` that has access to a `Context`. Each time there's a new value emitted, we poke at the current `Context` and ask it for the value that should be in the context, the string `value1`.

```
package rsb.reactor;
```

```java
import lombok.extern.log4j.Log4j2;
import org.junit.Assert;
import org.junit.Test;
import reactor.core.publisher.Flux;
import reactor.core.publisher.Signal;
import reactor.core.publisher.SignalType;
import reactor.util.context.Context;

import java.time.Duration;
import java.util.concurrent.ConcurrentHashMap;
import java.util.concurrent.CountDownLatch;
import java.util.concurrent.atomic.AtomicInteger;

@Log4j2
public class ContextTest {

    @Test
    public void context() throws Exception {
        var observedContextValues = new ConcurrentHashMap<String, AtomicInteger>();
        var max = 3;
        var key = "key1";
        var cdl = new CountDownLatch(max);
        Context context = Context.of(key, "value1");
        Flux<Integer> just = Flux//
                .range(0, max)//
                .delayElements(Duration.ofMillis(1))//
                .doOnEach((Signal<Integer> integerSignal) -> { ①
                    Context currentContext = integerSignal.getContext();
                    if (integerSignal.getType().equals(SignalType.ON_NEXT)) {
                        String key1 = currentContext.get(key);
                        Assert.assertNotNull(key1);
                        Assert.assertEquals(key1, "value1");
                        observedContextValues
                                .computeIfAbsent("key1", k -> new AtomicInteger(0))
                                .incrementAndGet();
                    }
                })//
                .subscriberContext(context);
        just.subscribe(integer -> {
            log.info("integer: " + integer);
            cdl.countDown();
        });

        cdl.await();
```

```
            Assert.assertEquals(observedContextValues.get(key).get(), max);
    }
}
```

① The doOnEach operator is a handy way to gain access to the current Context, whose contents you can then inspect.

5.10. Control Flow

Earlier, we talked about the distinction between assembly vs. execution time. The time we define a Publisher<T> is not the same as the time it is executed. This distinction affords Reactor some time to intervene on our behalf. It can do amazing things like merging similar operations onto the same thread (called "operator fusion"), and it can modify our stream for us. Reactor has time to change the way the pipes of our stream are connected together.

In this section, we're going to look at some patterns and operators that support the natural composition of streams of data.

We couldn't hope to cover all of them, but there are a few that I find myself reaching for all the time for common microservice orchestration use cases. We'll talk about some of these in more depth in subsequent chapters, but let's introduce some of them here.

5.10.1. Error Handlers

If a reactive stream results in an error, then you can trap that error and decide what happens using various operators whose name usually starts with on*.

Use the onErrorResume operator to produce a Publisher that should be emitted starting from the place where the error was encountered.

```java
package rsb.reactor;

import org.junit.Test;
import reactor.core.publisher.Flux;
import reactor.test.StepVerifier;

public class OnErrorResumeTest {

    private final Flux<Integer> resultsInError = Flux.just(1, 2, 3).flatMap(counter -> {
        if (counter == 2) {
            return Flux.error(new IllegalArgumentException("Oops!"));
        }
        else {
            return Flux.just(counter);
        }
    });

    @Test
    public void onErrorResume() {
        Flux<Integer> integerFlux = resultsInError
                .onErrorResume(IllegalArgumentException.class, e -> Flux.just(3, 2, 1));
        StepVerifier.create(integerFlux).expectNext(1, 3, 2, 1).verifyComplete();
    }

}
```

Use the onErrorReturn operator to produce a single value to be emitted starting from the place where the error was encountered.

```java
package rsb.reactor;

import lombok.extern.log4j.Log4j2;
import org.junit.Test;
import reactor.core.publisher.Flux;
import reactor.test.StepVerifier;

@Log4j2
public class OnErrorReturnTest {

    private final Flux<Integer> resultsInError = Flux.just(1, 2, 3).flatMap
(counter -> {
        if (counter == 2) {
            return Flux.error(new IllegalArgumentException("Oops!"));
        }
        else {
            return Flux.just(counter);
        }
    });

    @Test
    public void onErrorReturn() {
        Flux<Integer> integerFlux = resultsInError.onErrorReturn(0);
        StepVerifier.create(integerFlux).expectNext(1, 0).verifyComplete();
    }

}
```

Use onErrorMap if you want to normalize errors or, for some reason, map one error to another. You can use it with other operators to filter particular errors, then canonicalize them, then route to a shared error handler.

```java
package rsb.reactor;

import org.junit.Assert;
import org.junit.Test;
import reactor.core.publisher.Flux;
import reactor.test.StepVerifier;

import java.util.concurrent.atomic.AtomicInteger;

public class OnErrorMapTest {

    @Test
    public void onErrorMap() throws Exception {
        class GenericException extends RuntimeException {

        }
        var counter = new AtomicInteger();
        Flux<Integer> resultsInError = Flux.error(new
IllegalArgumentException("oops!"));
        Flux<Integer> errorHandlingStream = resultsInError
                .onErrorMap(IllegalArgumentException.class, ex -> new
GenericException())
                .doOnError(GenericException.class, ge -> counter
.incrementAndGet());
        StepVerifier.create(errorHandlingStream).expectError().verify();
        Assert.assertEquals(counter.get(), 1);
    }

}
```

5.10.2. Retry

I like to think I'm pretty young, but I've also definitely lived in a world where computers were not everywhere. Today, it's funny even to ponder it, but there was a time when cars, phones, TVs, and other things were mechanical and otherwise devoid of CPUs. But not in my day. If something mechanical didn't work, you could sometimes just whack it on the side, and it would work again. The .retry() operator reminds me of that. It lets you specify that you want to try to re-subscribe to a Publisher<T>. It attempts to recreate the source if any errors occur the first time around when processing the data. The network is the computer, sure, but computers aren't perfect. Things break. The network isn't infinitely fast. Hosts there were there a minute ago may no longer be there now. Whatever the cause, you may need to retry.

Let's suppose you've got a fallen service, and you're trying to obtain a result from the service. If the service experiences some sort of transient error - you know the type: out of disk, no more file descriptors, broken network link, etc. - then you could probably get a correct result if you just retry the request after a (usually small) delay. If that service's deployed on Cloud Foundry or Kubernetes, it'll be up and running in no time; the platform will ensure that a new instance of the application is started and deployed.

```java
package rsb.reactor;

import lombok.extern.log4j.Log4j2;
import org.junit.Test;
import reactor.core.publisher.Flux;
import reactor.test.StepVerifier;
import reactor.tools.agent.ReactorDebugAgent;

import java.util.concurrent.atomic.AtomicBoolean;

@Log4j2
public class ControlFlowRetryTest {

    @Test
    public void retry() {

        var errored = new AtomicBoolean();
        Flux<String> producer = Flux.create(sink -> {
            if (!errored.get()) {
                errored.set(true);
                sink.error(new RuntimeException("Nope!"));
                log.info("returning a " + RuntimeException.class.getName() + "!");
            }
            else {
                log.info("we've already errored so here's the value");
                sink.next("hello");
            }
            sink.complete();
        });

        Flux<String> retryOnError = producer.retry();
        StepVerifier.create(retryOnError).expectNext("hello").verifyComplete();
    }

}
```

The retry demonstrated above is a simple example. It will retry the request if there are any errors and only if there any errors. You can retry up until a certain number of times, at which point an error will be produced. For many transient errors, this solution is workable. There is a potential risk that too many of your clients will approach this service, causing more issues, and contributing to the load that ultimately results in the services being unable to respond in a timely fashion. The *thundering-herd problem* - where the stability of a service or process is impaired due to an overwhelming burst of demand - has struck again!

Introduce a growing backoff period, spacing out each subsequent request, to avoid the thundering herd problem. If the backoff period were identical across all nodes, then this alone wouldn't help simply delay the thundering herds. You need to introduce a *jitter* - sometime to randomize (ever so subtly) the intervals between requests. Retry supports this with the `retryBackoff(long times, Duration duration)` operator.

What if a `Publisher<T>` emits no data and doesn't produce an error? Use `repeatWhenEmpty()`, which will attempt to re-subscribe in the event of an empty `Publisher<T>` If the `Publisher<T>` is empty, and you don't want to re-subscribe, and just want to produce a default value, use `defaultIfEmpty(T default)`.

5.10.3. Merge

I include the `merge(Publisher<Publisher<T>>... publishers)` operator here because it works a bit like `flatMap(Publisher t)`, in that it flattens the `Publisher<T>` elements given to it. Suppose you invoked three times a web service that returned a `Mono<Customer>` Now you've got three `Mono<Customer>` instances. You can create a `Publisher<T>` out of them and then use `merge` to flatten them, producing a `Publisher<Customer>` on which you can now operate in aggregate.

```
package rsb.reactor;

import org.junit.Test;
import reactor.core.publisher.Flux;
import reactor.test.StepVerifier;

import java.time.Duration;

public class ControlFlowMergeTest {

    @Test
    public void merge() {
        Flux<Integer> fastest = Flux.just(5, 6);
        Flux<Integer> secondFastest = Flux.just(1, 2).delayElements(Duration.ofMillis(2));
        Flux<Integer> thirdFastest = Flux.just(3, 4).delayElements(Duration.ofMillis(20));
        Flux<Flux<Integer>> streamOfStreams = Flux.just(secondFastest, thirdFastest,
                fastest);
        Flux<Integer> merge = Flux.merge(streamOfStreams);
        StepVerifier.create(merge).expectNext(5, 6, 1, 2, 3, 4).verifyComplete();
    }

}
```

5.10.4. Zip

The zip operator is beneficial in scatter-gather kinds of processing. Suppose you've issued a call to one database for a sequence of orders (passing in their order IDs), ordered by their ID, and you've made another call to another database for customer information belonging to a given order. So you've got two sequences, of identical length, ordered by the same key (order ID). You can use `zip` to merge them into a `Publisher<T>` of `Tuple*` instances. There are several overloaded versions of this method, each taking a long list of arguments for common scenarios. In this example, we'd only need the variant that takes two `Publisher<T>` elements and returns a `Tuple2` element. Given `Flux<Customer>` customers and `Flux<Order>` orders, we could call `zip(orders, customers)` and would be given a `Flux<Tuple2<Order,Customer>>` in return. The `zip` operator takes one element from the stream on the left, and another operator from the stream on the right, and assigns them (typed!) ordinal positions.

This next example how to use the `zip` operator to take one element from each of one or more streams and emit a new stream with items from each of the source stream. The `zip` operator moves in lockstep, taking emitted values and grouping them.

```java
package rsb.reactor;

import org.junit.Test;
import reactor.core.publisher.Flux;
import reactor.test.StepVerifier;

public class ControlFlowZipTest {

    @Test
    public void zip() {
        Flux<Integer> first = Flux.just(1, 2, 3);
        Flux<String> second = Flux.just("a", "b", "c");
        Flux<String> zip = Flux.zip(first, second)
                .map(tuple -> this.from(tuple.getT1(), tuple.getT2()));
        StepVerifier.create(zip).expectNext("1:a", "2:b", "3:c")
.verifyComplete();
    }

    private String from(Integer i, String s) {
        return i + ":" + s;
    }

}
```

5.10.5. Timeout and First

I've put two operators in this section, `timeout(Duration)` and `first(Publisher<T> a, Pubisher<T> b, Publisher<T> c, ⋯)`. They can be used independently, but I think they're really great as a combo.

The timeout should be fairly obvious: if a value isn't recorded from a `Publisher<T>` within a particular time, a `java.util.concurrent.TimeoutException` is returned. This is an excellent last-line-of-defense for making potentially slow, shaky, service-to-service calls.

There is any number of possible reasons why a service might be down. Suffice it to say that the service to which you've made the request is down, and you've got a client that's depending on the response from this downstream service, pronto. Many organizations have strict service level agreements (SLAs) that they must abide by. An SLA might require that a response be returned within a specific time period. The `timeout` operator is great if you want to timebox potentially error-prone or stalled requests, aborting if the request takes longer than your SLA budget affords you.

```java
package rsb.reactor;

import lombok.extern.log4j.Log4j2;
import org.junit.Assert;
import org.junit.Test;
import reactor.core.publisher.Flux;
import reactor.test.StepVerifier;

import java.time.Duration;
import java.util.concurrent.TimeoutException;

@Log4j2
public class ControlFlowTimeoutTest {

    @Test
    public void timeout() throws Exception {

        Flux<Integer> ids = Flux.just(1, 2, 3).delayElements(Duration
.ofSeconds(1))
                .timeout(Duration.ofMillis(500)).onErrorResume(this::given);

        StepVerifier.create(ids).expectNext(0).verifyComplete();
    }

    private Flux<Integer> given(Throwable t) {
        Assert.assertTrue(
                "this exception should be a " + TimeoutException.class
.getName(),
                t instanceof TimeoutException);
        return Flux.just(0);
    }

}
```

Timeouts work well in shallow service topologies, where one service calls maybe one other service. Suppose, hypothetically, and for the purposes of simple math, that service A advertises an SLA of 10 seconds. If service A calls service B, the timeout could be used in two different ways. In the first scenario, it might be used to return an error value after ten seconds. Simple enough: just wait ten seconds and then return on timeout. It's acting sort of like a circuit breaker, where the error condition is the passing of an interval of time. A slightly more ambitious client might not simply default to an error, but retry the call. In this scenario, though, the client would make the call and then abort with enough time to retry the request at least once. The client may only retry the request one time. So, service A has an SLA of 10 seconds. It follows then that service B would need to have an SLA of 5 seconds, so that service A could try the call and then retry it and still be within its SLA.

Now suppose service B in turn calls service C. The same calculations apply. Service C will need to respond within 2.5 seconds so that service B can retry! Wouldn't it be nice if every client could get as much of the timeout as possible?

The `first` operator gives us a worthy alternative. The `first` operator is the closest thing I can find to the POSIX `select` function. In POSIX, `select` function returns when one or more file descriptors are ready for a class of input and output operations without blocking. Put another way: it can block until data is available in any of a number of file descriptors. The `first` operator doesn't block, of course, but it can help you achieve the same effect: it returns the first `Publisher<T>` from among a number of `Publisher<T>` instances that emits data. Even better, `first` applies backpressure to the other `Publisher<T>` instances. At first, I admit, it's hard to see why you might use this, but it is critical in supporting one of my favorite patterns: service hedging.

Suppose you need to guarantee you meet your SLA when calling a downstream service. If the request is idempotent - that is, the request is a read or can be made many times without any undue observable side-effects - then service hedging can be a handy pattern to have in your toolbox. You can lessen the risk of a slow response by calling the same service, otherwise identically deployed on a number of hosts, and preserving the fastest response. Even if one node is slowed, one of the others is bound to produce a response in time.

```java
package rsb.reactor;

import lombok.extern.log4j.Log4j2;
import org.junit.Test;
import reactor.core.publisher.Flux;
import reactor.test.StepVerifier;

import java.time.Duration;

@Log4j2
public class ControlFlowFirstTest {

    @Test
    public void first() {
        Flux<Integer> slow = Flux.just(1, 2, 3).delayElements(Duration
.ofMillis(10));
        Flux<Integer> fast = Flux.just(4, 5, 6, 7).delayElements(Duration
.ofMillis(2));
        Flux<Integer> first = Flux.first(slow, fast);
        StepVerifier.create(first).expectNext(4, 5, 6, 7).verifyComplete();
    }

}
```

5.11. Debugging

Reactive programming gives you a lot of benefits (which I've established and on which I will harp endlessly for the balance of this book!), but if I had to pick one thing that might pose a small problem to overcome, it's that reactive applications can be hard to debug. Where do errors happen? How do I trace the error to the source of the bug? What can Reactor do to help me find bugs? And, given that Reactor enjoys an enviable position at the heart of all reactive operations in my code, what visibility can it give me into the behavior of my applications that I didn't already have, if any?

If you want to capture detailed information about the logs of a given expectation, use `Hooks.onOperatorDebug()`. It'll turn your stack traces into something more intelligible. `Hooks.onOperatorDebug` gives you extra runtime information in the event of an error, albeit at a cost to your performance.

```java
package rsb.reactor;

import lombok.extern.log4j.Log4j2;
import org.junit.Assert;
import org.junit.Test;
import reactor.core.publisher.Flux;
import reactor.core.publisher.Hooks;
import reactor.core.publisher.Mono;
import reactor.test.StepVerifier;

import java.io.PrintWriter;
import java.io.StringWriter;
import java.time.Duration;
import java.util.concurrent.atomic.AtomicReference;

@Log4j2
public class HooksOnOperatorDebugTest {

    @Test
    public void onOperatorDebug() {
        Hooks.onOperatorDebug();
        var stackTrace = new AtomicReference<String>();
        var errorFlux = Flux//
                .error(new IllegalArgumentException("Oops!"))//
                .checkpoint()//
                .delayElements(Duration.ofMillis(1));

        StepVerifier //
                .create(errorFlux) //
                .expectErrorMatches(ex -> {//
                    stackTrace.set(stackTraceToString(ex));
                    return ex instanceof IllegalArgumentException;
                })//
                .verify();
        Assert.assertTrue(stackTrace.get()
                .contains("Flux.error     at " + HooksOnOperatorDebugTest
.class.getName()));
    }

    private static String stackTraceToString(Throwable throwable) {
        try (var sw = new StringWriter(); var pw = new PrintWriter(sw)) {
            throwable.printStackTrace(pw);
            return sw.toString();
        }
        catch (Exception ioEx) {
            throw new RuntimeException(ioEx);
        }
```

        }
    }

The `Hooks.onOperatorDebug()` call is expensive though! It adds overhead to every single operation. If you want more fine-grained isolation of errors in a stream, use the `checkpoint()` feature.

```
package rsb.reactor;

import lombok.extern.log4j.Log4j2;
import org.junit.Assert;
import org.junit.Test;
import reactor.core.publisher.Flux;
import reactor.core.publisher.Mono;
import reactor.test.StepVerifier;

import java.io.PrintWriter;
import java.io.StringWriter;
import java.time.Duration;
import java.util.concurrent.atomic.AtomicReference;

@Log4j2
public class CheckpointTest {

    @Test
    public void checkpoint() {

        var stackTrace = new AtomicReference<String>();

        var checkpoint = Flux//
                .error(new IllegalArgumentException("Oops!")).checkpoint() //
                .delayElements(Duration.ofMillis(1));

        StepVerifier //
                .create(checkpoint) //
                .expectErrorMatches(ex -> {
                    stackTrace.set(stackTraceToString(ex));
                    return ex instanceof IllegalArgumentException;
                })//
                .verify();

        Assert.assertTrue(stackTrace.get()//
                .contains("Error has been observed at the following site(s): "));
```

```
    }

    private static String stackTraceToString(Throwable throwable) {
        try (var sw = new StringWriter(); var pw = new PrintWriter(sw)) {
            throwable.printStackTrace(pw);
            return sw.toString();
        }
        catch (Exception ioEx) {
            throw new RuntimeException(ioEx);
        }
    }
}
```

The `checkpoint` operator can be more efficient at runtime than `Hooks.onOperatorDebug()` because it isolates the places where Reactor captures stack traces to the site where you've placed a `checkpoint`. That said, wouldn't it be nice if you could get the best of both worlds? Fast, production-optimized performance *and* the rich, detailed stack traces present in the debug information shown before?

What if you really want the operator debug information on all operators, but you also want to avoid the operator's performance costs? Good news, we can have our cake and eat it too! Add the Reactor Tools dependency to your classpath. Reactor Tools is a very useful library and you'll find it required for almost all of the things we're discussing in this section. Add the following dependency:

- `io.projectreactor : reactor-tools`

You'll need to call `ReactorDebugAgent.init();` early on in your code. You might consider the `public static void main(String [] args)` method for your Spring Boot application. Let's look at Blockhound, which helps you to find any code in the application that blocks a thread.

The Reactor Tools are delivered as a sort of Java agent that acts on your code before it's loaded into the JVM. We provide another such library, Blockhound, which helps you ferret out calls to blocking APIs. It'll throw an exception anywhere you invoke a blocking operation. Add the library to the classpath.

Add the following dependency to your build:

- io.projectreactor.tools:blockhound:1.0.1.RELEASE

It's pretty simple to see Blockhound in action: just block where you shouldn't block!

```java
package rsb.reactor;

import lombok.SneakyThrows;
import lombok.extern.log4j.Log4j2;
import org.junit.*;
import reactor.blockhound.BlockHound;
import reactor.blockhound.integration.BlockHoundIntegration;
import reactor.core.publisher.Mono;
import reactor.core.scheduler.Schedulers;
import reactor.test.StepVerifier;

import java.util.ArrayList;
import java.util.List;
import java.util.ServiceLoader;
import java.util.Spliterator;
import java.util.concurrent.atomic.AtomicBoolean;
import java.util.stream.StreamSupport;

import static reactor.blockhound.BlockHound.builder;

// NB: if you want to run this on Java 13 in your IDE, make sure to add
//
// to the "VM Options"
// the Maven build already handles this for you
//
@Log4j2
public class BlockhoundTest {

    private final static AtomicBoolean BLOCKHOUND = new AtomicBoolean();

    @Before
    public void before() {

        BLOCKHOUND.set(true);
        var integrations = new ArrayList<BlockHoundIntegration>();
        var services = ServiceLoader.load(BlockHoundIntegration.class);
        services.forEach(integrations::add);
```

```
        integrations.add(builder -> builder.blockingMethodCallback
(blockingMethod -> {
            if (BLOCKHOUND.get()) {
                throw new BlockingCallError(blockingMethod.toString());
            }
        }));

        BlockHound.install(integrations.toArray(new BlockHoundIntegration[0]
));
    }

    private static class BlockingCallError extends Error {

        BlockingCallError(String msg) {
            super(msg);
        }

    }

    @After
    public void after() {
        BLOCKHOUND.set(false);
    }

    @Test
    public void notOk() {
        StepVerifier//
                .create(this.buildBlockingMono().subscribeOn(Schedulers
.parallel())) //
                .expectErrorMatches(e -> e instanceof BlockingCallError/*
                                                                        * &&
                                                                        *
e.getMessage().
                                                                        *
contains("Blocking call!"
                                                                        * )
                                                                        */
)//
                .verify();
    }

    @Test
    public void ok() {
        StepVerifier//
                .create(this.buildBlockingMono().subscribeOn(Schedulers
.elastic())) //
                .expectNext(1L)//
```

```
            .verifyComplete();
    }

    Mono<Long> buildBlockingMono() {
        return Mono.just(1L).doOnNext(it -> block());
    }

    @SneakyThrows
    void block() {
        Thread.sleep(1000);
    }

}
```

If you are using Java 13 or later, you'll need to add
-XX:+AllowRedefinitionToAddDeleteMethods to your VM options when running the JVM. I've configured a Maven profile in the build that adds the virtual machine options and responds to Java 13 or later if detected. You don't need to explicitly specify the profile using -P.

This Maven configuration demonstrates how to conditionally configure the build to support Blockhound if Java 13 or later is detected when running the tests.

```
<profile>
    <id>blockhound-java-13</id>
    <activation>
        <jdk>[13,)</jdk>
    </activation>
    <build>
        <plugins>
            <plugin>
                <groupId>org.apache.maven.plugins</groupId>
                <artifactId>maven-surefire-plugin</artifactId>
                <configuration>
                    <argLine>-XX:+AllowRedefinitionToAddDeleteMethods</argLine>
                </configuration>
            </plugin>
        </plugins>
    </build>
</profile>
```

With these tools in place, it should be much easier to isolate and understand errors in your reactive pipelines.

5.12. Next Steps

In this chapter, we've looked at how to build reactive streams using Project Reactor. We've looked at factories to create new instances. We've looked at ways to adapt one kind of stream to another. We've looked at ways to control the flow of data in a reactive pipeline. We've looked at ways to compose or combine the pipelines. We also looked at ways to debug reactive streams. You're going to use what you've learned in this chapter *a lot* in your day to day work with reactive APIs. The rest of this book assumes that you've gone through and absorbed most of this chapter. We'll expand in subsequent chapters on some of the ideas introduced here.

Reactive Spring

Chapter 6. Data Access

If your application is the body, then the brain of any application today is its database. Data is also the lifeblood of your application. Your application today spends a good deal of its time processing data, and doing so efficiently is of paramount importance.

In this chapter, we'll look at how to consume data in a natively reactive manner. Reactive data access drivers and clients use asynchronous IO and support backpressure. They should be able to scale out reads and writes independent of threads.

Spring Data can help us here. Spring Data is an umbrella project comprised of numerous modules supporting NoSQL and RDBMS connectivity for different data access clients. As with certain RDBMSes, Cassandra, MongoDB, Couchbase, and Redis, Spring Data supports both a traditional blocking option and a reactive, non-blocking option. These reactive alternatives are built from the ground-up using an asynchronous or reactive driver. For this reason, we don't necessarily have a reactive alternative to some of the non-reactive Spring Data modules yet. There's already talk of a Spring Data Neo4j reactive module, for instance.

We're going to spend this chapter looking at some of the reactive options. Reactive modules are not drop-in replacements for the traditional and blocking options, and so inherent in this chapter is the reality that you'll possibly need to refactor existing data access code to support reactivity. It's non-trivial work, too!

6.1. Why Should You Go Reactive?

So, *why* would you? *Why* should you go reactive when processing data. Data is *the* primary motivation when considering reactive programming. Reactive programming supports the more efficient use of threads and allows nodes in a system to handle more IO-bound work at the same time. Reactive programming gives you cleaner APIs for processing streams of data. It lets you more naturally join, split, filter, and otherwise transform streams of data. Reactive programming surfaces both error handling and backpressure in the APIs themselves, giving consumers a consistent, surface-level API to handle the corner cases that contribute to system instability.

That last point is essential. Keep in mind that all systems have had this instability, but we, more often than not, fail to address it in our blocking code. Our simplifying abstractions have left us blind to the realities of the machine and the network. The insight here is that we're good developers, but it's been entirely too easy not to see these issues. Reactive programming allows us to confront these issues in a consistent, well-understood way.

Data-centric applications are *de rigueur* these days. Organizations are moving more and more data over the wire from one service to another, and they're generating more data, and at an increasing rate. Sensor data, the mobile web, social network activity, big data, and analytics, click stream tracking, machine learning, AI, and the dwindling cost of storing redundant data have all contributed to the growth of data produced in our applications and organizations. Reactive programming lets us manage as much of this data as possible, as efficiently as possible.

Bottom line: reactive programming might offer a more elegant way to process data, and it might offer a way to handle more users with the same resources - connections, threads, and hardware.

Reactive programming requires you to rethink the way you work with a datastore. It's not a drop-in replacement, and so some things fundamental to the way we work with data requires revision.

6.2. What About Transactions?

A database transaction is a logical unit of work that executes independently and discretely. In many databases, database transactions are ACID-compliant. They support atomicity, consistency, isolation, and durability. A transaction lets clients begin a unit of work, write multiple, discrete, records to a database within that unit of work, and then choose to either commit those writes (atomically) or roll them all back, reversing the writes. A client independently connecting to the database would either see the state of the database before the write (no observable changes) or see all the writes to the database. When we say the writes are atomic, we mean that the client would *not* see the database in an inconsistent state, with only some of the writes applied.

SQL datastores are ACID compliant. They support atomically committing or reversing transactions. Whatever approach we use for SQL data access needs to support transactions when working with a SQL datastore. Obviously.

It's a common misconception that NoSQL datastores don't support transactions. While there's historically been some truth to that, the situation is improving. Google's Spanner, for example, famously purports to support distributed transactions on a geographically distributed scale. Neo4J supports transactions. MongoDB 4.0 introduced transaction support, too.

For synchronous or blocking APIs, Spring has long supported the `PlatformTransactionManager` abstraction for resource-local transaction demarcation. When a NoSQL datastore introduces transaction support, we're quick to provide an implementation of the `PlatformTransactionManager` abstraction for that particular resource. Spring Data supports many different resource-local transaction types, beyond those concerned with JDBC-centric data access like `DataSourceTransactionManager`. There are implementations for, among many others, Apache Geode (`GemfireTransactionManager`), Neo4J (`Neo4jTransactionManager`), and - usefully for us - MongoDB (`MongoTransactionManager`). Spring's `PlatformTransactionManager` abstraction helps developers consistently integrate transaction demarcation into a non-reactive Spring application seamlessly.

```
package org.springframework.transaction;

import org.springframework.lang.Nullable;

public interface PlatformTransactionManager extends TransactionManager {

 TransactionStatus getTransaction(@Nullable TransactionDefinition var1)
 throws TransactionException;

 void commit(TransactionStatus var1) throws TransactionException;

 void rollback(TransactionStatus var1) throws TransactionException;
}
```

A transaction's life is short: the transaction starts, work done is committed in the scope of that transaction, or rolled back (usually because some exception has happened). There are try/catch blocks and exceptions, and bits of error handling involved. You need to instantiate the transaction itself and then manage it. It's all pretty yawn-inducing stuff that leaves most people yearning for the simpler, fancy-free world of client-side programming, to which they flee only to then find themselves managing infinitely more complex state machines in the form UI binding frameworks. However, I digress.

You can simplify the work of managing transactions with Spring's `TransactionTemplate`. A `TransactionTemplate` instance manages the state machine for you and lets you focus on the unit-of-work to be done in the transaction, enclosing your unit of work block in a transaction. If there are no exceptions in the enclosed block, then Spring commits the transaction. Otherwise, Spring rolls back the transaction. Imperative transaction management at its finest! Spring's support is excellent for when you need to manage individual units of work within the scope of a given method.

Add `@EnableTransactionManagement` to a `@Configuration`-annotated class to enable declarative transaction management. You can annotate individual methods, or entire classes, with `@Transactional`. Spring automatically encloses your method invocations in a transaction. If the method completes without exception, Spring commits the transaction, and all the work in the body of the method invocation goes with it. Spring rolls back the

Chapter 6. Data Access

transaction if there are any exceptions.

Spring's `PlatformTransactionManager` binds the state for the current transaction to the current thread using a `ThreadLocal`. Any work done in a transaction needs to happen on that one thread. Do you see the wrinkle? This transaction-per-thread approach isn't going to be a fit for reactive data access where execution can, and often does, jump threads.

Spring Framework 5.2 introduces a new hierarchy, rooted in the `ReactiveTransactionManager` type, to support transactions.

```java
package org.springframework.transaction;

import reactor.core.publisher.Mono;

import org.springframework.lang.Nullable;

public interface ReactiveTransactionManager extends TransactionManager {

    Mono<ReactiveTransaction> getReactiveTransaction(@Nullable TransactionDefinition definition)
            throws TransactionException;

    Mono<Void> commit(ReactiveTransaction transaction) throws TransactionException;

    Mono<Void> rollback(ReactiveTransaction transaction) throws TransactionException;

}
```

The `ReactiveTransactionManager` and all of Spring's reactive transaction management support rely on the Reactor `Context` to propagate transactional state across threads. Spring provides the `TransactionalOperator` to imperatively manage reactive transactions.

Spring also supports declarative transaction demarcation using the `@Transactional` annotation so long as the annotated method returns a `Publisher<T>`.

We'll return to the discussion of transaction management in the context of each of the datastores we introduce shortly.

6.3. Reactive SQL Data Access

I've been talking to engineers far-and-wide for the last few years as I introduce organization after organization to reactive programming, and invariably the first question is: does it support JDBC? Is there a way to use JDBC reactively? The answer I've always had to give was brutally honest, if disappointing: JDBC is a fundamentally synchronous and blocking API. It would serve no one if the Spring team were to wrap it and adapt it in the Reactive Streams types. It wouldn't be any more scalable, and the API would be more cumbersome since you'd have to scale out the transactions using threads. Not to mention, it doesn't even integrate with the broader ecosystem of tools that were expecting JDBC in the first place. Why bother?

Some people would slump away, visibly frustrated that I'd helped them to that "aha!" moment with reactive programming only to then have so thoroughly dashed their hopes. Reactive programming was not a solution for them; they despaired. Not yet. A bit of a pity! Done right, a reactive SQL client could offer some of the things sought in NoSQL datastores, namely performance and scalability.

So: for the moment, JDBC is not a very good choice for reactive data access. Now, that's not to say that you can't talk to a SQL datastore reactively - quite the contrary. You can't do that with JDBC. If you really, *really* want to use JDBC, though, you might have some, em, *psuedo-reactive*. Lightbend has an exciting project in this vein called Slick [http://slick.lightbend.com/]. Slick, ultimately, adapts JDBC and tries to hide some of the threading for you. Its primary purpose isn't to give you a reactive API for SQL-based data access, it seems, but instead to support a friendly, Scala-centric, and typesafe abstraction for working with SQL datastores. It also gives you a programming model that works well in reactive code, and through the use of the scheduler, it can even hide some of the client's blocking code. You don't get the scale-out benefits reactive programming should enable, but at least the programming model is friendly. It's a half-step, but it might be worth your consideration.

6.3.1. Reactive Relational Database Connectivity (R2DBC)

There are some options, apart from JDBC, that endeavor to natively support asynchronous IO and even reactive programming.

One option for reactive database access might be Oracle's ADBA project [https://blogs.oracle.com/java/jdbc-next:-a-new-asynchronous-api-for-connecting-to-a-database]. Oracle announced the ADBA (the Asynchronous Database API) project at JavaOne 2016. It wasn't usable at that point, but at least there was an acknowledgment that something was needed to plug this gap. A year later, at JavaOne 2017, Oracle had a prototype project based on things like Java 8's `CompletionStage`. `CompletionStage` (and `CompletableFuture`) support asynchronous resolution of a single value. They don't support asynchronous resolution of streams of values, and neither supports backpressure. They're not *reactive*.

The Java 9 released added the core interfaces from the Reactive Streams specification to the `java.util.concurrent.Flow` type, as nested types. So, `org.reactivestreams.Publisher` becomes `java.util.concurrent.Flow.Publisher`, `org.reactivestreams.Subscriber` becomes `java.util.concurrent.Flow.Subscriber`, and `org.reactivestreams.Processor` becomes `java.util.concurrent.Flow.Processor`. In the middle of 2018, the team behind ADBA finally saw fit to revise their effort to support the reactive types in the JDK.

In the meantime, a team at Pivotal started down the path of prototyping a reactive SQL data access API called R2DBC (short for *Relational Reactive Database Connectivity*). R2DBC is an open-source project [http://github.com/r2dbc] to which many have already contributed. We discuss R2DBC in this chapter.

As of this writing, both ADBA and R2DBC are in their early days and are not (yet) production-worthy. R2DBC also contains an adapter module that integrates ADBA modules with R2DBC so that if ADBA ever becomes production-worthy, there's no shortage of options for those that build on R2DBC.

R2DBC seeks to define a reactive SPI for SQL-based datastore access. It is *not* a facade on top of existing JDBC, but meant instead to leverage the rare natively-reactive SQL database driver. Emphasis on *rare*! There are implementations of the SPI for many common databases, including H2, Microsoft SQL Server, and PostgreSQL that were driven by the Pivotal engineering team. There's also an R2DBC implementation for MySQL supported by a third-party project called JAsync. I know that many of the other large database vendors are also working on R2DBC support. As of this writing, at least five other database vendors are developing R2DBC drivers. (No, not one of them, as far as I know, is Oracle).

Broadly, when I refer to R2DBC, I refer to at least three levels of abstraction. The low-level SPI works more or less like the raw JDBC API. The `DatabaseClient` is more or less like Spring's `JdbcTemplate`. Finally, Spring Data R2DBC provides an ORM-like experience with the declarative mapping of entities to records and support for declarative repository objects built-in.

6.3.2. Making a Connection

Let's build an application that connects to PostgreSQL using R2DBC.

You need to add the relevant R2DBC driver and the appropriate Spring Boot starter supporting necessary R2DBC integration, akin to using the `JdbcTemplate` directly, or the integration supporting Spring Data R2DBC.

- `org.springframework.boot` : `spring-boot-starter-data-r2dbc`
- `io.r2dbc` : `r2dbc-postgresql`

The `ConnectionFactory` is the heart of the R2BDC SPI. It connects the client to the appropriate data store. Spring Boot's auto-configuration can do it for you, or you can override the default auto-configuration and do it yourself. I'd much rather let the auto-configuration do the heavy lifting; define a property, `spring.r2dbc.url`, and away you go! Here's the configuration on my local machine:

The R2DBC URL for the PostgreSQL database running on my local machine. You should customize this to your particular environment.

```
spring.r2dbc.url=r2dbc:postgresql://orders:orders@localhost:5432/orders
spring.r2dbc.username=orders
spring.r2dbc.password=orders
```

You'd probably not want to keep that information in a property file baked into your application archive. Instead, consider externalizing it. You could use -- arguments, environment variables, the Spring Cloud Config Server, Hashicorp Vault, and more.

6.3.3. The Database Schema

In the following example, we're going to assume that you have a database (orders) with a username (orders) and password (0rd3rz) configured. If you have logged into your administrator account, you can execute the following statements to create the required role and database.

The DDL to create the orders *role and database in PostgreSQL*

```
CREATE ROLE orders WITH LOGIN PASSWORD '0rd3rz' ;
ALTER ROLE orders CREATEDB ;
CREATE DATABASE orders;
```

Next, you need a table with data you can read. Install the schema from src/main/resources/schema.sql in our tests before each run (more on that in a bit). Here's the DDL for our table, customer. We're going to map an object to this table.

```
drop table customer;
create table customer (
    id    serial  not null primary key,
    email varchar not null
);
```

6.3.4. The Repository Interface

Let's build a repository to manage access to our data. A repository insulates higher-level business logic from the lower-level persistence and data management chores. To best demonstrate the unique application of the various R2DBC abstractions, we'll implement the same repository interface three times. The repository pattern describes classes that encapsulate the logic required to access data sources. They centralize standard data access requirements (creating, reading, updating, deleting), providing better maintainability and decoupling the infrastructure used to access databases from the domain model layer.

Here's the repository interface to which we'll hew on our tour. It supports various common use-cases, including finding records, saving (or updating) records, and deleting records.

```java
package rsb.data.r2dbc;

import org.springframework.data.repository.NoRepositoryBean;
import reactor.core.publisher.Flux;
import reactor.core.publisher.Mono;

@NoRepositoryBean
public interface SimpleCustomerRepository {

    Mono<Customer> save(Customer c);

    Flux<Customer> findAll();

    Mono<Customer> update(Customer c);

    Mono<Customer> findById(Integer id);

    Mono<Void> deleteById(Integer id);

}
```

We'll introduce the various implementations momentarily.

6.3.5. The Customer Entity

The repository manipulates an entity's instances, Customer, that maps to the data in a table in our PostgreSQL database, customers. Here's the definition for that entity.

```java
package rsb.data.r2dbc;

import lombok.AllArgsConstructor;
import lombok.Data;
import lombok.NoArgsConstructor;
import org.springframework.data.annotation.Id;

@Data
@AllArgsConstructor
@NoArgsConstructor
public class Customer {

    @Id
    private Integer id;

    private String email;

    Customer(String email) {
        this.email = email;
    }

}
```

The entity is relatively spartan. An id field mapped with Spring Data's @Id annotation. We don't need that annotation for now, but we'll use it later when introducing Spring Data R2DBC.

6.3.6. Tests

We'll use tests to exercise the various repository implementations.

Let's look first at a base test for our repository implementations. We'll implement multiple repositories, and so our tests all extend our base tests and use the template pattern to swap out the repository implementations.

```java
package rsb.data.r2dbc;

import lombok.extern.log4j.Log4j2;
import org.junit.Assert;
import org.junit.Before;
import org.junit.Test;
import org.springframework.beans.factory.annotation.Autowired;
import org.springframework.beans.factory.annotation.Value;
import org.springframework.core.io.Resource;
import org.springframework.util.FileCopyUtils;
import reactor.core.publisher.Flux;
import reactor.core.publisher.Mono;
import reactor.test.StepVerifier;

import java.io.InputStreamReader;

@Log4j2
public abstract class BaseCustomerRepositoryTest {

    ①
    public abstract SimpleCustomerRepository getRepository();

    ②
    @Autowired
    private CustomerDatabaseInitializer initializer;

    ③
    @Value("classpath:/schema.sql")
    private Resource resource;

    private String sql;

    @Before
    public void setupResource() throws Exception {
        Assert.assertTrue(this.resource.exists());
        try (var in = new InputStreamReader(this.resource.getInputStream())) {
            this.sql = FileCopyUtils.copyToString(in);
        }
    }

    @Test
    public void delete() {

        var repository = this.getRepository();
        var data = repository.findAll().flatMap(c -> repository.deleteById(c.getId()))
```

```
                .thenMany(Flux.just( //
                        new Customer(null, "first@email.com"), //
                        new Customer(null, "second@email.com"), //
                        new Customer(null, "third@email.com"))) //
                .flatMap(repository::save); //

        StepVerifier //
                .create(data) //
                .expectNextCount(3) //
                .verifyComplete();

        StepVerifier //
                .create(repository.findAll().take(1)
                        .flatMap(customer -> repository.deleteById(customer
.getId())))
                .verifyComplete(); //

        StepVerifier //
                .create(repository.findAll()) //
                .expectNextCount(2) //
                .verifyComplete();
    }

    @Test
    public void saveAndFindAll() {

        var repository = this.getRepository();

        StepVerifier.create(this.initializer.resetCustomerTable())
.verifyComplete();

        var insert = Flux.just( //
                new Customer(null, "first@email.com"), //
                new Customer(null, "second@email.com"), //
                new Customer(null, "third@email.com")) //
                .flatMap(repository::save); //

        StepVerifier //
                .create(insert) //
                .expectNextCount(2) //
                .expectNextMatches(customer -> customer.getId() != null
                        && customer.getId() > 0 && customer.getEmail() !=
null)
                .verifyComplete(); //

    }
```

```java
    @Test
    public void findById() {

        var repository = this.getRepository();

        var insert = Flux.just( //
                new Customer(null, "first@email.com"), //
                new Customer(null, "second@email.com"), //
                new Customer(null, "third@email.com")) //
                .flatMap(repository::save); //
        var all = repository.findAll().flatMap(c -> repository.deleteById(c.getId()))
                .thenMany(insert.thenMany(repository.findAll()));

        StepVerifier.create(all).expectNextCount(3).verifyComplete();

        var recordsById = repository.findAll()
                .flatMap(customer -> Mono.zip(Mono.just(customer),
                        repository.findById(customer.getId())))
                .filterWhen(tuple2 -> Mono.just(tuple2.getT1().equals(tuple2.getT2())));

        StepVerifier.create(recordsById).expectNextCount(3).verifyComplete();
    }

    @Test
    public void update() {
        var repository = this.getRepository();

        StepVerifier //
                .create(this.initializer.resetCustomerTable()) //
                .verifyComplete(); //

        var email = "test@again.com";
        var save = repository.save(new Customer(null, email));
        StepVerifier //
                .create(save) //
                .expectNextMatches(p -> p.getId() != null) //
                .verifyComplete();
        StepVerifier //
                .create(repository.findAll()) //
                .expectNextCount(1) //
                .verifyComplete();
        var updateFlux = repository //
                .findAll() //
                .map(c -> new Customer(c.getId(), c.getEmail().toUpperCase()
)) //
```

```
                    .flatMap(repository::update);
        StepVerifier //
                .create(updateFlux) //
                .expectNextMatches(c -> c.getEmail().equals(email.
 toUpperCase())) //
                .verifyComplete();
    }

}
```

① Each test provides a reference to a `SimpleCustomerRepository` implementation through a template method.

② The `CustomerDatabaseInitializer`, which we'll look at momentarily, does the bulk of the work of resetting our database; it creates the schema for our table if it doesn't exist and it deletes everything in it if it does.

③ The schema to be registered on the database lives in `src/main/resources/schema.sql`.

As we look at R2DBC, we'll introduce each new level of abstraction to implement this `SimpleCustomerRepository` interface. I won't revisit each of those tests because they all serve only to extend the existing test, swapping in implementation of `SimpleCustomerRepository` by overriding the `getRepository()` method. The bulk of the implementation is in this core test class. The test reads in the data definition language (DDL) for a table and then exercises various methods using the `StepVerifier`. Be sure to check out our chapter on testing.

Now that we have a test harness, let's implement the `SimpleCustomerRepository` interface.

A Basic Repository Using the `ConnectionFactory`

In this first implementation, we'll inject a `ConnectionFactory` instance directly and use it for vending a new `Connection` to the data source. In a non-trivial example, we'd use a connection pool. So the Spring Boot autoconfiguration wraps our `ConnectionFactory` in a connection pool for us, assuming we have a valid `ConnectionFactory` defined somewhere.

The first example we'll look at is the lowest-level way to interact with our database. The flow is the same for all of the `SimpleCustomerRepository` interface methods in this implementation:

- We'll create a statement.
- Optionally bind parameters to the statement.
- Optionally specify the intent of the statement (is it an addition? A deletion?)
- Execute the statement.

```java
package rsb.data.r2dbc.basics;

import io.r2dbc.spi.Row;
import io.r2dbc.spi.RowMetadata;
import lombok.RequiredArgsConstructor;
import lombok.extern.log4j.Log4j2;
import org.springframework.stereotype.Repository;
import reactor.core.publisher.Flux;
import reactor.core.publisher.Mono;
import rsb.data.r2dbc.Customer;
import rsb.data.r2dbc.SimpleCustomerRepository;

import java.util.function.BiFunction;

@Repository ①
@Log4j2
@RequiredArgsConstructor
class CustomerRepository implements SimpleCustomerRepository {

    ②
    private final ConnectionManager connectionManager;

    private final BiFunction<Row, RowMetadata, Customer> mapper = (row,
            rowMetadata) -> new Customer(row.get("id", Integer.class),
                    row.get("email", String.class));

    @Override
    public Mono<Customer> update(Customer customer) {
        ③
        return connectionManager.inConnection(conn -> Flux
                .from(conn.createStatement("update customer set email = $1 where id = $2") //
                        .bind("$1", customer.getEmail()) //
                        .bind("$2", customer.getId()) //
```

Chapter 6. Data Access

```
                        .execute()))
                .then(findById(customer.getId()));
    }

    @Override
    public Mono<Customer> findById(Integer id) {
        ④
        return connectionManager
                .inConnection(conn -> Flux
                        .from(conn.createStatement("select * from customer where id = $1")
                                .bind("$1", id)//
                                .execute()))
                .flatMap(result -> result.map(this.mapper))//
                .single()//
                .log();
    }

    @Override
    public Mono<Void> deleteById(Integer id) {
        return connectionManager.inConnection(conn -> Flux
                .from(conn.createStatement("delete from customer where id = $1") //
                        .bind("$1", id) //
                        .execute()) //
        ) //
                .then();
    }

    @Override
    public Flux<Customer> findAll() {
        return connectionManager.inConnection(conn -> Flux
                .from(conn.createStatement("select * from customer ").execute())
                .flatMap(result -> result.map(mapper)));
    }

    @Override
    public Mono<Customer> save(Customer c) {

        return connectionManager
                .inConnection(
                        conn -> Flux
                                .from(conn
                                        .createStatement(
                                                "INSERT INTO customer(email) VALUES($1)")
```

```
                                    .bind("$1", c.getEmail()) //
                                    .returnGeneratedValues("id").execute
())
                          .flatMap(r -> r.map((row, rowMetadata) -> {
                              var id = row.get("id", Integer.class);
                              return new Customer(id, c.getEmail());
                          }))) //
                  .single() //
                  .log();
    }
}
```

① `@Repository` is another Spring stereotype annotation. It's meta-annotated with `@Component`. It is little more than documentation; it's functionally just a `@Component`.

② The `ConnectionManager` is the primary interface through which connections are obtained (and recycled). The `ConnectionManager#inConnection` method accepts a callback that does work on the `Connection`. The callback mechanism allows connection pools to work efficiently, as well.

③ The first method, `update`, creates a statement, binds the parameter against the positional parameters (a number starting with a dollar sign, $1, $2, and so on), and then execute the statement. Most writes or updates to the database look like this.

④ The following method, `findById`, queries the database, and when the results arrive, it maps those results using a `BiFunction<Row, RowMetadata, Customer>`. Most methods that query or read from the database look like this.

Reactive R2DBC code comes once you see you can express whole pipelines of interactions fluently. It is undoubtedly a whole ton cleaner to work with than, say, raw JDBC code. I'm sorely tempted to include a raw JDBC example, just for reference! However, I won't, so thank you next.

The `DatabaseClient`

The `DatabaseClient` is the reactive equivalent to Spring's `JdbcTemplate`. It provides convenience methods for everyday operations, reducing boilerplate. The `DatabaseClient` methods usually return references to a builder object against which you can chain method invocations.

Let's look at the new implementation of our `CustomerRepository`, backed by the `DatabaseClient`. The autoconfiguration should provide a reference to the `DatabaseClient` for you, but it's trivial to create your own if you'd like.

```java
package rsb.data.r2dbc.dbc;

import lombok.RequiredArgsConstructor;
import lombok.extern.log4j.Log4j2;
import org.springframework.data.r2dbc.core.DatabaseClient;
import org.springframework.stereotype.Component;
import reactor.core.publisher.Flux;
import reactor.core.publisher.Mono;
import rsb.data.r2dbc.Customer;
import rsb.data.r2dbc.SimpleCustomerRepository;

@Component
@RequiredArgsConstructor
@Log4j2
public class CustomerRepository implements SimpleCustomerRepository {

    private final DatabaseClient databaseClient;

    ①
    @Override
    public Flux<Customer> findAll() {
        return databaseClient.select() //
                .from(Customer.class) //
                .fetch() //
                .all();
    }

    ②
    @Override
    public Mono<Customer> save(Customer c) {
        return this.databaseClient.insert() //
                .into(Customer.class) //
                .table("customer") //
                .using(c) //
                .map((row, rowMetadata) -> new Customer(row.get("id",
 Integer.class),
                        c.getEmail()))//
                .first();
```

```java
    }

    @Override
    public Mono<Customer> update(Customer c) {
        return databaseClient.update().table(Customer.class).using(c).fetch()
                .rowsUpdated().filter(countOfUpdates -> countOfUpdates > 0)
                .switchIfEmpty(Mono.error(
                        new IllegalArgumentException("couldn't update " + c
.toString())))
                .thenMany(findById(c.getId())).single();
    }

    @Override
    public Mono<Customer> findById(Integer id) {
        return this.databaseClient.execute("select * from customer where id =
$1") //
                .bind("$1", id) //
                .fetch() //
                .first() //
                .map(map -> new Customer(Integer.class.cast(map.get("id")),
                        String.class.cast(map.get("email"))));
    }

    ③
    @Override
    public Mono<Void> deleteById(Integer id) {
        return this.databaseClient.execute("DELETE FROM customer where id =
$1") //
                .bind("$1", id) //
                .then();
    }
}
```

① The first method returns all the `Customer` records from the connected database table called `customers`.

② The save method is one method I'd wished we'd had in the `JdbcTemplate`. It takes a POJO, maps the fields from that POJO to column names, then takes those values and uses them in an insert statement, the result of which we map to `Customer` objects for return from the method. I don't see how this could be cleaner! You'd end up doing a fair bit of work to achieve the same effect with one of the longer variants of the `JdbcTemplate`'s `execute(···.)` methods. Is this an ORM? No. However, it's remarkable what you can get done with a smidge of the ever-so convenient convention.

③ The delete method is the only one to use bound parameters in this implementation, but it's otherwise not that interesting.

This example is markedly svelter than the previous one, which itself wasn't all that overwhelming.

6.3.7. Spring Data R2DBC

Thus far, we've used the R2DBC libraries directly. Let's look now at Spring Data R2DBC. All that we'd need is provided for us by the autoconfiguration to use the Spring Data module just like any other (reactive) Spring Data module.

```
package rsb.data.r2dbc.springdata;

import org.springframework.data.r2dbc.repository.Query;
import org.springframework.data.repository.reactive.ReactiveCrudRepository;
import reactor.core.publisher.Flux;
import rsb.data.r2dbc.Customer;

①
interface CustomerRepository extends ReactiveCrudRepository<Customer, Integer> {

    ②
    @Query("select id, email from customer c where c.email = $1")
    Flux<Customer> findByEmail(String email);

}
```

① Everything we need to support our test lives in the ReactiveCrudRepository.

② So why do we need the findByEmail? We don't! I just wanted to show you how easy it'd be to define a custom finder method with a custom query and to bind parameters in those finder methods to the query itself. In this case, email is a parameter for the query created behind the scenes.

That's it! Spring Data R2DBC could map other tables. We'd need more entities and more repositories. See? Even given `SimpleCustomerRepository` and `R2dbcConfiguration`, we're *still* ahead of the first, basic `CustomerRepository`, in terms of lines-of-code! *Way* ahead. This new version even supports a custom finder method, delivering more than we had before. Not bad for a few minutes of work.

A big reason for the manifold reduction in complexity is the base interface from which our repository extends, `ReactiveCrudRepository`. You'll see this interface a lot in Spring Data. Its definition looks like this:

```java
package org.springframework.data.repository.reactive;

import reactor.core.publisher.Flux;
import reactor.core.publisher.Mono;

import org.reactivestreams.Publisher;
import org.springframework.data.repository.NoRepositoryBean;
import org.springframework.data.repository.Repository;

@NoRepositoryBean
public interface ReactiveCrudRepository<T, ID> extends Repository<T, ID> {
  <S extends T> Mono<S> save(S entity);
  <S extends T> Flux<S> saveAll(Iterable<S> entities);
  <S extends T> Flux<S> saveAll(Publisher<S> entityStream);
  Mono<T> findById(ID id);
  Mono<T> findById(Publisher<ID> id);
  Mono<Boolean> existsById(ID id);
  Mono<Boolean> existsById(Publisher<ID> id);
  Flux<T> findAll();
  Flux<T> findAllById(Iterable<ID> ids);
  Flux<T> findAllById(Publisher<ID> idStream);
  Mono<Long> count();
  Mono<Void> deleteById(ID id);
  Mono<Void> deleteById(Publisher<ID> id);
  Mono<Void> delete(T entity);
  Mono<Void> deleteAll(Iterable<? extends T> entities);
  Mono<Void> deleteAll(Publisher<? extends T> entityStream);
  Mono<Void> deleteAll();
}
```

This interface defines many useful methods with which you'll become familiar, one way or another. These methods support the usual suspects -

finding, saving, deleting, and creating records. The interface exposes querying for records by ID.

None of these methods accept a String sql parameter, though.

In Spring Data, you use finder methods, as we did in our repository interface and often annotated with @Query, to express queries. These sorts of finder methods are very convenient because they remove all the boilerplate resource initialization and acquisition logic. They remove the work of mapping records to objects. All we need to do is provide the query and optionally parameters in the finder method's prototype.

You might protest: "why show us those first two approaches if you're just going to end up here?" Fair question! Relational Database Management Systems (RDBMS) occupy a special place in the hearts of developers. Statistically, most of us doing any back-end or server-side, work started our journey with an RDBMS. It is the most entrenched kind of database and the one with which you'll need to be most familiar in your career, for at least the foreseeable future. There are debates in the community about the role of ORM in an application's architecture. There are a dozen different ways to work with RDBMSes, too. Are you using yours for analytics and data warehousing? OLTP? As a store for transactions? Do you use the SQL '99 features or are you knee-deep in PostgreSQL PL/pgSQL [https://www.postgresql.org/docs/8.4/plpgsql-porting.htm] or Oracle PL/SQL? Are you using the PostgreSQL XML types or PostGIS geospatial indexes? Are you using stored procedures? The richness of your typical RDBMS makes it difficult to prescribe a particular level of abstraction. I prefer to work with these technologies in terms of Spring Data repositories, first, and be able to drop down to a lower level of abstraction should the need arise.

We've got a repository. What about our tests? The astute reader notes that our repository doesn't implement the SimpleCustomerRepository interface. I didn't want to complicate things, so I've adapted the native Spring Data repository to the SimpleCustomerRepository interface, forwarding invocations to the underlying Spring Data repository.

```java
package rsb.data.r2dbc.springdata;

import lombok.RequiredArgsConstructor;
import org.springframework.stereotype.Component;
import reactor.core.publisher.Flux;
import reactor.core.publisher.Mono;
import rsb.data.r2dbc.Customer;
import rsb.data.r2dbc.SimpleCustomerRepository;

@Component
@RequiredArgsConstructor
class SpringDataCustomerRepository implements SimpleCustomerRepository {

    private final CustomerRepository repository;

    @Override
    public Mono<Customer> save(Customer c) {
        return repository.save(c);
    }

    @Override
    public Mono<Customer> update(Customer c) {
        return repository.save(c);
    }

    @Override
    public Mono<Customer> findById(Integer id) {
        return repository.findById(id);
    }

    @Override
    public Mono<Void> deleteById(Integer id) {
        return repository.deleteById(id);
    }

    @Override
    public Flux<Customer> findAll() {
        return repository.findAll();
    }

}
```

Reactive SQL data access opens up doors previously closed to us. Whole galaxies of existing workloads based on SQL databases might now be candidates for reactive programming. The choice is a stark one.

Reactive programming could:

- make your application more efficient.
- make your application more cost-effective.
- be the cutting edge you need to continue using a SQL database, confident that it'll scale as you need it.
- prolong the natural life of some applications.

Nothing is free. You'd have to refactor to reactive. If you're using an ORM, or perhaps even using Spring Data already and you're using something like Spring Data JPA, then it might not be such a big deal to move to Spring Data R2DBC. If you're using Spring Data JDBC, it'll be trivial to move to Spring Data R2DBC. If you're using something like JOOQ, it might be possible to move to R2DBC or Spring Data R2DBC. Lukas Eder, the founder of JOOQ, has mused about possibly supporting R2DBC one day. If you're using the JdbcTemplate, this is a more non-trivial, but workable, migration. If you're using straight JDBC, then this is painful. Very, very painful. It'll also be a valuable opportunity to refactor and clean up your code. Moving from raw JDBC to JdbcTemplate or R2DBC offers heaps more functionality with markedly less code, either way.

6.4. More Efficient, Reactive Data Access in NoSQL Pastures

What motivates a move if you have an existing application based on these select few technologies for which there are reactive alternatives? Why switch from traditional MongoDB to reactive MongoDB? Why did you embrace something like MongoDB in the first place? MongoDB is a full-featured database with tons of features. You might've chosen it simply because it ticks a box you can't otherwise get ticked. Maybe you wanted to use its scalable filesystem abstraction, GridFS? Alternatively, the geospatial indexing (GIS) support? Maybe you genuinely do want the ability to have schemaless documents? Whatever the reason, you chose MongoDB because it maps naturally to the type of data you need to manage. (Well done!) If you're otherwise happy with your datastore and your performance is up-to-snuff, then I don't know that there's a compelling argument to be made to support refactoring to reactive.

All the usual reasons apply, of course. Reactive types would promote a uniform abstraction for dealing with data and errors. It would surface network integration issues in the API itself. These are wins, sure. Are they worth refactoring everything? Perhaps.

You might choose a NoSQL data store for the vaunted scale and speed characteristics of the technology. MongoDB is (notoriously) "web scale." Its ability to scale large amounts of data is a feature that might alone justify its use. Indeed, many technologies out there exist to support scale. Some NoSQL options trade on less-flexible data models for the concession that you'll get better performance and better scale. Map/reduce, for example, is a primitive way to process data, but one that naturally supports large amounts of data. I feel the same way about columnar databases like Apache HBase and Apache Cassandra. It's not the path of least resistance for most people to model data using columnar datastores. It's not easier for most people than, say, PostgreSQL or some other RDBMS.

Are these sometimes less flexible data models that path of least resistance? No. However, they offer performance and scale, and if that's a concern that motivates your decisions, you should consider reactive programming. It'll let you squeeze every last efficiency out of your database client code.

The bigger the data, the more beneficial reactive programming. Reactive programming is most valuable when something might otherwise monopolize threads. Reactive database clients might be the difference between one web server node and five!

6.4.1. Reactive Transactions in R2DBC

Building a repository is fine, but it's intentionally low-level. It deals with data-in and data-out. Business logic tends to live at a higher-level, as part of the service tier. Let's build a service that provides coarse-grained operations supporting the normalization of all emails in the system, and upserts of records by email.

Chapter 6. Data Access

This service features two operations that operate on many discrete records. These operations should be atomic - we don't want them to commit any changes unless everything succeeds. This is a natural opportunity for us to introduce transactions.

```java
package rsb.data.r2dbc;

import lombok.RequiredArgsConstructor;
import lombok.extern.log4j.Log4j2;
import org.reactivestreams.Publisher;
import org.springframework.stereotype.Service;
import org.springframework.transaction.annotation.Transactional;
import org.springframework.transaction.reactive.TransactionalOperator;
import reactor.core.publisher.Flux;
import reactor.core.publisher.Mono;

@Service
@Log4j2
@RequiredArgsConstructor
public class CustomerService {

    private final SimpleCustomerRepository repository;

    private final TransactionalOperator operator;

    private final CustomerDatabaseInitializer initializer;

    public Publisher<Void> resetDatabase() {
        return this.initializer.resetCustomerTable();
    }

    ①
    public Flux<Customer> upsert(String email) {
        var customers = this.repository.findAll()
                .filter(customer -> customer.getEmail().equalsIgnoreCase(email))
                .flatMap(match -> this.repository
                        .update(new Customer(match.getId(), email)))
                .switchIfEmpty(this.repository.save(new Customer(null, email
)));
        var validatedResults = errorIfEmailsAreInvalid(customers);
        return this.operator.transactional(validatedResults);
    }

    ②
```

177

```
    @Transactional
    public Flux<Customer> normalizeEmails() {
        return errorIfEmailsAreInvalid(this.repository.findAll()
                .flatMap(x -> this.upsert(x.getEmail().toUpperCase())));
    }

    private static Flux<Customer> errorIfEmailsAreInvalid(Flux<Customer> input) {
        return input.filter(c -> c.getEmail().contains("@"))
                .switchIfEmpty(Mono.error(new IllegalArgumentException(
                        "the email needs to be of the form a@b.com!")));
    }

}
```

① the `upsert` finds an existing record by its email or, if it doesn't exist, adds a new one

② the `normalizeEmails` method iterates through all the data in the database and confirms that each record's emails are correct.

The first operation, `upsert`, delegates to an underlying instance of a `SimpleCustomerRepository` to find all records in the existing database (yes, I realize we should probably have just used a SQL query with a predicate), filtering in Java code to find the record whose email matches the `email` parameter. If there's a record found, then it's updated. If there is no record found, then a new one is inserted.

It's crucial to take every opportunity to validate the results. This method passes the results through the `errorIfEmailsAreInvalid` method which, intuitively, returns an error - an `IllegalArgumentException` - if there are any errors in validating that the email has a `@` character in it.

We revert the writes - all of them - if any of the validation fails. The validation logic runs *after* the database writes. The write is an atomic operation: either *all* the writes succeed, or *none* do. The `upsert` method uses the `TransactionalOperator#transactional` method to envelop the reactive pipeline in a transaction. The writes are rolled back if the validation logic results in an error anywhere in the reactive pipeline.

The distinction between a cold stream (one that does not have any subscribers) and a hot stream (one that has at least one subscriber) is useful because it means we can define the reactive stream and then, later, envelope it in a transaction before any data flows through the stream.

The `TransactionalOperator` is like Spring's `TransactionTemplate`. It's ideal for explicit, fine-grained transaction demarcation, operating on distinct streams within a given scope.

If you want the resulting return value stream from a method enclosed in a transaction, you can decorate that method with `@Transactional`, the approach taken with `normalizeAllEmails`.

You can use both or either of these approaches out yourself: try to get away with an invalid email somewhere in your data and see what happens. I *dare* you!

6.4.2. MongoDB

We've reasonably well looked at the best option for reactive RDBMS-centric SQL programming in the Spring ecosystem. Now let's look at reactive NoSQL options. Few technologies - *ahem* - *spring* to mind as readily as MongoDB when exploring the NoSQL space. Its notoriety is due in part to its qualifications and the hilarious community that's developed around it. Using MongoDB a decade ago would've been a controversial choice. Still, these days it's become a successful business that's catering increasingly to the same enterprise markets as Oracle, IBM, and Microsoft pursue and often at similar revenue levels. MongoDB is but one of many entries in the NoSQL space, but it's the one on which we'll focus on this example because it's familiar, useful, and simple to pick up.

I don't want to give the impression that a MongoDB is interchangeable with any of the numerous alternatives in the NoSQL space - quite the contrary! NoSQL data stores are typical, well, atypical. Their only unifying quality is that they're not SQL-centric RDBMSes. So, this section isn't meant to be an introduction to NoSQL with Spring. Instead, it's meant to introduce some of the idioms of a reactive Spring Data module.

MongoDB is an exemplary integration for a reactive NoSQL datastore, but it's also an interesting one in that it has several features that feel more naturally expressed using reactive programming. Let's look at some examples, first of typical Spring Data idioms as applied to a NoSQL datastore, and then to some of MongoDB's specifics that shine in a reactive world.

6.4.3. Basic Spring Data MongoDB

Let's first set the stage. We've got a few of the more common things you'd expect in a Spring Data integration: an object mapped to a record in the datastore and supported with a repository. In MongoDB, records are called *documents*, and they're mostly rows of tables (called _collection_s in MongoDB). We'll start with a document-mapped entity called `Order`.

```
package rsb.data.mongodb;

import lombok.AllArgsConstructor;
import lombok.Data;
import lombok.NoArgsConstructor;
import org.springframework.data.annotation.Id;
import org.springframework.data.mongodb.core.mapping.Document;

@Data
@AllArgsConstructor
@NoArgsConstructor
@Document ①
class Order {

    @Id ②
    private String id;

    private String productId;

}
```

① The Spring Data MongoDB-specific `@Document` annotation marks this object as a document in a MongoDB collection.

② The Spring Data `@Id` annotation marks this field as a key for the document.

Simple enough. Now we'll need a repository implementation, `OrderRepository`.

Chapter 6. Data Access

```
package rsb.data.mongodb;

import org.springframework.data.repository.reactive.ReactiveCrudRepository;
import reactor.core.publisher.Flux;

①
interface OrderRepository extends ReactiveCrudRepository<Order, String> {

    Flux<Order> findByProductId(String productId);

}
```

① This repository extends the `ReactiveCrudRepository` interface, just as with R2DBC. There is a `ReactiveMongoRepository` interface with some specific repository support for MongoDB, but you probably won't need it.

There's nothing incredibly unique about this arrangement; we don't need to configure anything in particular to make Spring Data work. The Spring Boot autoconfiguration takes care of that.

We've got a test case for the `OrderRepository`, too.

```
package rsb.data.mongodb;

import org.junit.Before;
import org.junit.Test;
import org.junit.runner.RunWith;
import org.springframework.beans.factory.annotation.Autowired;
import org.springframework.boot.test.autoconfigure.data.mongo.DataMongoTest;
import org.springframework.test.context.junit4.SpringRunner;
import reactor.core.publisher.Flux;
import reactor.test.StepVerifier;

import java.util.Arrays;
import java.util.Collection;
import java.util.UUID;
import java.util.function.Predicate;

@DataMongoTest
@RunWith(SpringRunner.class)
public class OrderRepositoryTest {
```

181

```java
@Autowired
private OrderRepository orderRepository;

private final Collection<Order> orders = Arrays.asList(
        new Order(UUID.randomUUID().toString(), "1"),
        new Order(UUID.randomUUID().toString(), "2"),
        new Order(UUID.randomUUID().toString(), "2"));

private final Predicate<Order> predicate = order -> //
this.orders //
        .stream() //
        .filter(candidateOrder -> candidateOrder.getId()
                .equalsIgnoreCase(order.getId()))//
        .anyMatch(candidateOrder -> candidateOrder.getProductId()
                .equalsIgnoreCase(order.getProductId()));

@Before
public void before() {

    Flux<Order> saveAll = this.orderRepository.deleteAll()
            .thenMany(this.orderRepository.saveAll(this.orders));

    StepVerifier ①
            .create(saveAll) //
            .expectNextMatches(this.predicate) //
            .expectNextMatches(this.predicate) //
            .expectNextMatches(this.predicate) //
            .verifyComplete();
}

@Test
public void findAll() {
    StepVerifier ②
            .create(this.orderRepository.findAll()) //
            .expectNextMatches(this.predicate) //
            .expectNextMatches(this.predicate) //
            .expectNextMatches(this.predicate) //
            .verifyComplete();
}

@Test
public void findByProductId() {
    StepVerifier ③
            .create(this.orderRepository.findByProductId("2")) //
            .expectNextCount(2) //
            .verifyComplete();
}
```

```
}
```

① Write some data to the database

② Then confirm that what we've written into the database out again

③ Then confirm that our custom query works as designed, in this case returning the records whose `productId` matches the `productId` on the `Order` entity.

Setting Up MongoDB for Transactions and Tailable Queries

We've got a fundamental working repository going. The repository would work with any old instance of a 4.0 or later version of MongoDB. We're going to look at some of the more agreeable opportunities for reactive developers using MongoDB, transactions, and tailable queries that require that you launch MongoDB with a replica set. A replica set is a mechanism for distribution. You can run a replica set with only one node, which is sufficient for development, but you'll need to do at least that to try these features out.

Here's the script I use to start a single-instance replica set on my machine. I do something similar for my continuous integration setup, too.

Initializing a single-node replica set with MongoDB.

```
mongo --eval "rs.initiate({_id: 'rs0', members:[{_id: 0, host: '127.0.0.1:27017'}]});"
```

Reactive Transactions in MongoDB

So far, so good. A common question people ask about both MongoDB and reactive programming is: what about *transactions*?

Many NoSQL data stores support transactions, and Spring supports resource-local transaction management in a non-reactive context where appropriate. There is also a `ReactiveTransactionManager` hierarchy implementation for MongoDB in a reactive context.

The use of transactions in MongoDB is interesting, though mostly optional, because updates to a single document and its subdocuments are atomic. MongoDB supports and arguably encourages denormalized and embedded subdocuments to capture relationships between data. MongoDB's transaction support comes in handy for updates to multiple, discrete documents or when you want consistency between reads to multiple documents.

We first need to configure a few beans to demonstrate transactions with MongoDB.

```
package rsb.data.mongodb;

import org.springframework.context.annotation.Bean;
import org.springframework.data.mongodb.ReactiveMongoDatabaseFactory;
import org.springframework.data.mongodb.ReactiveMongoTransactionManager;
import org.springframework.transaction.ReactiveTransactionManager;
import org.springframework.transaction.annotation.EnableTransactionManagement;
import org.springframework.transaction.reactive.TransactionalOperator;

@EnableTransactionManagement
class TransactionConfiguration {

    ①
    @Bean
    TransactionalOperator transactionalOperator(ReactiveTransactionManager txm) {
        return TransactionalOperator.create(txm);
    }

    ②
    @Bean
    ReactiveTransactionManager reactiveMongoTransactionManager(
            ReactiveMongoDatabaseFactory rdf) {
        return new ReactiveMongoTransactionManager(rdf);
    }

}
```

① You've already seen this before...

② We configure the MongoDB-specific variant of the `ReactiveTransactionManager` hierarchy.

We've already got an `OrderRepository` that handles individual interactions with the database - everyday data operations like queries, inserts, updates, and reads. Let's build an `OrderService` service on top of the `OrderRepository` that supports writing multiple records to the database. We'll use this to demonstrate transactions by rolling back writes if a given parameter is `null`. If we write N records where the N-1 record is `null`, it results in an error that, in turn, rolls back all N writes, `null` and all.

```
package rsb.data.mongodb;

import lombok.RequiredArgsConstructor;
import org.springframework.data.mongodb.core.ReactiveMongoTemplate;
import org.springframework.stereotype.Service;
import org.springframework.transaction.reactive.TransactionalOperator;
import org.springframework.util.Assert;
import reactor.core.publisher.Flux;
import reactor.core.publisher.Mono;

import java.util.function.Function;

@Service
@RequiredArgsConstructor
class OrderService {

    private final ReactiveMongoTemplate template;

    private final TransactionalOperator operator;

    ①
    public Flux<Order> createOrders(String... productIds) {
        return this.operator
                .execute(status -> buildOrderFlux(template::insert,
productIds));
    }

    private Flux<Order> buildOrderFlux(Function<Order, Mono<Order>> callback,
            String[] productIds) {
        return Flux //
                .just(productIds) //
                .map(pid -> {
                    Assert.notNull(pid, "the product ID shouldn't be null");
                    return pid;
                }) //
                .map(x -> new Order(null, x)) //
                .flatMap(callback);
    }

}
```

① The createOrders method uses the TransactionalOperator#execute method. We've already looked at declarative transa

Let's exercise the service in a test.

Chapter 6. Data Access

```java
package rsb.data.mongodb;

import lombok.extern.log4j.Log4j2;
import org.assertj.core.api.Assertions;
import org.junit.Before;
import org.junit.BeforeClass;
import org.junit.Test;
import org.junit.runner.RunWith;
import org.reactivestreams.Publisher;
import org.springframework.beans.factory.annotation.Autowired;
import org.springframework.boot.test.autoconfigure.data.mongo.DataMongoTest;
import org.springframework.context.annotation.Import;
import org.springframework.core.io.FileSystemResource;
import org.springframework.core.io.Resource;
import org.springframework.data.mongodb.core.ReactiveMongoTemplate;
import org.springframework.test.context.junit4.SpringRunner;
import org.springframework.util.StreamUtils;
import reactor.core.publisher.Flux;
import reactor.core.publisher.Mono;
import reactor.test.StepVerifier;

import java.io.File;
import java.nio.charset.Charset;

@RunWith(SpringRunner.class)
@DataMongoTest ①
@Log4j2
@Import({ TransactionConfiguration.class, OrderService.class })
public class OrderServiceTest {

    @Autowired
    private OrderRepository repository;

    @Autowired
    private OrderService service;

    @Autowired
    private ReactiveMongoTemplate template;

    ②
    @BeforeClass
    public static void warn() throws Exception {
        Resource script = new FileSystemResource(
                new File("..", "ci/bin/setup-mongodb.sh"));
        Assertions.assertThat(script.exists()).isTrue();
        Charset charset = Charset.defaultCharset();
```

```
        String instructions = StreamUtils.copyToString(script.getInputStream
(), charset);
        log.warn("Be sure MongoDB supports replicas. Try:\n\n" +
instructions);
    }

    ③
    @Before
    public void configureCollectionsBeforeTests() {
        Mono<Boolean> createIfMissing = template.collectionExists(Order.
class) //
                .filter(x -> !x) //
                .flatMap(exists -> template.createCollection(Order.class)) //
                .thenReturn(true);
        StepVerifier //
                .create(createIfMissing) //
                .expectNextCount(1) //
                .verifyComplete();
    }

    ④
    @Test
    public void createOrders() {

        Publisher<Order> orders = this.repository //
                .deleteAll() //
                .thenMany(this.service.createOrders("1", "2", "3")) //
                .thenMany(this.repository.findAll());

        StepVerifier //
                .create(orders) //
                .expectNextCount(3) //
                .verifyComplete();
    }

    ⑤
    @Test
    public void transactionalOperatorRollback() {
        this.runTransactionalTest(this.service.createOrders("1", "2", null));
    }

    private void runTransactionalTest(Flux<Order> ordersInTx) {
        Publisher<Order> orders = this.repository //
                .deleteAll() //
                .thenMany(ordersInTx) //
                .thenMany(this.repository.findAll());
```

```
        StepVerifier //
                .create(orders) //
                .expectNextCount(0) //
                .verifyError();

        StepVerifier //
                .create(this.repository.findAll()) //
                .expectNextCount(0) //
                .verifyComplete();
    }

}
```

① This test uses the @DataMongoTest test slice.

② This doesn't do anything besides print out a reminder that transactions require MongoDB replica sets. It demonstrates a script that can be used to demonstrate those replicas.

③ This code reactively checks for a MongoDB collection and, if it's not there, creates it.

④ This test demonstrates the happy path and confirms that writing three non-null values should result in three new records.

⑤ This test demonstrates that writing three records, one of which is null, results in a rollback with no observable side effects.

Multi-document transactions are available for replica sets only. Transactions for sharded clusters are scheduled for MongoDB 4.2.x or later.

Tailable Queries

In a 24/7 always-on and interconnected world, data is changing all the time. Batch-centric processing limits data to time-boxed windows, meaning there's always some frame of as-yet unprocessed data. This lag is problematic if the expectation is that a system is always available. Organizations are increasingly moving to stream-processing models where feeder clients process data from data sources as the data becomes available. Streaming data processing inverts the traditional, batch-centric approach to data processing. In a streaming architecture, the data is *pushed* to the clients wherein a more traditional batch-centric model, and the data is *pulled* from the source, accumulated in batches, and then processed.

A data stream is a continuously evolving sequence of events where each event represents new data. A client subscribed to a stream needs only to process the new data, avoiding costly reprocessing of existing data. Stream-centric processing mitigates the need for expensive client-side polling.

Does this vague description of stream processing sound familiar? To my mind, it sounds like reactive programming. We could take the idea further, extending it out to complex event processing (CEP) with Reactor's windowing functions.

Stream processing has many benefits. There are a couple of ways to achieve stream processing. One approach uses a staged-event driven architecture wherein a component polls the data source and then publishes the deltas to downstream clients. A component still polls, but the polling is done once on behalf of all the clients and multiple subscribers. This approach reduces the load on the data source, since there is only one polling query while simplifying downstream clients' work - they don't need to worry about tracking deltas themselves.

Some data sources can *tell* the clients what's changed; they can tell the client about new data that matches a predicate or query. Apache Geode [https://geode.apache.org/] and Oracle Coherence are both types of distributed data grids. They support *continuous queries*. Continuous queries invert the traditional polling arrangement between the client and the data source. A client registers a continuous query with the data grid, and the data grid asserts any new data in the grid against the query. If any new data matches the query, the data grid notifies the subscribed clients.

MongoDB supports something like continuous queries but gives it the equally as descriptive name *tailable queries*. It's analogous to using the `tail -f` command on the command line to follow the file's output. In MongoDB, a client connects to the database and issues the query. Tailable queries ignore indexes, so the first reads may be slow, depending on how much data matches the query. The client's cursor remains connected to the data source even after reading the initial result set, and clients consume any new subsequent records.

You might *really* want that index. I understand! You'll need to re-query the records manually, using the last offset of the records to retrieve only those records inserted after the offset.

Now, let's suppose you have decided to use MongoDB's tailable queries. There are many possibilities here! You could use MongoDB to do lightweight publish/subscribe integration. You could implement a chat system. You could broadcast sensor data or stock tickers.

Whatever you decide to do, it's trivially easy to get it done with tailable queries. Let's look at an example. We'll query all documents in a given collection, customers, whose name attribute matches a given value.

Tailable queries require capped collections. A capped collection is a fixed-size collection that supports high-throughput operations that insert and retrieve documents based on insertion order. Capped collections work in a way similar to circular buffers. Once a collection fills its allocated space, it makes room for new documents by overwriting the oldest documents in the collection.

Let's look first at the Customer entity - nothing surprising here.

```
package rsb.data.mongodb;

import lombok.AllArgsConstructor;
import lombok.Data;
import lombok.NoArgsConstructor;
import org.springframework.data.annotation.Id;
import org.springframework.data.mongodb.core.mapping.Document;

@Data
@AllArgsConstructor
@NoArgsConstructor
@Document
public class Customer {

    @Id
    private String id;

    private String name;

}
```

The repository is where things get interesting - it's the first place we communicate the idea that we will create a tailable query to MongoDB.

```
package rsb.data.mongodb;

import org.springframework.data.mongodb.repository.ReactiveMongoRepository;
import org.springframework.data.mongodb.repository.Tailable;
import reactor.core.publisher.Flux;

public interface CustomerRepository extends ReactiveMongoRepository<Customer, String> {

    @Tailable  ①
    Flux<Customer> findByName(String name);

}
```

① The `@Tailable` annotation tells Spring Data not to close the client cursor when executing the query derived from the finder method.

Tailable queries require capped collections. We'll need to make sure to create the capped collection before we start using it. We can't rely on Spring Data to automatically create the capped collection for us. We'll do so explicitly in the following test, in the `@Before` method. You might implement this as an initialization step somewhere else. In a production environment, it might get done as part of the scripting involved in deploying the database in the first place. Capped collections are one of the few things in MongoDB that involve the ahead-of-time configuration for MongoDB. MongoDB is schemaless, but that eliminates all upfront configuration.

```
package rsb.data.mongodb;

import com.mongodb.reactivestreams.client.MongoCollection;
import lombok.extern.log4j.Log4j2;
import org.assertj.core.api.Assertions;
import org.bson.Document;
import org.junit.Before;
import org.junit.Test;
import org.junit.runner.RunWith;
import org.springframework.beans.factory.annotation.Autowired;
import org.springframework.boot.test.autoconfigure.data.mongo.DataMongoTest;
import org.springframework.data.mongodb.core.CollectionOptions;
```

```java
import org.springframework.data.mongodb.core.ReactiveMongoTemplate;
import org.springframework.test.context.junit4.SpringRunner;
import reactor.core.publisher.Mono;
import reactor.test.StepVerifier;

import java.util.Queue;
import java.util.UUID;
import java.util.concurrent.ConcurrentLinkedQueue;

@Log4j2
@DataMongoTest
@RunWith(SpringRunner.class)
public class TailableCustomerQueryTest {

    @Autowired
    private ReactiveMongoTemplate operations;

    @Autowired
    private CustomerRepository repository;

    @Before
    public void before() {

        ①
        CollectionOptions capped = CollectionOptions.empty().size(1024 * 1024)
                .maxDocuments(100).capped();

        Mono<MongoCollection<Document>> recreateCollection = operations
                .collectionExists(Order.class)
                .flatMap(exists -> exists ? operations.dropCollection(Customer.class)
                        : Mono.just(exists))
                .then(operations.createCollection(Customer.class, capped));

        StepVerifier.create(recreateCollection).expectNextCount(1).verifyComplete();
    }

    @Test
    public void tail() throws InterruptedException {
        ②
        Queue<Customer> people = new ConcurrentLinkedQueue<>();

        ③
        StepVerifier //
                .create(this.write().then(this.write())) //
```

```
                .expectNextCount(1) //
                .verifyComplete();

        ④
        this.repository.findByName("1") //
                .doOnNext(people::add) //
                .doOnComplete(() -> log.info("complete")) //
                .doOnTerminate(() -> log.info("terminated")) //
                .subscribe();

        Assertions.assertThat(people).hasSize(2);

        ⑤
        StepVerifier.create(this.write().then(this.write())) //
                .expectNextCount(1) //
                .verifyComplete(); //

        ⑥
        Thread.sleep(1000);
        Assertions.assertThat(people).hasSize(4);
    }

    private Mono<Customer> write() {
        return repository.save(new Customer(UUID.randomUUID().toString(), "1"));
    }

}
```

① We explicitly create a capped collection

② This test accumulates results from the capped collection and the tailable query into a Queue.

③ Write two records to the now pristine collection to the database.

④ Run the tailable query which returns a Publisher<Customer>, to which we'll subscribe. As new records arrive, we capture them in the previously defined Queue.

⑤ Once subscribed, confirm that the first two records are in the collection, let's write two more records.

⑥ Confirm the updates to the Queue (without having to re-run the query.)

Pretty cool, eh? Now, keep in mind, a tailable cursor *will* disconnect under certain conditions. If the query returns no records, then the cursor becomes dead. If a cursor returns the document at the "end" of the collection and then the application deletes that document, then the cursor also becomes dead.

MongoDB is nothing if not versatile. It can transactionally persist and query records and relationships. Did I mention that it also supports a scalable filesystem? You can use MongoDB's GridFS to write file-like data and scale it out safely.

MongoDB also supports geospatial queries. Foursquare provides applications, like Swarm and Foursquare, that aim primarily to let your friends know where you are and figure out where they are. Foursquare gamified geography. Foursquare contributed a lot to the initial geospatial support in MongoDB.

6.5. Review

In this chapter, we've introduced reactive SQL and NoSQL data access. We introduced the `ReactiveTransactionManager` hierarchy and its support in Spring Framework 5.2+. We looked at R2DBC, a new SPI and supporting implementations for reactive R2DBC-centric data access. I think it's very cool that, this close to 2020 as we are, we still get to talk about SQL and transactions in a brave new (reactive) context. We also looked at reactive NoSQL, focusing on MongoDB. We looked at transaction demarcation, and we looked at tailable queries, both things that are unique to MongoDB among the supported reactive NoSQL options.

6.6. Next Steps

In this chapter, we've looked at how to use reactive programming to connect to SQL-based datastores (with R2DBC and Spring Data R2DBC) and to connect to one of the many supported NoSQL datastores, MongoDB. Reactive programming makes it easier for developers to consume data efficiently. Reactive programming is necessary because data is at the heart of virtually all applications. It doesn't matter how reactive your web tier and security and gateways are if you're going to throttle at the data access layer.

Chapter 7. HTTP

In this chapter, we're going to look at how Spring supports building reactive HTTP-centric services. I say centric because we're going to look at concerns that emanate from HTTP-based applications as are typical of web applications, including but not limited to WebSockets, REST, and more.

> This chapter focuses on concepts and details in HTTP 1.1.

7.1. HTTP Works

HTTP is a pretty simple protocol. It's got one purpose to support document retrieval. It's purpose-built for this. It supports the request-response interaction model but doesn't support any application-level flow control mechanism. In HTTP, requests are sent to a server, which then responds with a response.

7.1.1. HTTP Requests

An HTTP request message starts off with a start-line that includes an HTTP verb (like `PUT`, `POST`, `GET`, `OPTIONS`, and `DELETE`), a target URI and an HTTP version. Headers then follow the start line. Headers are key-value pairs (separated by : and space) that live on different lines. HTTP responses do not have some headers (like `Host`, `User-Agent`, and `Accept*`) otherwise included in HTTP requests. Two line breaks follow the headers. Finally, an HTTP request might have an HTTP body. An HTTP body might contain one single resource, like a JSON document. It might also contain multiple resources, called a multipart body, each containing a different bit of information. HTML forms commonly have multipart bodies.

A sample HTTP request

```
GET /rc/customers HTTP/1.1
Host: localhost:8080
User-Agent: the-reactive-spring-book/1.0.0
Accept: */*
```

This request asks for the data available at the /rc/customers resource.

7.1.2. HTTP Responses

The start line of an HTTP response is called the status line. It contains the HTTP protocol version, a status code, and status text. There are many common status codes like 200 ("OK"), 201 ("CREATED"), 404 ("ERROR"/"NOT FOUND"), 401 ("UNAUTHORIZED"), and 302 ("FOUND"). The status text is a textual description of the status code to help humans understand the HTTP message.

Next, come the HTTP headers, which look just like the headers in a request.

Finally comes an optional body element. A web server may send a response with a body all-at-once in a single resource of known length, or it may send the response as a single resource of unknown length, encoded by chunks with Transfer-Encoding set to chunked, or as a multipart body.

A sample HTTP response

```
HTTP/1.1 200 OK
transfer-encoding: chunked
Content-Type: application/hal+json;charset=UTF-8

[
 {"id":"5c8151c4c24dae6677437751","name":"Dr. Who"},
 {"id":"5c8151c4c24dae6677437752","name":"Dr. Strange"}
]
```

7.1.3. HTTP Aims to Serve… Pages

If you're in the business of serving HTTP documents, then HTTP is purpose-built for you and has a ton of excellent features. Here are some of the things HTTP controls.

Caching: Caching describes how clients cache documents. This determination includes what to cache and for how long.

Authentication: Some pages are intended only for a specific client whose identity the HTTP request encodes in a standard way. A web server sends the `WWW-Authenticate` header detailing what type of authentication is supported and the `401` status code indicating that the client is unauthorized. The client then sends the `Authorization` header containing credentials to obtain access.

Proxying and Tunneling: Clients or servers are often located on intranets and mask their real IP address. HTTP requests can be proxied transparently from one node to another.

Sessions: HTTP cookies are containers for data initiated at the request of either the client or the server that then resides in the client. A client automatically re-transmits the HTTP cookies to a service on subsequent requests. Services use this permanent state to correlate otherwise discrete requests.

HTTP provides all the primitives to build a platform for (securely) retrieving resources efficiently.

7.2. HTTP Scales

HTTP scales pretty well. Before the stunning obviousness of that assertion moves you to reach in disgust for your book-burning lighter (why do you even have a book-burning lighter, hmm?) or your Kindle's ready-and-willing erase button, let me clarify. The web scaled because HTTP is a stateless protocol. When a client makes a request, the server is free to forget everything it has ever known about the client just as soon as the client has disconnected.

Our amnesiac web servers may not care about the client-specific state, but we developers sure do! We find ways to correlate client-requests to server-side state using HTTP sessions, cookies, and OAuth. Let's ignore these possibilities for now and focus on otherwise stateless HTTP.

Any node can handle any request if there is no assumption that the request requires state resident on a particular node, that the request is stateless. If a client hits one endpoint on server A and then hits refresh, there's not necessarily any state in the server that needs to be replicated to server B for the next identical request to be handled on server B a nanosecond later.

Each client connects to the web server, and the server sends bytes back in response. Each time there's a new client, the server replies with a new stream of bytes. If there are two requests, then the server has to send back two data streams simultaneously. The server can create a new thread for each request. Adding threads to accommodate requests works well so long as we can produce replies faster than we get new requests. If the rate of new requests exceeds the number of available threads, the server becomes constrained. This traditional approach to building applications has scaled pretty well. HTTP requests have traditionally been short-lived (how much data could your single .html page have, after all?) and infrequent (how often do you click from one HTTP page to another, after all?)

Application developers take advantage of this scalability by designing APIs over HTTP. REST, short for *representational state transfer*, is a constraint on HTTP designed to prescribe how resources necessary to applications are represented using HTTP. REST APIs enjoy the same scalability as HTTP.

In my book, O'Reilly's *Cloud Native Java*, I argue for microservices. Microservices are small, self-contained APIs usually built with REST. Microservices are easily scaled as capacity demands because we keep the APIs as stateless as possible. However, all good things come to an end. With microservices and big data, and the internet-of-things (IoT), suddenly, the dynamics of scaling web applications change. The average web server now contends with tons of HTTP calls for every single .html page rendered. Megabytes and megabytes of JavaScript alone! Much of that JavaScript, in turn, makes HTTP calls (remember "Ajax"?) to HTTP endpoints, only making things worse. What used to be intermittent and relatively small requests between user clicks are now frequent and extensive requests being.

We scale HTTP services by adding more nodes to a load-balancer rotation. It's cheap, but not free, to scale-out services built in this stateless fashion using cloud platforms like Cloud Foundry, Amazon Web Services, Microsoft Azure, and Google Cloud. This sort of scale-out is a nice middle-ground. It allows us to handle more requests per second and at a reasonably low price. It doesn't require us to rethink the way we write software.

We might be able to do better, to handle a more significant number of requests, by moving to asynchronous I/O and reactive programming. I don't have to convince you of that! Otherwise, you wouldn't be reading this book, *Reactive Spring*! Traditional Servlet-based applications used synchronous and blocking IO. The web server reads the incoming requests from an `InputStream` and writes the response in an `OutputStream`. Every byte read or written blocks one of the web servers' precious few threads. The bottleneck here, the number of threads we can create, becomes problematic long before they might otherwise using asynchronous I/O and reactive programming.

What's needed is a web framework and runtime that supports asynchronous IO and reactive programming. Spring Webflux, a net new reactive web runtime and framework in Spring Framework 5, is how we get from legacy to lightspeed. Spring Webflux refers to both a component model and framework, which runs on top of a web server, *and* a Netty-based runtime.

7.3. REST

REST is a constraint on the HTTP protocol. In a minimal implementation of REST, the lifecycle of data maps to HTTP verbs. You POST to an HTTP resource to create a new entity. DELETE to a resource to delete an entity. PUT to update an entity. GET to read an entity or entities. HTTP status codes are used to signal to the client that an operation has succeeded or failed. HTTP supports content negotiation where, using headers, a client and a server can agree on the types of content types they can intelligibly exchange.

HTTP supports URIs. URIs are strings that uniquely address individual resources. These URIs give resources on the web a canonical address that makes them referenceable and navigable. You've no doubt used HTTP URIs if you've ever clicked on an HTML document link. HTTP links are a natural way of relating one resource to another. REST, as introduced by Dr. Roy Fielding in his doctoral dissertation, emphasizes the use of links as a way to surface relationships for HTTP resources. While this was part of REST's original definition, it's not so common a practice as it should be. HATEOAS (Hypermedia as the Engine of Application State) is commonly used to distinguish truly REST-compliant APIs from those that don't use links to related resources.

7.4. Spring WebFlux: a Net-New Reactive Web Runtime

Spring MVC builds on the Servlet specification. The default assumption in the Servlet specification blocks threads that things are synchronous. The Servlet specification assumes that requests blocks threads or that requests are short-lived interactions that don't require asynchronous I/O. If you want asynchronous I/O, it's possible to get it, but it's not the default, and it's relatively limited. The rest of the Servlet API - for retrieving HTTP sessions and cookies, for example - doesn't support asynchronous I/O. Spring Framework 5 introduced a net-new reactive web runtime based on Netty (whew! What a mouthful! Try saying that ten times fast!) and a framework called Spring WebFlux. Spring Framework 5 assumes the presence of Java 8 and lambdas.

Spring Webflux assumes that everything is asynchronous by default. There are interesting implications to the fact that everything in Spring Webflux is reactive by default. If you want to return a simple JSON stanza with eight records, you return a `Publisher<T>`. Simple enough. If you want to do something long-lived, like WebSockets or server-sent events, for which asynchronous I/O is a better choice, you also use a `Publisher<T>`! (I use this handy mnemonic: *when you're not sure, use a publisher*!)

Life's much simpler now. In Spring MVC, the way you create long-lived server-sent event responses is entirely different from creating other HTTP responses. Ditto WebSockets. Websockets are a completely different programming model. The experience feels more familiar to developers using Apache Kafka or RabbitMQ than those using Spring MVC! In Spring MVC, server-sent events and WebSockets require developers to get into the business of managing threads... In a Servlet container. It all *works*, but you'd be forgiven for thinking that the Servlet specification, and Spring MVC atop it, are optimized for the synchronous, blocking cases.

7.4.1. A Simple Sample

Before we get too far down the road, let's introduce a sample domain entity, Customer, and a supporting repository, CustomerRepository. Let's suppose we have an entity, Customer, with two fields, id and name:

```
package rsb.http.customers;

import lombok.Data;
import lombok.NoArgsConstructor;

@Data
@NoArgsConstructor
class Customer {

    private String id, name;

    Customer(String i, String n) {
        this.id = i;
        this.name = n;
    }

    Customer(String name) {
        this.name = name;
    }

}
```

Nothing too fancy here. Moving on. We also have a mock repository that handles the "persistence" of the Customer entity with a Map<K, V> implementation:

```java
package rsb.http.customers;

import org.springframework.stereotype.Component;
import org.springframework.stereotype.Repository;
import reactor.core.publisher.Flux;
import reactor.core.publisher.Mono;

import java.util.Map;
import java.util.UUID;
import java.util.concurrent.ConcurrentHashMap;

@Repository
public class CustomerRepository {

    private final Map<String, Customer> data = new ConcurrentHashMap<>();

    Mono<Customer> findById(String id) {
        return Mono.just(this.data.get(id));
    }

    Mono<Customer> save(Customer customer) {
        var uuid = UUID.randomUUID().toString();
        this.data.put(uuid, new Customer(uuid, customer.getName()));
        return Mono.just(this.data.get(uuid));
    }

    Flux<Customer> findAll() {
        return Flux.fromIterable(this.data.values());
    }

}
```

Good stuff. Let's start building HTTP APIs using this entity.

7.4.2. Building Spring MVC-Style HTTP Endpoints

There are a couple of ways to build HTTP endpoints in Spring Webflux. The first - as a class with endpoints mapped to handler methods - is familiar to anybody who's ever worked with Spring MVC. Create a class, annotate it with `@Controller` (for regular old HTTP endpoints that don't need message conversion by default), or `@RestController` (for more REST-ful HTTP endpoints) and then define handler methods. Let's look at an example.

Chapter 7. HTTP

```
package rsb.http.customers;

import org.springframework.http.ResponseEntity;
import org.springframework.web.bind.annotation.*;
import reactor.core.publisher.Flux;
import reactor.core.publisher.Mono;

import java.net.URI;

@RestController  ①
@RequestMapping(value = "/rc/customers")  ②
class CustomerRestController {

    private final CustomerRepository repository;

    CustomerRestController(CustomerRepository cr) {
        this.repository = cr;
    }

    @GetMapping("/{id}")  ③
    Mono<Customer> byId(@PathVariable("id") String id) {
        return this.repository.findById(id);
    }

    @GetMapping  ④
    Flux<Customer> all() {
        return this.repository.findAll();
    }

    @PostMapping  ⑤
    Mono<ResponseEntity<?>> create(@RequestBody Customer customer) {  ⑥
        return this.repository.save(customer)//
                .map(customerEntity -> ResponseEntity//
                        .created(URI.create("/rc/customers/" + customerEntity.getId())) //
                        .build());
    }

}
```

① `@RestController` is a stereotype annotation (itself also ultimately meta-annotated with `@Component`) that indicates to Spring that this bean should have any of its annotated methods registered as HTTP handlers

② The `@RequestMapping` annotation tells Spring how to map any method on which it's configured to a particular type of HTTP request. If you place the @RequestMapping on the controller class itself, every subordinate, method-specific mapping inherits its mapping configuration from the class mapping. You can use @RequestMapping or the HTTP method-specific annotation variants like @GetMapping and @PostMapping. These annotations are themselves also annotated with @RequestMapping.

③ When an HTTP GET request arrives at http://localhost:8080/rc/customers/23, the framework invokes this handler. The framework matches arbitrary values after ···/customers/, extracts it, and passes it in as a parameter to the handler method. The framework gives the extracted path variable {id} to the handler method parameter annotated with @PathVariable("id").

④ This endpoint returns all Customer entities when an HTTP GET request to /rc/customers arrives

⑤ This endpoint accepts incoming HTTP POST request. POST requests typically contain HTTP bodies converted to a type of Customer automatically and made available as a request parameter. Customer customer.

There's much power here! The @RequestMapping annotation can match a good many types of requests. You can specify the HTTP methods (sometimes called *verbs*) to which a handler should respond. If you don't specify a method, then it matches *all* methods. You can specify the path of the resource. You can specify what headers must be present in the incoming request ("this request must have an Accept header that specifies application/json), and you can provide header values for the response ("the Content-Type for this resource is `application/xml`"). You can require those specific parameters are present. It is my experience that you'll be able to match most of your requests declaratively. I've rarely experienced a situation where I couldn't get done what I wanted to get done.

There are variants of @RequestMapping, like @GetMapping and @PostMapping, that are otherwise identical to @RequestMapping but do not require method. These are convenience annotations and aren't offered for all the HTTP methods, only the most common ones. You can always substitute a slightly more verbose @RequestMapping for one of the more specific and perhaps shorter variants.

This controller is otherwise straightforward. It introduces a lot of critical concepts. *Handler methods* are invoked to handle incoming HTTP requests. Which HTTP requests are handled by which handler methods are governed by the *request mapping* annotations. In this model, we hang all of this off a Spring bean, an object, with methods and annotations. Methods and annotations are familiar if you're using Spring. These concepts are vital to using Spring in the web tier.

This class may look familiar if you've ever used Spring MVC, but it is worth stressing that this is *not* Spring MVC. Indeed if you consult the logs, you'll see there's no Servlet engine. While things are hopefully familiar, don't be lulled into thinking the existing code works unchanged 100% of the time.

One key difference: by the time a handler method returns in Spring MVC, for most cases, everything that needs to be resolved to manifest a response is present. The notable exception is for the occasional asynchronous use cases like WebSockets or server-sent events. In Spring Webflux, the opposite is usually so. In Spring Webflux, most return values from a handler method are Publisher<T> instances that have yet to materialize. The framework will eventually .subscribe() to the instance and materialize the response, but you shouldn't write code that assumes as much. It *should* happen right after the handler method returns, but on what thread? For how long? All the assumptions you might've made in a Servlet environment, such as pinning things to a ThreadLocal, no longer hold. Instead, you'll need to use the Reactor Context object.

7.4.3. Functional Reactive Endpoints

I like Spring MVC-style controllers. They're familiar, and if you have many collocated handler methods, as you might if you had a handful of handlers supporting different HTTP methods for the same resource, it makes sense to define them all in the same class. The different endpoints typically share common dependencies, like the CustomerRepository here. You can define as many controller classes as you like, each supporting different resources, typically in different packages partitioned along business verticals.

There are some limitations, however.

Suppose you wanted to customize further how the framework matches requests. Suppose you wanted case insensitivity for the URI's path, or to match only on some condition in some database matches? As-is, the request matching is informed by the specifications in the declarative annotations. The annotations are data and don't imply functionality. Spring looks at the annotations and turns your stipulations into a matcher that enacts your configuration. The annotations don't mean anything in a vacuum. They're data, not verbs. You could customize how requests match, but you'd have to drop one level of abstraction into the request handling machinery. It's at this point that the abstraction would feel *leaky* like you're solving a related problem in a non-related way. The disorienting feeling of using a leaky abstraction is best explained by the protagonist Dorothy in the film *The Wizard of Oz*: "Toto, I've got a feeling we're not in Kansas anymore."

Suppose you wanted to dynamically register new resources (and their associated request matching and handler logic). As-is, endpoints correspond one-to-one with methods in a class. You can't iterate through a for-loop and add new methods to a class! Indeed, this isn't easy. (No, nobody wants to see your straightforward trick using class bytecode generation with ByteBuddy, Chad! We talked about this! Stop trying to make simple byte code manipulation happen!)

Lastly, I'd argue that the existing controller structure is fine if you plan to have more than one HTTP endpoint off a given class. However, what if you genuinely have one endpoint? Also, what if that one endpoint is a trivial String - "Hello world!"? You'd end up having a class, maybe a constructor, fields, annotations, and a method to express what ends up being one request mapping and one request handler. Sure, languages like Kotlin can clean a lot of this up. It's the principal of the thing! A *whole object* to express what could be a method call and a lambda parameter. We can do better.

Are you typically going to build single HTTP endpoint applications? NO. Of course not. Perhaps after a handful of collocated endpoints, the line-count is amortized over the similar handler methods all in the same class. That sort of amortization is possible with method or function-invocations too.

In the Java ecosystem and the .NET ecosystem, it's common to express HTTP handler logic as methods on (sometimes stateful) objects. ASP.NET MVC and WebForms, Java Server Faces, and Apache Struts all work this way. So did WebWork. So does Spring MVC. Frameworks are reflections of their host language's capabilities. Frameworks built before Java supported lambdas reflect that. They were reflections of the Java language's capabilities.

Lambdas and Method References, Oh My!

Languages with first-class lambda support often support pairing a request matching predicate with a functional style handler. It isn't difficult to find examples. Sinatra in the Ruby ecosystem, Ratpack in the Groovy ecosystem, Scalatra in the Scala ecosystem, Express.js in the Node.js ecosystem, and Flask in the Python ecosystem all work this way. Java was short on options here until the relatively recent release of Java 8. Java 8 gave us a kind of lambda, and Spring Framework 5 defines a Java 8 baseline. Moreover, Spring Framework 5 is the first release to formalize the Spring team's embrace of Kotlin, bringing the languages for which Spring has first-class support to three: Java, Groovy, and now Kotlin. All three of these languages have good (or excellent) lambda support.

It's only natural that, with this lambda-friendly, functional-friendly foundation, Spring Webflux also supports functional, lambda-ready, reactive HTTP handlers. Let's look at some examples.

```
package rsb.http.routes;

import org.springframework.context.annotation.Bean;
import org.springframework.context.annotation.Configuration;
import org.springframework.stereotype.Component;
import org.springframework.web.reactive.function.server.HandlerFunction;
import org.springframework.web.reactive.function.server.RouterFunction;
import org.springframework.web.reactive.function.server.ServerRequest;
import org.springframework.web.reactive.function.server.ServerResponse;
import reactor.core.publisher.Mono;

import static
org.springframework.web.reactive.function.server.RouterFunctions.route;
import static
org.springframework.web.reactive.function.server.ServerResponse.ok;

@Configuration
class SimpleFunctionalEndpointConfiguration {

    @Bean
    RouterFunction<ServerResponse> simple(GreetingsHandlerFunction handler) {
①

        ②
        return route() //
                .GET("/hello/{name}", request -> { ③
                    var namePathVariable = request.pathVariable("name");
                    var message = String.format("Hello %s!", namePathVariable);
                    return ok().bodyValue(message);
                }) //
                .GET("/hodor", handler) ④
                .GET("/sup", handler::handle) ⑤
                .build();
    }

}
```

① You can register as many beans of type RouterFunction<ServerResponse as you like.

② Routes are defined using the static factory methods, like route(), on RouterFunctions. A result is a builder object to which you can add new route definitions dynamically.

③ The first registration (/hello/{name}) matches incoming HTTP GET requests. The route expects path variables ({name}) using the given ServerRequest parameter, request. The handler logic, to be invoked when a request matches, is provided as a lambda. The handler returns a non-reactive HTTP response. The server sends the response with an HTTP status 200 (OK).

④ If an inline lambda becomes more extensive than an expression or a couple of lines, it can become hard to figure out what's happening with so much collocated business logic. It's common to extract this business logic into either an implementation of the functional interface, HandlerFunction<ServerResponse> or...

⑤ method references, with structurally similar signatures (same input types and return types).

This example depends on a bean of type GreetingsHandlerFunction:

The GreetingsHandlerFunction implements the functional interface for handlers and the host for a method reference to be used as a handler.

```
package rsb.http.routes;

import org.springframework.stereotype.Component;
import org.springframework.web.reactive.function.server.HandlerFunction;
import org.springframework.web.reactive.function.server.ServerRequest;
import org.springframework.web.reactive.function.server.ServerResponse;
import reactor.core.publisher.Mono;

import static org.springframework.web.reactive.function.server.ServerResponse.ok;

@Component
class GreetingsHandlerFunction implements HandlerFunction<ServerResponse> {

    @Override
    public Mono<ServerResponse> handle(ServerRequest request) {
        return ok().syncBody("Hodor!");
    }

}
```

In this functional reactive example, all the registrations and the business logic for those registrations live nearby. Routing logic is centralized here, in stark contrast to Spring MVC-style controllers, where routing logic is strewn about the codebase, attached to the handler methods in various objects, in various packages. If I wanted to rewrite all the URLs or change the resource URIs' strings, I'd need not look any further than this single bean definition. If you've only got one or two endpoints, then this may not matter. It might matter considerably more if you're trying to manage hundreds of endpoints.

The examples I've shown you so far demonstrate a typical progression I see in my code. I tend to use inline lambdas first, but collocating business logic with the routes results in a monolithic `RouterFunction` bean definition packed with inline lambdas. It quickly becomes, eh, *difficult* to follow the code.

Use method references to factor out the handler logic. A standard convention is to extract these handler methods out to an object, a *handler class*. Handler classes aren't a specific thing, like a `@RestController` or a `@Service`, in Spring. They're just regular old objects hosting methods to whom we delegate the handling of HTTP requests for functional reactive endpoints. In this first example, I've extracted the handler logic to a bean of type `GreetingsHandlerFunction`, whose definition I show below. The `GreetingsHandlerFunction` bean gets used in two different ways: as an object that implements the functional interface and as an object that hosts a valid method, compatible with the functional interface, that we reference.

This example demonstrates how to use the functional reactive style to define routes. These routes hang off of the `RouterFunctions.Builder` builder that's defined for us by the `route(…)` method. In this example, I chain the registrations together for the more concise code. Still, there's no reason you couldn't store the intermediate builder in a variable and then, in a for-loop or as a result of a database query, register new endpoints on the builder dynamically.

When you call `GET(…)`, it registers a `RequestPredicate`. A `RequestPredicate` matches incoming requests. In these examples, we're using the static factory methods to describe common kinds of requests with implementations of `RequestPredicate`. You can match the incoming path, HTTP method, headers, path extensions, query parameters, etc. We'll look more at `RequestPredicates`, and how to write your own, momentarily.

In the previous example, all the HTTP registrations were discrete. They didn't have much in common and didn't depend on another. Spring Webflux also supports hierarchical (nested) registrations, with top-level registrations governing how nested registrations match. Nested request predicates can inherit from their parent request predicates. You might want to define different handlers for different HTTP methods against the same resource path. You might want to define different handlers against a root URI (`/foo`) and then differentiate nested registration paths (like `/foo/{id}` and `/foo/{id}/bars`). You might want to distinguish different handlers by the accepted incoming media types. Whatever your use case, Spring Webflux has your back. Let's look at how we can use nested registrations to describe a hierarchy more naturally and avoid redundant configuration.

Here's what we want to describe.

HTTP Method	Root Path	Sub Path (if any)	Media-Type
GET	/nested	``	application/json
GET	/nested	``	text/event-stream
GET	/nested	`/{pv}	application/json

Here is how we can hierarchically describe that.

```
package rsb.http.routes;

import org.springframework.context.annotation.Bean;
import org.springframework.context.annotation.Configuration;
import org.springframework.web.reactive.function.server.RouterFunction;
import org.springframework.web.reactive.function.server.ServerResponse;

import static org.springframework.http.MediaType.*;
import static
org.springframework.web.reactive.function.server.RequestPredicates.accept;
import static
org.springframework.web.reactive.function.server.RequestPredicates.path;
import static
org.springframework.web.reactive.function.server.RouterFunctions.route;

@Configuration
class NestedFunctionalEndpointConfiguration {

    @Bean
    RouterFunction<ServerResponse> nested(NestedHandler nestedHandler) {

        ①
        var jsonRP = accept(APPLICATION_JSON).or(accept(
APPLICATION_JSON_UTF8));
        var sseRP = accept(TEXT_EVENT_STREAM);

        return route() //
                .nest(path("/nested"), builder -> builder //
                        .nest(jsonRP, nestedBuilder -> nestedBuilder //
                                .GET("/{pv}", nestedHandler::pathVariable) ②
                                .GET("", nestedHandler::noPathVariable) ③
                        ) //
                        .add(route(sseRP, nestedHandler::sse)) ④
                ) //
                .build();

    }

}
```

① jsonRP is a RequestPredicate that responds to incoming requests that accept application/json or application/json;charset=UTF-8. sseRP is a RequestPredicate that responds to incoming requests that accept text/event-stream (server-sent events).

② This is a nested handler function that responds only if the client accepts application/json or application/json;charset=UTF-8 *and* if the client requests the path /nested/{pv} with the HTTP method GET.

③ This is a nested handler function that responds only if the client accepts application/json or application/json;charset=UTF-8 *and* if the client requests the path /nested (with no trailing path variable) with the HTTP method GET.

④ This is a nested handler function that responds only if the client accepts text/event-stream *and* if the client requests the path /nested (with no trailing path variable) with the HTTP method GET.

The exciting thing here is the nesting of endpoint definitions. I've used tabs to make clear the sort of implied hierarchy in the definitions.

The definitions start at /nested; it's the root. We're going to define three endpoints that have that for their root. Under that, two endpoints return application/json data. This first registration registers a handler that returns a default value. The next handler registration expects a sub-path, the person's name to greet, relative to /nested: /nested/{pv}.

```
curl -H"accept: application/json" http://localhost:8080/nested
```

```
curl -H"accept: application/json" http://localhost:8080/nested/World
```

The final handler hangs off /nested but produces a server-sent event (SSE) stream (text/event-stream) data. Server-sent events are a convenient way to describe a never-ending stream of data sent to the client. We'll look at SSE in a bit more depth shortly.

```
curl -H"accept: text/event-stream" http://localhost:8080/nested
```

You can express all sorts of hierarchies using the RouterFunction<ServerResponse> DSLs. In this example, we defer to method references in a handler object, NestedHandler.

```java
package rsb.http.routes;

import org.springframework.stereotype.Component;
import org.springframework.web.reactive.function.server.ServerRequest;
import org.springframework.web.reactive.function.server.ServerResponse;
import reactor.core.publisher.Mono;
import rsb.utils.IntervalMessageProducer;

import java.util.Map;
import java.util.Optional;

import static org.springframework.http.MediaType.TEXT_EVENT_STREAM;
import static org.springframework.web.reactive.function.server.ServerResponse.ok;

@Component
class NestedHandler {

    Mono<ServerResponse> sse(ServerRequest r) {
        return ok() //
                .contentType(TEXT_EVENT_STREAM) //
                .body(IntervalMessageProducer.produce(), String.class);
    }

    Mono<ServerResponse> pathVariable(ServerRequest r) {
        return ok().syncBody(greet(Optional.of(r.pathVariable("pv"))));
    }

    Mono<ServerResponse> noPathVariable(ServerRequest r) {
        return ok().syncBody(greet(Optional.ofNullable(null)));
    }

    private Map<String, String> greet(Optional<String> name) {
        var finalName = name.orElse("world");
        return Map.of("message", String.format("Hello %s!", finalName));
    }

}
```

There's nothing novel to establish in the `NestedHandler`. Let's return to our Customer HTTP API; this time implemented using the functional reactive style.

Chapter 7. HTTP

```
package rsb.http.customers;

import org.springframework.context.annotation.Bean;
import org.springframework.context.annotation.Configuration;
import org.springframework.web.reactive.function.server.RouterFunction;
import org.springframework.web.reactive.function.server.ServerResponse;

import static
org.springframework.web.reactive.function.server.RequestPredicates.path;
import static
org.springframework.web.reactive.function.server.RouterFunctions.route;

@Configuration
class CustomerApiEndpointConfiguration {

    @Bean
    RouterFunction<ServerResponse> customerApis(CustomerHandler handler) {
        return route() //
                .nest(path("/fn/customers"), builder -> builder //
                        .GET("/{id}", handler::handleFindCustomerById)
                        .GET("", handler::handleFindAll)
                        .POST("", handler::handleCreateCustomer))
                .build();
    }

}
```

The registrations defined here behave identically in functionality to those in `CustomerRestController`, except they start with /fn, not /rc. The logic for each endpoint lives in a handler object, `CustomerHandler`.

```
package rsb.http.customers;

import org.springframework.stereotype.Component;
import org.springframework.web.reactive.function.server.ServerRequest;
import org.springframework.web.reactive.function.server.ServerResponse;
import reactor.core.publisher.Flux;
import reactor.core.publisher.Mono;

import java.net.URI;

import static
org.springframework.web.reactive.function.server.ServerResponse.created;
import static
org.springframework.web.reactive.function.server.ServerResponse.ok;

@Component
class CustomerHandler {

    private final CustomerRepository repository;

    CustomerHandler(CustomerRepository repository) {
        this.repository = repository;
    }

    Mono<ServerResponse> handleFindAll(ServerRequest request) {
        var all = this.repository.findAll(); ①
        return ok().body(all, Customer.class); ②
    }

    Mono<ServerResponse> handleFindCustomerById(ServerRequest request) {
        var id = request.pathVariable("id");
        var byId = this.repository.findById(id);
        return ok().body(byId, Customer.class);
    }

    Mono<ServerResponse> handleCreateCustomer(ServerRequest request) {
        return request.bodyToMono(Customer.class) //
                .flatMap(repository::save) //
                .flatMap(saved -> created(URI.create("/fn/customers/" + saved.getId()))
                        .build());
    }

}
```

① Return a `Publisher<Customer>`.

② The response is built using statically imported methods on the `ServerResponse` object, like `ok(…)` and `created(…)`. `ServerResponse.created(URI)` is one of many convenience methods on `ServerResponse` for common scenarios. It's common in an HTTP API to return 201. 201 indicates that a POST has resulted in creating some state on the server. The next question a client has after reading the 201 status code is, "all right, so where do I find the newly created resource?" Communicate that using a URI.

The handler methods depend on our reactive Spring Data MongoDB repository. Each response derives from `Publisher<T>`. The ultimately subscribes to our `Publisher<T>` instances. You can return a `Publisher<T>` for small payloads (like our endpoints serving `application/json`) or streaming payloads (like the endpoints serving `text/event-stream`).

Request Predicates

Thus far, we've used the built-in DSL to create request predicates that match common types of requests, distinguishing by HTTP method or accepted media types, to a given URI. These are just `RequestPredicate` implementations that we've constructed using the DSL and static factory methods on the `RequestPredicates` class. The thing is, you're not limited to those variants provided by the framework. You can add your own or mix-and-match others.

Let's look at how we can customize the matching of incoming requests. I confess I had a tough time trying to imagine a use-case that was not already served out-of-the-box. Thankfully, and as with most things, the community helped! I was talking to someone at a conference who asked about case-insensitive matching. Out of the box, both Spring MVC and Spring Webflux are case-sensitive when they match paths. That's a good, caring default, but sometimes, well, you want something a little more *insensitive*.

```
package rsb.http.routes;

import lombok.extern.log4j.Log4j2;
import org.springframework.context.annotation.Bean;
```

```java
import org.springframework.context.annotation.Configuration;
import org.springframework.http.MediaType;
import org.springframework.web.reactive.function.server.HandlerFunction;
import org.springframework.web.reactive.function.server.RouterFunction;
import org.springframework.web.reactive.function.server.ServerRequest;
import org.springframework.web.reactive.function.server.ServerResponse;

import java.util.Set;

import static org.springframework.web.reactive.function.server.RequestPredicates.GET;
import static org.springframework.web.reactive.function.server.RequestPredicates.accept;
import static org.springframework.web.reactive.function.server.RouterFunctions.route;
import static org.springframework.web.reactive.function.server.ServerResponse.ok;
import static rsb.http.routes.CaseInsensitiveRequestPredicate.i;

@Log4j2
@Configuration
class CustomRoutePredicates {

    private final HandlerFunction<ServerResponse> handler = //
            request -> ok().syncBody(
                    "Hello, " + request.queryParam("name").orElse("world") +
"!");

    @Bean
    RouterFunction<ServerResponse> customRequestPredicates() {

        var aPeculiarRequestPredicate = GET("/test") ①
                .and(accept(MediaType.APPLICATION_JSON_UTF8)) //
                .and(this::isRequestForAValidUid);

        var caseInsensitiveRequestPredicate = i(GET("/greetings/{name}")); ②

        return route() //
                .add(route(aPeculiarRequestPredicate, this.handler)) //
                .add(route(caseInsensitiveRequestPredicate, this.handler)) //
                .build();
    }

    boolean isRequestForAValidUid(ServerRequest request) {
        var goodUids = Set.of("1", "2", "3");
        return request //
                .queryParam("uid") //
```

```
                .map(goodUids::contains) //
                .orElse(false);
    }

}
```

① This example demonstrates that you can compose (or negate, or both) RequestPredicate implementations. A RequestPredicate can express conditions like "match an HTTP GET request *and* match a custom request predicate." Here we substitute a method reference for a RequestPredicate.

② Here, with the static i() factory method that I've created, I wrap and adapt a RequestPredicate with another implementation that lowercases the request's URI. Tada! Case-insensitive request matching. We'll explore the implementation details momentarily.

The last example introduces a custom RequestPredicate wrapper that wraps incoming requests and normalizes their URI so that they match our all-lowercase RequestPredicate implementations, regardless of the case of the incoming URI. I created a factory method, rsb.http.routes.CaseInsensitiveRequestPredicate.i (i is for *insensitive*), that takes a target RequestPredicate and adapts it.

Here's the RequestPredicate implementation.

```java
package rsb.http.routes;

import org.springframework.web.reactive.function.server.RequestPredicate;
import org.springframework.web.reactive.function.server.ServerRequest;

class CaseInsensitiveRequestPredicate implements RequestPredicate {

    private final RequestPredicate target;

    public static RequestPredicate i(RequestPredicate rp) {
        return new CaseInsensitiveRequestPredicate(rp);
    }

    CaseInsensitiveRequestPredicate(RequestPredicate target) {
        this.target = target;
    }

    @Override
    public boolean test(ServerRequest request) { ①
        return this.target.test(new LowercaseUriServerRequestWrapper(request));
    }

    @Override
    public String toString() {
        return this.target.toString();
    }

}
```

① Our wrapper `RequestPredicate` simply wraps the incoming `ServerRequest` with a `LowercaseUriServerRequestWrapper` and forwards it to the target `RequestPredicate`

The `ServerRequest` wrapper does the hardest work. You may want to extend, wrap and adapt a request so Spring Webflux ships with a convenient base class called `ServerRequestWrapper` that already has storage for the target `ServerRequest`. We'll use that to wrap an incoming request, normalize its URI, and then proceed.

```
package rsb.http.routes;

import org.springframework.http.server.PathContainer;
import org.springframework.web.reactive.function.server.ServerRequest;
import
org.springframework.web.reactive.function.server.support.ServerRequestWrapper
;

import java.net.URI;

public class LowercaseUriServerRequestWrapper extends ServerRequestWrapper {

    public LowercaseUriServerRequestWrapper(ServerRequest target) {
        super(target);
    }

    ①
    @Override
    public URI uri() {
        return URI.create(super.uri().toString().toLowerCase());
    }

    @Override
    public String path() {
        return uri().getRawPath();
    }

    @Override
    public PathContainer pathContainer() {
        return PathContainer.parsePath(path());
    }

}
```

① Lower-case the request URI and return that.

Now, assuming your `RequestPredicate` implementations all use lowercase `Strings`, this gives you case-insensitive request matching. Issue a request to the `/greetings/{name}` endpoint and confirm it still works. Uppercase the request and try again. You should see the same result.

7.4.4. Filters

A custom request predicate is one way to achieve case-insensitive URIs.

Another might be introducing a filter - an object that intercepts all incoming HTTP requests intended for downstream Spring Webflux components - and operates on it or transforms it somehow. There are a few different ways to introduce filter-like functionality into a Spring Webflux application. You can use a `WebFilter`, generically, and for all types of handlers, or a `HandlerFilterFunction` for functional reactive endpoint handlers.

I'd start with the `WebFilter` approach as it's generally applicable and should be reasonably familiar.

Let's revisit our case-insensitivity use case. We'll lowercase incoming request URIs using the `.mutate()` operation on the `ServerWebExchange` representing the incoming HTTP request.

Chapter 7. HTTP

```
package rsb.http.filters;

import org.springframework.stereotype.Component;
import org.springframework.web.server.ServerWebExchange;
import org.springframework.web.server.WebFilter;
import org.springframework.web.server.WebFilterChain;
import reactor.core.publisher.Mono;

import java.net.URI;

@Component
class LowercaseWebFilter implements WebFilter {

    @Override
    public Mono<Void> filter(ServerWebExchange currentRequest, WebFilterChain chain) {

        ①
        var lowercaseUri = URI
                .create(currentRequest.getRequest().getURI().toString().toLowerCase());

        var outgoingExchange = currentRequest.mutate() ②
                .request(builder -> builder.uri(lowercaseUri)).build();

        return chain.filter(outgoingExchange); ③
    }

}
```

① lowercase incoming HTTP requests

② mutate the incoming request, forwarding it on with a lowercase URI

③ forward the request onward in the filter chain

The `WebFilter` API is a great way to introduce generic, cross-cutting concerns like security, timeouts, compression, message enrichment, etc. You can try this out by invoking some other endpoint, like /test with both lowercase and uppercase.

I like the generic `WebFilter` approach because it lets me intercept *all* requests into my application and potentially contribute something to them before anything can respond. `WebFilter` instances are ideal places for things like security.

Spring Webflux also supports targeted filters that hang off a specific RouterFunction<ServerResponse> itself. The framework invokes filters *after* a particular URI has matched, too late to normalize a URI as we did in the WebFilter. The targeted filters - hooks - are still great fits for cross-cutting functionality like security. Let's look at some of the hooks that Spring Webflux extends for processing incoming requests.

```java
package rsb.http.filters;

import lombok.extern.log4j.Log4j2;
import org.springframework.context.annotation.Bean;
import org.springframework.context.annotation.Configuration;
import org.springframework.web.reactive.function.server.RouterFunction;
import org.springframework.web.reactive.function.server.ServerRequest;
import org.springframework.web.reactive.function.server.ServerResponse;
import reactor.core.publisher.Mono;

import java.util.UUID;

import static org.springframework.web.reactive.function.server.RouterFunctions.route;
import static org.springframework.web.reactive.function.server.ServerResponse.badRequest;
import static org.springframework.web.reactive.function.server.ServerResponse.ok;

@Log4j2
@Configuration
class LowercaseWebConfiguration {

    @Bean
    RouterFunction<ServerResponse> routerFunctionFilters() {
        var uuidKey = UUID.class.getName();
        return route() ①
                .GET("/hi/{name}", this::handle) //
                .GET("/hello/{name}", this::handle) //
                .filter((req, next) -> {②
                    log.info(".filter(): before");
                    var reply = next.handle(req);
                    log.info(".filter(): after");
                    return reply;
                }) //
```

Chapter 7. HTTP

```
                    .before(request -> {
                        log.info(".before()"); ③
                        request.attributes().put(uuidKey, UUID.randomUUID());
                        return request;
                    }) //
                    .after((serverRequest, serverResponse) -> {
                        log.info(".after()"); ④
                        log.info("UUID: " + serverRequest.attributes().get
(uuidKey));
                        return serverResponse;
                    }) //
                    .onError(NullPointerException.class, (e, request) ->
badRequest().build()) ⑤
                    .build();
        }

    Mono<ServerResponse> handle(ServerRequest serverRequest) {
        return ok().syncBody(
                String.format("Hello, %s!", serverRequest.pathVariable("name
")));
    }

}
```

① This configuration defines two HTTP endpoints

② The `filter(HandlerFilterFunction<ServerResponse, ServerResponse>)` method looks similar to our earlier `WebFilter`.

③ `before()` lets you pre-process a request. I use this opportunity to stash data associated with the request in the attributes.

④ `after()` lets you post-process a request. I can pull out that request attribute and confirm it's still there.

⑤ `onError()` supports two variants that support matching specific types of exceptions and providing a response for them and another variant that provides a default response.

So, if you configure `.before()` and `.filter()` and `.after()`, you may wonder, which happens first? In the example above, we can see through the logging the following order:

- `.filter()`: before
- `.before()`

227

- .filter(): after
- .after()

The HandlerFilterFunction is invoked earlier than .before() and earlier than .after(). In this example, I also configure an onError() callback that returns an HTTP 400 if something should go wrong with the request. The onError() method lets me keep tedious error handling and cleanup logic separate from the endpoint handler functions themselves; they can throw an Exception and have it bubble up to the centralized error-handling routine in onError.

Error Handling for Functional Reactive Endpoints

The .filter() operator is a great place to centralize error handling routine for all endpoints hanging off a RouterFunction<ServerResponse>. The best part? We can use the same functional reactive idioms with which we're already familiar. Let's look at a simple example with an endpoint to read a Product record by their ID, /products/{id}. Request ID 1 or 2, and you trigger a ProductNotFoundException. Everything else returns successfully. We'll attach some error handling logic to the RouterFunction to trap ProductNotFoundException exceptions and translate them into an HTTP 404 (Not Found) response.

```
package rsb.http.filters;

import lombok.Data;
import lombok.RequiredArgsConstructor;
import org.springframework.context.annotation.Bean;
import org.springframework.context.annotation.Configuration;
import org.springframework.web.reactive.function.server.RouterFunction;
import org.springframework.web.reactive.function.server.ServerResponse;
import reactor.core.publisher.Mono;

import java.util.Set;

import static org.springframework.web.reactive.function.server.RouterFunctions.route;
import static org.springframework.web.reactive.function.server.ServerResponse.notFound;

@Configuration
```

```
class ErrorHandlingRouteConfiguration {

    @Bean
    RouterFunction<ServerResponse> errors() {
        var productIdPathVariable = "productId";
        return route() //
                .GET("/products/{" + productIdPathVariable + "}", request -> {
                    var productId = request.pathVariable
(productIdPathVariable);
                    if (!Set.of("1", "2").contains(productId)) {
                        return ServerResponse.ok().syncBody(new Product
(productId));
                    }
                    else {
                        return Mono.error(new ProductNotFoundException
(productId));
                    }
                }) //
                .filter((request, next) -> next.handle(request)) ①
                    .onErrorResume(ProductNotFoundException.class,
                            pnfe -> notFound().build())) ②
                .build();
    }

}

@Data
@RequiredArgsConstructor
class Product {

    private final String id;

}

@Data
@RequiredArgsConstructor
class ProductNotFoundException extends RuntimeException {

    private final String productId;

}
```

① We forward the request processing to the next filter down the chain.

② If something goes wrong at any point in the request processing chain, we can use familiar Reactor operators to trap the exception and handle it. In this case, we return an HTTP 404 (Not Found).

I've inlined these handlers as lambdas, but you could, and more than likely, should extract them out to method references.

7.5. Long-Lived Client Connections

So far, we've mostly looked at how to build HTTP endpoints that respond to requests and then disconnect. We've got a unique opportunity, with asynchronous IO and reactive programming, to serve endpoints that support long-lived client connections. Why would we do this? Reactivity! As soon as the client disconnects from an endpoint, the server can't send anything to it. For the client to see an updated server state, it needs to reconnect. This reconnection is inefficient, and it means that the client needs to ask the service to replay any missed updates since the last connection.

Why would you need this? Imagine any use case where the liveliness of the data is paramount: stock tickers, sensor updates, chat messages, presence notifications. All of these things assume the immediacy of the updates consumed.

There are a few good options available to us in the HTTP stack: server-sent events and WebSockets.

Before we dive in and demonstrate some of these concepts, I've built a utility class that publishes a never-ending stream of events. You'll see this again in short order so let's establish it here for reference.

```
package rsb.utils;

import lombok.Data;
import reactor.core.publisher.Flux;
import java.time.Duration;
import java.util.concurrent.atomic.AtomicLong;

public abstract class IntervalMessageProducer {

    public static Flux<String> produce(int c) {
        return produce().take(c);
    }

    public static Flux<String> produce() {
        return doProduceCountAndStrings().map(CountAndString::getMessage);
    }

    private static Flux<CountAndString> doProduceCountAndStrings() {
        var counter = new AtomicLong();
        return Flux //
                .interval(Duration.ofSeconds(1)) ①
                .map(i -> new CountAndString(counter.incrementAndGet())); //
    }

}

@Data
class CountAndString {

    private final String message;

    private final long count;

    CountAndString(long c) {
        this.count = c;
        this.message = "# " + this.count;
    }

}
```

① This endpoint produces new `CountAndString` values every second using the `Flux.interval` operator.

Let's look at one of two viable options for never-end streams of data.

7.6. Server-Sent Events (SSE)

Server-sent events (SSE) are a convenient way to describe a (potentially never-ending) data stream sent to a client. The client sees the content type, `text/event-stream`, and knows not to disconnect. It knows that it should keep the socket open and continue to read the data. SSE is an excellent way to send updates to a client asynchronously. It's a unidirectional means of communication, meaning that it is suitable only for the producer (the server) to communicate to the consumer (the client). If the client wants to respond, it should just send a message to another HTTP endpoint. It's a simple protocol where two newlines delineate the payload and then the text `data:`. Some textual representation then follows that.

Simple, but it works. There's no concept of headers in the messages themselves, beyond what HTTP supports for the overall message. A server-sent event is an HTTP payload, so it requires textual payloads.

We've got our `IntervalMessageProducer`. What is required to adapt it to a server-sent event stream? Not so much, it turns out! Here's an example.

```
package rsb.sse;

import lombok.extern.log4j.Log4j2;
import org.springframework.context.annotation.Bean;
import org.springframework.context.annotation.Configuration;
import org.springframework.http.MediaType;
import org.springframework.web.reactive.function.server.RouterFunction;
import org.springframework.web.reactive.function.server.ServerRequest;
import org.springframework.web.reactive.function.server.ServerResponse;
import reactor.core.publisher.Mono;
import rsb.utils.IntervalMessageProducer;

import static
org.springframework.web.reactive.function.server.RouterFunctions.route;

@Log4j2
@Configuration
class SseConfiguration {

    private final String countPathVariable = "count";

    @Bean
    RouterFunction<ServerResponse> routes() {
        return route() //
                .GET("/sse/{" + this.countPathVariable + "}", this::
handleSse) //
                .build();
    }

    Mono<ServerResponse> handleSse(ServerRequest r) {
        var countPathVariable = Integer.parseInt(r.pathVariable(this
.countPathVariable));
        var publisher = IntervalMessageProducer.produce(countPathVariable)
                .doOnComplete(() -> log.info("completed"));

        return ServerResponse //
                .ok() //
                .contentType(MediaType.TEXT_EVENT_STREAM) ①
                .body(publisher, String.class);

    }
}
```

① The *only* thing that's interesting here is that we're using the text/event-stream media type. Everything else is as you've seen before.

I wrote this example using the functional reactive style. If I'd used a `@RequestMapping` variant like `@GetMapping`, I'd have specified `produces = MediaType.TEXT_EVENT_STREAM_VALUE`.

You can consume server-sent events from HTML and JavaScript using the `EventSource` object in JavaScript. Now, because I care and want you to appreciate the potential, I'm going to do something I wouldn't normally do in polite company: JavaScript. (Stand back!)

```
function log(msg) {
    var messagesDiv = document.getElementById('messages');
    var elem = document.createElement('div');
    var txt = document.createTextNode(msg);
    elem.appendChild(txt);
    messagesDiv.append(elem);
}

window.addEventListener('load', function (e) {
    log("window has loaded.");
    var eventSource = new EventSource('http://localhost:8080/sse/10'); ①
    eventSource.addEventListener('message', function (e) {
        e.preventDefault();
        log(e.data);
    });
    eventSource.addEventListener('error', function (e) { ②
        e.preventDefault();
        log('closing the EventSource...')
        eventSource.close();
    });
});
```

① This program connects to our SSE endpoint, requesting a finite series of elements, with the JavaScript `EventSource` object and registers a listener for the `message` event. As new messages arrive, the handler calls `log` which appends a new line of text to the `div` element having `id` named messages.

② The JavaScript client triggers errors when the SSE endpoint runs out of elements. Here, we use that as an opportunity to disconnect.

Here's the HTML page that hosts the JavaScript.

```
<!DOCTYPE html>
<html lang="en">
<head>
    <meta charset="utf-8">
    <title> Server-Sent Events</title>
</head>
<body>
<script src="/sse.js"></script>
<div id="messages"></div>
</body>
</html>
```

7.7. Websockets

Server-sent events and HTTP might be all you need. It's a little odd having to correlate HTTP requests and outgoing server-sent events; it makes conversational protocols more difficult unless you're willing to thread together incoming HTTP requests and server-sent events.

Server-sent events are not particularly significant for binary data since every payload is encoded text.

Websockets offers a better way forward if you need something more bi-directional. Websockets are a different protocol than HTTP, but they work well with HTTP. A WebSocket client connects to an HTTP endpoint and then negotiates an upgrade to the WebSocket protocol. Websockets are also well supported in JavaScript.

Websocket applications are slightly more complicated than what we've seen so far, but not by much. In general, WebSocket-based applications require three different beans.

- a `WebSocketHandler`: this is where the business logic for your application lives. It's the thing that's unique from one WebSocket application to another.
- a `WebSocketHandlerAdapter`: this is machinery that's required by the framework to do its work. If I'm honest, I haven't ever needed to

configure this or tailor it, but you might need to, and that's why it's not defaulted for you.

- a `HandlerMapping`: this bean tells Spring how to mount the WebSocket logic to a URI.

For both of these applications, the `WebSocketHandlerAdapter` is invariant, so I'll reproduce its configuration here, just once. The `WebSocketHandlerAdapter` is what takes an incoming HTTP request and handles the upgrade. You can override this and the downstream `WebsocketService`, which Spring Boot automatically configures for us if you like. I don't, so I won't.

```
package rsb.ws;

import org.springframework.context.annotation.Bean;
import org.springframework.context.annotation.Configuration;
import org.springframework.web.reactive.socket.server.support.WebSocketHandlerAdapter;

@Configuration
public class WebsocketConfiguration {

    @Bean
    WebSocketHandlerAdapter webSocketHandlerAdapter() {
        return new WebSocketHandlerAdapter();
    }

}
```

I've defined this once for all my WebSocket endpoints in the application.

Let's look at a few WebSocket examples.

7.7.1. Echos of Websockets Past

This first example is a slightly more involved twist on the classic echo protocol. The server initiates the stream of data, sending it to the client, who then replies with the same value suffixed with `reply`. In this case, the consumer is the thing doing the echoing. To generate values, we'll again turn to `IntervalMessageProducer`.

```
package rsb.ws.echo;

import lombok.extern.log4j.Log4j2;
import org.springframework.context.annotation.Bean;
import org.springframework.context.annotation.Configuration;
import org.springframework.web.reactive.HandlerMapping;
import org.springframework.web.reactive.handler.SimpleUrlHandlerMapping;
import org.springframework.web.reactive.socket.WebSocketHandler;
import org.springframework.web.reactive.socket.WebSocketMessage;
import reactor.core.publisher.Flux;
import reactor.core.publisher.SignalType;
import rsb.utils.IntervalMessageProducer;

import java.util.Map;

@Log4j2
@Configuration
class EchoWebsocketConfiguration {

    ①
    @Bean
    HandlerMapping echoHm() {
        return new SimpleUrlHandlerMapping(Map.of("/ws/echo", echoWsh()), 10
);
    }

    ②
    @Bean
    WebSocketHandler echoWsh() {
        return session -> {  ③

            Flux<WebSocketMessage> out = IntervalMessageProducer //
                    .produce() //
                    .doOnNext(log::info) //
                    .map(session::textMessage)  ④
                    .doFinally(
                            signalType -> log.info("outbound connection: " +
signalType));  ⑤

            Flux<String> in = session //
                    .receive() //
                    .map(WebSocketMessage::getPayloadAsText)  ⑥
                    .doFinally(signalType -> {
                        log.info("inbound connection: " + signalType);
                        if (signalType.equals(SignalType.ON_COMPLETE)) {
                            session.close().subscribe();
```

```
                    }
                 }).doOnNext(log::info);
            return session.send(out).and(in); ⑦
        };
    }
}
```

① It used to require *three* separate lines to construct this object, before Spring Framework 5.2. I filed an issue [https://github.com/spring-projects/spring-framework/issues/23362], and the team added this constructor! See how nice that is? And you can do the same. Sometimes all you have to do is ask nicely, friends!

② This is the essential work done.

③ A `WebsocketHandler` is given a reference to a `WebSocketSession`, which you can stash for reference later on if you want. You can pump data into that `WebSocketSession` in other threads, too. The `WebSocketSession` is created once per client, a bit like an HTTP session.

④ On connection, this handler creates a cold stream of data, a `Flux<WebSocketMessage>`, by mapping each of the generated messages from the `IntervalMessageProducer` to a `WebSocketMessage` using the `WebSocketSession.textMessage` factory method. There's a variant, `WebSocketSession.binaryMessage` that conveys binary data.

⑤ There might be application state to dismantle when the WebSocket client, like a JavaScript application in a browser, disconnects or the user navigates to another page. Use the `doFinally` operator to intervene.

⑥ We can ask the `WebSocketSession` to give us a publisher to start receiving data. This example takes any incoming request, turns the payload into text, and log it in the `doOnNext` operator.

⑦ Chain the two cold streams and make them hot using `and(Publisher<T>)` to compose them into a `Mono<Void>`.

That's it! Granted, it may seem like a lot, but it's only three beans, and the only one of any real import is the `WebsocketHandler`. Let's now look at another HTML example that looks similar in structure to the SSE example before.

```
function log(msg) {
    var messagesDiv = document.getElementById('messages');
    var elem = document.createElement('div');
    var txt = document.createTextNode(msg);
    elem.appendChild(txt);
    messagesDiv.append(elem);
}

var websocket = null;

document
    .getElementById('close')
    .addEventListener('click', function (evt) {
        evt.preventDefault();
        websocket.close();
        return false;
    });

window.addEventListener('load', function (e) {
    ①
    websocket = new WebSocket('ws://localhost:8080/ws/echo');
    websocket.addEventListener('message', function (e) {
        var msg = e.data;
        log(msg);
        websocket.send(msg + ' reply'); ②
    });
});
```

① This program connects to the WebSocket endpoint using a JavaScript WebSocket and the ws:// protocol.

② When the JavaScript program sees a new incoming message, it logs it out and then uses the WebSocket object to send it right back, suffixed with `reply`.

Let's now look at the HTML page that hosts the JavaScript program.

A page, /echo.html, and requisite HTML elements

```html
<!DOCTYPE html>
<html lang="en">
<head>
    <meta charset="utf-8">
    <title>
        this is a test
    </title>
</head>
<body>

<a href="#" id="close"> Close Session </a>

<script src="/echo.js"></script>

<div id="messages"></div>

</body>
</html>
```

Alrighty! That was a good chapter, gang! Good game. I'll see you in the next chapter!

…

What're you still doing here? Get! Go!

…

All right! All right! Fine. I didn't want to do this, but I know what you want. What you *need*. The last example capably demonstrates the moving parts in a typical WebSocket application. You're thinking, surely, that we *need* a chat example! We couldn't possibly finish this discussion of WebSockets without the requisite chat example. And I am happy to oblige.

7.7.2. The Chatastic Websocket Example

Is whatever it is we're about to look at going to displace ye ole favorite chat application? Probably not. It does work. This example is a reasonably long toy application or a tiny production application. Let's work through it.

The chat works with `Connection` instances, which are wrappers for a given client connection and its corresponding `WebSocketSession`.

```
package rsb.ws.chat;

import lombok.Data;
import lombok.RequiredArgsConstructor;
import org.springframework.web.reactive.socket.WebSocketSession;

@Data
@RequiredArgsConstructor
class Connection {

    private final String id;

    private final WebSocketSession session;

}
```

When a client sends a message in, we adapt it to a `Message` object. `Message` instances store a client ID, the text of the message itself, and a timestamp.

```
package rsb.ws.chat;

import lombok.Data;
import lombok.RequiredArgsConstructor;

import java.util.Date;

@Data
@RequiredArgsConstructor
class Message {

    private final String clientId;

    private final String text;

    private final Date when;

}
```

The bulk of the chat implementation lives in `ChatWebsocketConfiguration`.

```java
package rsb.ws.chat;

import com.fasterxml.jackson.databind.ObjectMapper;
import lombok.SneakyThrows;
import org.springframework.context.annotation.Bean;
import org.springframework.context.annotation.Configuration;
import org.springframework.web.reactive.HandlerMapping;
import org.springframework.web.reactive.handler.SimpleUrlHandlerMapping;
import org.springframework.web.reactive.socket.WebSocketHandler;
import org.springframework.web.reactive.socket.WebSocketMessage;
import reactor.core.publisher.Flux;
import reactor.core.publisher.SignalType;

import java.util.Date;
import java.util.Map;
import java.util.concurrent.BlockingQueue;
import java.util.concurrent.ConcurrentHashMap;
import java.util.concurrent.Executors;
import java.util.concurrent.LinkedBlockingQueue;

@Configuration
class ChatWebsocketConfiguration {

    ①
    ChatWebsocketConfiguration(ObjectMapper objectMapper) {
        this.objectMapper = objectMapper;
    }

    ②
    private final Map<String, Connection> sessions = new ConcurrentHashMap<>();

    ③
    private final BlockingQueue<Message> messages = new LinkedBlockingQueue<>();

    private final ObjectMapper objectMapper;

    @Bean
    WebSocketHandler chatWsh() {

        ④
        var messagesToBroadcast = Flux.<Message>create(sink -> {
            var submit = Executors.newSingleThreadExecutor().submit(() -> {
                while (true) {
                    try {
                        sink.next(this.messages.take());
```

Chapter 7. HTTP

```
                }
                catch (InterruptedException e) {
                    throw new RuntimeException(e);
                }
            }
        });
        sink.onCancel(() -> submit.cancel(true));
    }) //
            .share();

    return session -> { ⑤

        var sessionId = session.getId();

        this.sessions.put(sessionId, new Connection(sessionId, session));

        var in = session ⑥
                .receive() //
                .map(WebSocketMessage::getPayloadAsText) //
                .map(this::messageFromJson) //
                .map(msg -> new Message(sessionId, msg.getText(), new
Date())) //
                .map(this.messages::offer)//
                .doFinally(st -> { ⑦
                    if (st.equals(SignalType.ON_COMPLETE)) {//
                        this.sessions.remove(sessionId);//
                    }
                }); //

        var out = messagesToBroadcast ⑧
                .map(this::jsonFromMessage)//
                .map(session::textMessage);

        return session.send(out).and(in);
    };
}

⑨
@SneakyThrows
private Message messageFromJson(String json) {
    return this.objectMapper.readValue(json, Message.class);
}

@SneakyThrows
private String jsonFromMessage(Message msg) {
    return this.objectMapper.writeValueAsString(msg);
}
```

```
    @Bean
    HandlerMapping chatHm() {
        return new SimpleUrlHandlerMapping() {
            {
                this.setUrlMap(Map.of("/ws/chat", chatWsh()));
                this.setOrder(2);
            }
        };
    }

}
```

① We're going to use Jackson's `ObjectMapper` in a few different places

② Storage for new `Connection` instances. `Connection` is a holder for a given connection's ID and a `WebSocketSession`. We'll need a reference to all connected `WebSocketSession` connections to broadcast messages to everyone in a given chat.

③ As clients send messages into the application, enqueue them for delivery in that `Queue<Message>`. We create a `Publisher<T>` from this `Queue<T>` later and use that to broadcast messages to other WebSocket sessions.

④ This is probably the trickiest part of the whole application. We'll revisit this use of `Flux.create` momentarily. This example demonstrates how we bridge an external event source with our reactive APIs. It's how to turn a `Queue<T>` into a `Publisher<T>`.

⑤ The `WebSocketHandler` interface has one abstract method that takes a reference to the `WebSocketSession` created when a client connects to the application. You can stash a reference to that `WebSocketSession` and use it to send messages to an individual client. We do just that here by taking the incoming session, recording its ID and wrapping it in a `Connection` instance, and then storing that connection in the `Map<String, Connection>` established earlier. Each new WebSocket client results in another entry in this `Map<String, Connection>`. We'll have to make sure that this `Map<String, Connection>` not only expands for new connections but contracts as clients disconnect or navigate away from the page.

⑥ There are two concerns here, so I've extracted them into two different pipelines. The first deals with incoming messages, turns them into text,

⑦ When the client disconnects, the browser sends a signal to the server, and we handle that disconnect with the `doFinally` operator, wherein we take care to remove the `WebSocketSession` associated with the current session from the `Map<String, Connection>` storage.

⑧ The outbound stream of data taps the global, shared `messsagesToBroadcast Publisher<T>`, takes each new value as they arrive, turns them into a `String`, and then turns those `String`s into `WebSocketMessage` instances using the `WebSocketSession`.

⑨ There's a fair bit of marshaling `String` objects to `Message` objects and marshaling `Message` objects back into JSON `String`s. I've tucked that logic away in these little helper methods.

The use of `Flux.create` is worth reviewing. This method takes a `Consumer<FluxSink<T>>`. It is our job in the `Consumer` to stash the reference to the `FluxSink<T>` for use later on. You can stash this reference for use in any other thread. Anybody with a reference to it can emit items that subscribers to this `Publisher<T>` see. This method is ideal for bridging event-centric systems. One possibility is hanging an outbound adapter off an `IntegrationFlow` in Spring Integration and, for each new message delivered, forwarding that message into the `FluxSink<T>`. Spring Integration talks to all manner of event sources and sinks. You could build a WebSocket application that notifies you when a new file drops on an FTP server, or an XMPP message arrives, an email sends, or a Tweet mentions a user. The possibilities are endless!

In this example, `T` refers to instances of `Message`. We're defining this `Publisher<Message>` one time in the entire application. This loop runs and continually polls the `Queue<T>`. `Queue.take()` blocks (hisses!) the thread of control until there's an item to return. It's for this reason that we need to keep this loop in a separate thread. This while loop drains items from `Queue<T>` when new items arrive and then hands them to the `FluxSink<T>` for publication.

The example had a few major components:

- Bridging one event-centric system to reactive code.
- The ferrying of streams of data around the `WebSocketHandler` itself
- The explicit bookkeeping of client sessions

This example only has one, global, "room" (or "topic"), but there's no reason you couldn't link individual clients to rooms and then broadcast requests to only those clients associated with a particular room.

If you understood all that, then the rest is easy. Let's look at the JavaScript and HTML client supporting our chat.

```html
<!DOCTYPE html>
<html lang="en">
<head>
    <meta charset="utf-8">
    <title>Chat</title>
    <meta name="viewport" content="width=device-width, initial-scale=1">
    <link rel="stylesheet" href="chat.css"/>
</head>
<body style="padding: 10px">
<div id="messages"></div>
<div>
    <textarea name="message" id="message"></textarea>
    <button id="send">Send</button>
</div>
<script src="/chat.js"></script>
</body>
</html>
```

The HTML page defines a messages element that contains new, appended messages. It also defines a textbox in which the user composes messages. The page depends on CSS styling to improve the look-and-feel (only slightly!), and it depends on JavaScript to connect it to our WebSocket code.

```
window
    .addEventListener('load', function (e) {

        var messages = document.getElementById('messages');
        var button = document.getElementById('send');
        var message = document.getElementById('message');
        var websocket = new WebSocket('ws://localhost:8080/ws/chat');  ①

        websocket.addEventListener('message', function (e) {
            var element = document.createElement('div');
            element.innerText = e.data;
            messages.appendChild(element);
        });

        ②
        function send() {
            var value = message.value;
            message.value = '';
            websocket.send(JSON.stringify({'text': value.trim()}));
        }

        ③
        message.addEventListener('keydown', function (e) {
            var key = e.key;
            if (key === 'Enter') {
                send();
            }
        });

        button.addEventListener('click', function (e) {
            send();
            e.preventDefault();
            return false;
        });
    })
;
```

① The JavaScript `WebSocket` object connects to our chat endpoint and listens for new messages.

② The send function takes whatever text is in the textbox and sends it to the server using the stashed `WebSocket` reference.

③ The rest of the application concerns wiring up elements in the UI to the send function. Hit Enter in the textbox, click the Send button, and publish your message.

I'm not going to bother reproducing the style information for the application as it's both minimal and irrelevant to the application's functioning. Also, it's terrible. Just *terrible*. A veritable cascade of sad styles. Confoundingly subpar styles. CSS. I need help with my CSS, and I'm not too big to admit it.

7.8. Reactive Views with Thymeleaf

We've looked at WebSockets and server-sent events and introduced a few server-side endpoints. Whatever user interfaces we've seen thus far are limited to static .html, .js, and .css in the src/main/resources/static folder, as static assets.

In this section, we're going to look at reactive server-side views, focusing on Thymeleaf.

Thymeleaf is an exciting technology because it's a rendering template designed to promote round-tripping user-interfaces with server-side business logic. It reminds me of Apache Tapestry or Apache Wicket, both of which promote roundtrip-able templates. Thymeleaf templates are, in contrast to many other templating engines, valid HTML markup, which previews clearly in HTML designers like Adobe Dreamweaver.

Thymeleaf is a reasonably new entry into the world of templating engines with other options, like Apache Velocity and Apache Freemarker, both more than a decade old. (Both Apache Velocity and Apache Freemarker are *epic* rendering engines, and you should use them if that's your inclination.)

Thymeleaf was developed with integration for Spring-based applications front-and-center in its design goals, and its creator, Daniel Fernandez, is a friend to the Spring community. He and the team working on Thymeleaf work hard to make sure Thymeleaf integrates well, and quickly, into the latest-and-greatest versions of Spring.

So, I love Thymeleaf, but I'll level with you. I wasn't sure if I needed to include this section in the book. The prevailing wisdom seems to be that there's less need for server-side views these days with the rich client-side user interfaces (UI) possible with rich-web frameworks like Vue.js, Angular, and React. These rich client-side applications are often served up from content-delivery networks (CDNs), calling endpoints in a server-side API gateway or backend, server-side HTTP application. For that approach to work, you'd need to handle all user-interface concerns - like templating - in the client-side technology. It's possible, but you might find it more convenient to build a rich UI that lives as a sort of island on a page whose templating and theme the application drives with server-side views powered by the likes of Thymeleaf. You can more easily secure server-side views with Spring Security. Server-side views simplify the work of building progressively richer UI elements that degrade well. It makes it easier to start with the skills you know and add more dynamic behavior as you need to. As you'll see in this section, you can still do some pretty dynamic things this way.

7.8.1. How Spring's View Resolution Works with Thymeleaf

Add the Spring Boot starter for Thymleaf to your build:

- `org.sprinframework.boot` : `spring-boot-starter-thymeleaf`

The arrangement for Spring's template rendering is the same for both Spring MVC and Spring Webflux. A request comes in for a Spring handler method, `/some-url.do`, which invokes a Spring handler method. The handler method's job is to construct a model, basically a `Map<String, Object>` containing keys and model attributes. Then, provide that model and a view template for the framework to turn into a rendered template. Usually, the view template reference is some canonical string that gets plugged into a view resolver that turns the abstract, canonical string into a `View` object backed by some templating engine. Spring Boot auto-configures most of this for you. Spring Boot's Thymeleaf integration resolves `src/main/resources/templates/foo.html` given a string foo.

Let's look at a simple `.html` page with a reactive model attribute.

7.8.2. A Simple HTML View with a Reactive Stream

The simplest thing you could do is render a page with a `Publisher<T>`-backed model attribute. Thymeleaf treats a `Publisher<T>` like any other collection-like model attribute, letting you iterate over the results. Let's revisit our sample `Customer` application. We'll look at both functional reactive endpoints and a `@Controller`-stereotype-based example. Both of these handlers use the following template.

The `customers.html` *Thymeleaf template*

```
<!DOCTYPE html>
<html>①
<head>
    <title>
        A Reactive Thymeleaf View
    </title>
</head>
<body>

<h1>
    [[${type}]]②
    Customers
</h1>
<ol>
    <li data-th-each="customer : ${customers}">③
        [[${customer.id}]]
        [[${customer.name}]]
    </li>
</ol>
</body>
</html>
```

① There's a Thymeleaf HTML namespace, and if we were using that variant, we'd define it here. I prefer to use the custom, and more HTML5-like, custom attributes for my templates.

② type is a string model attribute that we're inlining on the page using the special [[…]] syntax.

③ The model attribute customers is a `Publisher<Customer>`, too. The data-th-each element iterates over elements in the `Publisher<Customer>` attribute, rendering the element's body for each element in the stream. Each time through the loop, the attribute customer is made available to the nested template and contains the current value in the iteration. We visit each customer in the customers attribute and render information about the customer, including the ID and the name.

Let's look at the first implementation, CustomerViewController.

```java
package rsb.http.customers;

import org.springframework.stereotype.Controller;
import org.springframework.ui.Model;
import org.springframework.web.bind.annotation.GetMapping;

import java.util.Map;

@Controller
class CustomerViewController {

    private final CustomerRepository repository;

    CustomerViewController(CustomerRepository repository) {
        this.repository = repository;
    }

    @GetMapping("/c/customers.php")
    String customersView(Model model) {①
        var modelMap = Map.of("customers", repository.findAll(), //
                "type", "@Controller"); ②
        model.addAllAttributes(modelMap);③
        return "customers";④
    }

}
```

① You can inject a Model, a glorified Map<String, Object>, in your handler methods

② We've got two attributes specified here, type and customers

③ This copies all the attributes from the Map<String, Object> to the Model

④ The return value is a string, the view name to be resolved using a view resolver.

Easy enough. Let's look at the functional reactive handler.

```java
package rsb.http.customers;

import org.springframework.context.annotation.Bean;
import org.springframework.context.annotation.Configuration;
import org.springframework.web.reactive.function.server.RouterFunction;
import org.springframework.web.reactive.function.server.ServerResponse;

import java.util.Map;

import static org.springframework.web.reactive.function.server.RouterFunctions.route;

@Configuration
class CustomerViewEndpointConfiguration {

    @Bean
    RouterFunction<ServerResponse> customerViews(CustomerRepository repository) {

        return route() //
            .GET("/fn/customers.php", r -> {
                var map = Map.of(//
                    "customers", repository.findAll(), ①
                    "type", "Functional Reactive" //
                );
                return ServerResponse.ok().render("customers", map); ②
            }) //
            .build();
    }

}
```

① We'll need a model, just as before....

② ...and when we're done we'll render a particular template, `customers`.

So, assuming you have a `Publisher<T>` of finite duration, Thymeleaf accumulates everything in memory and render the page, and everything's fine. What if you have a `Publisher<T>` of infinite duration, like the one produced by our `IntervalMessageProducer`? In this case, we'd be in a bit of a pickle! People start clicking away after just two seconds. I start falling asleep three seconds into a discussion on.... *zzzzzzz*. AH! Can you imagine having to wait all of eternity to check the sports scores? I don't have that kind of time. No, no. Instead, we need to update the view - *in-situ* - as new results arrive.

7.8.3. A Reactive View

Suppose you have a part of a page whose contents need to update to reflect new, ever-changing values - a stock ticker, or status information, or chat messages. Server-sent events, WebSockets, or JavaScript, are ideal solutions for these sort of liveliness requirements. Whatever solution we end up pursuing would end up reconstructing the UI DOM on each new message in JavaScript code. It would be a pity as we already have a templating engine and templating logic in place. If Thymeleaf predominantly drives our pages, it'd be wasteful to reproduce the templating in a client-side JavaScript approach. Thymeleaf can help us here.

In Thymeleaf, a fragment is an HTML markup section that can be referenced and manipulated as a block. Like little islands of user interface logic. It's even possible to pass fragments into other fragments as parameters. You can do some pretty impressive things without needing a full-blown component model. Thymeleaf also lets you re-render a page fragment against newly published values in a `Publisher<T>` and stream the updated fragments as a server-sent stream. Do you see the possibilities? Thymeleaf renders the markup and the page. We lay the page almost exactly as if we had no dynamic element. We need to introduce a sprinkle of JavaScript to make it work, but nothing too crazy.

Let's look at an example that continuously re-renders the markup whenever the stream created by `IntervalMessageProducer` publishes a new item. There are two parts: the template and the controller endpoints behind it. Let's first look at the template.

```
<!DOCTYPE html>
<html>
<head><title>Tick Tock</title></head>
<body>

①
<div id="updateBlock">
    ②
    <h1 data-th-each="update : ${updates}">
        [[${update}]]
    </h1>
</div>


<script src="/ticker.js"></script>

</body>
</html>
```

① The document object model (DOM) has a `div` element named `ticktock` which we'll reference in our JavaScript code *and* our Java controller later.

② Inside the `div` element is a pretty typical loop - indicated by the Thymeleaf-specific `data-th-text` attribute - that iterates over the elements in the `updates` model attribute. Importantly, if there is no attribute named `updates`, then nothing inside the loop is rendered.

The JavaScript code powers the more dynamic logic in /ticker.js.

```
window.addEventListener('load', function (e) {
    var tickTockBlock = document.getElementById('updateBlock');
    var es = new EventSource('http://localhost:8080/ticker-stream');
    es.addEventListener('message', function (update) {
        tickTockBlock.innerHTML = update.data;   ①
    });
})
```

① The page updates the aforementioned `div` element, `updateBlock`, whenever a new value comes in from the server-sent event stream residing at /ticker-stream.

You've seen all this before - JavaScript, server-sent events, DOM manipulation, and HTML pages. Nothing too scary. Let's now turn to the definition of the server-side controller.

```java
package rsb.views;

import org.springframework.stereotype.Controller;
import org.springframework.ui.Model;
import org.springframework.web.bind.annotation.GetMapping;
import org.thymeleaf.spring5.context.webflux.ReactiveDataDriverContextVariable;
import rsb.utils.IntervalMessageProducer;

import static org.springframework.http.MediaType.TEXT_EVENT_STREAM_VALUE;

@Controller
class TickerSseController {

    ①
    @GetMapping("/ticker.php")
    String initialView() {
        return "ticker";
    }

    ②
    @GetMapping(produces = TEXT_EVENT_STREAM_VALUE, value = "/ticker-stream")
    String streamingUpdates(Model model) {
        var producer = IntervalMessageProducer.produce();
        var updates = new ReactiveDataDriverContextVariable(producer, 1); ③
        model.addAttribute("updates", updates);
        return "ticker :: #updateBlock"; ④
    }

}
```

① This first controller renders the initial view of the template. It does *not* provide a value for the updates model attribute. A client could request /ticker.php and get the template layout. When the template loads, it'll run the JavaScript, which will stream the updated markup from...

② ...this server-sent event stream that uses a ReactiveDataDriverContextVariable to wrap the Publisher<T> and set it as the updates model attribute for the returned view. The controller's return value is in a special format used by Thymeleaf to signify that it should render a fragment - in this case, that fragment refers to the `div` element, `updateBlock`, containing our loop - found inside a containing view, `ticker`.

That example looks like a standard controller view except, saliently, that the mapping stipulates that this endpoint produces `TEXT_EVENT_STREAM_VALUE` updates, not your typical `text/html` markup you'd expect from a controller.

When you update and then load `/customers.php` in your browser, you'll see the number in that element incrementing ever upward, one second at a time.

Not bad, eh? I think about client-side programming a lot these days, mostly because it's become more complicated than server-side programming. The pendulum has swung, and nowadays, it is not uncommon to find browser-based client applications that are substantially JavaScript, with all routing and rendering happening in the browser. HTML markup, styling, and more are all defined in terms of the JavaScript code, which is especially common when using Angular and React, for example. The client-side has been getting progressively more dynamic. Google and other search engines want markup to index. They don't have as easy a time indexing the resulting rendered page after all the JavaScript has run. Some clients still don't support dynamic JavaScript behavior. So, isomorphic applications - applications that render in the client and pre-render on the server-side and serve the pre-rendered view and then start introducing dynamic behavior on the client - have become more common. Most of the time, when people talk about isomorphic applications, they're talking about taking the client-side Javascript renderer and using it on the server with Node.js. I like to think that this example, using server-sent events to update HTML markup reactively, demonstrates that you can get isomorphic applications, going the other way around for straightforward applications, and use server-side rendering that is a bit more dynamic on the client.

7.9. A Reactive Servlet Container

Thus far, everything we've seen and everything we will see runs on the default reactive web runtime, Spring Webflux's Netty HTTP-based web server. This runtime - fast, lean, and mean - is a newly developed runtime that we shipped in Spring Framework 5.0. It is, crucially, *not*, based on the Servlet API. Suppose you want to run on a Servlet container? The Spring team tries to be pragmatic, and so it is possible to run on top of a Servlet container. You can run reactive code on Apache Tomcat by changing a few dependencies.

- `org.springframework.boot : spring-boot-starter-tomcat`
- `org.springframework.boot : spring-boot-starter-webflux`

When you add `spring-boot-starter-webflux`, be sure to exclude `org.springframework.boot : spring-boot-starter-reactor-netty` from its transitive dependencies.

And... that's it! You're now running on Apache Tomcat and can take advantage of it as usual. Here's a trivial functional-reactive HTTP endpoint, just for good measure.

```
package test;

import org.springframework.boot.SpringApplication;
import org.springframework.boot.autoconfigure.SpringBootApplication;
import org.springframework.context.annotation.Bean;
import org.springframework.http.MediaType;
import org.springframework.web.reactive.function.server.HandlerFunction;
import org.springframework.web.reactive.function.server.RouterFunction;
import org.springframework.web.reactive.function.server.ServerRequest;
import org.springframework.web.reactive.function.server.ServerResponse;
import reactor.core.publisher.Mono;

import static
org.springframework.web.reactive.function.server.RequestPredicates.GET;
import static
org.springframework.web.reactive.function.server.RouterFunctions.route;
import static
org.springframework.web.reactive.function.server.ServerResponse.ok;

@SpringBootApplication
public class TomcatWebfluxApplication {

    @Bean
    RouterFunction<ServerResponse> routes() {
        return route()//
                .GET("/hello",
                        r ->
ok().contentType(MediaType.TEXT_PLAIN).bodyValue("Hi!"))
                .build();
    }

    public static void main(String args[]) {
        SpringApplication.run(TomcatWebfluxApplication.class, args);
    }

}
```

I don't know if I'd do this, but you might need to do this for compatibility reasons. Isn't it cool that you can?

7.10. The Reactive Client

So far, we've focused on building HTTP endpoints on the server, but we can't conclude this chapter without discussing someway we can talk to other HTTP-based services. Spring provides a venerable client, the `WebClient`, to help. The `WebClient` is the reactive successor to the `RestTemplate`, but it has substantial differences, which I think make it a more exciting option. It's a reactive, non-blocking client. You can use it, of course, to talk to non-reactive HTTP services, where you would've used the `RestTemplate` before, or to reactive HTTP services. The client speaks HTTP, so it doesn't care whether you're using synchronous or asynchronous I/O on the other side of the HTTP protocol.

The venerable `RestTemplate` has tons of template-style methods optimized for the common cases and supported callbacks to support more complex requests. It always felt like things got very complicated, very quickly, from there. Many of the callbacks took the position that you don't want the `RestTemplate` to do anything for you, so would drop you into a place where you could (and had to) do everything. Spring Framework 3.0 introduced the `RestTemplate` in 2009 when people were first moving to HTTP-centric RESTful services. It defaulted to synchronous and blocking IO, a familiar posture for the time.

The `WebClient` is a builder-style client. You chain together method invocations to define and further customize a given request. The result is that simple requests are straightforward, and slightly more complex requests are only slightly more complicated. It stair-steps upwards in complexity linearly.

The `WebClient` can do everything that the `RestTemplate` could, and some things that it couldn't. An example: it is notoriously hard to get the `RestTemplate` to stream over server-sent events since the default behavior of the `RestTemplate` is to wait for the complete response and then attempt to convert it using the configured `HttpMessageConverters`. It's not a problem now!

7.10.1. An HTTP Endpoint

We're going to exercise the `WebClient`, but we need something to issue requests. We'll set up three endpoints: one that returns stock-standard JSON and another endpoint that returns server-sent event stream.

```
package rsb.service;

import org.reactivestreams.Publisher;
import org.springframework.http.MediaType;
import org.springframework.security.core.Authentication;
import org.springframework.web.bind.annotation.GetMapping;
import org.springframework.web.bind.annotation.PathVariable;
import org.springframework.web.bind.annotation.RestController;
import reactor.core.publisher.Flux;
import reactor.core.publisher.Mono;
import rsb.client.Greeting;

import java.time.Duration;
import java.time.Instant;
import java.util.stream.Stream;

@RestController
class HttpController {

    ①
    @GetMapping(value = "/greet/single/{name}")
    Publisher<Greeting> greetSingle(@PathVariable String name) {
        return Mono.just(greeting(name));
    }

    ②
    @GetMapping(value = "/greet/many/{name}", produces = MediaType.TEXT_EVENT_STREAM_VALUE)
    Publisher<Greeting> greetMany(@PathVariable String name) {
        return Flux //
                .fromStream(Stream.generate(() -> greeting(name)))
                .delayElements(Duration.ofSeconds(1));
    }

    private Greeting greeting(String name) {
        return new Greeting("Hello " + name + " @ " + Instant.now());
    }

}
```

① The first HTTP endpoint produces a response of content-type application/json

② The second HTTP endpoint produces a response of content-type text/event-stream

There is also an otherwise empty `public static void main(String [] args)` class used to run the application.

7.10.2. Take a Walk on the Client-Side

Let's change our perspective and see what it looks like to work with the non-blocking HTTP `WebClient`. Our client invokes our service. You'll need to ensure that you've launched the `HttpServiceApplication` application is running.

Configuration

The host and the port and the username and password are all specified, and you can use the defaults, but if you change anything, you'll need to update configuration values for the client. I've created a simple `@ConfigurationProperties`-annotated bean to capture those values.

```
package rsb.client;

import lombok.AllArgsConstructor;
import lombok.Data;
import lombok.NoArgsConstructor;
import org.springframework.boot.context.properties.ConfigurationProperties;

@Data
@AllArgsConstructor
@NoArgsConstructor
@ConfigurationProperties(prefix = "client")
public class ClientProperties {

    private Http http = new Http();

    @Data
    public static class Http {

        private Basic basic = new Basic();

        private String rootUrl; ①

        @Data
        public static class Basic {

            private String username, password; ②

        }

    }

}
```

① This captures a value for the root URL of all requests (the host and port, essentially).

② This captures the username and password for the authenticated endpoint, as well.

7.10.3. It's Your (HTTP) Call

We'll look at three scenarios, each demonstrating something interesting. In each of these HTTP calls, we'll inject a `WebClient.Builder` and initialize it and then use the builder to build a `WebClient`. I initialize the `WebClient` in the constructor because they're expensive, and I don't want to recreate them each time I request. You might very reasonably go a step further and pull up your `WebClient` object into a `@Bean` provider method so you can inject the shared reference anywhere you need them. In this example, I need two `WebClient` instances: one pre-configured for authentication and one not. I could have easily pulled them into separate bean methods and used qualifiers to inject the right one. This approach serves to make the examples clearer and more concise.

In each of these instances, we inject the `WebClient.Builder` and then further customize it, a familiar pattern. Spring Boot defines the `WebClient.Builder`, but not the `WebClient`, because it might be that some auto-configuration wants to contribute something to the `WebClient`, such as a filter before you finally create the `WebClient`. Those auto-configurations need only inject the `WebClient.Builder` and customize that. In this way, all clients are subsequently built with that `WebClient.Builder` benefits from that configuration. Spring Cloud supports client-side load-balancing using this mechanism. You could configure an OAuth-aware client, too. It's important to customize the `WebClient.Builder` instance before anybody uses it to build a `WebClient`. Spring Boot provides the `WebClientCustomizer` interface. Register a bean of type `WebClientCustomizer`, and you'll be allowed to customize the `WebClient.Builder` reference as early as possible. Spring Boot will invoke the customizer, providing you a reference to the current `WebClient.Builder`.

The first demonstrates a single `application/json` response.

The second demonstrates a `text/event-stream` server-sent event stream and is a particularly compelling use case to me. The `RestTemplate`, the first HTTP client to be packaged in Spring, could not easily be made to support this kind of use case since it was designed to take the entire response, pass the whole thing through an `HttpMessageConverter` and through that yield an object. An HTTP request came in, and one, and *only* one, object emerged. This worked fine for most scenarios. But not for server-sent events. I think I got it working once, and it was horrific. Spring has supported server-sent events on the server-side for *years*! Spring only lacked an easy way to consume that server-sent event stream. Naturally, the intended use case for server-sent events has always been JavaScript clients. Still! The asymmetry of it all! Oh, how I've waited for this demo!

Let's take a look at these two.

We'll inject and configure two unique `WebClient` instances and two clients that use these `WebClient` instances. The first instance has its base URL specified so that we don't need to respecify it for each subsequent request.

```
package rsb.client;

import lombok.extern.log4j.Log4j2;
import org.springframework.context.annotation.Bean;
import org.springframework.context.annotation.Configuration;
import org.springframework.web.reactive.function.client.WebClient;

@Log4j2
@Configuration
public class DefaultConfiguration {

    @Bean
    DefaultClient defaultClient(WebClient.Builder builder, ClientProperties properties) {
        var root = properties.getHttp().getRootUrl();
        return new DefaultClient(builder.baseUrl(root).build()); ①
    }

}
```

① Inject the required `WebClient.Builder` to configure the `DefaultClient`

```java
package rsb.client;

import lombok.RequiredArgsConstructor;
import lombok.extern.log4j.Log4j2;
import org.springframework.web.reactive.function.client.WebClient;
import reactor.core.publisher.Flux;
import reactor.core.publisher.Mono;

import java.util.Map;

@Log4j2
@RequiredArgsConstructor
public class DefaultClient {

    private final WebClient client;

    public Mono<Greeting> getSingle(String name) {
        ①
        return client.get()//
                .uri("/greet/single/{name}", Map.of("name", name))// "Stéphane Maldini"
                .retrieve()//
                .bodyToMono(Greeting.class);
    }

    public Flux<Greeting> getMany(String name) {
        ②
        return client.get()//
                .uri("/greet/many/{name}", Map.of("name", name))// "Madhura Bhave"
                .retrieve()//
                .bodyToFlux(Greeting.class)//
                .take(10);
    }

}
```

① Consume a single (application/json) value

② Consume *multiple* (potentially infinite!) values from a server-sent event stream. The code isn't dramatically different. That's the magic trick. It's just a stream that emits more items.

Not bad, eh? The WebClient has tons of builder methods that specify things like the HTTP verb (here we used .get(), but there are others) and attributes, headers, and cookies that you want to send. You can even plugin custom filters, which - as we'll see when we review security - will be handy.

7.10.4. Teaching Your `WebClient` New Tricks

There are many useful filters available there, including one that handles HTTP BASIC authentication, one that generates an error signal if an error occurs, and limits the response's size and cancels if any more return. Spring tries to anticipate the common requirements, but you can create your own `ExchangeFilterFunction`, for your purposes, too. Let's look at a trivial example that logs the beginning of a request and the request's end.

There are three moving parts to this solution. The first is a `WebClientCustomizer` that registers an `ExchangeFilterFunction` with the builder.

```
package rsb.client.timer;

import lombok.extern.log4j.Log4j2;
import org.springframework.boot.web.reactive.function.client.WebClientCustomizer;
import org.springframework.stereotype.Component;
import org.springframework.web.reactive.function.client.WebClient;

@Log4j2
@Component
class TimingWebClientCustomizer implements WebClientCustomizer {

    @Override
    public void customize(WebClient.Builder webClientBuilder) {
        webClientBuilder.filter(new TimingExchangeFilterFunction()); ①
    }

}
```

① We merely register the `rsb.client.timer.TimingExchangeFilterFunction` as a filter here.

The `TimingExchangeFilterFunction` takes the current request, wraps it in a wrapper class (`rsb.client.timer.TimingClientResponseWrapper`), and then lets all subsequent filters in the filter chain have their crack at the current request.

```
package rsb.client.timer;

import org.springframework.web.reactive.function.client.ClientRequest;
import org.springframework.web.reactive.function.client.ClientResponse;
import org.springframework.web.reactive.function.client.ExchangeFilterFunction;
import org.springframework.web.reactive.function.client.ExchangeFunction;
import reactor.core.publisher.Mono;

class TimingExchangeFilterFunction implements ExchangeFilterFunction {

    @Override
    public Mono<ClientResponse> filter(ClientRequest request,
ExchangeFunction next) {
        return next.exchange(request)
                .map(currentResponse -> new
TimingClientResponseWrapper(currentResponse));①
    }

}
```

① Take the current response, the result of letting all subsequent filters in the filter chain have a crack at the current request, and wrap it using `TimingClientResponseWrapper`

The wrapper does the real work of intercepting the body's production and tapping into the reactive lifecycle of the resulting Reactor `Mono<T>` or `Flux<T>`.

```
package rsb.client.timer;

import lombok.extern.log4j.Log4j2;
import org.springframework.core.ParameterizedTypeReference;
import org.springframework.http.client.reactive.ClientHttpResponse;
import org.springframework.web.reactive.function.BodyExtractor;
import org.springframework.web.reactive.function.client.ClientResponse;
import org.springframework.web.reactive.function.client.support.ClientResponseWrapper;
import reactor.core.publisher.Flux;
import reactor.core.publisher.Mono;
```

```
import java.time.Instant;

@Log4j2
class TimingClientResponseWrapper extends ClientResponseWrapper {

    TimingClientResponseWrapper(ClientResponse delegate) {
        super(delegate);
    }

    private void start() {
        log.info("start @ " + Instant.now().toString());
    }

    private void stop() {
        log.info("stop @ " + Instant.now().toString());
    }

    ①
    private <T> Mono<T> log(Mono<T> c) {
        return c.doOnSubscribe(s -> start()).doFinally(s -> stop());
    }

    private <T> Flux<T> log(Flux<T> c) {
        return c.doOnSubscribe(s -> start()).doFinally(s -> stop());
    }

    ②
    @Override
    public <T> T body(BodyExtractor<T, ? super ClientHttpResponse> extractor)
{
        T body = super.body(extractor);
        if (body instanceof Flux) {
            return (T) log((Flux) body);
        }
        if (body instanceof Mono) {
            return (T) log((Mono) body);
        }
        return body;
    }

    @Override
    public <T> Mono<T> bodyToMono(Class<? extends T> elementClass) {
        return log(super.bodyToMono(elementClass));
    }

    @Override
    public <T> Mono<T> bodyToMono(ParameterizedTypeReference<T>
```

```
    elementTypeRef) {
        return log(super.bodyToMono(elementTypeRef));
    }

    @Override
    public <T> Flux<T> bodyToFlux(Class<? extends T> elementClass) {
        return log(super.bodyToFlux(elementClass));
    }

    @Override
    public <T> Flux<T> bodyToFlux(ParameterizedTypeReference<T> elementTypeRef) {
        return log(super.bodyToFlux(elementTypeRef));
    }

}
```

① The methods named log simply take a Reactor Mono or Flux and wrap them.

② The methods starting with body* intercept the current request and wraps them.

Run the client application with these in place, and you'll see the timing on the console. Easy!

7.11. Security

Security is a non-trivial concern that - even if one were so inclined - one should *not* have to hand roll. The Spring web stack, generally, integrates very well with Spring Security. Indeed, you could even say that Spring Security lives on the web. Remember, the first lines of Spring were concerned with building web applications! And so it was only natural that when Australian Ben Alex decided to create Acegi Security, a framework built on Spring to secure web applications, the most exciting new capabilities introduced supported building web applications. Acegi Security was, of course, later renamed Spring Security, and it has enjoyed a prominent role in almost every application out there. Indeed, before Spring Boot came along, Spring Security was the second most popular Spring module, after Spring Framework itself, and perhaps only because Spring Security, in turn, depended on Spring Framework. Hard to say.

To what did Spring Security owe its immense popularity? Of course, I can only speculate, but this is my sense of the world in the early 2000s when Spring rose to prominence (for the first time). The JVM ecosystem was then a bit like the JavaScript ecosystem today, with new web frameworks cropping up virtually every other day, it seemed. J2EE (as Jakarta EE was then called) introduced the absolute minimum support for application security, leaving it up to individual application servers to fill in the considerable gaps. The implication was that you had to pay your application server vendor a truckload of money to get adequate security. Of course, whatever arrangement you arrived at was going to be proprietary to that application server. Spring Security offered a consistent interface that worked in a truly portable fashion across all application servers. It *also* supported applications that were not otherwise Spring-based applications. You could use Spring Security to secure an Apache Struts application or any other Servlet-based application. Apache Tomcat was quickly becoming the most ubiquitous web server in the JVM ecosystem (as it remains today, in 2020).

There was a lot of promise in this formula: Write applications using your web framework of choice. Use Spring to handle the transactional service component model. Perhaps bring in Hibernate to manage persistence. Use Spring Security to secure the whole thing. Who needed EJBs? Since then, Spring Security has become the sort of de-facto standard. There are some alternatives in the JVM ecosystem that are interesting. Still, while we can argue about the subtle improvements here or there, there's nothing that's better in every way and - more importantly - nothing that comes close to providing the breadth of integrations as Spring Security does.

"Alright, Josh. We get it! Spring Security's going to be big!" I hear you exclaim, exasperated. And that, my friends, is precisely the point. It's *huuuge*. It's got integrations for *everything*: OAuth, Active Directory, LDAP, OIDC, SAML, etc.

This richness of integrations is lovely if you're building applications that work compatibly with all those integrations. Reactive programming changes things. Remember: we've already established that some things don't lend themselves to a reactive application. Spring Security has traditionally used Java `ThreadLocal<T>` instances to stash the current authenticated `java.security.Principal` in a way that all downstream component code would be able to find it. That won't work anymore! Gotta use the Reactor `Context`. And of course, we have the question of cryptography, which is innately CPU-bound work. You can't do that anymore! Or at least, we can't do that on a Reactor `Scheduler`'s non-blocking threads.

Spring Security 5 introduces new support for propagating the authenticated `java.security.Principal` with the Reactor `Context`, where necessary. And it adds a `ReactiveAuthenticationManager`, which moves the cryptography-heavy act of authentication to a blocking thread pool for us. So, the good news is that, from an API perspective, things work as well as they can. But they don't *actually* work. That is, there's no magic bullet here. We can't just rub reactive on our security and have it become exponentially more scalable. When you build reactive applications, you need to care for when and where you introduce blocking cryptography. This has always been true - BCrypt can add entire seconds to the hot path of a request if you're not paying attention! At least now, in Reactor-based APIs, we have the tools and conventions to support doing the right thing.

We can and should use this paradigm shift to reevaluate how we do security. Do we *need* to do painfully slow cryptography on every request in our services' threadpool? Or could we switch to OAuth and validate the token per request, delegating to a standalone authorization service that we could both more easily scale horizontally? It's rare in life to get a better scalability result *and* to get a better security posture. Things like OAuth in a reactive application give us this, and I encourage you to explore OAuth and Spring Security 5.0's OAuth support.

In this example, however, we're going to keep things as simple as possible for a demonstration. You need to understand that Spring Security addresses two orthogonal concerns: authentication (who is making a given request) and authorization (what permissions, or rights, or authorities, or entitlements does a given client have to in a system).

So, we'll use Spring Security to address both of these concerns for our trivial HTTP API. To get started, we'll need to add the Spring Security dependency to our build.

- `org.springframework.boot` : `spring-boot-starter-security`

To keep things simpler, I've put both the client and the service implementation into the same Maven module in our code. I'll load configuration under a property file (`application-service.properties`) to configure a specific port for the service and override the default set port (0, which tells Spring Boot to find any random, unused port) in `application.properties`.

First, let's look at the `main` class for our service.

```
package rsb.security.service;

import org.springframework.boot.SpringApplication;
import org.springframework.boot.autoconfigure.SpringBootApplication;

@SpringBootApplication
public class ServiceApplication {

    public static void main(String args[]) {
        System.setProperty("spring.profiles.active", "service");  ①
        SpringApplication.run(ServiceApplication.class, args);
    }

}
```

① This profile results in `application-service.properties` loading and the application will run on a fixed port, 8080.

Now, let's introduce the configuration for Spring Security.

Chapter 7. HTTP

```
package rsb.security.service;

import org.springframework.context.annotation.Bean;
import org.springframework.context.annotation.Configuration;
import org.springframework.security.config.Customizer;
import org.springframework.security.config.web.server.ServerHttpSecurity;
import org.springframework.security.core.userdetails.MapReactiveUserDetailsService;
import org.springframework.security.core.userdetails.User;
import org.springframework.security.core.userdetails.UserDetails;
import org.springframework.security.web.server.SecurityWebFilterChain;

@Configuration
class SecurityConfiguration {

    ①
    @Bean
    MapReactiveUserDetailsService authentication() {
        UserDetails jlong = User.withDefaultPasswordEncoder().username("jlong")
                .password("pw").roles("USER").build();
        UserDetails rwinch = User.withDefaultPasswordEncoder().username("rwinch")
                .password("pw").roles("USER", "ADMIN").build();
        return new MapReactiveUserDetailsService(jlong, rwinch);
    }

    ②
    @Bean
    SecurityWebFilterChain authorization(ServerHttpSecurity http) {
        return http//
                .httpBasic(Customizer.withDefaults())③
                .authorizeExchange(ae -> ae④
                        .pathMatchers("/greetings").authenticated()⑤
                        .anyExchange().permitAll()⑥
                )//
                .csrf(ServerHttpSecurity.CsrfSpec::disable)//
                .build();
    }

}
```

① This first bean establishes a hardcoded (*gasp!*) in-memory repository of users and passwords. Do *not* do this in a production application! It's the simplest thing that could work. If you understand how everything we've seen figures into a Spring Security application, you understand what you're looking for when you substitute other more mature authentication (a.k.a. identity providers).

② This bean installs a filter that will ensure that only the authorized have access to the /greetings endpoint. This bean provides authorization for our application.

③ In this application, we'll use straight HTTP BASIC, a username and password-based scheme.

④ the authorizeExchange configuration method tells Spring Security how to lockdown various resources - endpoints - in the application.

⑤ We want the /greetings endpoint, explicitly, to reject unauthenticated requests. This is a particular and very specific configuration.

⑥ This fallthrough rule says that every other endpoint is accessible.

Let's revisit the familiar GreetingsController, access to which we will restrict and use the current authenticated user principal information to inform what name is shown in the response's message.

```
package rsb.security.service;

import org.springframework.security.core.annotation.AuthenticationPrincipal;
import org.springframework.security.core.userdetails.UserDetails;
import org.springframework.web.bind.annotation.GetMapping;
import org.springframework.web.bind.annotation.RestController;
import reactor.core.publisher.Mono;

import java.time.Instant;
import java.util.Map;

@RestController
class GreetingController {

    @GetMapping("/greetings")
    Mono<Map<String, String>> greet(@AuthenticationPrincipal Mono<UserDetails> user) { ①
        return user//
                .map(UserDetails::getUsername)//
                .map(name -> Map.of("greetings",
                        "Hello " + name + " @ " + Instant.now() + "!"));
    }

}
```

① The `@AuthenticationPrincipal` annotation tells Spring to inject the current authenticated `Principal` as a parameter in the web controller handler method. You could alternatively call `principal()` when you the functional reactive style. This endpoint will respond with the authenticated user's name in the greetings.

Let's look at the client.

```
package rsb.security.client;

import lombok.extern.log4j.Log4j2;
import org.springframework.boot.SpringApplication;
import org.springframework.boot.autoconfigure.SpringBootApplication;
import org.springframework.boot.context.event.ApplicationReadyEvent;
import org.springframework.context.ApplicationListener;
import org.springframework.context.annotation.Bean;
import org.springframework.core.ParameterizedTypeReference;
import
```

```java
org.springframework.web.reactive.function.client.ExchangeFilterFunctions;
import org.springframework.web.reactive.function.client.WebClient;

import java.util.Map;

@Log4j2
@SpringBootApplication
public class ClientApplication {

    public static void main(String args[]) {
        SpringApplication.run(ClientApplication.class, args);
    }

    ①
    @Bean
    WebClient webClient(WebClient.Builder builder) {
        var username = "jlong";
        var password = "pw";
        var basicAuthentication = ExchangeFilterFunctions.basicAuthentication(username,
                password);
        return builder//
                .filter(basicAuthentication)②
                .build();//
    }

    ②
    @Bean
    ApplicationListener<ApplicationReadyEvent> client(WebClient secureHttpClient) {
        return event -> secureHttpClient//
                .get()//
                .uri("http://localhost:8080/greetings")//
                .retrieve()//
                .bodyToMono(new ParameterizedTypeReference<Map<String, String>>() {
                })③
                .subscribe(map -> log.info("greeting: " + map.get("greetings")));

    }

}
```

① Here we build the reactive `WebClient` and configure a filter...

② ...to handle HTTP BASIC authentication

③ The data that we expect back is JSON, and while we could've used the familiar `GreetingResponse`, I figured we could just as easily have converted it to a `Map<String, String>` from which we could dereference the one key, `greeting`. (Just trying to keep you on your toes!)

That was easy! Run the service, then run the client, and you'll see a greeting for `jlong`, the user's name, on the console. We've only just begun to scratch the surface of Spring Security as it applies to HTTP-based services. There's a whole other book to be written here! Or, at the very least, a lot to say when we look at RSocket and Spring Security later.

7.12. Next Steps

This chapter looks at how to build reactive HTTP applications with REST endpoints, controllers, and views. We looked at the new functional-reactive endpoint style. We've looked at WebSockets to build lively, interactive HTTP clients. We learned how to use the `WebClient`, a new non-blocking HTTP client. We learned how to use the net-new reactive component-model, Spring Webflux, on a Servlet container. This is just the beginning. HTTP forms the foundational layer for modern microservice applications. What you've learned here will serve you when we investigate edge services, testing, and more.

Reactive Spring

Chapter 8. Testing

I love testing, and so should you.

8.1. How I Stopped Worrying and Learned to Love Testing

It took me a while to get into TDD. Pivotal Labs is a tip-of-the-spear consulting business and practices TDD. Pivotal Labs has been around for *decades*. It was a consulting business that has become associated with *agile*; it's founder Rob Mee is legendary in the big-A and little-a "agile" communities as one of the principal drivers of the methodology earliest days. Pivotal Labs, through VMware, doesn't do a lot of advertising, and we sometimes turn some of the requests we get down. The reason is simple: we don't need the business. People come to us, and if we're going to take on new work, it must be that the work we do is transformative to an organization. We have no interest in helping an organization build, let's say, a conference room scheduling system, if such an application won't help the business. We have offices *everywhere* - New York, Tokyo, San Francisco, London, Singapore, Berlin, Boston, Atlanta, Toronto, and a zillion other locations [https://pivotal.io/locations]. At any given time, our Pivotal Labs offices all around the world are almost always fully booked.

We're not staff augmentation. People engage Pivotal Labs not just to help them write some software, but to teach them *how* to write software. People that work with us arrive by 9 am if they want to take their free breakfast with us. By 9:07 am, our office-wide morning standup starts. It's usually no more than five minutes. Then each team, working on different customer projects, breaks out into their standups. These are *actual* standups - *very* quick! By 9:15 am or 9:20 am, we're off to the races. In Pivotal Labs, people are clustered into teams supporting different projects. We have representation from the customers onsite. We have engineering from the projects onsite.

Each day people take work from the backlog and start on it, and they work in pairs. Typically, it's one "Pivot," as we affectionately call ourselves, and one member from a client paired together. The pairings may change daily. Perhaps today, I'd like to work with Jacques to learn the Go programming language's peculiarities. Tomorrow I'd like to work with Natalie to learn more about Android, and the day after, I'd work with Alex to learn more about Concourse. We all bring unique skills to a given effort, and through this constant pairing, we get a chance to share those skills. To absorb and diffuse them. The client, of course, best understands the business domain, too. So we often pair one Pivot and one member of the client team. It helps spread skills around; it means that no single member of the team is irreplaceable. This is an important dynamic. We want to promote sustainable development. We want everyone to have mastery and ownership of the code.

Pivots, in this case, a collective noun that refers to everyone working in a Pivotal Labs location, typically do "red-green refactoring" where one of the pairs writes the test that fails (the test is *red*) and then the other pair writes the code that makes the failing test pass. We keep doing this until the work is done! Or until lunch, whichever comes first. Lunch is at a fixed hour across the entire office. When you pair program, the last thing you want is people wandering off for lunch dates that take longer than usual. So, you work until lunch, take your lunch, and then are back in your chairs pair-programming until the work is done, or the end of the day, whichever comes first. The day ends at 18:00 / 6 pm. Not 6:01 pm. Not 5:59 pm. 6:00pm. After this point, the office is a *ghost* town. The goal here is to promote sustainable development.

Pivotal Labs doesn't issue company laptops. People come to work and login to a machine. Any machine! We require that people check their opinions at the door. We don't give a *damn* about your awful Active Directory configurations and your Eclipse key-bindings and your so-locked-down-as-to-be-useless corporate Windows installations. At Pivotal Labs, *everyone* uses the same machine with the same configuration: macOS, IntelliJ IDEA, etc. We have custom tools for things like `git` so we can sign commits with the names of both pairs on the same machine. Once the day's done, we expect people to go home and not work on this until the next day. Again, *sustainable development*!

When we first introduced Spring Boot, I spent a lot of time going to different Pivotal Labs offices trying to help them level up on Spring Boot and, sure, we got there together, but what surprised me was how much *I* learned. I walked away from the experience feeling *really* productive! I loved it. I learned (well, at least, I started to learn) how the masters wrote software using a process that supported people who weren't masters. The process was so useful because it provided many checks for quality. It provided a framework for building quality into the system by optimizing opportunities to ensure that quality.

Pivotal Labs developers were, at the time of the Pivotal formation, not necessarily using Spring. They were avid Ruby-on-Rails developers. They never had a mandate to use Spring because the Spring R & D group lived within the same corporate structure as Pivotal Labs. No. If Spring Boot were to succeed, it would be because it was useful to them. It would be because they genuinely felt they could recommend it with confidence to our clients.

I confess that I had some bias in the whole thing. Pivotal Labs people are typically young and carefree. They're happy! These were *not* the jaded and chiseled enterprise developers with which I was familiar. No sirree! They couldn't possibly be up to the task of managing "real" enterprise software! What did *they* know about WebSphere? What did *they* know about Axway Integrator? What did *they* know about SOAP?

Turns out: *nothing*! And thank goodness for that! Their job was, and always has been, to deliver good software that supports the business' needs, *not* to implement garbage tools agreed upon by some CIO over golf with a vendor. They delivered quality by embracing a process that has constant checks for quality. Suppose you do that enough, then its easy enough to get mastery-level code from amateurs fresh out of college, and quickly, too. This last fact was fascinating to me. I misunderstood things. I had incorrectly assumed that we enterprise types on the Spring team would have to level up the Pivotal Labs folks, but they ended up teaching us a ton! It turns out that if you take an amateur developer (nobody at Pivotal Labs is an amateur, of course) and drop them into the forest armed with only Spring Boot and a process supported and guided by rapid feedback and testing, they do just fine! Indeed, I think I'd prefer their Spring Boot-based code over that of a good deal of the "enterprise architects" with whom I've worked in my life!

One thing that fell out of this ongoing discussion was that, compared to the Ruby on Rails community, at least, the Java community's tools for testing weren't nearly so sophisticated. Yah. It hurts just admitting that! I mean, we had frickin' JUnit before everybody else! Everybody else's X-Unit was a JUnit-alike! How had we fallen so behind? I think a big part of it was that we, in the Java community, never really had a serious effort to embrace TDD. We never really had a serious effort to make programming in Java accessible for everyone. Not like the Rails community did, certainly. Java being complicated was a feature, not a bug. Spring Boot has changed things here. Spring Boot has given people an opinionated, full-stack approach to building software that scaled nicely, and it embraced testing. Indeed, every single project generated from the Spring Initializr [http://start.spring.io] has included in its dependencies supporting testing. There is no *opt-out*. It *embraces* test-driven development! So, what is test-driven development?

8.2. Test-Driven Development

Of course, we walk the walk: we practice continuous integration (CI) and continuous delivery (CD). We do test-driven development. We use cloud computing. All these things translate into better results, faster, so it's hard to write a chapter like this one, focused on testing, seemingly excluding all these other beautiful practices. We're going to focus on testing, and we're even going to try to do test-driven development (TDD).

TDD is, simply, the act of writing tests first. Before you've written a line of production code, you write tests that test the production code, which is hard to do if you've not written the production code because there are no types against which to compile. So you end up having to write the minimum to get the compiler happy, then going back to flesh out the test. But you don't want to write too much of the test. You're just trying to prove out one thing in the production code, after all. So, you end up in this tight loop that might seem at first very frustrating.

With a statically typed language like Java, you end up in continuous loop writing tests, then write the code to make the test compile and then pass and then go back to test code. At first, this seems to constrain. You'll like it once you get the hang of it. TDD has some profound benefits. A team doing

TDD is at most a few cmd/ctrl + Z's away from green, production-worthy code. A team doing TDD gets the tests done at the same time as the feature is implemented. The endorphin hit of successfully implementing a feature arrives simultaneously when the team members otherwise get the code tested. It no longer feels like a *chore*, like documentation, which must be cared for but feels like a lesser priority. The agile manifesto says, "value working code *over* comprehensive documentation." With TDD, you have working code *and* proof that the code works at the same time. If you use something like JavaDocs and TDD, you can get pretty good documentation concurrently as you deliver the functional tests! For more on Spring REST Docs, you might check out O'Reilly's *Cloud Native Java*.

So, clearly, I'm a big fan of TDD, but it can be hard to demonstrate its execution in a book! So, here's what I'm going to do. We'll introduce the test code first, as the need arises, and then look at the production code that satisfies the tests. I (mostly) won't introduce fragments of tests. It's *really* tedious to do TDD in a book!

8.3. Inside-Out or Outside-In

It depends, I suppose, on the team and their style and the individual's style. You have to decide whether you want to write tests for the inner-most components first and then work your way out to the API-layer and UI - testing as you go, or whether you want to do things in reverse, starting with the UI and then working your way inwards. The inside-out approach has sometimes been called "Chicago-style."

Here are, as best as I can understand, the differences in approach. Imagine you're building a complex system. In an inside-out approach, you'd start with the individual entities and start fleshing out their behaviors at higher layers. Eventually, at higher layers, you'd start assembling individual pieces. Now, some might say that this assembly, this *integration*, is where the risk is, and that definition should be cared for first before you get into the small and perhaps even meaningless entities that support the integration. I'd argue that it is more straightforward to parallelize work if you start from the inside-out; people can pick a part of the application they'd like to work on, and workstreams converge at the integration tier.

I like to go inside-out: I'll start fleshing out the business entity and work my way towards the interface. If you're just building an API (an HTTP API or an RPC API), that API is the "interface." In this way, I'm deferring potentially risky integrations until a little later and hopefully - in a microservices world - that integration is still relatively small and controlled by folks on the same team. That is, "integration" isn't as scary if it's all being done by the same person or set of folks on a small enough team.

Microservices are all about achieving autonomy and reducing the cost of coordination, but that doesn't mean you eliminate coordination! Just reduce it. Your mileage may vary, and I'm here to tell you that I don't have a very strong opinion about it one way or another; I just want to provide background about how I'm going to approach this chapter: inside-out.

We're going to build two things: an API producer and an API consumer.

8.4. The `Customer` Object is Always Right (Right?)

We're going to need to instantiate and manage objects of type `Customer` to map to the domain model. Let's first ensure that we have a valid object that can successfully hold the data we expect to be there. We're not interested in whether this object is a valid entity that maps to data in a database. We *just* want to assert some basic things about the object's state and see how Spring supports us here.

Making some basic assertions about a `Customer` *object*

```
package rsb.testing.producer;

import org.assertj.core.api.Assertions;
import org.hamcrest.Matchers;
import org.junit.Assert;
import org.junit.Test;

public class CustomerTest {

    @Test
    public void create() {
        Customer customer = new Customer("123", "foo");  ①
        Assert.assertEquals(customer.getId(), "123");  ②
        Assert.assertThat(customer.getId(), Matchers.is("123"));  ③
        Assertions.assertThat(customer.getName()).
isEqualToIgnoringWhitespace("foo");  ④
    }

}
```

① all we're doing is new-ing up a new record of type `Customer`, assigning it a UUID for the `id` and a value for the `name`

② here we use plain ol' JUnit 4's `Assert` methods to confirm that the value we stashed in the `id` property, 123, is the value we get back when accessing it via a property accessor. Put another way: can we put data in and get it back out again in one piece? We're using JUnit 4, but it doesn't matter. The `Assert` class has existed in JUnit for *decades*.

③ If you end up doing more complicated tests, everything ends up boiling down into `Assert.assertTrue( boolean )` calls where the test's recipe is encoded somewhere reusable - a method returning a `boolean`, perhaps? This can get tedious after a while because the *why* of the test - *why* this test failed - gets lost to time. We have to remember to name whatever method we're using for the test in a meaningful way and then write a relevant message for the `assertTrue(String, boolean)` overload. All we have to show for things is the `boolean`. We can do better. JUnit's `assertThat` variant supports a `Matcher` object that couples the error reporting condition. Hamcrest, a third-party library that ships with Spring Boot's default testing support, provides several useful `Matchers`

for us. Here, we assert things about the equality of two operands.
④ Finally, there is AssertJ. AssertJ is yet another third-party library supporting testing that ships with Spring Boot. It provides convenient type-safe tests that flow fluidly from the types given. Here, it was kind enough to offer us an `isEqualToIgnoringWhitespace(String)` method for the argument to `Assertions.assertThat(String)`.

Not bad? This test ought to be easy enough to satisfy! Let's see the production code for such a thing.

A plain ol' `Customer` *object with some Lombok annotations*

```
package rsb.testing.producer;

import lombok.AllArgsConstructor;
import lombok.Data;
import lombok.NoArgsConstructor;
import org.springframework.data.annotation.Id;
import org.springframework.data.mongodb.core.mapping.Document;

①
@Data
@AllArgsConstructor
@NoArgsConstructor
class Customer {

    ②
    private String id;

    private String name;

}
```

① These annotations come from Lombok, a compile-time annotation processor that will synthesize our getters, setters, constructors, and more for us. This just saves us a ton of code related to storing and retrieving data in this object. You'll need a plugin for IntelliJ or Eclipse, though. Sorry.

② I *could* annotate this class with Spring Data MongoDB's `@Document` annotation and annotate this field with Spring Data Commons' `@Id` annotation, but Spring Data's pretty darned smart! It'll figure it out for us.

8.5. A Repository of (Untested) Knowledge

I was of two minds about this section. Should we look at what it is to test just the fact of Spring Data MongoDB's ability to persist this entity? We're not taking advantage of the lifecycle that Spring Data MongoDB, the object mapper, gives us. We're not doing anything, really, besides constructing an object. It might've been an exciting excuse to introduce the `ReactiveMongoTemplate`, but the steps we're going to see in this next section apply equally to anything we'd do with the `ReactiveMongoTemplate`. Besides - we've already looked at it (and more besides) in our discussion of reactive data in another chapter. Let's instead turn to test reactive repositories.

"Wait a minute!" I hear you exclaim, "why would I test a Spring Data repository? I thought the whole point was that they *just worked*?" And you'd be right! I wouldn't worry too much about testing a repository itself. The standard CRUD-supporting methods implied in that repository, like `findById` and `save`, work just fine and have been tested *millions* of times. They work as advertised. Instead, we will confine our tests to any custom queries we might define in our repository. It's trivial to express a custom query by convention - just the name the method declared on a repository interface according to the documented conventions - or explicitly with a `@Query` annotation on the declared finder-methods. These queries, which rely on the object's structure, may occasionally fall out of sync with the object's structure and so you must test these manually.

8.5.1. The Spring Test Framework

The goal here is to test that the business logic concerned with persisting documents to the MongoDB database works as we hope and have configured. So, besides just instantiating an instance of the object, `Customer`, we'll also need to instantiate all the Spring Data MongoDB machinery, at a minimum.

Sounds like a buzz kill. I don't want to spend my day trying to recreate the recipe to set up Spring Data MongoDB and correctly wire things up! Spring

Boot already knows how to do that. We could manually new-up a Spring `ApplicationContext` in our tests, but that would be inelegant. Besides, I'd love to inject relevant dependencies into my test class, instead of asking for it by type from the resulting `ApplicationContext`.

JUnit has an integration mechanism, the `@RunWith` annotation, that tells it to defer to a particular class to manage the test class's lifecycle. In this way, Spring can do everything except instantiate our unit test itself and execute the actual test methods. The result is a streamlined integration that lets us think about the code we're trying to test and much less about Spring itself. If we only use the `@RunWith(SpringRunner.class)` and `@SpringBootTest` annotations on a test class in the same package as our production Spring Boot application, then the entire Spring application will automatically be started when the test is run and any field-dependencies declared with `@Autowired` in the class satisfied.

> Yeah. I know. *Bleargh*! Field injection? I don't love it either. Now's a good time to mention that this is a limitation of JUnit 4, which's been lifted in JUnit 5, led by Sam Brannen. The very same Sam Brannen that leads the Spring Test Framework integration. Now's *also* an excellent time to mention that we're using JUnit 4 because it's the default in Spring Boot, for the moment, but that JUnit 5 works perfectly with Spring Boot and its use is well-documented.

8.5.2. Test Slices

A Spring Data repository typically lives in a Spring Boot application, which in turn might lives alongside a web server, a web framework, the Spring Boot Actuator, and more. The last thing we want is to launch all those pieces just to test the persistence logic and our Spring Data MongoDB code.

Spring Boot provides *test slices* that carve up a Spring Boot application context into logical layers. There are many *slices* in Spring Boot, but they mostly have the same basic structure: they are delivered as annotations to add to your test context code. They then turn around and disable most (if not all) of Spring Boot's autoconfiguration and then selectively re-introduce the autoconfiguration related to the logical layer you're testing. They sometimes define component filters that tell Spring Boot, which beans to introduce in this new application context. So, if you were to test Spring Data MongoDB code, such a filter would only include components related to Spring Data MongoDB and ignore, for example, any Servlet or Spring WebFlux code. Test slices make it easy for us to isolate the things under test from the invariants.

8.5.3. Flapdoodle

It's not always true that there exists a reliable, embedded database option that we can use instead of requiring a deployed database. If it is true, then you should take advantage of that option. We can use Flapdoodle, a third-party project with which Spring Boot already integrates. All you need to do is add it to the classpath, and Spring's test support will wire everything up. Add the following dependency to your application's pom.xml:

- de.flapdoodle.embed : de.flapdoodle.embed.mongo.

Make sure that you give it a test scope. This way, even if you don't have MongoDB installed, your test code reliant upon MongoDB will work.

Let's look at an example of a simple test that writes some data to the database and then pulls it back out.

Data in, data out...

```
package rsb.testing.producer;

import org.junit.Test;
import org.junit.runner.RunWith;
import org.reactivestreams.Publisher;
import org.springframework.beans.factory.annotation.Autowired;
import org.springframework.boot.test.autoconfigure.data.mongo.DataMongoTest;
import org.springframework.test.context.junit4.SpringRunner;
import reactor.core.publisher.Flux;
import reactor.test.StepVerifier;

import java.util.function.Predicate;
```

```
@RunWith(SpringRunner.class) ①
@DataMongoTest ②
public class CustomerRepositoryTest {

    ③
    @Autowired
    private CustomerRepository customerRepository;

    ④
    @Test
    public void findByName() {
        String commonName = "Jane";
        Customer one = new Customer("1", commonName);
        Customer two = new Customer("2", "John");
        Customer three = new Customer("3", commonName);

        Publisher<Customer> setup = this.customerRepository //
                .deleteAll() //
                .thenMany(this.customerRepository.saveAll(Flux.just(one, two, three))) //
                .thenMany(this.customerRepository.findByName(commonName));

        Predicate<Customer> customerPredicate = customer -> ⑤
        commonName.equalsIgnoreCase(customer.getName());

        StepVerifier ⑥
                .create(setup) //
                .expectNextMatches(customerPredicate) //
                .expectNextMatches(customerPredicate) //
                .verifyComplete();

    }

}
```

① the Spring Test Framework integration (you'll use this on every class)

② the `@DataMongoTest` is the relevant test-slice for working with Spring Data and MongoDB in particular.

③ we can autowire Spring beans; here we inject the `CustomerRepository` (whose implementation we'll look at momentarily)

④ a standard test method. Now, consider that we're working with reactive data pipelines in which the setup logic for our test happens asynchronously. The tear-down logic might also be asynchronous. Thus,

I've found that while I could factor out the logic itself into a separate method, I'd want to plug in the resulting `Publisher<T>` into the code under test, as I do in this test. For this reason, I don't have a lot of `@Before`- or `@After`-annotated methods in my reactive test code.

⑤ This is a regular Java 8 `Predicate<T>` that we will use with the centerpiece for all reactive testing, the `StepVerifier`.

⑥ the `StepVerifier` expects some definition of a `Publisher` to watch and then lets us assert certain things about what we expect the `Publisher` might emit. In this test, we assert that we expect that the `Publisher<Customer>` will emit two records, both of which have a name that matches `commonName`. The `StepVerifier` will drain the `Publisher` once we call `verifyComplete`.

This test class's basic arrangement should be familiar: we establish some pre-requisites and ensure that they are met. Then, we do the thing about which we are uncertain and trying to test. Then, confirm that the thing we did worked. We *didn't* have to configure all of the Spring Data MongoDB machinery, though. We didn't have to figure out from the Spring `ApplicationContext` those things that changed. We didn't have to figure out how to wait for the reactive publisher to emit items of interest and then assert them.

This test confirmed that our repository, `CustomerRepository`, and a custom finder method `findByName(String name)`, worked as expected. Here's the repository's implementation.

```
package rsb.testing.producer;

import org.springframework.data.mongodb.repository.ReactiveMongoRepository;
import reactor.core.publisher.Flux;

interface CustomerRepository extends ReactiveMongoRepository<Customer, String> {

    ①
    Flux<Customer> findByName(String name);

}
```

① We could've used a custom BSON query here, using the `@Query` annotation, if we'd liked. Either way, we benefit from having a valid test.

8.6. On The Web, No One Knows You're a Reactive Stream

But we *do* need to be able to test it, anyway! We've got a working data access layer. We've confirmed that we can roundtrip data to MongoDB, and so now we're confronted with an existential question, something with which I'm sure you all wrestled in university. If I (reactively) write data to the database but don't have an API by which to access it, did we, in point of fact, actually write it? The answer is one best decided by philosophers. I'm going to take the tact that the we need to build an API that supports successfully (with HTTP status code 200/OK) retrieving the data as `application/json` in response to an HTTP GET. That's what I'm expecting, anyway! Let's confirm as much with the reactive `WebTestClient` support.

In this test, we're interested in proving that the web tier works as designed. We're interested in confirming that the payload coming back from the Spring WebFlux web runtime looks and feels like what we're expecting. We're *not* interested in proving that MongoDB works. We already did that! In this test, we'll use the `@WebFluxTest` test-slice to isolate the web tier from everything else. We've established the Spring test slices can selectively include Spring beans for use in an application, allowing the test to load only the machinery related to the thing we care about. The `@WebFluxTest` slice won't include anything related to persistence. This is a good thing and a bad thing. It means that our code is focused, but it also means that our functional reactive handler, which depends on the `CustomerRepository`, is doomed to fail unless we can give it a valid repository reference.

What's needed here is a *mock*; we want to swap out part of the object graph with something empty. It's there to stand in for a real `CustomerRepository`. That's halfway right. Our repository doesn't just need to return `null` and `0` and `false`. It's not just an empty husk of an object. It needs to return a reactive `Publisher<Customer>` when asked. So, we need a *stub* - an object that's been pre-programmed to return results of a specific shape to accommodate our test. We're going to use @MockBean to achieve this. Ultimately, @MockBean mocks out references with Mockito [https://site.mockito.org/] mocks and allows us to pre-program their responses as a stub. Mockito is another excellent third-party library that already ships on the test classpath of a Spring Boot application.

Test time:

A test for the customer HTTP GET endpoint

```
package rsb.testing.producer;

import org.junit.Test;
import org.junit.runner.RunWith;
import org.mockito.Mockito;
import org.springframework.beans.factory.annotation.Autowired;
import org.springframework.boot.test.autoconfigure.web.reactive.WebFluxTest;
import org.springframework.boot.test.mock.mockito.MockBean;
import org.springframework.context.annotation.Import;
import org.springframework.http.MediaType;
import org.springframework.test.context.junit4.SpringRunner;
import org.springframework.test.web.reactive.server.WebTestClient;
import reactor.core.publisher.Flux;

@WebFluxTest ①
@Import(CustomerWebConfiguration.class) ②
@RunWith(SpringRunner.class)
public class CustomerWebTest {

    @Autowired
    private WebTestClient client; ③

    @MockBean ④
    private CustomerRepository repository;

    @Test
    public void getAll() {

        ⑤
        Mockito.when(this.repository.findAll())
                .thenReturn(Flux.just(new Customer("1", "A"), new Customer("2", "B")));

        ⑥
        this.client.get() //
```

```
                .uri("/customers") //
                .accept(MediaType.APPLICATION_JSON).exchange() //
                .expectStatus().isOk().expectHeader()
                .contentType(MediaType.APPLICATION_JSON) //
                .expectBody() //
                .jsonPath("$.[0].id").isEqualTo("1") //
                .jsonPath("$.[0].name").isEqualTo("A") //
                .jsonPath("$.[1].id").isEqualTo("2")//
                .jsonPath("$.[1].name").isEqualTo("B") //
        ;
    }
}
```

① The `@WebFluxTest` slice lets you isolate the web tier machinery from everything else in the Spring application context

② The `CustomerWebConfiguration` declares the `RouterFunction<ServerResponse>` instance.

③ The Spring Test Framework defines the reactive `WebTestClient`, which is sort of the reactive analog to the `MockMvc` mock client from the Servlet-centric Spring MVC world

④ `@MockBean` tells Spring to either replace any bean in the bean registry with a Mockito mock bean of the same type as the annotated field *or* to add a Mockito mock bean to the bean registry if no such bean exists.

⑤ Here, we turn our mock object into a stub by pre-programming the `CustomerRepository#findAll` call. Now, when the code under test injects the `CustomerRepository` and calls the `findAll` method, it'll always be given the `Publisher<Customer>` defined here with the static, known *apriori* results. We could've as quickly put this line in a method annotated with `@Before`.

⑥ This is where the rubber meets the road: the test confirms that there's an HTTP `GET`-accessible endpoint that produces `application/json` and that responds with HTTP status `200`. We also poke at the returned payload a little using JSON Path expressions to confirm two entries in the resulting JSON whose values line up with the values we pre-programmed the stub to return.

Our test is a fair bit more complicated than the implementation itself! Let's look at it. All of it is defined in the `CustomerWebConfiguration`.

A test for the customer HTTP GET endpoint

```java
package rsb.testing.producer;

import org.springframework.context.annotation.Bean;
import org.springframework.context.annotation.Configuration;
import org.springframework.web.reactive.function.server.RouterFunction;
import org.springframework.web.reactive.function.server.ServerResponse;

import static
org.springframework.web.reactive.function.server.RequestPredicates.GET;
import static
org.springframework.web.reactive.function.server.RouterFunctions.route;
import static
org.springframework.web.reactive.function.server.ServerResponse.ok;

@Configuration
class CustomerWebConfiguration {

    @Bean  ①
    RouterFunction<ServerResponse> routes(CustomerRepository customerRepository) {
        return route(GET("/customers"),  ②
                request -> ok().body(customerRepository.findAll(), Customer.class));
    }

}
```

① You've seen this before: it's a bean that defines functional reative HTTP routes. Just one, in this case.

② The HTTP route listens to HTTP `GET` requests for `/customers` and returns all the `Customer` records in the MongoDB `CustomerRepository`. When this runs in the test code, our injected `CustomerRepository` reference will be a Mockito mock that's been pre-programmed to return fixed data.

The `@WebFluxTest` code autoconfigures the `WebTestClient`, Spring WebFlux itself, caching support, and includes only WebFlux-tier Spring beans like `@Controller`, `@ControllerAdvice`, `@JsonComponent`, `Converter`/`GenericConverter`, and `WebFluxConfigurer` beans. We must use things like `@Import` and `@MockBean` to bring in collaborating objects for the code under test.

It might very well be that you *want* all of the Spring application context for your tests. Maybe you're trying to do more of an integration test. In this case, you should prefer the generic `@SpringBootTest` and `@AutoconfigureWebTestClient`.

Pretty straightforward, eh? Run all the tests so far, and I think you'll agree - things are looking up! We've managed to test the data access tier and the web tier. Our tests run quickly. What else could we ask for? I think we're ready to build a client!

8.7. The `Customer` is Always Right!

A client is a set of distributable types that let another application talk to our API. You might agree as an organization to build and maintain one "blessed" client library, or you might let each team build their own. Either way, the result is the same. There's code designed to support working with an API that must be maintained separate and apart from the API. It is here that we risk *drift* - the client code becoming inconsistent with the service code.

It's an age-old problem: how do we test client code to confirm that it works reliably against the service API?

We face tension. We want to ensure that the client works with the service, but we also need to test the client without running the full system to ensure compliance. We want speed in using our client, but we *also* want consistency. We want the guarantee that our client will work with the API that it targets.

I've always thought it incredibly rude to welcome someone new to a new job with the words, "now please deploy this massively distributed system to test your API." It feels offensive in other languages, not just English, too! Such a declaration tells me that the velocity of a contributor is not valued. It tells me that no care has gone into defining the seams of the components in the system.

Imagine it. You move to microservices, ostensibly to gain velocity and autonomy, and the first thing you are told to do is to reproduce the entire working system on your local machine. In any kind of non-trivial system, this could mean dozens or hundreds of services and their databases, message queues, caches, and more. This isn't a sustainable ask for anybody, least of all someone working on something utterly unrelated, like an edge service supporting an iPhone application.

Let's take a few whacks at this problem. We're going to do this work in a new module, `consumer`. The new project will have the following dependencies on the classpath.

- `org.springframework.boot` : `spring-boot-starter-webflux`
- `org.projectlombok` : `lombok` with optional set to `true`
- `org.springframework.boot` : `spring-boot-starter-test` with scope test
- `io.projectreactor` : `reactor-test` with scope test
- `org.springframework.cloud` : `spring-cloud-starter-contract-stub-runner` with scope test

If you use the Spring Initializr to generate the project, you'll automatically be given a `pom.xml` with the Spring Cloud bill-of-materials (BOM) dependency. If not, make sure that you add it.

At this point, we should agree that deploying the whole system isn't a solution. We could use Wiremock to mock out the system. Wiremock is a third-party API that's well supported by Spring Cloud Contract. It's easy to use Wiremock to mock out an HTTP service. In this case, when we say "mock," we mean that it'll stand up an HTTP server and respond with whatever pre-programmed response we give it. Wiremock is excellent for when you want to mock out a partner's hopefully slowly evolving API. Some good candidates are the Facebook API or a cloudy vendor's public-facing API.

Let's look at a simple test that uses Wiremock.

```
package rsb.testing.consumer;

import com.github.tomakehurst.wiremock.client.WireMock;
import lombok.extern.log4j.Log4j2;
```

```
import org.junit.Before;
import org.junit.Test;
import org.junit.runner.RunWith;
import org.springframework.beans.factory.annotation.Autowired;
import org.springframework.boot.test.context.SpringBootTest;
import org.springframework.cloud.contract.wiremock.AutoConfigureWireMock;
import org.springframework.context.annotation.Import;
import org.springframework.core.env.Environment;
import org.springframework.test.context.junit4.SpringRunner;
import reactor.core.publisher.Flux;
import reactor.test.StepVerifier;

import static org.springframework.http.HttpHeaders.CONTENT_TYPE;
import static org.springframework.http.MediaType.APPLICATION_JSON_UTF8_VALUE;

@RunWith(SpringRunner.class)
@Import(ConsumerApplication.class)
@SpringBootTest(webEnvironment = SpringBootTest.WebEnvironment.RANDOM_PORT)
① 
@AutoConfigureWireMock(port = 0) ②
public class WiremockCustomerClientTest {

    ③
    @Autowired
    private CustomerClient client;

    @Autowired
    private Environment environment;

    @Before
    public void setupWireMock() {

        String base = String.format("%s:%s", "localhost",
                this.environment.getProperty("wiremock.server.port", Integer
.class));
        this.client.setBase(base);

        String json = "[{ \"id\":\"1\", \"name\":\"Jane\"},"
                + "{ \"id\":\"2\", \"name\":\"John\"}]";

        ④
        WireMock.stubFor( //
                WireMock.get("/customers") //
                        .willReturn(WireMock.aResponse() //
                                .withHeader(CONTENT_TYPE,
 APPLICATION_JSON_UTF8_VALUE) //
                                .withBody(json)));
```

```java
    }

    @Test
    public void getAllCustomers() {
        Flux<Customer> customers = this.client.getAllCustomers();
        StepVerifier.create(customers) //
                .expectNext(new Customer("1", "Jane")) //
                .expectNext(new Customer("2", "John")) //
                .verifyComplete();
    }

}
```

① This is a stock-standard Spring Boot test that will run on a random HTTP port.

② The `@AutoConfigureWireMock` annotation installs the necessary WireMock machinery and stipulates on which port it should run. The WireMock HTTP server won't return anything in particular until we customize it.

③ This test will exercise our `CustomerClient`, which we'll introduce momentarily.

④ Here's where the rubber meets the road. We use the Java WireMock API to define how we expect our mock HTTP service to respond, given an HTTP GET request to /customers. This is a bit like how we customize the Mockito mock, turning it into a stub.

The test exercises a `CustomerClient` which is meant to be the typed Java client on which other teams can depend. It is expected that we'll perform whatever network communication in this `CustomerClient`.

```
package rsb.testing.consumer;

import lombok.extern.log4j.Log4j2;
import org.springframework.stereotype.Component;
import org.springframework.web.reactive.function.client.WebClient;
import reactor.core.publisher.Flux;

@Log4j2
@Component
class CustomerClient {

    private final WebClient webClient;

    private String base = "localhost:8080";

    public void setBase(String base) {
        this.base = base;
        log.info("setting base to " + base);
    }

    CustomerClient(WebClient webClient) {
        this.webClient = webClient;
    }

    Flux<Customer> getAllCustomers() {
        return this.webClient  ①
                .get()  ②
                .uri("http://" + this.base + "/customers")  ③
                .retrieve()  ④
                .bodyToFlux(Customer.class);  ⑤
    }

}
```

① The `WebClient` is the reactive HTTP client, analagous to the `RestTemplate`, like how R2DBC's `DatabaseClient` is the reactive SQL database client, analagous to the `JdbcTemplate`. We need to produce a bean of this type somewhere.

② It supports convenient methods for all the standard HTTP verbs. Here, we issue an HTTP GET.

③ We issue a request to our URL…

④ and tell the reactive `WebClient` to issue the request…

⑤ ...and transform the JSON results into a `Flux<Customer>`

The `CustomerClient` assumes the presence of a `WebClient` bean somewhere in the context. It's not hard to manufacture an instance of this bean - `WebClient.builder().build()` will work - but `WebClient` instances are essential and potentially shared resources across any of several beans. We might want to centralize configuration for things like compression, client-side load-balancing, authentication, and more. Spring Cloud, for example, can configure client-side load-balancing with Ribbon. So, while Spring Boot doesn't automatically build a `WebClient`, it automatically builds an object of type `WebClient.Builder` to which other configurations can contribute filters and error handlers. We can inject that builder, optionally further customize the `WebClient`, and then build the resulting instance.

```
package rsb.testing.consumer;

import org.springframework.context.annotation.Bean;
import org.springframework.context.annotation.Configuration;
import org.springframework.web.reactive.function.client.WebClient;

@Configuration
class CustomerClientConfiguration {

    @Bean
    WebClient myWebClient(WebClient.Builder builder) {
        return builder.build();
    }

}
```

Run that test, and everything should work to plan. Our consumer test is green. Our producer test is green. They're both green! Things are so green that they're golden! We can ship it, take a long lunch, and then take the day off because we're done, surely? Not so fast, sparky! We've sort of hand-waived away one part of the code that's important: the `Customer` class.

This consumer is a separate codebase from the producer. We're not sharing the definition of that class across the two projects. First, we can't guarantee that they'd be in the same language or even deployed on the same platform.

A tangent: why would anybody use anything besides Spring and the JVM to ship service-oriented software? I regard the very possibility of that with the same guarded caution as scientists at CERN. They regarded the possibility of the Higgs Boson particle when the idea of it was first announced as was distinctly possible, but they couldn't be sure! It seems logical to your humble author that people would use Spring, but sometimes people want to watch the world burn and use PHP...

Anyway, it's a hypothetical worth entertaining. We know that the producer and the consumer are both implemented in Java and Spring. But that may not always (**gasp**!) be true. Even if it were true, we shouldn't share the type definition across producers and consumers because their purposes differ. The `Customer` definition in the producer is a class designed to support persisting the document in MongoDB. It's pretty minimal, but it could be considerably more involved. It could support validation, auditing, and data life cycle methods, all of which should exist only in the producer. The consumer needs a simple data transfer object (DTO) to support ferrying the data to and from the service.

So, two types for two purposes. What happens if the implementation in the consumer should differ substantively from the implementation in the producer? Suppose that the producer evolves the record type and decides to refactor. What if, in version 2.0, the `name` field is split into two fields, `familyName` and `givenName`? The HTTP REST API would now reflect this new data, but the client wouldn't! But both producer and consumer would still build, and our tests would be green since they test only themselves, indifferent to other parties.

How insidious! It would seem we're back to square one. We want to know for sure that both sides agree. We could write exhaustive integration tests that deploy both producer and consumer and then run an end-to-end test. That would make it easier to sleep at night, but we'd lose out in agility. We've moved to microservices ostensibly for agility. Surely, we can do better than redeploy the whole cluster just for confidence that two system actors are correct? Also: this specific situation sure seems a heckuva lot more complicated than in the monolith where we could just use Mockito!

There has got to be a better way!

8.8. The `Customer` Is Not Always Right

So, Wiremock is a fantastic approach if you're mocking out a relatively stable API or, in a pinch, if you're mocking out a third party API - fast-moving or not - over which you have no control. In this particular example, we can change both the producer and the consumer. It may be that we can effect change by cooperating with other teams or affect change directly.

Let's use consumer-driven contract testing (CDCT) and Spring Cloud Contract to design a test that will confirm the structure of our reactive HTTP API *and* produce an artifact against which we can test our client. Spring Cloud Contract supports many different workflows, and this chapter isn't meant to address them all. What we want to look at is how to test reactive Spring WebFlux-based endpoints using Spring Cloud Contract.

The idea behind CDCT is simple: we define *contracts* (not schemas!) used to assert certain things about a network service interface at *test time*. If the assertions are valid, we can then use the contract to stand up a mock network service that complies with the contract's assertions, against which a client could reasonably make calls and expect valid responses back. When I say network service, I mean an HTTP API or a messaging API powered by Spring Integration or Apache Camel.

Typically, I define a contract file for the producer, configure the Maven plugin for Spring Cloud Contract (in the producer), define any setup logic in a base class, and then rework the client tests to substitute the use of Wiremock for the Spring Cloud Contract Stubrunner.

Add the Spring Cloud Contract Contract verfifier dependency to the Maven build for the producer:

- `org.springframework.cloud`:`spring-cloud-starter-contract-verifier` with scope test

8.8.1. Defining the Contract

This part's the easiest, for me at least. It's just code! You write the contract for the API using a typesafe Groovy, Java, or Kotlin-based DSL. Contracts typically live in src/main/resources/contracts in either the producer module or in a mutually shared contracts module that both producer and consumer can change. In CDCT, the assumption is that the client will define and contribute to the producer's contract definition to build. After all, why would you want to build an API that no client wants? You should define a contract for every little thing you want to capture for every change that could break across versions. Contracts are particularly effective when you want to capture potentially breaking changes across API versions. Contracts help you ensure compatibility for older clients depending on older APIs until you can migrate them to the new version. Let's look at a contract that captures our HTTP endpoint's behavior, /customers.

```
import org.springframework.cloud.contract.spec.Contract
import org.springframework.cloud.contract.spec.internal.HttpMethods

Contract.make {
    ①
    request {
        method HttpMethods.HttpMethod.GET
        url "/customers"

    }
    ②
    response {
        ③
        body(
        """
            [
            { "id": 1, "name" : "Jane" },
            { "id": 2, "name" : "John" }
            ]
        """
        )
        status(200)
        headers {
            contentType(applicationJson())
        }
    }
}
```

① define what we expect a request to this endpoint to look like

② assert what we expect to be returned assuming that the code in the reactive HTTP endpoint is run *and* assuming that any setup logic we plugin later is run.

Pretty straightforward, right? If you're using IntelliJ IDEA with the Groovy support, you get autocompletion when you make changes to this contract definition.

This contract is executed during the tests *if* you configure the correct plugin for either Gradle or Maven.

8.8.2. Configure the Spring Cloud Contract Maven plugin

In a system of law, a *contract* is only as valid as the system of validation and enforcement that governs it. In this case, that governor - the thing that ensures the results' integrity - is a build-time plugin. We're using Maven, so we'll configure the Maven version of the plugin.

The Spring Cloud Contract Maven plugin configuration

```xml
<plugin>
    <groupId>org.springframework.cloud</groupId>
    <artifactId>spring-cloud-contract-maven-plugin</artifactId>
    <version>${spring-cloud-contract-maven-plugin.version}</version>
    <extensions>true</extensions>
    <configuration>
        ①
        <baseClassForTests>
            rsb.testing.producer.BaseClass
        </baseClassForTests>
        ②
        <testMode>WEBTESTCLIENT</testMode>
        <!--            <testMode>EXPLICIT</testMode>-->
    </configuration>
</plugin>
```

① This plugin will transpile our contract definition - which we'll explore in just a moment - into a test case. An actual, honest-to-goodness JUnit class that will be compiled and run with all of our other tests. This declarative contract will result in a test that pokes at the structure of our reactive HTTP endpoint almost identically to what we did earlier in rsb.testing.producer.CustomerWebTest. This new test class will require that we set up any machinery required for the test to work, just as we had to do in `CustomerWebTest`. We'll put that setup logic in a base-class.

② Our HTTP API is powered by a reactive Spring WebFlux endpoint instead of a non-reactive HTTP Servlet-based application. This configuration switch helps the Spring Cloud Contract Maven plugin understand that fact.

The plugin version changes from version to version. Here's the Maven property defining the version that we're using for the code in this book.

The Spring Cloud Contract Maven plugin version

```
<spring-cloud-contract-maven-plugin.version>
    2.2.4.RELEASE
</spring-cloud-contract-maven-plugin.version>
```

The Maven plugin will transpile our contract file into a unit test that will extend the provided base class. The base class must setup the Spring Cloud Contract testing machinery and provide any of the mock collaborators needed for the test to work, just as we provided mock collaborators in our `CustomerWebTest`.

8.8.3. Defining the Base Class

There are several ways we could provide base classes for the transpiled Spring Cloud Contract tests. We could use conventions based on the contracts' names, based on package names, and more. Here, I've chosen a straightforward strategy: I'll map all transpiled tests to one base class. This clearly won't scale, but it's an excellent way to get started.

```
package rsb.testing.producer;

import io.restassured.module.webtestclient.RestAssuredWebTestClient;
import org.junit.Before;
import org.junit.runner.RunWith;
import org.mockito.Mockito;
import org.springframework.beans.factory.annotation.Autowired;
import org.springframework.boot.test.context.SpringBootTest;
import org.springframework.boot.test.mock.mockito.MockBean;
```

```java
import org.springframework.boot.web.server.LocalServerPort;
import org.springframework.context.annotation.Configuration;
import org.springframework.context.annotation.Import;
import org.springframework.test.context.junit4.SpringRunner;
import org.springframework.web.reactive.function.server.RouterFunction;
import reactor.core.publisher.Flux;

①
@RunWith(SpringRunner.class)
②
@SpringBootTest(webEnvironment = SpringBootTest.WebEnvironment.RANDOM_PORT,
properties = "server.port=0")
public class BaseClass {

    ③
    @LocalServerPort
    private int port;

    ④
    @MockBean
    private CustomerRepository customerRepository;

    @Autowired
    private RouterFunction<?>[] routerFunctions;

    @Before
    public void before() throws Exception {

        ⑤
        Mockito.when(this.customerRepository.findAll()).thenReturn(
                Flux.just(new Customer("1", "Jane"), new Customer("2", "John
")));

        ⑥
        RestAssuredWebTestClient.standaloneSetup(this.routerFunctions);
    }

    ⑦
    @Configuration
    @Import(ProducerApplication.class)
    public static class TestConfiguration {

    }

    // RestAssuredWebTestClient.standaloneSetup(new
ProducerController(personToCheck ->
    // personToCheck.age >= 20));
```

```
}
```

① This is a regular Spring-powered JUnit test

② We instruct the Spring Boot testing machinery to start the web application under test on a random port

③ We'll need to know in our tests on what port the application eventually settles. Inject that here using the `@LocalServerPort` annotation.

④ Use `@MockBean` to mock out the `CustomerRepository` collaborating object...

⑤ ...whose pre-programmed stub behavior we'll configure in the usual way

⑥ Spring Cloud Contract, in turn, uses a third-party project called RestAssured. We point the RestAssured machinery to our running web application here

⑦ the Spring Test framework needs to understand how to construct a Spring application context to discover the beans under test. Import the root Spring Boot configuration class here.

We're done with the producer side. On your command line, run `mvn clean install`. The build should be green, and you should see the console's output, towards the end of the build, that looks something like the following.

installing the Spring Cloud Contract producer stubs...

```
...
[INFO]
[INFO] --- maven-install-plugin:2.5.2:install (default-install) @ producer
---
[INFO] Installing /Users/joshlong/reactive-spring-
book/code/testing/producer/target/producer-0.0.1-SNAPSHOT.jar to
/Users/joshlong/.m2/repository/rsb/producer/0.0.1-SNAPSHOT/producer-0.0.1-
SNAPSHOT.jar
[INFO] Installing /Users/joshlong/reactive-spring-
book/code/testing/producer/pom.xml to
/Users/joshlong/.m2/repository/rsb/producer/0.0.1-SNAPSHOT/producer-0.0.1-
SNAPSHOT.pom
[INFO] Installing /Users/joshlong/reactive-spring-
book/code/testing/producer/target/producer-0.0.1-SNAPSHOT-stubs.jar to
/Users/joshlong/.m2/repository/rsb/producer/0.0.1-SNAPSHOT/producer-0.0.1-
SNAPSHOT-stubs.jar
[INFO]
------------------------------------------------------------------------
[INFO] BUILD SUCCESS
[INFO]
------------------------------------------------------------------------
[INFO] Total time: 13.564 s
...
```

Scan the output, and you'll see the usual suspects: it's installed the pom.xml and the producer-0.0.1-SNAPSHOT.jar, naturally. But there's also one more thing of interest: it's installed *stubs*! These stubs communicate the information that an API consumer will need to stand up a mock version of this API. Consumers can discover these stubs in many ways: through the local Maven ~/.m2/repository (LOCAL), as an artifact on the (test) CLASSPATH, or through a shared artifact repository (REMOTE) hosted in your organization.

Let's review the expected and ideal workflow. You'll make changes to your producer and your contracts. You'll run the build locally. If everything is green, you'll commit the changes and then do a git push. The CI environment will run the same tests as you run locally. It will run more exhaustive integration tests. If everything's green, the CI environment will push the code into the CD pipeline. That will (one hopes) result in a build that's been deployed to production where the code in your new API now represents the code with which all clients must integrate since that is what they can expect to confront when moving to production. At the same time, your CI build will do a `mvn deploy`, promoting the binaries and stubs to your organization's artifact repository.

> As we've worked through this example, we've taken for granted that you've set up a CD pipeline. If you haven't, then do! You might also refer to O'Reilly's *Cloud Native Java* for more on the topic.

For our purposes, for this example, our "artifact repository" is just `~/.m2/repository`. Let's revisit our consumer code and rework it in the light of Spring Cloud Contract.

8.8.4. Use the Spring Cloud Contract Stubrunner in the Client Test

This part's easy! It's my favorite part, even. We get to *delete* code! Here's a new test that's virtually identical to what we had before except that we've removed everything to do with Wiremock and we've replaced it with a simple annotation, `@AutoConfigureStubRunner`.

```
package rsb.testing.consumer;

import lombok.extern.log4j.Log4j2;
import org.junit.Test;
import org.junit.runner.RunWith;
import org.springframework.beans.factory.annotation.Autowired;
import org.springframework.boot.test.context.SpringBootTest;
import org.springframework.cloud.contract.stubrunner.spring.AutoConfigureStubRunner;
import org.springframework.cloud.contract.stubrunner.spring.StubRunnerPort;
import org.springframework.cloud.contract.stubrunner.spring.StubRunnerProperties;
import org.springframework.test.annotation.DirtiesContext;
import org.springframework.test.context.junit4.SpringRunner;
import reactor.core.publisher.Flux;
import reactor.test.StepVerifier;

@SpringBootTest( //
```

```
            webEnvironment = SpringBootTest.WebEnvironment.MOCK, //
            classes = ConsumerApplication.class //
)
@RunWith(SpringRunner.class)
@Log4j2
@DirtiesContext
@AutoConfigureStubRunner(//
        ids = StubRunnerCustomerClientTest.PRODUCER_ARTIFACT_ID, ①
        stubsMode = StubRunnerProperties.StubsMode.LOCAL ②
)
public class StubRunnerCustomerClientTest {

    final static String PRODUCER_ARTIFACT_ID = "rsb:producer";

    @Autowired
    private CustomerClient client;

    @StubRunnerPort(StubRunnerCustomerClientTest.PRODUCER_ARTIFACT_ID)
    private int portOfProducerService; ③

    @Test
    public void getAllCustomers() {

        var base = "localhost:" + this.portOfProducerService;
        this.client.setBase(base);
        log.info("setBase( " + base + ')');

        Flux<Customer> customers = this.client.getAllCustomers();
        StepVerifier //
                .create(customers) //
                .expectNext(new Customer("1", "Jane")) //
                .expectNext(new Customer("2", "John")) //
                .verifyComplete();
    }

}
```

① The @AutoConfigureStubRunner annotation loads the stub's artifact *at runtime* and turns it into a mock HTTP API whose responses are what we pre-programmed in the contract definition. It uses the Ivy Maven-compatible dependency resolver to load the stub. We provide coordinates in the ids attribute. This coordinate syntax should be familiar if you've ever used Ivy (the horror!) or Gradle: it is groupId:artifactId:version. The + means *use use the latest*, which is what we want since, by definition, in a continuous delivery environment, the latest version of the stub also corresponds to what's in production. The last argument, 8080, tells the stub-runner to run our mock HTTP server, just like Wiremock, on port 8080.

② `StubsMode.LOCAL` signals to the stub runner that we want to resolve the stubs by looking in the local `~/.m2/repository` folder, as opposed to in an organization artifact repository on the CLASSPATH for the running application.

③ The stub runner will launch the endpoint for us. We can find out where using the `@StubRunnerPort` annotation and providing the coordinates for the producer artifact - the same coordinates we specify for the `@AutoConfigureStubRunner` itself.

Besides configuring `@AutoConfigureStubRunner`, we also removed the `Wiremock` code, leaving only the essence of the thing we wanted to test: given a request to the `/customers` HTTP endpoint, confirm that the results we know to contain `Jane` and `John` do contain those records. The stub runner starts and stops the mock HTTP endpoint for the lifetime of our tests. It's *infinitely* lighter and cheaper to run that mock HTTP service than it is to deploy a full production cluster.

If your `Customer` DTO in the consumer contains an inconsistent field name, then your test will now fail because the mock data being returned in the client reflects the shape of the JSON produced by the producer. Problem solved!

8.8.5. Bonus: Use the Spring Cloud Contract Stubrunner Boot `.jar`

Alright - this is all well and good for anybody using Spring. Spring Cloud Contract helps the folks behind both producers and consumers who are using Spring to get home to their families on time. But what about the hypothetical non-Spring and non-JVM developers? What about those building iPhone applications and Android applications and HTML5, browser-based applications? Indeed they have families too! Think of the children!

We can use the Spring Cloud Contract Stub Runner Boot `.jar`. We must download and use it to run a mock HTTP API just as the `@AutoconfigureStubRunner` annotation does for our tests. You can download the `.jar` from Maven Central or any of the other usual spots.

Using the Spring Cloud Contract Stub Runner Boot `.jar`

```
$ wget -O stub-runner.jar
'https://search.maven.org/remotecontent?filepath=org/springframework/cloud/sp
ring-cloud-contract-stub-runner-boot/{srb-version}/spring-cloud-contract-
stub-runner-boot-{srb-version}.jar'
$ java -jar spring-cloud-contract-stub-runner-boot-{srb-version}.jar \
    --stubrunner.ids=rsb:producer:+:8080 \  ①
    --stubrunner.stubsMode=LOCAL --server.port=0
```

① We specify the same coordinates as we did when using the `@AutoconfigureStubRunner` annotation

An alternative approach is just to build your own Stub Runner Boot Server `` `.jar` `` the old fashioned way by building a new Spring Boot project from the Spring Initializr, add `Cloud Bootstrap`, and then click `Generate` to get a new Spring Boot `.jar`. Open it up and add the following dependency to the Maven build:

- `org.springframework.cloud` : `spring-cloud-starter-contract-stub-runner`

Then- and this last step is important - make sure to annotate the main class with `org.springframework.cloud.contract.stubrunner.server.EnableStubRunnerServer`. Finally, compile and enjoy!

Once the process is up and running, you can invoke your mock HTTP API at `http://localhost:8080/customers`. There, you'll see the records `Jane` and `John` just as we'd specified in our contract. So, now, instead of telling someone to deploy a Kubernetes cluster just to test their HTML 5 application, give them a copy of the Stub Runner Boot `.jar` and the coordinates for the stubs in your organization's artifact repository.

8.9. Next Steps

Testing is how you move forward with confidence. Imagine being increasingly uncertain as you move forward in time about the work you did yesterday, the day before, and so on? You'd be a bundle of nerves and regret in no time! Testing is the antidote. It's how you live with yourself and face your peers with confidence. Reactive programming flips a few assumptions about the observability of behavior in code on its head, but Reactor, and Spring on top of it, provide the tools to help.

In this chapter, we've seen how to evolve a reactive Spring-based application with confidence from service to system.

What we've reviewed in this chapter will serve us as we explore other reactive APIs.

Chapter 9. RSocket

You've probably heard about RSocket. Certainly, we on the Spring team have been talking it up, but if not, then this is the chapter for you! RSocket is a binary, cross-platform, cross-language network protocol that maps naturally to the Reactive Streams API.

9.1. Motivations for RSocket

Thus far, we've looked at using the Reactive Streams specification to describe how we conduct data between producers and consumers. This API gives us a protocol - a way to understand the relationship between two actors in a system. It does not necessarily describe a network protocol that implements the API or even imply network communication. Most of the things we've seen thus far, in this book, adapt existing protocols that can be faithfully implemented in terms of the Reactive Streams APIs. We have looked at asynchronous IO-centric data access, asynchronous IO-centric HTTP services, and WebSocket services, etc. It's a pretty good bet that if an API wraps an asynchronous IO-centric foundation, it can be mapped to a Reactive Streams-compatible API. Well, usually. Not all protocols are designed equally. The mapping is not always exact. HTTP is not an ideal fit with the ideas behind Reactive Streams.

9.1.1. HTTP or Not HTTP

HTTP doesn't truly understand backpressure at the network protocol level. The best that we can hope for is that when an HTTP client disconnects from a reactive HTTP service, the HTTP service perceives that a client socket has disconnected and propagates backpressure to all the complicated things producing the HTTP response. The best that we can hope for is something like org.reactivestreams.Subscription#cancel. That's a one time deal: it ignores one of the best parts of the Reactive Streams specification: Subscription#request, which gives us a mechanism to resume our requests when we're most able. A request must be retried if it ends up canceled. Imagine how cool it would be to call Subscription#request(long), process those emitted values, and then - while unable to handle any more - simply hold off on calling `request` again for a while, while waiting for things to stabilize. If later things settle down, the client resumes the requests from the last offset. Session resumption is convenient, especially in microservices and internet-of-things (IoT), where nodes are continually communicating and run a real risk of one node overwhelming another.

HTTP only supports one message exchange pattern: request/response. A client connects to a service, and the client initiates the request that results in a response. The opposite is impossible with HTTP; the client node must first connect to a service. It's impossible to do fire-and-forget messaging - where a client sends a message, and then neither waits for nor expects an acknowledgment of the request or a response from the service. There will *always* be a response - even if it's just an `HTTP 200 OK` to acknowledge the request. The Reactive Streams specification assumes that things will be asynchronous - that systems compose more naturally when we assume asynchronous, message-passing centric interactions. HTTP presumes synchronous, request-response centric interactions, a model that's not necessarily better for request-response centric communications. It is clearly paradigm-limiting for things like notifications that imply an asynchronous architecture.

HTTP 1.x is inefficient with connections. HTTP 1.0 only allowed one request to be processed per connection at a time. HTTP 1.1 improved things a bit with pipelining where requests are serialized on a connection, but this is only a minor improvement. Large or slow responses could still block others behind it. In concrete terms, this is a problem because browsers have a finite number of connections (from four to eight, in my experience) that they can dedicate to a single origin. HTTP pages often require dozens (or hundreds!) of HTTP resources to fully and correctly render. The requests have to be divided across the number of connections and then queued up. Want to render the DOM, but you haven't loaded the CSS files for the page? *Good luck*.

It's pretty cheap to create network connections (if you don't mind the constant network connection, setup, and destruction costs), but that doesn't mean its *free*. At some point, your operating system will have to prioritize connectivity, and this could impact other network applications on the system. Helpfully, HTTP 2.0 supports multiplexing - sending multiple requests and responses on the same connection.

9.1.2. RSocket: A Reactive Network Protocol

RSocket was designed with a blank slate and geared towards fast, scalable, and operations-friendly interactions between services. Work on RSocket started at Netflix and then continued when the engineers behind it moved to Facebook. It was motivated by the desire to replace HTTP, inefficient and inflexible, with a protocol that has less overhead.

In RSocket terminology, one node is a *requester* to another node's *responder*. Once connected, either side may initiate the conversation. RSocket avoids wherever possible the terms "client" or "server" as they imply that the client advances the conversational state where, in RSocket, either side can do so. I will use "client" and "service" a lot in my code in this chapter to clarify the logical role that these examples may play in architecture, even if technically, either side could play either role. RSocket supports several symmetric interaction models with asynchronous message passing over a single connection. They are:

- *Request/Response*: a requester may send a single request to a responder who may respond with a unique value.
- *Request/Stream*: a requester may send a single request to a responder who may respond with many (or infinite) values.
- *Channel*: a requester may send multiple values to a responder who may return with multiple values. This describes a bi-directional stream of interactions.
- *Fire-and-forget*: a requester may send a request to a responder, which does not produce a response.

RSocket connections are stateful; once a requester connects to a responder, it stays connected. Connections are multiplexed, so there is no need to consistently set up and dismantle network connections. One connection can be used for multiple logical transactions. RSocket also supports session resumption; a requester may resume long-lived streams across different transport connections. This can be useful for mobile-to-server interactions where connectivity may be fragile and non-persistent.

The RSocket protocol uses a lower-level transport protocol to carry RSocket frames. RSocket can run on transports such as TCP, WebSockets, HTTP/2 Streams, and Aeron. All RSocket transport protocols must support reliable unicast delivery. They must be connection-oriented and preserve frame ordering. Frame A sent before Frame B must arrive in source order. RSocket transport protocols are assumed to support FCS (Frame check sequence) [https://en.wikipedia.org/wiki/Frame_check_sequence] at either the transport protocol or at each MAC layer hop. In this chapter, we'll just assume the default TCP implementation.

That said, the other transports are exciting and worth your exploration. The WebSocket implementation, in particular, means that you could build HTML 5 clients that speak RSocket. Did I mention that RSocket is cross-platform, and there are clients available in many languages, including but not limited to C++ [https://github.com/rsocket/rsocket-cpp], Java [https://github.com/rsocket/rsocket-java], and JavaScript [https://github.com/rsocket/rsocket-js]? Thus, JavaScript applications can speak to Java applications using RSocket.js and RSocket Java with frames transported over WebSockets. Usefully: the RSocket client for the JVM is built on Project Reactor.

A *frame* is a single message containing a request, response, or protocol processing. A *fragment* is a portion of an application message that has been partitioned for inclusion in a *frame*. A *stream* is a unit of operation (request/response, channel, etc.). RSocket implementations may support frame check sequences (FCS) [https://en.wikipedia.org/wiki/Frame_check_sequence]. FCS is an error-detecting code added to a frame.

Each request or response has zero or more payloads associated with a stream. RSocket doesn't care what you put in the payload on the wire. It could be Google Protocol Buffs, CBOR, JSON, XML, etc. It's up to you to encode and decode that payload. A request or response may carry multiple payloads. In a Reactive Streams context, the `Subscriber` processes each payload in the `Subscriber#onNext(T)` method. The `Subscriber#onComplete()` event signals the successful completion of the stream.

RSocket payloads may contain data and metadata. Metadata may be encoded differently than the data itself. Metadata is correlated with both the connection (at connection setup) and with individual messages.

Metadata is a natural place to propagate out-of-band information like security tokens. You can put anything you want in the metadata payload, sort of like headers in other protocols.

9.2. Common Infrastructure for Raw RSocket

Throughout this chapter, we're going to look at a *ton* of different examples. We're going to reuse some things in the various examples, so I've extracted them into an autoconfiguration module. The autoconfiguration activates responds to configuration properties in a class called `BootifulProperties`. These properties will be useful later, as they give us a way to specify the host and port for all of our many RSocket services.

```java
package rsb.rsocket;

import lombok.Data;
import org.springframework.boot.context.properties.ConfigurationProperties;

@Data
@ConfigurationProperties("bootiful") ①
public class BootifulProperties {

    private final RSocket rsocket = new RSocket();

    @Data
    public static class RSocket {

        private String hostname = "localhost"; ②

        private int port = 8182; ③

    }
}
```

① The prefix for all my custom properties in this chapter will be `bootiful`

② The default hostname will be `localhost`, though you can change it with `bootiful.hostname`

③

the default port will be `port`, though you can change it with `bootiful.port`

We'll use these values mostly in the first section of the chapter, where we look at low-level RSocket and have to stand up certain infrastructure manually. I've provided some default values for these configuration properties. You can still override them (if you've already got something running on the default port or want to address your service with another network interface) the usual ways.

The autoconfiguration registers our configuration properties and a bean of type `EncodingUtils` that I will use to make short work of encoding and decoding payloads in the section looking at raw RSocket. Here is the autoconfiguration.

```java
package rsb.rsocket;

import com.fasterxml.jackson.databind.ObjectMapper;
import org.springframework.boot.context.properties.EnableConfigurationProperties;
import org.springframework.context.annotation.Bean;
import org.springframework.context.annotation.Configuration;

@Configuration
@EnableConfigurationProperties(BootifulProperties.class)
class BootifulAutoConfiguration {

    @Bean
    ①
    EncodingUtils encodingUtils(ObjectMapper objectMapper) {
        return new EncodingUtils(objectMapper);
    }

}
```

① We'll need to handle the encoding of data and metadata ourselves, especially in the beginning, so this convenient helper reduces some of the monotony.

The central conceit of `EncodingUtils` is to absolve us of all the tedious exception handing associated with using the Jackson `ObjectMapper` to read arbitrary values for data payloads and to read `Map<String, T>` values for metadata.

```java
package rsb.rsocket;

import com.fasterxml.jackson.core.type.TypeReference;
import com.fasterxml.jackson.databind.ObjectMapper;
import com.fasterxml.jackson.databind.ObjectReader;
import lombok.SneakyThrows;

import java.util.Map;

public class EncodingUtils {

    private final ObjectMapper objectMapper;

    private final ObjectReader objectReader;

    private final TypeReference<Map<String, Object>> typeReference = new TypeReference<>() {
    };

    public EncodingUtils(ObjectMapper objectMapper) {
        this.objectMapper = objectMapper;
        this.objectReader = this.objectMapper.readerFor(typeReference);
    }

    @SneakyThrows
    public <T> T decode(String json, Class<T> clazz) {
        return this.objectMapper.readValue(json, clazz);
    }

    @SneakyThrows
    public <T> String encode(T object) {
        return this.objectMapper.writeValueAsString(object);
    }

    @SneakyThrows
    public String encodeMetadata(Map<String, Object> metadata) {
        return this.objectMapper.writeValueAsString(metadata);
    }

    @SneakyThrows
    public Map<String, Object> decodeMetadata(String json) {
        return this.objectReader.readValue(json);
    }

}
```

I'd just as soon have Spring Boot worry about installing all of this for me, so I'll stuff it into its own `.jar` and create a `META-INF/spring.factories` file that we can add to the classpath of the examples in this chapter.

9.3. Raw RSocket

We can do some exciting things out of the box using low-level RSocket and Project Reactor. It's instructional to look at some simple examples in this light before getting to the more powerful, native component model and integration in Spring, starting with Spring Framework 5.2 and Spring Boot 2.2. I spent more than a year doing live-coding demonstrations of Spring and RSocket before Spring shipped its simplifying component model. It's not that difficult - even I can do it!

I debated even writing this section to look at low-level RSocket. I didn't give HTTP a similar treatment in the HTTP chapter for this book. I figured you've become acquainted with HTTP at this point in your career (or even just your life as a human being). You've no doubt used it in a browser if nothing else. You hopefully even know some of the HTTP verbs and their use and HTTP concepts (headers, bodies, cookies, sessions, etc.). It's unlikely, however, that you already have a similar familiarity with RSocket.

In most, if not all, of those examples, we'll look at two code pieces, a `client` and a `service`. And yes, I know that I just spent some time making the case that one of the benefits for RSocket is that it doesn't require client and service topologies; that two RSocket nodes once connected are *requester* and *responder*. That remains true. But you'll undoubtedly use RSocket in a service-oriented style, and it helps to make things clearer to distinguish which calls which first. In these examples, when you see `service`, you will know it should be run before the `client`.

I've chosen to keep the `client` and the `service` as separate Spring Boot applications *within* the same Maven module. This is more for ease of reference and implementation. It spares me from having to set up redundant Maven projects. You would undoubtedly tease the service out into a separate deployable artifact from the client in a proper service-oriented architecture.

The first thing you'll need to do when using RSocket is to connect to another node. Let's look at a simple request/response example, as this will be the simplest to grasp.

9.3.1. A Request/Response Example

Let's look at the skeletal Spring Boot application class for our first service. Almost all of our applications will have a class identical to this one. There's only one important thing worth noting here: we've got to keep the Java process running because our RSocket service won't. I've resorted to the simplest thing that could work: System.in.read(). That's it.

> Make sure your services all have a System.in.read() call to keep them running; otherwise, they'll start and promptly quit before anything interesting happens!

```
package rsb.rsocket.requestresponse.service;

import lombok.SneakyThrows;
import org.springframework.boot.SpringApplication;
import org.springframework.boot.autoconfigure.SpringBootApplication;

@SpringBootApplication
public class RequestResponseApplication {

    @SneakyThrows
    public static void main(String[] arrrImAPirate) {
        SpringApplication.run(RequestResponseApplication.class,
arrrImAPirate);
        System.in.read();①
    }

}
```

① The call to System.in.read() forces the client thread to join, waiting for user input. Don't accidentally run this and then type a character in the shell for this service!

That is the last time we'll see that file for the next several examples, as they would be redundant.

Chapter 9. RSocket

The request/response service implementation follows.

```java
package rsb.rsocket.requestresponse.service;

import io.rsocket.*;
import io.rsocket.transport.netty.server.TcpServerTransport;
import io.rsocket.util.DefaultPayload;
import lombok.RequiredArgsConstructor;
import lombok.extern.log4j.Log4j2;
import org.springframework.boot.context.event.ApplicationReadyEvent;
import org.springframework.context.ApplicationListener;
import org.springframework.core.Ordered;
import org.springframework.stereotype.Component;
import reactor.core.publisher.Mono;
import rsb.rsocket.BootifulProperties;

@Log4j2
@Component
@RequiredArgsConstructor
class Service
        implements SocketAcceptor, Ordered, ApplicationListener<ApplicationReadyEvent> {

    private final BootifulProperties properties;

    ①
    @Override
    public void onApplicationEvent(ApplicationReadyEvent applicationReadyEvent) {
        log.info("starting " + Service.class.getName() + '.');
        RSocketFactory //
                .receive()②
                .acceptor(this)③
                .transport(TcpServerTransport.create(④
                        this.properties.getRsocket().getHostname(),
                        this.properties.getRsocket().getPort()))//
                .start() ⑤
                .subscribe();//
    }

    @Override ⑥
    public Mono<RSocket> accept(ConnectionSetupPayload connectionSetupPayload,
            RSocket rSocket) {
        var rs = new AbstractRSocket() {⑦
```

```
            @Override
            public Mono<Payload> requestResponse(Payload payload) {⑧
                return Mono
                        .just(DefaultPayload.create("Hello, " + payload
.getDataUtf8()));
            }
        };

        return Mono.just(rs);
    }

    @Override
    public int getOrder() {
        return Ordered.HIGHEST_PRECEDENCE;
    }

}
```

① Most of our applications install themselves and start serving in response to the `ApplicationReadyEvent` Spring context event.

② All services `receive()` connections.

③ `SocketAcceptor` instances accept incoming connections. This class implements `SocketAcceptor`. This interface handles the initial connection and installs the subsequent request handling logic.

④ On what transport do we want to handle requests? Here we use the `TcpServerTransport` to use the TCP transport, though - as we alluded to earlier - other transports support at least Aeron and WebSockets.

⑤ The `start` method kicks off the processing and returns a `Publisher<T>` which we then subscribe to.

⑥ The payload for the accept method consists of metadata associated with setting up a new connection and the actual RSocket instance representing the client's connection to the service. It is the requester of our responder.

⑦ Given an RSocket representing the connection associated with the incoming request, return an RSocket instance that can provide the incoming requests' answers. It's a handshake.

⑧ Each RSocket instance can respond in any of the usual ways - request/response, fire-and-forget, stream, etc. - by overriding one of the methods provided in `AbstractRsocket`. We override the callback method to respond to requests with a single incoming `Payload`, providing a unique `Payload` response.

Turning to the client, we also have a boilerplate class to house our `main` method, just as with the service.

```java
package rsb.rsocket.requestresponse.client;

import lombok.SneakyThrows;
import org.springframework.boot.SpringApplication;
import org.springframework.boot.autoconfigure.SpringBootApplication;

@SpringBootApplication
public class RequestResponseApplication {

    @SneakyThrows
    public static void main(String[] arrrImAPirate) {
        SpringApplication.run(RequestResponseApplication.class, arrrImAPirate);
        System.in.read();
    }

}
```

I won't reprint the `main` classes for each client example, which would be redundant. Let's look at the actual client, which - structurally - is reasonably similar to the service. It's the service's mirror image.

```java
package rsb.rsocket.requestresponse.client;

import io.rsocket.Payload;
import io.rsocket.RSocketFactory;
import io.rsocket.transport.netty.client.TcpClientTransport;
import io.rsocket.util.DefaultPayload;
import lombok.RequiredArgsConstructor;
import lombok.extern.log4j.Log4j2;
import org.springframework.boot.context.event.ApplicationReadyEvent;
import org.springframework.context.ApplicationListener;
import org.springframework.core.Ordered;
import org.springframework.stereotype.Component;
import reactor.core.publisher.Flux;
import rsb.rsocket.BootifulProperties;
```

```
@Log4j2
@Component
@RequiredArgsConstructor
class Client implements ApplicationListener<ApplicationReadyEvent>, Ordered {

    private final BootifulProperties properties;

    @Override
    public void onApplicationEvent(ApplicationReadyEvent
applicationReadyEvent) {
        log.info("starting " + Client.class.getName() + '.');
        Flux<String> reply = RSocketFactory//
                .connect()①
                .transport(TcpClientTransport.create(
                        this.properties.getRsocket().getHostName(),
                        this.properties.getRsocket().getPort()))//
                .start()//
                .flatMapMany(socket -> { ②
                    var reactiveSpring = DefaultPayload.create("Reactive Spring");
                    return socket//
                            .requestResponse(reactiveSpring)//
                            .map(Payload::getDataUtf8);
                });
        reply.subscribe(log::info);
    }

    @Override
    public int getOrder() {
        return Ordered.LOWEST_PRECEDENCE;
    }

}
```

① We use the `connect` method to connect to our service, not the `receive` method as we did when building the service.

② The result of the `start` method is an RSocket instance representing the service's connection. We can then use it to interact with the service. In this case, we use a method to start a request/response interaction with our service. We take the payload that's returned and then unpack the data as a UTF-8 encoded string, which we then log out.

If you understood everything so far, good news! Almost all the other message exchange patterns are virtually identical. The delta from this example to a fire-and-forget, request/stream, or channel example is virtually nill. Let's review some others, if only for posterity.

9.3.2. A Fire-and-Forget Example

A fire-and-forget call is one where the client does not expect or receive a response from the service. It is an excellent choice when you don't *need* the acknowledgment of the message. This is typical when you're dealing with potentially ephemeral, non-critical data. There are tons of examples of this in architecture.

- *location updates*: suppose your client plots someone's marathon run on a fixed course or their movements on a video game field. You may miss one message, but that's fine because the next one won't be too long in coming.

- *Heartbeat events*: Most services have some sort of heartbeat event for stateful clients. Too many missed heartbeats may trigger a disconnect, but it's probably acceptable to miss one.

- *Click stream processing*: want to do complex-event processing on the user's mouse's real-time movement on your application or HTTP service? Great. But you'll still be able to paint a comprehensive picture if you miss a few pixels.

- *Video frames*: sure, you'd *like* to have all 30 or 60 frames per second, but the user probably won't notice one or two missed frames, and by the time they do, they're already well into the next few seconds of footage.

- *Obserability events*: This is a common outcome for the tell-don't-ask architecture (or CQRS) where components broadcast state changes. In this case, it might be interesting for other parties, other microservices, in your system to be aware of a state change in your component. Still, you don't need to be responsible for ensuring that they do. All you can do is throw state changes out there and hope they're all-consuming them.

- *Fire-and-forget* messaging: yes, I know this seems redundant, but if you're using reactive APIs to talk to something else that supports fire-and-forget semantics, like an RPC service that returns void, or a message queue (like Apache Kafka, Apache RocketMQ, RabbitMQ, etc.) for which you are not awaiting a response, then this is a natural mapping.

Understanding *why* you'd use fire-and-forget is far more interesting than *how* you'd use it. How you'd use it is trivially different from request-and-response. Here's our fire-and-forget service.

```java
package rsb.rsocket.fireandforget.service;

import io.rsocket.*;
import io.rsocket.transport.netty.server.TcpServerTransport;
import lombok.RequiredArgsConstructor;
import lombok.extern.log4j.Log4j2;
import org.springframework.boot.context.event.ApplicationReadyEvent;
import org.springframework.context.ApplicationListener;
import org.springframework.stereotype.Component;
import reactor.core.publisher.Mono;
import rsb.rsocket.BootifulProperties;

@Log4j2
@Component
@RequiredArgsConstructor
class Service implements SocketAcceptor, ApplicationListener
<ApplicationReadyEvent> {

    private final BootifulProperties properties;

    @Override
    public void onApplicationEvent(ApplicationReadyEvent
applicationReadyEvent) {
        log.info("starting " + Service.class.getName() + '.');
        RSocketFactory //
                .receive()//
                .acceptor(this)//
                .transport(TcpServerTransport.create(
                        this.properties.getRsocket().getHostname(),
                        this.properties.getRsocket().getPort()))//
                .start() //
                .subscribe();
    }

    @Override
    public Mono<RSocket> accept(ConnectionSetupPayload
```

```
connectionSetupPayload,
            RSocket rSocket) {
        var rs = new AbstractRSocket() {

            @Override
            public Mono<Void> fireAndForget(Payload payload) {
                log.info("new message received: " + payload.getDataUtf8());
                return Mono.empty(); ①
            }
        };

        return Mono.just(rs);
    }
}
```

① The only thing worth noting is that we're returning `Mono<Void>`. That's *it*!

Here's our client.

```java
package rsb.rsocket.fireandforget.client;

import io.rsocket.RSocketFactory;
import io.rsocket.transport.netty.client.TcpClientTransport;
import io.rsocket.util.DefaultPayload;
import lombok.RequiredArgsConstructor;
import lombok.extern.log4j.Log4j2;
import org.springframework.boot.context.event.ApplicationReadyEvent;
import org.springframework.context.ApplicationListener;
import org.springframework.stereotype.Component;
import rsb.rsocket.BootifulProperties;

@Log4j2
@Component
@RequiredArgsConstructor
class Client implements ApplicationListener<ApplicationReadyEvent> {

    private final BootifulProperties properties;

    @Override
    public void onApplicationEvent(ApplicationReadyEvent applicationReadyEvent) {
        log.info("starting " + Client.class.getName() + '.');
        RSocketFactory//
                .connect()//
                .transport(TcpClientTransport.create(
                        this.properties.getRsocket().getHostname(),
                        this.properties.getRsocket().getPort()))//
                .start()//
                .flatMapMany(socket -> socket
                        .fireAndForget(DefaultPayload.create("Reactive Spring")))①
                .subscribe(log::info);
    }
}
```

① There's no follow-through! That's bad in golf but great in high frequency messaging. The only useful thing we can do with the `Mono<Void>` returned from this method is to `subscribe` to it, which we ultimately do.

9.3.3. A Streaming (Channel) Example

The next example is a bit more involved. Both sides will send a stream - a

Flux<T> - of results. We'll use it here to demonstrate the classic game of ping/pong. Channels streams are a great way to model constant, conversational state. There are a lot of interactions that benefit from this dynamic. Your typical WebSocket interaction looks like this. Chat applications look like this. Game state changes in a video game look like this. We're starting to stray away from some of the message exchange patterns with which we may be most comfortable coming from HTTP.

In this example, the *service* is the Pong class, which will respond when it receives a ping from the client Ping class. Here's the service, err, Pong, class.

```
package rsb.rsocket.channel.service;

import io.rsocket.*;
import io.rsocket.transport.netty.server.TcpServerTransport;
import io.rsocket.util.DefaultPayload;
import lombok.RequiredArgsConstructor;
import lombok.extern.log4j.Log4j2;
import org.reactivestreams.Publisher;
import org.springframework.boot.context.event.ApplicationReadyEvent;
import org.springframework.context.ApplicationListener;
import org.springframework.stereotype.Component;
import reactor.core.publisher.Flux;
import reactor.core.publisher.Mono;
import rsb.rsocket.BootifulProperties;

@Log4j2
@Component
@RequiredArgsConstructor
class Pong implements SocketAcceptor, ApplicationListener
<ApplicationReadyEvent> {

    private final BootifulProperties properties;

    @Override
    public void onApplicationEvent(ApplicationReadyEvent
applicationReadyEvent) {

        RSocketFactory //
                .receive()//
                .acceptor(this)//
                .transport(TcpServerTransport.create(
                        this.properties.getRsocket().getHostname(),
                        this.properties.getRsocket().getPort()))
```

```
                    .start() //
                    .subscribe();
    }

    @Override
    public Mono<RSocket> accept(ConnectionSetupPayload
connectionSetupPayload,
            RSocket rSocket) {

        var rs = new AbstractRSocket() {

            @Override
            public Flux<Payload> requestChannel(Publisher<Payload> payloads)
{ ①
                return Flux //
                        .from(payloads) //
                        .map(Payload::getDataUtf8) //
                        .doOnNext(
                                str -> log.info("received " + str + " in " +
getClass())) //
                        .map(request -> "pong") ②
                        .map(DefaultPayload::create);
            }
        };

        return Mono.just(rs);
    }
}
```

① Given an infinite stream of incoming payloads (all of them ping)...

② Return an infinite stream of outgoing ` pong`s.

And here's the client, err, Ping, class.

```
package rsb.rsocket.channel.client;

import io.rsocket.Payload;
import io.rsocket.RSocketFactory;
import io.rsocket.transport.netty.client.TcpClientTransport;
import io.rsocket.util.DefaultPayload;
import lombok.RequiredArgsConstructor;
import lombok.extern.log4j.Log4j2;
import org.springframework.boot.context.event.ApplicationReadyEvent;
import org.springframework.context.ApplicationListener;
```

```
import org.springframework.stereotype.Component;
import reactor.core.publisher.Flux;
import rsb.rsocket.BootifulProperties;

import java.time.Duration;

@Log4j2
@Component
@RequiredArgsConstructor
class Ping implements ApplicationListener<ApplicationReadyEvent> {

    private final BootifulProperties properties;

    @Override
    public void onApplicationEvent(ApplicationReadyEvent applicationReadyEvent) {

        Flux<Payload> ping = Flux ①
                .interval(Duration.ofSeconds(1)).map(i -> DefaultPayload.create("ping"));

        RSocketFactory//
                .connect()//
                .transport(TcpClientTransport.create(
                        this.properties.getRsocket().getHostname(),
                        this.properties.getRsocket().getPort()))//
                .start()//
                .flatMapMany(socket -> socket②
                        .requestChannel(ping)//
                        .map(Payload::getDataUtf8)//
                        .doOnNext(str -> log
                                .info("received " + str + " in " + getClass().getName()))//
                        .take(10))//
                .subscribe();
    }

}
```

① The client generates an infinite stream of `ping` messages...

② and fires them off using the client RSocket instance.

Responding to the client is as simple as `map` or `flatMap`'ing the incoming stream into a stream of responses and then directing the stream right back at the client. It took me a long time to appreciate this simplicity. In this trivial example, I am sending back a `String`, but there's no reason I couldn't initiate a database call or call some other RSocket endpoint, and then `flatMap` the result.

There is another message exchange pattern - request/stream - that is a specialization of the channel case; a client sends a single `Payload`, to which the service responds with a `Flux<Payload>`. I won't bother with an example.

Thus far, we've done everything in terms of one node initiating a request, which may or may not yield a response. The real power of RSocket is that it lets either side start a request at whatever point they want. Let's explore that possibility.

9.3.4. A Bidirectional Example

This next example takes things a bit further. In this example, both client and service produce a stream of values. The client connects to the service and requests a stream of `GreetingResponse`'s. The service connects to the client and requests a stream of `ClientHealthState` instances representing the client's health. The service will produce an infinite stream of `GreetingResponse` instances, but only so long as the client telemetry stream indicates no errors. We'll test each result from the client stream with a filter to see if it indicates an error. Ideally, every result from that stream will indicate that everything is fine. If we filtered out all the `ClientHealthState` instances except the errors, then ideally, the stream would be empty. As soon as the client stream is non-empty, which indicates an error, the service should stop streaming. So, in effect, there are *two* ongoing interactions between the two nodes. The client initiates the conversation with the service, but the service then begins communication with the client in a side channel. This is what we mean by a bidirectional exchange. Even better, this example requires one stream of communication to change or react to the other.

This example features two ongoing interactions, each of which may be any of the already examined message exchange patterns: fire-and-forget, request-response, request-stream, or channel. What is novel here is not the message exchange patterns *per se*; it's that there are two of them and that each side initiates one. The concept of a "client" or "service" blurs as both sides are clients, and both sides are services. They are both requester and responder.

This example requires a few common types. The service (the first responder) produces an infinite stream of `GreetingResponse` objects when given a `GreetingRequest` instance. We're going to see these types many more times in this chapter, so I won't reprint them for each successive example. I've put them in a common package to both the `client` and the `service` code.

Here is the type for the request:

```java
package rsb.rsocket.bidirectional;

import lombok.AllArgsConstructor;
import lombok.Data;
import lombok.NoArgsConstructor;

@Data
@AllArgsConstructor
@NoArgsConstructor
public class GreetingRequest {

    private String name;

}
```

Here is the type for the response:

```
package rsb.rsocket.bidirectional;

import lombok.AllArgsConstructor;
import lombok.Data;
import lombok.NoArgsConstructor;

@Data
@AllArgsConstructor
@NoArgsConstructor
public class GreetingResponse {

    private String message;

}
```

The client starts to stream `ClientHealthState` instances to the service as soon as the client connects to the service.

```
package rsb.rsocket.bidirectional;

import lombok.Data;

@Data
public class ClientHealthState {

    public static final String STARTED = "started";

    public static final String STOPPED = "stopped";

    private final String state;

    public ClientHealthState() {
        this.state = STARTED;
    }

    public ClientHealthState(String s) {
        this.state = s;
    }

}
```

While the implementations have more code, they're only lengthier because they're doing two things simultaneously. They combine the concepts we've

Chapter 9. RSocket

already encountered. Here is the service.

```java
package rsb.rsocket.bidirectional.service;

import io.rsocket.*;
import io.rsocket.transport.netty.server.TcpServerTransport;
import io.rsocket.util.DefaultPayload;
import lombok.RequiredArgsConstructor;
import lombok.extern.slf4j.Slf4j;
import org.springframework.boot.context.event.ApplicationReadyEvent;
import org.springframework.context.ApplicationListener;
import org.springframework.stereotype.Component;
import reactor.core.publisher.Flux;
import reactor.core.publisher.Mono;
import rsb.rsocket.BootifulProperties;
import rsb.rsocket.EncodingUtils;
import rsb.rsocket.bidirectional.ClientHealthState;
import rsb.rsocket.bidirectional.GreetingRequest;
import rsb.rsocket.bidirectional.GreetingResponse;

import java.time.Duration;
import java.time.Instant;
import java.util.stream.Stream;

import static rsb.rsocket.bidirectional.ClientHealthState.STOPPED;

@Slf4j
@Component
@RequiredArgsConstructor
class Service implements ApplicationListener<ApplicationReadyEvent>,
    SocketAcceptor {

    private final BootifulProperties properties;

    private final EncodingUtils encodingUtils;

    @Override
    public void onApplicationEvent(ApplicationReadyEvent are) {
        log.info("starting " + this.getClass().getName());
        RSocketFactory//
                .receive()//
                .acceptor(this)//
                .transport(TcpServerTransport.create(
                        this.properties.getRsocket().getHostname(),
                        this.properties.getRsocket().getPort()))//
                .start()//
```

```
            .subscribe();
    }

    @Override
    public Mono<RSocket> accept(ConnectionSetupPayload setup, RSocket clientRsocket) {

        ①
        return Mono.just(new AbstractRSocket() {

            @Override
            public Flux<Payload> requestStream(Payload payload) {

                ②
                var clientHealthStateFlux = clientRsocket//
                        .requestStream(DefaultPayload.create(new byte[0]))//
                        .map(p -> encodingUtils.decode(p.getDataUtf8(),
                                ClientHealthState.class))//
                        .filter(chs -> chs.getState().equalsIgnoreCase(STOPPED));

                ③
                var replyPayloadFlux = Flux//
                        .fromStream(Stream.generate(() -> {
                            var greetingRequest = encodingUtils
                                    .decode(payload.getDataUtf8(),
                GreetingRequest.class);
                            var message = "Hello, " + greetingRequest.getName() + " @ "
                                    + Instant.now() + "!";
                            return new GreetingResponse(message);
                        }))//
                        .delayElements(Duration
                                .ofSeconds(Math.max(3, (long) (Math.random() * 10))))//
                        .doFinally(signalType -> log.info("finished."));

                return replyPayloadFlux ④
                        .takeUntilOther(clientHealthStateFlux)//
                        .map(encodingUtils::encode)//
                        .map(DefaultPayload::create);
            }
        });
    }
}
```

① I've said this before, but it's worth repeating: this is an ideal point to do some connection setup. You might have different clients, and each client has their own RSocket connection. YOu could store that connection mapping here in a `Map<K, V>` and then use that to hold onto session state for each client.

② This stream will only emit a value if there's a `ClientHealthState.STOPPED` event. If that event never occurs, then this stream is virtually empty.

③ This will emit an infinite stream of `GreetingResponse` values, but we want it to stop, eventually...

④ We use the handy `takeUntilOther` operator to take new values only so long as the `ClientHealthState` stream is empty. As soon as there's a value in the `ClientHealthState` stream, the `GreetingResponse` stream stops emitting new values. Handy, eh?

I love this example! And how about *that operator*, eh? Awesome! This is another example of where Reactor's various operators can make life a breeze, and when life is otherwise so hard, why wouldn't you accept a little help from a friendly library? What we're doing is relatively complex, and would not be fun code to write in a multithreaded fashion in a non-reactive example.

The client is appealing, only in that it features things you've already seen before, just not in the standard arrangement that you've so far seen them. Our client is a client - in that it requests something of the service - but it's also a service - in that it implements `SocketAcceptor`; it both asks and answers questions.

```
package rsb.rsocket.bidirectional.client;

import io.rsocket.*;
import io.rsocket.transport.netty.client.TcpClientTransport;
import io.rsocket.util.DefaultPayload;
import lombok.RequiredArgsConstructor;
import lombok.extern.slf4j.Slf4j;
import reactor.core.publisher.Flux;
import reactor.core.publisher.Mono;
import rsb.rsocket.EncodingUtils;
import rsb.rsocket.bidirectional.ClientHealthState;
```

```java
import rsb.rsocket.bidirectional.GreetingRequest;
import rsb.rsocket.bidirectional.GreetingResponse;

import java.time.Duration;
import java.util.Date;
import java.util.stream.Stream;

import static rsb.rsocket.bidirectional.ClientHealthState.STARTED;
import static rsb.rsocket.bidirectional.ClientHealthState.STOPPED;

①
@RequiredArgsConstructor
@Slf4j
class Client implements SocketAcceptor {

    private final EncodingUtils encodingUtils;

    private final String uid;

    private final String serviceHostname;

    private final int servicePort;

    Flux<GreetingResponse> getGreetings() {
        var greetingRequestPayload = this.encodingUtils
                .encode(new GreetingRequest("Client #" + this.uid));
        return RSocketFactory//
                .connect()//
                .acceptor(this)//
                .transport(
                        TcpClientTransport.create(this.serviceHostname, this
.servicePort)) //
                .start()//
                .flatMapMany(instance -> instance ②
                        .requestStream(DefaultPayload.create
(greetingRequestPayload)) //
                        .map(payload -> encodingUtils.decode(payload
.getDataUtf8(),
                                GreetingResponse.class))//
                );
    }

    ③
    @Override
    public Mono<RSocket> accept(ConnectionSetupPayload setup, RSocket
serverRSocket) {
```

```java
        return Mono.just(new AbstractRSocket() {

            @Override
            public Flux<Payload> requestStream(Payload payload) {

                var start = new Date().getTime();

                var delayInSeconds = ((long) (Math.random() * 30)) * 1000;

                var stateFlux = Flux.fromStream(Stream.generate(() -> {
                    var now = new Date().getTime();
                    var stop = ((start + delayInSeconds) < now) && Math
.random() > .8;
                    return new ClientHealthState(stop ? STOPPED : STARTED);
                }))//
                        .delayElements(Duration.ofSeconds(5));

                return stateFlux//
                        .map(encodingUtils::encode)//
                        .map(DefaultPayload::create);
            }
        });
    }
}
```

① This client requires some parameters that aren't provided through normal Spring dependency injection. The `ClientLauncher` passes those values when it instantiates instances of the `Client` class. We'll get to that momentarily.

② We use the RSocket client instance to request a stream of `GreetingResponse`s from the service.

③ The `Client` class also implements `SocketAcceptor`, so it can itself respond to connections that have been made and provide a stream of values in response. Here, the client sends a stream of `ClientHealthState` objects that terminate after a random time window. The client responds with `ClientHealthState.STARTED` messages by default. There's a less than 20% chance that any single message after some part of 30 seconds will be a `ClientHealthState.STOPPED` message. So, you may need to wait a bit to see it stop. Which is great for a demo where we want to visualize what's happening.

To simulate actual, random, client activity against our service, we'll launch a few instances at random intervals from the `ClientLauncher` class.

```java
package rsb.rsocket.bidirectional.client;

import lombok.RequiredArgsConstructor;
import lombok.extern.slf4j.Slf4j;
import org.springframework.boot.context.event.ApplicationReadyEvent;
import org.springframework.context.ApplicationListener;
import org.springframework.stereotype.Component;
import reactor.core.publisher.Flux;
import rsb.rsocket.BootifulProperties;
import rsb.rsocket.EncodingUtils;
import rsb.rsocket.bidirectional.GreetingResponse;

import java.time.Duration;
import java.util.stream.IntStream;

@Slf4j
@Component
@RequiredArgsConstructor
class ClientLauncher implements ApplicationListener<ApplicationReadyEvent> {

    private final EncodingUtils encodingUtils;

    private final int maxClients = 10;

    private final BootifulProperties properties;

    @Override
    public void onApplicationEvent(ApplicationReadyEvent event) {
        var nestedMax = Math.max(5, (int) (Math.random() * maxClients));
        var hostname = this.properties.getRsocket().getHostname();①
        var port = this.properties.getRsocket().getPort();
        log.info("launching " + nestedMax + " clients connecting to " + hostname + ':'
                + port + ".");
        Flux.fromStream(IntStream.range(0, nestedMax).boxed())②
                .map(id -> new Client(this.encodingUtils, Long.toString(id), hostname,
                        port))③
                .flatMap(client -> Flux.just(client)
                        .delayElements(Duration.ofSeconds((long) (30 * Math.random()))))④
                .flatMap(Client::getGreetings)⑤
```

```
            .map(GreetingResponse::toString)⑥
            .subscribe(log::info);
    }
}
```

① Each client has a unique ID and receives the service's host and port to connect.

② The Java 8 Stream API gives us a handy way to create a range of values that we turn into a Flux<T>. (This is just a superfluous alternative to a for-loop!)

③ We'll instantiate each client here. NB: we're *not* starting, or launching, each client! Just constructing the instance.

④ This line wraps each Client instance in a Publisher<T> that is only emitted - made available for subscribers to process - after a simulated delay using the handy delayElements(Duration) operator.

⑤ We'll start each client as soon as each instance of the Client is emitted.

⑥ The last two lines map the emitted value to a String and then log it out.

9.3.5. Metadata

The next example is a straightforward evolution of everything we've seen thus far. We're going to push metadata to the service so that the consumer can use it. We'll need to encode the data, just as we did with the message's payload. Metadata is an opportunity for us to communicate out-of-band information as we would using HTTP headers or RabbitMQ headers. You can use it to transmit things like authentication, or trace information, and more. RSocket's metadata is meant to be *pushed* to the recipient, giving the other a chance to respond to state changes independent of whatever it is doing in the application's main flow. You can use metadata on a connection independently from whatever else you're doing with that connection.

We are going to need to handle encoding the metadata from the client to service. We will use the metadata to communicate some well-known headers whose keys well establish a separate class well share across the producer and the consumer.

We're going to assume that our metadata is actually a Java Map<K, V> whose keys are String values that we decode.

```
package rsb.rsocket.metadata;

public class Constants {

    public static String CLIENT_ID_HEADER = "client-id";

    public static String LANG_HEADER = "lang";

}
```

Let's look at our service. Most of this will be fairly identical to what we've seen before, with only a small delta concerned with transmitting metadata.

We're going to use the metadata to communicate what human language (or Locale) (Japanese, Chinese, French, etc.) the client wants to use. The service keeps a Map<String, Object> of client ID to human language. The client can update the preference by sending metadata to the service.

```
package rsb.rsocket.metadata.service;

import io.rsocket.*;
import io.rsocket.transport.netty.server.TcpServerTransport;
import lombok.RequiredArgsConstructor;
import lombok.extern.log4j.Log4j2;
import org.springframework.boot.context.event.ApplicationReadyEvent;
import org.springframework.context.ApplicationListener;
import org.springframework.stereotype.Component;
import reactor.core.publisher.Mono;
import rsb.rsocket.BootifulProperties;
import rsb.rsocket.EncodingUtils;
import rsb.rsocket.metadata.Constants;

import java.util.Map;

@Log4j2
@Component
@RequiredArgsConstructor
class Service implements SocketAcceptor, ApplicationListener
<ApplicationReadyEvent> {
```

```java
    private final EncodingUtils encodingUtils;

    private final BootifulProperties properties;

    @Override
    public void onApplicationEvent(ApplicationReadyEvent
applicationReadyEvent) {
        log.info("starting " + Service.class.getName() + '.');
        RSocketFactory //
                .receive()//
                .acceptor(this)//
                .transport(TcpServerTransport.create(
                        this.properties.getRsocket().getHostname(),
                        this.properties.getRsocket().getPort()))//
                .start() //
                .subscribe();
    }

    @Override
    public Mono<RSocket> accept(ConnectionSetupPayload
connectionSetupPayload,
            RSocket rSocket) {
        var rs = new AbstractRSocket() {

            @Override
            public Mono<Void> metadataPush(Payload payload) {
                var metadataUtf8 = payload.getMetadataUtf8();
                var metadata = encodingUtils.decodeMetadata(metadataUtf8);①
                return onMetadataPush(metadata);②
            }
        };
        return Mono.just(rs);
    }

    private Mono<Void> onMetadataPush(Map<String, Object> metadata) {
        var clientId = (String) metadata.get(Constants.CLIENT_ID_HEADER);
        var stringBuilder = new StringBuilder().append(System.lineSeparator(
));
        stringBuilder//
                .append(String.format("(%s) %s", clientId,
                        "----------------------------------"))//
                .append(System.lineSeparator());
        metadata.forEach((k, v) -> stringBuilder//
                .append(String.format("(%s) %s", clientId, k + '=' + v))//
                .append(System.lineSeparator()));
        log.info(stringBuilder.toString());
        return Mono.empty();
```

```
    }
}
```

① The service decodes incoming metadata into a `Map<K, V>`

② and then updates the local state accordingly.

The `Client` leverages the metadata facility to notify the service of its change of the locale with three different languages. Run both applications, and you should see the service logging new locale changes over a few seconds.

Metadata is a general-purpose mechanism that's meant to serve any of several use cases. What we communicate in the metadata payload and with what encoding we communicate it is entirely up to us. Later, we'll see that Spring leverages mime types and a composite metadata mechanism to make this particular nuisance short work.

We've covered all the message exchange patterns. We've covered concepts like metadata. We've also seen what we mean by the idea that RSocket applications are *requester* / *responder*-centric, not necessarily *client* / *server*-centric.

I could write this kind of code all day - it's just enough of an API to get something done with ease if I want to. Next, we'll see that things can and do become considerably more concise with Spring's help.

9.4. Bootiful RSocket

Everything introduced thus far works nicely all by its lonesome. Sure, everything ran in a Reactive Spring Boot-based application. But, I didn't *really* need Spring Boot to do what I did in those examples. I was mainly using Spring Boot to manage Maven dependencies and bean dependency injection. The code we examined could almost as quickly have existed in a raw `main` method. And precisely that's the point.

I would argue that the code is approachable. You could even begin to see how you would test the application. There are not many moving parts involved in making an RSocket requester or responder. It feels very similar to using a `java.net.(Server)Socket` to me. It's short and sweet - simple - because what you see is what you get. I did not introduce concepts for things that application developers need - like routing - because there is no core concept of routing. That has to be added later. I didn't introduce concepts like serialization because, unlike GRPC and HTTP, that's all entirely up to you. I didn't introduce concepts like security because that's really a convention you will need to figure out yourself. You have a *lot* more latitude than you'd typically have, but many more gaps to plug.

There are a ton of opportunities for something like Spring to provide value here. A *lot* is left to the user to handle themselves! Let's look at those opportunities. Let's see where Spring can simplify the code, and let's see where it can augment RSocket.

These things are not bugs in RSocket. Remember, the name is R..." Socket". It is *designed* to be a very flexible means of data exchange; to look and work much like whatever standard socket API you've ever used works. It's not designed to be a web framework or to offer a full-blown component model. Its only natural that there are some gaps that a framework like Spring can fill in for us. Let's revisit these basic examples and see what they look like when implemented in the Spring Framework and Spring Boot integrations.

First, we want something to handle the creation of the service machinery. I don't create my Apache Tomcat instance or Netty service, and I don't want to create my RSocket service. I want one that is centrally configured by the framework. One on top of which the rest of my application code naturally sits.

I want to leverage a familiar component model to craft RSocket handlers in the way that I've become accustomed to building HTTP endpoints in Spring MVC or Spring WebFlux. Spring provides a very convenient component model that builds upon the annotations you've probably used when working with any messaging types in Spring Framework itself. If you use Spring's WebSocket support in Spring Framework, then you have used these annotations.

I had to use the RSocket object directly, which implies a lot of resource initialization and acquisition ceremony that did much rather avoid. Spring Framework's `RSocketRequester` is a clean abstraction - it lets me easily map typical service interactions into the underlying RSocket.

As with the raw RSocket examples, we'll again depend on some common infrastructure. I'll still keep everything in a single module for ease of comprehension and management. We'll continue to depend on `BootifulProperties`. There's a fly in the ointment. Spring Boot makes some things - like the port assignment for the RSocket service - global.

This is where things are a little confusing, or at the very least asymmetrical. Spring Boot provides a property, `spring.rsocket.server.port`, that tells Spring Boot on which port it should expose an RSocket service. There is no default value for this, and so if you do not specify this, Spring Boot will not start an RSocket service. Setting the property has not only the effect of dictating the port for the service but of *enabling the service in the first place*. So, no property, no service. You need to *opt-in*.

This is very different than the familiar `server.port` property for HTTP-based services, which merely changes the port for an HTTP service that would run and start at port `8080` by default. When you have `spring-boot-starter-webflux` or `spring-boot-starter-web`, Spring Boot will start an HTTP service no matter what. No property, no problem. You need to *opt-out*.

Our examples will, as before, live in the same codebase and Maven module. We'll need some way to tell Spring Boot that our services should be installed as a service and assigned a network port, while our clients should not. We'll achieve this with some Spring profile trickery. We'll activate a Spring profile called `service`. Spring Boot will automatically try to load service-specific configuration like `application-service.properties` and the global configuration in `application.properties`. You'll see that I set the profile in the `main` method of each example. The configuration in `application.properties` is the same as before - it maps `bootiful.rsocket.port` to the auto-configured `BootifulProperties` configuration properties instance we'll then use to configure our RSocket clients. The `application-service.properties` file references the `bootiful.rsocket.port` property.

Let's look at these two configuration files. First, let's examine the global configuration.

```
bootiful.rsocket.port=8181
```

And then the service-specific configuration.

```
spring.rsocket.server.port=${bootiful.rsocket.port}
```

All of that explaining for what amounts to two tiny properties! Yikes! The good news is that this is about as tricky as things will get, and, even better, it won't affect you one bit in *your* clients and services because you'll do the right thing and put your code into separate Spring Boot projects, obviating the need for all of this funny business in the first place. *Right*?

9.4.1. Request/Response Example

Let's look at Spring Boot's RSocket support in action, in roughly the same progression as we did when we looked at raw RSocket. The first example is a simple request/response example. In the brave, new, and *bootiful* world of RSocket, you define RSocket endpoints with Spring's `@Controller` and `@MessageMapping`-centric component model. You might be familiar with this component model if you built WebSocket endpoints in Spring Framework 4.

Each of these examples, both the client and the service, have their own classes with their own `main` methods. I won't reprint any more of these beyond this first one. They're all equivalent. Just assume that they're required and that you can check the code online [https://github.com/reactive-spring-book/rsocket] for the full examples.

```
package rsb.rsocket.requestresponse.service;

import org.springframework.boot.SpringApplication;
import org.springframework.boot.autoconfigure.SpringBootApplication;

@SpringBootApplication
public class RequestResponseApplication {

    public static void main(String[] arrrImAPirate) {
        System.setProperty("spring.profiles.active", "service"); ①
        SpringApplication.run(RequestResponseApplication.class, arrrImAPirate);
    }

}
```

① This tells Spring Boot to load the configuration for the `service` profile, loading the service-specific confuguratino for the port.

Here's the substance of the service, a simple `@Controller`.

```
package rsb.rsocket.requestresponse.service;

import lombok.extern.log4j.Log4j2;
import org.springframework.messaging.handler.annotation.Headers;
import org.springframework.messaging.handler.annotation.MessageMapping;
import org.springframework.messaging.handler.annotation.Payload;
import org.springframework.stereotype.Controller;
import reactor.core.publisher.Mono;

import java.util.Map;

①
@Log4j2
@Controller
class GreetingController {

    ② ③
    @MessageMapping("greeting")
    Mono<String> greet(@Headers Map<String, Object> headers, ④
            @Payload String name⑤
    ) {
        headers.forEach((k, v) -> log.info(k + '=' + v));
        return Mono.just("Hello, " + name + "!");
    }

}
```

① This is indeed the exact same @Controller stereotype annotation from Spring's web tier component model

② We didn't see routes in the raw RSocket examples because they don't really exist as a first-class concept. The @MessageMapping annotation is a big improvement already. We'll explore this a bit more soon. Our RSocketRequester can address this endpoint handler with the greeting route.

③ This method returns a single value, Mono<String>, which we could've alternatively expressed as String. We could alternatively return a Flux<T> if we so desired.

④ We can inject any RSocket request headers using the @Headers annotation. This is optional.

⑤ And we can inject the request payload using the @Payload annotation.

Are you expecting a single `String`? Use a `String` or `Mono<String>`. The `@Payload` annotation is optional if there are no other ambiguous parameters.

Let's now look at the client. Our client code will be much more straightforward, thanks to the `RsocketRequester`. `RSocketRequester` instances are different from other clients you might have encountered (like the `WebClient`) because they are stateful: you connect them to the service of interest at the beginning of their lives, and that's it. All subsequent operations are assumed to be against the already connected client instance. If you want to talk to multiple hosts, then you need numerous `RSocketRequester` instances.

It's up to use to factory an `RSocketRequester` for each client application. The `RSocketRequester` is a client (a requester) that we can use to talk to our service (a responder). All the following examples will construct an `RSocketRequester` in the following fashion unless otherwise noted.

```
package rsb.rsocket.requestresponse.client;

import org.springframework.context.annotation.Bean;
import org.springframework.context.annotation.Configuration;
import org.springframework.messaging.rsocket.RSocketRequester;
import rsb.rsocket.BootifulProperties;

@Configuration
class ClientConfiguration {

    @Bean
    RSocketRequester rSocketRequester(BootifulProperties properties, ①
            RSocketRequester.Builder builder) {②
        return builder.connectTcp(properties.getRsocket().getHostname(),
                properties.getRsocket().getPort()).block();
    }

}
```

① You've seen `BootifulProperties` before - we use it to resolve the hostname and port to which our client should connect

② The `RSocketRequester.Builder` looks familiar! We used the

WebClient.Builder to factory a new HTTP client when we looked at building HTTP services.

The RSocketRequester is powerful because it's versatile; it boils down almost all the various message exchange patterns into some very simple formulations. It expects you to specify the route for the endpoint you want to invoke, provide data to be sent to the endpoint (typically a Publisher<T> of some sort), and to describe what data you expect to be returned to you as a result (usually a Flux<T> or Mono<T>). Here are some possible formulations.

Table 1. Message Exchange Pattern Formulations with the RSocketRequester

Pattern	In	Out
Request / Response	Mono<T>	Mono<T>
Stream	Mono<T>	Flux<T>
Fire and Forget	Publisher<T>	Mono<Void>
Channel	Flux<T>	Flux<T>

Our client pulls all of this together. You'll need a class with a main method, as before.

```
package rsb.rsocket.requestresponse.client;

import lombok.SneakyThrows;
import org.springframework.boot.SpringApplication;
import org.springframework.boot.autoconfigure.SpringBootApplication;

@SpringBootApplication
public class RequestResponseApplication {

    @SneakyThrows
    public static void main(String[] arrrImAPirate) {
        SpringApplication.run(RequestResponseApplication.class, arrrImAPirate);
        System.in.read();
    }

}
```

We won't reprint all the client `main` method classes as they're largely the same as the one we've just seen.

The core of this client class follows.

```java
package rsb.rsocket.requestresponse.client;

import lombok.RequiredArgsConstructor;
import lombok.extern.log4j.Log4j2;
import org.springframework.boot.context.event.ApplicationReadyEvent;
import org.springframework.context.ApplicationListener;
import org.springframework.messaging.rsocket.RSocketRequester;
import org.springframework.stereotype.Component;
import org.springframework.util.Assert;

@Log4j2
@Component
@RequiredArgsConstructor
class Client implements ApplicationListener<ApplicationReadyEvent> {

    private final RSocketRequester rSocketRequester;

    @Override
    public void onApplicationEvent(ApplicationReadyEvent are) {
        var rsocket = this.rSocketRequester.rsocket(); ①
        var availability = rsocket.availability();②
        Assert.isTrue(availability == 1.0,
                "the availability must be 1.0 in order to proceed!");
        log.info("the data mimeType is " + this.rSocketRequester.dataMimeType());③
        log.info("the metadata mimeType is " + this.rSocketRequester.metadataMimeType());
        this.rSocketRequester//
                .route("greeting")④
                .data("Reactive Spring")⑤
                .retrieveMono(String.class)⑥
                .subscribe(System.out::println);
    }

}
```

① You still can access the underlying RSocket.

② You can figure out if the service is available using the availability method, which returns 0.0 or 1.0

③ Encoding is handled for you out of the box. You can override it, but you probably won't need to. Use the `dataMimeType` and `metadataMimeType` methods to ascertain the mime type.

④ Every request starts by specifying a `route`...

⑤ ..and then the input data (a `T` or a `Publisher<T>`)...

⑥ ..and then the expected return data type. We can expect a `Mono<T>` using the `retrieveMono` method or a `Flux<T>` using the `retrieveFlux` method or a `Mono<Void>` for fire-and-forget exchanges using the special `send` method.

9.4.2. A Streaming (Channel) Example

The first example demonstrated one request, one response. Here's our ping-pong streaming example, where both requester and responder deal with an infinite `Flux<String>`. First, the service.

```java
package rsb.rsocket.channel.service;

import lombok.extern.log4j.Log4j2;
import org.springframework.messaging.handler.annotation.MessageMapping;
import org.springframework.messaging.handler.annotation.Payload;
import org.springframework.stereotype.Controller;
import reactor.core.publisher.Flux;

@Log4j2
@Controller
class PongController {

    @MessageMapping("pong")
    Flux<String> pong(@Payload Flux<String> ping) {
        return ping.map(request -> "pong").doOnNext(log::info);
    }

}
```

And then the client.

```java
package rsb.rsocket.channel.client;

import lombok.RequiredArgsConstructor;
import lombok.extern.log4j.Log4j2;
import org.springframework.boot.context.event.ApplicationReadyEvent;
import org.springframework.context.ApplicationListener;
import org.springframework.messaging.rsocket.RSocketRequester;
import org.springframework.stereotype.Component;
import reactor.core.publisher.Flux;

import java.time.Duration;

@Log4j2
@Component
@RequiredArgsConstructor
class Client implements ApplicationListener<ApplicationReadyEvent> {

    private final RSocketRequester rSocketRequester;

    @Override
    public void onApplicationEvent(ApplicationReadyEvent event) {
        var ping = Flux//
                .interval(Duration.ofSeconds(1))//
                .map(i -> "ping");
        rSocketRequester//
                .route("pong")//
                .data(ping)//
                .retrieveFlux(String.class)//
                .subscribe(log::info);
    }
}
```

See how much easier all of this is?

9.4.3. A Fire and Forget

One more time, with one more ever-so-slight variation: here's a fire-and-forget example.

```java
package rsb.rsocket.fireandforget.service;

import lombok.extern.log4j.Log4j2;
import org.springframework.messaging.handler.annotation.MessageMapping;
import org.springframework.stereotype.Controller;

@Log4j2
@Controller
class GreetingController {

    @MessageMapping("greeting")
    void greetName(String name) {
        log.info("new command sent to update the name '" + name + "'.");
    }

}
```

And then the client. The only thing different here, really, is that we're using the send method on the RSocketRequester.

```
package rsb.rsocket.fireandforget.client;

import lombok.RequiredArgsConstructor;
import lombok.extern.log4j.Log4j2;
import org.springframework.boot.context.event.ApplicationReadyEvent;
import org.springframework.context.ApplicationListener;
import org.springframework.messaging.rsocket.RSocketRequester;
import org.springframework.stereotype.Component;

@Log4j2
@Component
@RequiredArgsConstructor
class Client implements ApplicationListener<ApplicationReadyEvent> {

    private final RSocketRequester rSocketRequester;

    @Override
    public void onApplicationEvent(ApplicationReadyEvent applicationReadyEvent) {
        log.info("starting " + Client.class.getName() + '.');
        rSocketRequester.route("greeting").data("Reactive Spring").send().subscribe();
    }

}
```

9.4.4. Bidirectional Communication

Let's examine at a bidirectional example analogous in concept to the bidirectional example we looked at earlier. The client will connect to the service to consume a stream of `GreetingResponse` instances after the client sends a `GreetingRequest`, and only for so long as the client does not send a `ClientHealthState.STOPPED` value. It will also have the same simulation-like quality, with several random clients connecting to the service. That is where the similarities end, as we'll see.

Let's start with the service.

```
package rsb.rsocket.bidirectional.service;

import lombok.RequiredArgsConstructor;
import lombok.extern.log4j.Log4j2;
```

Chapter 9. RSocket

```java
import org.springframework.messaging.handler.annotation.MessageMapping;
import org.springframework.messaging.handler.annotation.Payload;
import org.springframework.messaging.rsocket.RSocketRequester;
import org.springframework.stereotype.Controller;
import reactor.core.publisher.Flux;
import reactor.core.publisher.Mono;
import rsb.rsocket.bidirectional.ClientHealthState;
import rsb.rsocket.bidirectional.GreetingRequest;
import rsb.rsocket.bidirectional.GreetingResponse;

import java.time.Duration;
import java.time.Instant;
import java.util.stream.Stream;

@Log4j2
@Controller
@RequiredArgsConstructor
class GreetingController {

    @MessageMapping("greetings")
    Flux<GreetingResponse> greetings(RSocketRequester client, ①
            @Payload GreetingRequest greetingRequest) {

        var clientHealthStateFlux = client//
                .route("health")②
                .data(Mono.empty())//
                .retrieveFlux(ClientHealthState.class)//
                .filter(chs -> chs.getState().equalsIgnoreCase
(ClientHealthState.STOPPED))③
                .doOnNext(chs -> log.info(chs.toString()));

        var replyPayloadFlux = Flux④
                .fromStream(Stream.generate(() -> new GreetingResponse(
"Hello, "
                        + greetingRequest.getName() + " @ " + Instant.now() +
"!")))
                .delayElements(
                        Duration.ofSeconds(Math.max(3, (long) (Math.random()
* 10))));

        return replyPayloadFlux//
                .takeUntilOther(clientHealthStateFlux)⑤
                .doOnNext(gr -> log.info(gr.toString()));
    }

}
```

① This `RSocketRequester` is connected to the client, the thing that's making the request of our service

② Initiate a request to the route `health` on the client

③ Filter each response from the client, preserving only the `ClientHealthState.STOPPED` instance

④ This stream is an infinite stream of `GreetingResponse` instances whose results are artificially staggered by some random delay

⑤ The controller provides a response only so long as we do *not* see a `ClientHealthState.STOPPED` value from the `clientHealthStateFlux` stream

The service is a relatively straightforward re-implementation of the service in our earlier example. The request comes in, and we ask the requesting client a question about its health. We've got the same key components: the same streams, the same logic, and operators.

The client supports fetching `GreetingResponse` instances, just as before. It's far fewer lines of code.

Chapter 9. RSocket

```java
package rsb.rsocket.bidirectional.client;

import lombok.RequiredArgsConstructor;
import lombok.extern.log4j.Log4j2;
import org.springframework.messaging.rsocket.RSocketRequester;
import reactor.core.publisher.Flux;
import rsb.rsocket.bidirectional.GreetingRequest;
import rsb.rsocket.bidirectional.GreetingResponse;

@Log4j2
@RequiredArgsConstructor
class Client {

    private final RSocketRequester rSocketRequester;

    private final String uid;

    Flux<GreetingResponse> getGreetings() { //
        return this.rSocketRequester//
                .route("greetings")//
                .data(new GreetingRequest("Client #" + this.uid))//
                .retrieveFlux(GreetingResponse.class);
    }

}
```

The client launcher launches instances of the `Client` class, also just as before.

```java
package rsb.rsocket.bidirectional.client;

import lombok.RequiredArgsConstructor;
import lombok.extern.slf4j.Slf4j;
import org.springframework.boot.context.event.ApplicationReadyEvent;
import org.springframework.context.ApplicationListener;
import org.springframework.messaging.rsocket.RSocketRequester;
import org.springframework.stereotype.Component;
import reactor.core.publisher.Flux;
import reactor.core.scheduler.Schedulers;
import rsb.rsocket.bidirectional.GreetingResponse;

import java.time.Duration;
import java.util.stream.IntStream;

@Slf4j
@Component
@RequiredArgsConstructor
class ClientLauncher implements ApplicationListener<ApplicationReadyEvent> {

    private final RSocketRequester rSocketRequester;

    private final int maxClients = 10;

    @Override
    public void onApplicationEvent(ApplicationReadyEvent event) {
        var nestedMax = Math.max(5, (int) (Math.random() * maxClients));
        log.info("launching " + nestedMax + " clients.");
        Flux.fromStream(IntStream.range(0, nestedMax).boxed())//
                .map(id -> new Client(this.rSocketRequester, Long.toString(id)))//
                .flatMap(client -> Flux.just(client)
                        .delayElements(Duration.ofSeconds((long) (30 * Math.random()))))//
                .flatMap(Client::getGreetings)⑤
                .subscribeOn(Schedulers.elastic())⑥
                .map(GreetingResponse::toString).subscribe(log::info);
    }

}
```

Things are a little more interesting in the client, even if the necessary arrangement of having a `ClientLauncher` launch some clients to talk to the service is basically the same. What we haven't seen yet is how the client produces the `ClientHealthState` stream. There are two parts involved in this. First, the `HealthController`:

```java
package rsb.rsocket.bidirectional.client;

import org.springframework.messaging.handler.annotation.MessageMapping;
import org.springframework.stereotype.Controller;
import reactor.core.publisher.Flux;
import rsb.rsocket.bidirectional.ClientHealthState;

import java.time.Duration;
import java.util.Date;
import java.util.stream.Stream;

import static rsb.rsocket.bidirectional.ClientHealthState.STARTED;
import static rsb.rsocket.bidirectional.ClientHealthState.STOPPED;

@Controller
class HealthController {

    @MessageMapping("health")
    Flux<ClientHealthState> health() {
        var start = new Date().getTime();
        var delayInSeconds = ((long) (Math.random() * 30)) * 1000;
        return Flux//
                .fromStream(Stream//
                        .generate(() -> {
                            var now = new Date().getTime();
                            var stop = ((start + delayInSeconds) < now)
                                    && Math.random() > .8;
                            return new ClientHealthState(stop ? STOPPED : STARTED);
                        }))//
                .delayElements(Duration.ofSeconds(5));
    }

}
```

Now we inject that `HealthController` and configure the `RSocketRequester` to expose those endpoints.

```java
package rsb.rsocket.bidirectional.client;

import org.springframework.context.annotation.Bean;
import org.springframework.context.annotation.Configuration;
import org.springframework.messaging.rsocket.ClientRSocketFactoryConfigurer;
import org.springframework.messaging.rsocket.RSocketRequester;
import org.springframework.messaging.rsocket.RSocketStrategies;
import org.springframework.messaging.rsocket.annotation.support.RSocketMessageHandler;
import rsb.rsocket.BootifulProperties;

@Configuration
class ClientConfiguration {

    ①
    @Bean
    ClientRSocketFactoryConfigurer clientRSocketFactoryConfigurer(
            HealthController healthController, RSocketStrategies strategies) {
        return RSocketMessageHandler.clientResponder(strategies, healthController);
    }

    @Bean
    RSocketRequester rSocketRequester(ClientRSocketFactoryConfigurer configurer,
            RSocketRequester.Builder builder, BootifulProperties properties) {

        return builder//
                .rsocketFactory(configurer)②
                .connectTcp(properties.getRsocket().getHostname(),
                        properties.getRsocket().getPort())//
                .block();
    }

}
```

① The `ClientRSocketFactoryConfigurer` depends upon the just defined `HealthController` and mounts it as a responder accessible to any requester.

② The `rsocketFactory` method allows us to customize the `RSocketRequester` to expose the `HealthController`. When the greetings service uses the

RSocketRequester of the incoming request to ask the client about its health, it calls the health endpoint against that RSocketRequester. It is this wiring that makes that work.

There are fewer code lines in this version and fewer things to worry about, so I consider it a significant improvement over the first, bidirectional, and raw RSocket example. The only thing of note is that last bit - where we expose the HealthController by wiring it up to the RSocketRequester. It took a few minutes for me to really understand what was happening. It feels a bit odd, doesn't it? Imagine having a Spring MVC controller tied to, or made available from, a RestTemplate! Odd! But it makes more sense when you consider other @MessageMapping implementations like WebSockets. It also makes more sense if you think about how actual sockets work. Either way, once I wrapped my head around it, I loved it. (I now wish that I could somehow expose a bidirectional HTTP endpoint with a RestTemplate.)

9.4.5. Setup Connections

Spring's component model provides special handling for setup logic to run when the connection is first established. The setup handlers are invoked whenever metadata is pushed and right after the connection is first created. You can use these setup handlers to establish any per-connection setup, in much the same way as we might've in the accept(ConnectionSetupPayload connectionSetupPayload, RSocket rSocket) method in the raw RSocket programming model.

> just remember: a new connection does *not* correspond to one new user! Connections are often shared by many users.

```java
package rsb.rsocket.setup.service;

import lombok.extern.log4j.Log4j2;
import org.springframework.messaging.handler.annotation.Headers;
import org.springframework.messaging.handler.annotation.Payload;
import org.springframework.messaging.rsocket.annotation.ConnectMapping;
import org.springframework.stereotype.Controller;

import java.util.Map;

@Log4j2
@Controller
class SetupController {

    @ConnectMapping("setup") ①
    public void setup(@Payload String setupPayload,
            @Headers Map<String, Object> headers) {②
        log.info("setup payload: " + setupPayload);
        headers.forEach((k, v) -> log.info(k + '=' + v));
    }

}
```

① Your setup handlers can have routes. Or not. It's worth noting that this same handler handles both the initial setup frame and all subsequent metadata push frames.

② They can also have headers and payloads, as before.

Our client does most of the work; constructing the `RSocketRequester` is enough to exercise the setup handler we just examined.

```java
package rsb.rsocket.setup.client;

import org.springframework.context.annotation.Bean;
import org.springframework.context.annotation.Configuration;
import org.springframework.messaging.rsocket.RSocketRequester;
import rsb.rsocket.BootifulProperties;

@Configuration
class ClientConfiguration {

    @Bean
    RSocketRequester rSocketRequester(BootifulProperties properties,
            RSocketRequester.Builder builder) {
        return builder//
                .setupData("setup data!")①
                .setupRoute("setup")②
                .connectTcp(properties.getRsocket().getHostname(),
                        properties.getRsocket().getPort())③
                .block();
    }

}
```

① You can specify data to be sent for the setp handler…

② And you can specify which route to invoke (optional)…

③ And then we finally address the client, as before

9.4.6. Routing

We've now seen the routing mechanism in play. The routing mechanism is general purpose and can even handle route variables, akin to the path variables of a Spring MVC or a Spring WebFlux HTTP URI. It makes it seem a little weird that I can only describe raw RSocket endpoints to the granularity of a host and port, and no further. In all of the examples we looked at earlier, we wrote the code with only one function for each service. The client connects, and there's only one response possible. Beyond that, we would have had to write a switch statement to dereference the incoming parameter and route it to a particular handler, in our own proprietary way. We would also have had to encode our own routing concept - is it a `String`, or is it a number? A URL? It'd be entirely up to us.

Routing in Spring is robust. It supports flat routes as well as parameterized routes.

Let's examine a controller with some routes in it.

```java
package rsb.rsocket.routing.service;

import org.springframework.messaging.handler.annotation.DestinationVariable;
import org.springframework.messaging.handler.annotation.MessageMapping;
import org.springframework.stereotype.Controller;
import reactor.core.publisher.Flux;
import reactor.core.publisher.Mono;
import rsb.rsocket.routing.Customer;

import java.util.Map;

①
@Controller
class RoutingController {

    private final Map<Integer, Customer> customers = Map.of(1, new Customer(1, "Zhen"), 2,
            new Customer(2, "Zhouyue"));

    @MessageMapping("customers")
    ②
    Flux<Customer> all() {
        return Flux.fromStream(this.customers.values().stream());
    }

    @MessageMapping("customers.{id}")
    ③
    Mono<Customer> byId(@DestinationVariable Integer id) {
        return Mono.justOrEmpty(this.customers.get(id));
    }

}
```

① The `RoutingController` exposes two endpoints operating on `Customer` data which - for ease of demonstration - I've hardcoded into a `Map`. The `Customer` type is a simple DTO in a common ancestor package of both the `client` and `service` package.

② `customers` returns all `Customer` data

③ `customers.{id}` returns the customer whose ID matches whatever is specified for the `DestinationVariable`. Spring intelligently handles conversion of the variable, as you would expect.

9.4.7. Encoding

In the last example, I explained that we're transmitting a DTO - `Customer` - from the client to the service. This just *works* because by default Spring's RSocket support uses CBOR to encode data. This aspect of Spring's RSocket support, like everything in Spring, is configurable.

In raw RSocket, serialization is left entirely to the user. In the raw examples we've looked at, it's mostly Strings. There's no concept of mime types or content-negotiation, or anything. This is doubly troublesome since serialization is a concern for both the data and the metadata, which we'll look at next.

Let's suppose we wanted to encode our data (for whatever reason) using Jackson and JSON instead of CBOR. This example has two POJOs - `GreetingRequest` and `GreetingResponse` - that are uninteresting. Getters, setters, etc. No encoding-specific concerns. We'll use the `RSocketStrategiesCustomizer` to override the default encoding and decoding in our RSocket service.

```java
package rsb.rsocket.encoding.service;

import org.springframework.boot.rsocket.messaging.RSocketStrategiesCustomizer;
import org.springframework.context.annotation.Bean;
import org.springframework.context.annotation.Configuration;
import org.springframework.core.Ordered;
import org.springframework.core.annotation.Order;
import org.springframework.http.codec.json.Jackson2JsonDecoder;
import org.springframework.http.codec.json.Jackson2JsonEncoder;

@Configuration
class ServiceConfiguration {

    @Bean
    @Order(Ordered.HIGHEST_PRECEDENCE)
    ①
    RSocketStrategiesCustomizer rSocketStrategiesCustomizer() { ②
        return strategies -> strategies //
                .decoder(new Jackson2JsonDecoder()) ③
                .encoder(new Jackson2JsonEncoder());
    }

}
```

① Our bean must be the last to override the configuration

② The `RSocketStrategiesCustomizer` callback interface gives you a chance to participate in the customization of the `RSocketStrategies.Builder` to customize codecs for an RSocket client or service.

③ There are several pre-provided encoders and decoders. We'll use the convenient `Jackson2Json(De|En)coder` variants.

Nothing else needs to change.

Here's the `GreetingController` as an example, but it's virtually identical to what we've seen before.

Chapter 9. RSocket

```java
package rsb.rsocket.encoding.service;

import lombok.extern.log4j.Log4j2;
import org.springframework.messaging.handler.annotation.Headers;
import org.springframework.messaging.handler.annotation.MessageMapping;
import org.springframework.messaging.handler.annotation.Payload;
import org.springframework.stereotype.Controller;
import reactor.core.publisher.Mono;
import rsb.rsocket.encoding.GreetingRequest;
import rsb.rsocket.encoding.GreetingResponse;

import java.util.Map;

@Log4j2
@Controller
class GreetingController {

    @MessageMapping("greetings")
    Mono<GreetingResponse> greet(@Payload GreetingRequest request,
            @Headers Map<String, Object> headers) {
        headers.forEach((k, v) -> log.info(k + '=' + v));
        return Mono.just(new GreetingResponse("Hello, " + request.getName() + "!"));
    }

}
```

The client-side is virtually the same: configure the `RSocketStrategiesCustomizer` and the `RSocketRequester`.

```java
package rsb.rsocket.encoding.client;

import org.springframework.boot.rsocket.messaging.RSocketStrategiesCustomizer;
import org.springframework.context.annotation.Bean;
import org.springframework.context.annotation.Configuration;
import org.springframework.core.Ordered;
import org.springframework.core.annotation.Order;
import org.springframework.http.codec.json.Jackson2JsonDecoder;
import org.springframework.http.codec.json.Jackson2JsonEncoder;
import org.springframework.messaging.rsocket.RSocketRequester;
import rsb.rsocket.BootifulProperties;

@Configuration
class ClientConfiguration {

    ①
    @Bean
    @Order(Ordered.HIGHEST_PRECEDENCE)
    RSocketStrategiesCustomizer rSocketStrategiesCustomizer() {
        return strategies -> strategies.decoder(new Jackson2JsonDecoder())
                .encoder(new Jackson2JsonEncoder());
    }

    @Bean
    RSocketRequester rSocketRequester(BootifulProperties properties,
            RSocketRequester.Builder builder) {
        return builder//
                .connectTcp(properties.getRsocket().getHostname(),
                        properties.getRsocket().getPort()) //
                .block();
    }

}
```

Then: use the `RSocketRequester` in the `Client`. Again, no changes!

```java
package rsb.rsocket.encoding.client;

import lombok.RequiredArgsConstructor;
import lombok.extern.log4j.Log4j2;
import org.springframework.boot.context.event.ApplicationReadyEvent;
import org.springframework.context.ApplicationListener;
import org.springframework.messaging.rsocket.RSocketRequester;
import org.springframework.stereotype.Component;
import rsb.rsocket.bidirectional.GreetingRequest;
import rsb.rsocket.encoding.GreetingResponse;

@Log4j2
@Component
@RequiredArgsConstructor
class Client implements ApplicationListener<ApplicationReadyEvent> {

    private final RSocketRequester rSocketRequester;

    @Override
    public void onApplicationEvent(ApplicationReadyEvent event) {
        this.rSocketRequester//
                .route("greetings")//
                .data(new GreetingRequest("Spring fans"))//
                .retrieveMono(GreetingResponse.class)//
                .subscribe(log::info);
    }
}
```

Pretty convenient, eh?

9.4.8. Metadata

In the setup example, in the controller, Spring injected headers coming to the controller from the client, but we didn't really customize or enrich the headers. Metadata is a natural place to encode out-of-band information about the message. You could use this to encode trace headers, security credentials, client IDs, checksums, sequence numbers, etc. Both the initial setup (connection) handlers and the regular handler endpoints support metadata.

Let's look at a controller with a @ConnectMapping-annotated handler to respond to newly connected clients, and that has a `@MessageMapping`-annotated handler to respond to incoming requests.

```java
package rsb.rsocket.metadata.service;

import lombok.RequiredArgsConstructor;
import lombok.extern.log4j.Log4j2;
import org.springframework.messaging.handler.annotation.Header;
import org.springframework.messaging.handler.annotation.Headers;
import org.springframework.messaging.handler.annotation.MessageMapping;
import org.springframework.messaging.rsocket.annotation.ConnectMapping;
import org.springframework.stereotype.Controller;
import reactor.core.publisher.Mono;
import rsb.rsocket.metadata.Constants;

import java.util.Map;

@Log4j2
@Controller
@RequiredArgsConstructor
class MetadataController {

    @ConnectMapping
    ①
    Mono<Void> setup(@Headers Map<String, Object> metadata) {
        log.info("## setup");
        return enumerate(metadata);
    }

    @MessageMapping("message")
    ②
    Mono<Void> message(@Header(Constants.CLIENT_ID_HEADER) String clientId,
            @Headers Map<String, Object> metadata) {
        log.info("## message for " + Constants.CLIENT_ID_HEADER + ' ' +
clientId);
        return enumerate(metadata);
    }

    private Mono<Void> enumerate(Map<String, Object> headers) {
        headers.forEach((header, value) -> log.info(header + ':' + value));
        return Mono.empty();
    }

}
```

① Setup requests can communicate headers.

② Ditto for regular requests. In this instance, I've extracted also extracted out an individual header to be passed as a specific parameter.

It all just works as you'd expect. Things get more interesting when building the client.

Spring supports content-negotiation and mime types. You can even specify the default mime type to assume (and we looked earlier at how to specify encoders and decoders) for metadata and data. If you do, you'll see the changed mime type reflected in the headers.

```
package rsb.rsocket.metadata.client;

import org.springframework.context.annotation.Bean;
import org.springframework.context.annotation.Configuration;
import org.springframework.messaging.rsocket.RSocketRequester;
import org.springframework.util.MimeTypeUtils;
import rsb.rsocket.BootifulProperties;

@Configuration
class ClientConfiguration {

    @Bean
    RSocketRequester rsocketRequester(BootifulProperties properties,
            RSocketRequester.Builder builder) {
        return builder//
                .dataMimeType(MimeTypeUtils.APPLICATION_JSON)①
                .connectTcp(properties.getRsocket().getHostname(),
                        properties.getRsocket().getPort())//
                .block();
    }

}
```

① We will encode the data using the `application/json` mime type.

It may be a bit odd, at first, that header values actually map to mime types. The *key* for a header is derived from a mime type. We'll encode two custom headers in this example, so I've extracted the relevant constant `String` values into a separate class, `Constants`.

```java
package rsb.rsocket.metadata;

import org.springframework.util.MimeType;

public class Constants {

    ①
    public static final String CLIENT_ID_HEADER = "client-id";

    public static final String CLIENT_ID_VALUE = "messaging/x.bootiful."
            + CLIENT_ID_HEADER;

    public static final MimeType CLIENT_ID = MimeType.valueOf(
CLIENT_ID_VALUE);

    ②
    public static final String LANG_HEADER = "lang";

    public static final String LANG_VALUE = "messaging/x.bootiful." +
LANG_HEADER;

    public static final MimeType LANG = MimeType.valueOf(LANG_VALUE);

}
```

① The first header is called `client-id`. I've then derived a mime type as both a String literal and a `MimeType` instance

② The second header is called `lang`. I've then derived a mime type as both a String literal and a `MimeType` instance.

The client sends two header values and so invokes the `metadata` method two consecutive times. The `metadata` signature takes a value and *then* a `MimeType`. We'll send in a `MimeType` from the client, but when we print out the headers in the controller, we'll see the header key is `client-id`, not the full-blown mime-type. The same mapping happens for the other header and its mime type.

It is up to us to teach Spring how to make that mapping. We do so with an `RSocketStrategiesCustomizer` in the service.

Chapter 9. RSocket

```java
package rsb.rsocket.metadata.service;

import org.springframework.boot.rsocket.messaging.RSocketStrategiesCustomizer;
import org.springframework.context.annotation.Bean;
import org.springframework.context.annotation.Configuration;
import org.springframework.core.codec.StringDecoder;
import rsb.rsocket.metadata.Constants;

@Configuration
class ServiceConfiguration {

    @Bean
    RSocketStrategiesCustomizer rSocketStrategiesCustomizer() {
        return strategies -> strategies//
                .metadataExtractorRegistry(registry -> {
                    ①
                    registry.metadataToExtract(Constants.CLIENT_ID, String.class,
                            Constants.CLIENT_ID_HEADER);
                    registry.metadataToExtract(Constants.LANG, String.class,
                            Constants.LANG_HEADER);
                })//
                .decoders(decoders -> decoders.add(StringDecoder.allMimeTypes()));
    }

}
```

① Given a mime type of `messaging/x.bootiful.client-id`, and a target type of `java.lang.String`, this metadta extractor should map to `client-id`.

The metadata-to-headers mechanism we've been looking at is supported in Spring, and is an extension to the core RSocket protocol. This arrangement is a little more work than you'd have to do for HTTP headers, *but* it does speak to the versatility of RSocket's API. Remember, in the raw RSocket APIs, metadata is just a blob of bytes with which we can do whatever we want. We can *still* do that if we wish to; just get ahold of the raw RSocket instance and do as you will.

```java
package rsb.rsocket.metadata.client;

import lombok.RequiredArgsConstructor;
import lombok.extern.log4j.Log4j2;
import org.springframework.boot.context.event.ApplicationReadyEvent;
import org.springframework.context.ApplicationListener;
import org.springframework.messaging.rsocket.RSocketRequester;
import org.springframework.stereotype.Component;
import reactor.core.publisher.Mono;
import rsb.rsocket.metadata.Constants;

import java.util.Locale;
import java.util.UUID;

@Log4j2
@Component
@RequiredArgsConstructor
class Client implements ApplicationListener<ApplicationReadyEvent> {

    private final RSocketRequester rSocketRequester;

    @Override
    public void onApplicationEvent(ApplicationReadyEvent event) {

        Mono<Void> one = this.rSocketRequester①
                .route("message")//
                .metadata(UUID.randomUUID().toString(), Constants.CLIENT_ID)//
                .metadata(Locale.CHINESE.getLanguage(), Constants.LANG)//
                .send();

        Mono<Void> two = this.rSocketRequester②
                .route("message")//
                .metadata(metadataSpec -> {
                    metadataSpec.metadata(UUID.randomUUID().toString(),
                            Constants.CLIENT_ID);//
                    metadataSpec.metadata(Locale.JAPANESE.getLanguage(),
Constants.LANG);//
                })//
                .send();

        one.then(two).subscribe();
    }

}
```

① Send zero or more headers by successively invoking the `metadata(Object, MimeType)` method

② Alternatively, we can send zero or more headers by invoking the `metadata` method against the `RSocketRequester.MetadataSpec` instance given to us in the `metadata` overload.

If we run the example, we'll see our custom headers and some handy headers provided out of the box:

- `rsocketRequester`: this is a reference, primarily, to the client RSocket (wrapped in an RSocketRequester)
- `lookupDestination`: the route used to address this handler
- `rsocketFrameType`: what kind of message exchange does this message represent? The call to `message` is a fire-and-forget exchange, so the frame type's value is `REQUEST_FNF`.
- `contentType`: what content type is being used to encode the data? We customized the content type when we created the RSocketRequester to see `application/json` here.
- `dataBufferFactory`: this is an instance of a `DataBufferFactory` that we can use to, at a much lower level, create custom `DataBuffer` instances. Hopefully, you won't need to do this, but it's nice to know that you can.

9.4.9. Error Handling

Error handling felt a bit slapdash when using the raw RSocket APIs. I'd prefer to centralize as much of that as possible. I don't want to have to worry about that in every controller. The whole point of having a framework is a central place in which to effect change! Why would error handling be any different? Thankfully Spring has us covered here.

The only reason I could imagine that you'd want to write all that ceremonial code directly is to learn about how you would and exert more control over the various resources' configuration. Well, we've learned how. So let's not do it again if we can help it. As to the last requirement of control - this is Spring: there is *always* a way to customize the relevant pieces of application infrastructure through callback interfaces. There are interfaces like `RSocketServerCustomzier`, `RSocktStrategiesCustomizer`, and more.

There are many ways to handle errors within Reactor itself. We've already looked at some error-handling patterns on any reactive stream, be it a network stream backed `Publisher<T>` or not. All I want is to centralize error handling, and Spring's `@MessageExceptionHandler` is ideally suited to the task.

```java
package rsb.rsocket.errors.service;

import lombok.extern.log4j.Log4j2;
import org.springframework.messaging.handler.annotation.MessageExceptionHandler;
import org.springframework.messaging.handler.annotation.MessageMapping;
import org.springframework.stereotype.Controller;
import reactor.core.publisher.Flux;
import reactor.core.publisher.Mono;

import java.time.Duration;
import java.util.stream.Stream;

@Log4j2
@Controller
class ErrorController {

    @MessageMapping("greetings")
    Flux<String> greet(String name) { ①
        return Flux//
                .fromStream(Stream.generate(() -> "hello " + name + "!"))//
                .flatMap(message -> {
                    if (Math.random() >= .5) {
                        return Mono.error(new IllegalArgumentException(
"Ooops!"));
                    } //
                    else {
                        return Mono.just(message);
                    }
                })//
                .delayElements(Duration.ofSeconds(1));
    }

    @MessageExceptionHandler ②
    void exception(Exception exception) {
        log.error("the exception is " + exception.getMessage());
    }

}
```

① This controller handler method returns a never-ending stream of results that has a 50% chance of failing.

② A `@MessageExceptionHandler`-annotated method in the controller will be given a chance to handle the error based on the exception handler method's signature. You can narrow the parameter types to handle more specific exceptions.

The client is like any other client. The only mildly amusing thing is that we're using the doOnError operator (which is a part of Reactor and thus any Mono<T> or Flux<T> will have it) to log errors, too.

```java
package rsb.rsocket.errors.client;

import lombok.RequiredArgsConstructor;
import lombok.extern.log4j.Log4j2;
import org.springframework.boot.context.event.ApplicationReadyEvent;
import org.springframework.context.ApplicationListener;
import org.springframework.messaging.rsocket.RSocketRequester;
import org.springframework.stereotype.Component;

@Log4j2
@Component
@RequiredArgsConstructor
class Client implements ApplicationListener<ApplicationReadyEvent> {

    private final RSocketRequester rSocketRequester;

    @Override
    public void onApplicationEvent(ApplicationReadyEvent event) {
        this.rSocketRequester//
                .route("greetings")//
                .data("Spring Fans")//
                .retrieveFlux(String.class)//
                .doOnError(log::error)//
                .subscribe(log::info);
    }
}
```

9.5. Security

Security is a non-trivial concern that - even if one were so inclined - one should *not* have to hand roll. Spring Security is well supported in the Spring web stack, but I was not looking forward to what this chapter would end up looking like when securing RSocket endpoints because when I first started this book, there was no support! I am so glad, then, that the Spring

Security team did *not* disappoint. By the time I got to writing this chapter, there was already outstanding support for two modes for authentication: SIMPLE and JWT-based authentication.

We'll look at SIMPLE-based authentication, but it's not much more challenging to make JWT-based authentication work. You need to understand that Spring Security addresses two orthogonal concerns: authentication (who is making a given request) and authorization (what permissions, or rights, or authorities, or entitlements does a given client have to in a system).

Let's revisit the familiar `GreetingsController`. We will restrict access to the endpoint and use the current authenticated user principal information to inform the response's message.

```java
package rsb.rsocket.security.service;

import org.springframework.messaging.handler.annotation.MessageMapping;
import org.springframework.security.core.annotation.AuthenticationPrincipal;
import org.springframework.security.core.userdetails.UserDetails;
import org.springframework.stereotype.Controller;
import reactor.core.publisher.Flux;
import reactor.core.publisher.Mono;
import rsb.rsocket.security.GreetingRequest;
import rsb.rsocket.security.GreetingResponse;

import java.time.Duration;
import java.util.stream.Stream;

@Controller
class GreetingsController {

    @MessageMapping("greetings")
    Flux<GreetingResponse> greet(@AuthenticationPrincipal Mono<UserDetails> user) {  ①
        return user//
                .map(UserDetails::getUsername)//
                .map(GreetingRequest::new)//
                .flatMapMany(this::greet);
    }

    private Flux<GreetingResponse> greet(GreetingRequest request) {
        return Flux
                .fromStream(Stream.generate(
                        () -> new GreetingResponse("Hello, " + request.getName() + "!")))
                .delayElements(Duration.ofSeconds(1));
    }

}
```

① This `@AuthenticationPrincipal` annotation instructs Spring Security to inject the current, validly authenticated user as a parameter. In this case, we're not expecting any payload. We don't care about the payload. There shouldn't be a payload. We want the current user, with whose username we'll generate an infinite stream of greetings.

The controller is fairly run of the mill. Let's look at the security-specific configuration required to make it all work.

```java
package rsb.rsocket.security.service;

import org.springframework.context.annotation.Bean;
import org.springframework.context.annotation.Configuration;
import org.springframework.messaging.rsocket.RSocketStrategies;
import org.springframework.messaging.rsocket.annotation.support.RSocketMessageHandler;
import org.springframework.security.config.Customizer;
import org.springframework.security.config.annotation.rsocket.RSocketSecurity;
import org.springframework.security.core.userdetails.MapReactiveUserDetailsService;
import org.springframework.security.core.userdetails.User;
import org.springframework.security.messaging.handler.invocation.reactive.AuthenticationPrincipalArgumentResolver;
import org.springframework.security.rsocket.core.PayloadSocketAcceptorInterceptor;

@Configuration
class SecurityConfiguration {

    ①
    @Bean
    MapReactiveUserDetailsService authentication() {
        return new MapReactiveUserDetailsService(
                User.withDefaultPasswordEncoder().username("rwinch").password("pw")
                        .roles("ADMIN", "USER").build(),
                User.withDefaultPasswordEncoder().username("jlong").password("pw")
                        .roles("USER").build());
    }

    ②
    @Bean
    PayloadSocketAcceptorInterceptor authorization(RSocketSecurity security) {
        return security//
                .simpleAuthentication(Customizer.withDefaults())//
                .build();
    }

    ③
    @Bean
```

```
    RSocketMessageHandler rSocketMessageHandler(RSocketStrategies strategies)
{
        var mh = new RSocketMessageHandler();
        mh.getArgumentResolverConfigurer()
                .addCustomResolver(new
AuthenticationPrincipalArgumentResolver());
        mh.setRSocketStrategies(strategies);
        return mh;
    }

}
```

① For authentication, I've configured an in-memory repository of usernames and passwords here using an implementation of the `ReactiveUserDetailsService` with two hardcoded users (jlong and rwinch). Don't do this, or you'll make Spring Security lead Rob Winch. Use something like OAuth.

② To address authorization, I've configured a `PayloadSocketAcceptorInterceptor` to intercept RSocket requests and provide an authorization filter using SIMPLE authentication.

③ By default, Spring Security doesn't know what to do when it sees the `@AuthenticationPrincipal` annotation in an RSocket controller, so we enable that functionality by plugging in an `RSocketMessageHandler`.

Run the service, and now let's look at the client that has to authenticate with the service. Authentication is just another kind of metadata, so it requires a `MimeType` and some form of credential.

When is the token and the credential required? Remember, RSocket connections are multiplexed. There's no reason you couldn't handle multiple client requests with the same connection. So, should the authentication be done once per connection, at setup time? Or should it be done per-transaction? Or both? It is an acceptable approach to authenticate on connection setup if you don't plan on sharing the connection for multiple users. You might also want to provide the authentication for each request. We'll look at both strategies.

```
    package rsb.rsocket.security.client;
```

Chapter 9. RSocket

```java
import io.rsocket.metadata.WellKnownMimeType;
import lombok.extern.log4j.Log4j2;
import org.springframework.boot.context.event.ApplicationReadyEvent;
import org.springframework.boot.rsocket.messaging.RSocketStrategiesCustomizer;
import org.springframework.context.ApplicationListener;
import org.springframework.context.annotation.Bean;
import org.springframework.context.annotation.Configuration;
import org.springframework.messaging.rsocket.RSocketRequester;
import org.springframework.security.rsocket.metadata.SimpleAuthenticationEncoder;
import org.springframework.security.rsocket.metadata.UsernamePasswordMetadata;
import org.springframework.stereotype.Component;
import org.springframework.util.MimeType;
import org.springframework.util.MimeTypeUtils;
import reactor.core.publisher.Mono;
import rsb.rsocket.BootifulProperties;
import rsb.rsocket.security.GreetingResponse;

@Log4j2
@Configuration
class ClientConfiguration {

    ①
    private final MimeType mimeType = MimeTypeUtils
            .parseMimeType(WellKnownMimeType.MESSAGE_RSOCKET_AUTHENTICATION.getString());

    private final UsernamePasswordMetadata credentials = new UsernamePasswordMetadata(
            "jlong", "pw");

    ②
    @Bean
    RSocketStrategiesCustomizer rSocketStrategiesCustomizer() {
        return strategies -> strategies.encoder(new SimpleAuthenticationEncoder());
    }

    @Bean
    RSocketRequester rSocketRequester(BootifulProperties properties,
            RSocketRequester.Builder builder) {
        return builder//
                .setupMetadata(this.credentials, this.mimeType) ③
                .connectTcp(properties.getRsocket().getHostname(),
                        properties.getRsocket().getPort())
```

```java
                .block();
    }

    @Bean
    ApplicationListener<ApplicationReadyEvent> ready(RSocketRequester greetings) {
        return args -> greetings//
                .route("greetings")//
                .metadata(this.credentials, this.mimeType)④
                .data(Mono.empty())//
                .retrieveFlux(GreetingResponse.class)//
                .subscribe(gr -> log.info("secured response: " + gr.toString()));
    }
}
```

① I've defined the authentication mime type and credential here as my client class variables. Naturally, you're going to derive a username and password in any other way. No matter what you do, *don't* hardcode the username and password in code as I have! This is a demo! Have I mentioned that you run the distinct risk of making Spring Security lead Rob Winch (@rob_winch) [https://twitter.com/rob_winch] sad? Don't do it, people! 2020 is sad enough already!

② We're going to need to tell RSocket about the kind of encoding required to send SIMPLE authentication metadata correctly, so we register a pre-provided `RSocketStrategiesCustomizer` implementation from Spring Security

③ If we want to configure authentication on connection setup, we can then do that when we build the `RSocketRequester`. Obviously, this is optional. You can also do it per request.

④ Here's what it looks like when we provide authentication per request, which I imagine will be your typical use-case.

And we're done! Now, if your client tries to make a request without that authentication information, it'll fail. It's one thing to have a nifty protocol, but Spring provides an end-to-end integration with RSocket, from fundamental interactions to production-minded concerns like security. I love it. And, best of all, I can go to production with it!

9.6. Spring Integration

Spring Integration, a module in the Spring ecosystem, supports *enterprise application interation* (EAI). It helps you build data flow pipelines that help adapt data - events or messages - from the real world and work with them in a unified fashion as `Message<T>` instances. A `Message<T>` has a payload and headers that describe the payload. Spring Integration brings to life enterprise application integration patterns, as defined in Gregor Hohpe and Bobby Woolf's landmark work *Enterprise Integration Patterns: Designing, Building, and Deploying Messaging Solutions 1st Edition* [https://www.amazon.com/o/asin/0321200683/ref=nosim/enterpriseint-20].

There are many patterns in the book, and we don't have nearly enough time to explain them or define their particular semantics in Spring Integration. (Bobby and Gregor wrote a thrilling 1000+ page book to explain the latter, and I, and many others, have already written books on the topic of Spring Integration. Suffice it to say that Spring Integration works by defining how messages flow from one component to another in a system. Components are specialized processors that act on each incoming message and then emit each message outbound for something downstream. Message in, message out. The output of one component is the input to another.

Spring Integration flows are event-driven. Something - an event or a message - kicks off the pipeline. An interaction flow ultimately terminates somewhere. So messages must enter the flow and must exit the flow. Where do messages arrive from? And go to? Why, some other flow, service, or system entirely, of course! The *real world*, perhaps?

Adapters are the simplest way to connect Spring Integration flows to the outside world. An inbound adapter is responsible for monitoring an external system's state and - on perceiving an event - turning it into a `Message<T>`, which then feeds into a Spring Integration flow as a `Message<T>`. An outbound adapter is responsible for taking a Spring `Message<T>` and writing it to an external system. There are adapters for any number of disparate systems and services, including file systems, e-mail, FTP, SFTP, Apache Kafka, Twitter, databases, TCP sockets, RabbitMQ, MQTT, etc. If you don't see something you'd like, it's straightforward to build your own.

Gateways are like adapters except that they're bidirectional, where adapters are unidirectional components. An outbound gateway sends a `Message<T>` to an external system and then processes whatever reply the external system might produce. An inbound gateway acts as the thing to which external messages are sent, and is then responsible for producing a reply. I see messages making a U-shape when I imagine these components in action.

Components connect to each other through **channels** (Spring Framework `MessageChannel` instances). You may have already seen `MessageChannel` instances in Spring. They're in Spring Framework now but started off into Spring Integration. Spring Integration has since rebased on top of the Spring Framework types.

The connection may be implicit (in which case Spring Integration connects one component with another) or explicit - you plug in your own `MessageChannel` to support whatever use-case you want: should the channel support publish/subscriber type of communication? Should it be backed by a JMS message broker? Should it be point-to-point? Synchronous? Asynchronous? These days, there's one more question: how does it handle reactive backpressure?

Spring Integration provides a veritable treasure trove of adapters and gateways, making it easy to connect our software with other systems. And, it offers a rich assortment of components supporting control flow. Suppose the Spring Integration team has done their job correctly. In that case, 90% of the work in a typical application integration scenario should be a function of how well you string together various Spring Integration bits to produce a solution. The various components in Spring Integration are functional, stateless, message-centric. A message comes in. A message goes out. This supports natural composition and reconfiguration of flows: so long as the downstream component expects whatever the upstream component produces, everything works out.

Does all of this sound a bit like building reactive pipelines? It should! You're going to find working with Spring Integration a breeze! And while

Spring Integration precedes reactive programming in the Spring ecosystem by a *decade*, it works well with reactive components. The new Spring Integration RSocket module means that Spring Integration works well with RSocket, too! So, let's look at a simple example to whet your appetite.

Remember, the world is weird, and as we move further in time, the surface area of "legacy" software grows. Spring Integration promotes a pipes-and-filters component model to support the assembly of easily-reconfigured pipelines. These pipelines may consist of disparate technologies, be they synchronous, asynchronous, blocking, non-blocking, etc. If you want to build a pipeline but want to talk to something that doesn't support reactivity, Spring Integration gives you the tools to do that and to accommodate reactive applications.

Spring Integration's RSocket module ships with both inbound and outbound gateways. We're only going to look at the outbound gateway; it'll allow us to issue a request to a downstream RSocket service and then process the reply in Spring Integration. It'll allow us to act as a client to an RSocket service.

The service is our old, and now familiar friend, the `GreetingController`.

```java
package rsb.rsocket.integration.service;

import org.springframework.messaging.handler.annotation.MessageMapping;
import org.springframework.stereotype.Controller;
import reactor.core.publisher.Flux;
import rsb.rsocket.integration.GreetingRequest;
import rsb.rsocket.integration.GreetingResponse;

import java.time.Duration;
import java.time.Instant;
import java.util.stream.Stream;

@Controller
class GreetingController {

    @MessageMapping("greetings")
    Flux<GreetingResponse> greet(GreetingRequest request) {
        return Flux//
                .fromStream(Stream.generate(() -> new GreetingResponse(
                        "Hello, " + request.getName() + " @ " + Instant.now()
+ "!")))//
                .take(10)①
                .delayElements(Duration.ofSeconds(1));
    }

}
```

① This only produces ten results

Start that service, and let's meet our client, the Spring Integration flow. Our integration flow will: * observe files deposited into a folder on our local filesystem * convert them into `String` values * and then send those `Strings` to our RSocket `GreetingsController`, producing a reactive stream of ten responses... * ...which we'll process in our integration flow.

```java
package rsb.rsocket.integration.integration;

import lombok.extern.log4j.Log4j2;
import org.springframework.beans.factory.annotation.Value;
import org.springframework.boot.SpringApplication;
import org.springframework.boot.autoconfigure.SpringBootApplication;
import org.springframework.context.annotation.Bean;
import org.springframework.integration.dsl.IntegrationFlow;
```

```java
import org.springframework.integration.dsl.IntegrationFlows;
import org.springframework.integration.dsl.MessageChannels;
import org.springframework.integration.file.dsl.Files;
import org.springframework.integration.file.transformer.FileToStringTransformer;
import org.springframework.integration.handler.GenericHandler;
import org.springframework.integration.rsocket.ClientRSocketConnector;
import org.springframework.integration.rsocket.RSocketInteractionModel;
import org.springframework.integration.rsocket.dsl.RSockets;
import org.springframework.messaging.MessageChannel;
import org.springframework.messaging.rsocket.RSocketStrategies;
import rsb.rsocket.BootifulProperties;
import rsb.rsocket.integration.GreetingRequest;
import rsb.rsocket.integration.GreetingResponse;

import java.io.File;

@Log4j2
@SpringBootApplication
public class IntegrationApplication {

    @Bean
    ClientRSocketConnector clientRSocketConnector(RSocketStrategies strategies,
            BootifulProperties properties) {①
        ClientRSocketConnector clientRSocketConnector = new ClientRSocketConnector(
                properties.getRsocket().getHostname(), properties.getRsocket().getPort());
        clientRSocketConnector.setRSocketStrategies(strategies);
        return clientRSocketConnector;
    }

    @Bean
    IntegrationFlow greetingFlow(@Value("${user.home}") File home,
            ClientRSocketConnector clientRSocketConnector) {

        var inboundFileAdapter = Files②
                .inboundAdapter(new File(home, "in"))//
                .autoCreateDirectory(true);

        return IntegrationFlows//
                .from(inboundFileAdapter,
                        poller -> poller.poller(pm -> pm.fixedRate(100)))③
                .transform(new FileToStringTransformer())④
                .transform(String.class, GreetingRequest::new)⑤
                .handle(RSockets//
```

```
                        .outboundGateway("greetings")⑥
                        .interactionModel(RSocketInteractionModel
.requestStream)//
                        .expectedResponseType(GreetingResponse.class)//
                        .clientRSocketConnector(clientRSocketConnector)//
                )//
                .split()⑦
                .channel(this.channel()) ⑧
                .handle((GenericHandler<GreetingResponse>) (payload, headers)
-> {⑨
                    log.info("-----------------");
                    log.info(payload.toString());
                    headers.forEach((header, value) -> log.info(header + "="
+ value));
                    return null;
                })//
                .get();
    }

    @Bean
    MessageChannel channel() {
        return MessageChannels.flux().get();⑩
    }

    public static void main(String[] args) {
        SpringApplication.run(IntegrationApplication.class, args);
    }

}
```

① First things first: we need to tell Spring Integration how to define an RSocketRequester. If we were using an inbound gateway, we would specify a ServerRSocketConnector.

② The integration flow originates messages from an inbound file adapter that will monitor a directory for any new files. As soon as a file arrives, the adapter publishes a Message<File> into the integration flow.

③ Spring Integration's pollers tell it how frequently it should fetch any new messages from a source like a file system directory which doesn't otherwise really have any way to *volunteer* the presence of a new file. The inbound adapter needs to scan the directory and compute the delta between this scan and the last scan.

④ The outcome of the inbound file adapter is a Message<File>. But we don't want a `Message<File>` - we want a `Message<String>` where each `String` represents a name that we intend to greet. The `FileToStringTransformer` (provided out-of-the-box in Spring Integration) handles the conversion for us

⑤ The next step is to convert the `String` into a `GreetingRequest`..

⑥ that's destined for the `greetings` endpoint in our RSocket service. The RSockets factory builds an outbound gateway that will invoke the downstream RSocket endpoint and return a `Flux<GreetingResponse>` to the next handler. But we don't want to process the whole `Flux<GreetingResponse>`; we want to process each individual `GreetingResponse`.

⑦ The `split()` operator enables this - it usually splits `Collection<T>` or `Iterator<T>`'s, but it now knows what to do given a `Publisher<T>` like our `Flux<GreetingResponse>`. It operates kind of like the `flatMap` operator on a `Flux<T>`.

⑧ The thing is, we're now squarely in the realm of reactive programming, and so downstream components must support backpressure and asynchronous processing. So, rather than accept the default `MessageChannel`, we've explicitly plugged in a `Flux<T>`-aware `MessageChannel` whose definition is defined in a bean further down the page.

⑨ Finally, we work with each constituent `GreetingResponse`. The integration flow terminates at the first component to return `null` for a given `Message<T>`. We're ending the flow merely by printing out the results. We could use some other Spring Integration adapter to write data to an external system via an outbound adapter or another gateway!

⑩ There are many `MessageChannel` implementations available on the `MessageChannels` facotry class, but we use `flux()` for this reactive implementation.

Overall, I was pleased how nicely the reactive support in Spring Integration came together, and even more pleased with how beautifully the RSocket support in Spring Integration worked out. It maps to what we're doing while also affording us the ability to - in a sane, well understand structure - integrate with other things that may not be reactive.

9.7. Next Steps

RSocket is well supported across the various Spring frameworks, core Spring Framework to Spring Boot and Spring Security and Spring Integration. But there's still more to come.

9.7.1. An RSocket Broker

RSocket is a fledgling project of the Reactive Foundation [https://reactive.foundation/], which counts as its members the Spring team (a part of VMware), Lightbend, Alibaba, Facebook, and Vlingo. We're building an RSocket broker that can act as a hub to mediate connections from RSocket requesters to RSocket responders. This hub can handle things like routing, load-balancing, security, and so much more. Such a hub could handle many use-cases typically associated with service registries, message queues, load balancers, etc. I can't wait to see what becomes of this.

9.7.2. A Declarative RSocket Client

Have you ever used Spring Cloud Feign? It's a way to turn an interface with Spring MVC mapping annotations (traditionally used in the HTTP service tier) into a declarative HTTP client. It's based on OpenFeign [https://github.com/OpenFeign/feign]. Feign is useful, even if it's not particularly reactive. Some also argue that it's inappropriate since it implies RPC semantics for HTTP endpoints when HTTP clients *should* use HATEOAS (hypermedia). RPC semantics are entirely appropriate for RSocket, however. So - with a bit of inspiration from Mario Gray (@MarioGray) [http://twitter.com/MarioGray] - I built a Feign- or Retrofit-like declarative client for RSocket, which I'm calling Retrosocket. It's even an experimental Spring project, and you can learn more about it here at github.com/spring-projects-experimental/spring-retrosocket [https://github.com/spring-projects-experimental/spring-retrosocket].

The basic concept is that, given an `RSocketRequester` in the Spring context, the project could create declarative RSocket clients.

```
@RSocketClient
interface GreetingClient {

    @MessageMapping("greetings.{formal}")
    Flux<GreetingResponse> greet(
            @DestinationVariable("formal") boolean formal,
            @Payload Mono<String> payload);
}
```

That use case and many others already work. Hopefully, by the time you're reading this, that project will have gone even further. It won't get to where it needs to go without you, dear community, so I encourage you to check it out and feedback.

9.7.3. A Super Handy RSocket CLI

Toshiaki Maki (@making) [http://twitter.com/making] built an RSocket Client CLI (called RSC) [https://github.com/making/rsc] that aims to be a `curl` for RSocket. It's very convenient! With it, you can quickly interact with your RSocket endpoints. Here is a sample interaction.

The RSC RSocket client in action making a request to the `hello` *route*

```
rsc tcp://localhost:8080 --request --route hello -d Foo --debug
```

Reactive Spring

Chapter 10. Service Orchestration and Composition

I struggled with the naming for this chapter. Anytime you bring in the word "service" or "orchestration," people lose their minds. I'm not interested in drudging up the long and storied arguments about SOA vs. microservices or anything of that sort. I am not here to refresh the definitions of choreography and orchestration. I did a lot of that in my last book, *Cloud Native Java*. I want to focus on what it looks like to compose services reactively.

It's not that you couldn't do what we're going to do here without reactive programming; it's more that it would be far more tedious and costly.

Traditional service orchestration and composition is a continuum: you can optimize your implementation for scalability or brevity of the code's expression, but not both. Reactive programming, I think, gives us the best of both dimensions: it gives us a concise way to express the intrinsically independent, potentially asynchronous, nature of distributed actors in a system.

Service orchestration and composition is one of the wheelhouses for reactive programming; it's one of the main reasons you should embrace it. Anytime you have multiple, distinct services talking to each other, you benefit from using reactive APIs. It makes concurrent and parallel programming more accessible. It is also one of the reasons we made sure to also support reactive programming inside of Spring MVC. We knew that one of the first drivers for reactive programming would be service orchestration and composition using the reactive `WebClient`. People would want to be able to return a `Publisher<T>` from their MVC controller handler methods, even if they didn't have time to try to rework their code to be a native Spring Webflux application.

In this chapter, we will look at all the concerns that fall out of trying to do service orchestration and discovery. We'll look at discovering other services. We'll look at routing. We'll look at service composition. It's going to be a networked journey, and the only way to get from here to there is to start.

10.1. Service Registration and Discovery

We're going to work with a lot of different services in this chapter, which brings up the very first concern we'll need to address: *finding* the services. Many of the patterns we'll investigate benefit from knowing which services exist in the system. We'll look at Spring Cloud's service registration and discovery support to make short work of finding the services. A **service registry** is an infrastructure service that keeps track of which instances of which services exist and where they are. Think of it as a phone book: given a service name, the service registry will give us back all the name instances. There are many service registries, including Apache Zookeeper, Hashicorp Consul, Netflix's Eureka, etc. Spring Cloud provides a low-level abstraction - the `ReactiveDiscoveryClient` - which we can use to programmatically interact with the service registries given an appropriate implementation. There's a ton of support that builds on top of this lowest level interface, as well see shortly.

If this sounds a bit like DNS, that's for a good reason. There are some pros and cons to using service registration and discovery over DNS. Service registration lets us programmatically interrogate the state of the system. It gives us a way to ask which services exist and how many of them are out there. DNS only provides us with a way to ask where a service is supposed to live. Service registration and discovery mechanisms are typically application-specific - your code leverages it instead of your networking stack. Some service registries - like Hashicorp Consul - can act as a DNS service *and* a programmatic phone type thing. So cloud-native applications built using Spring Cloud can do exciting things with individual instances, but other services will at least get a valid instance from the Consul registry's DNS.

You can use any of several different service registries. Still, because I want to keep this code as easy-to-use as possible out of the box, I will use Spring Cloud to code up a single instance of a Netlfix Eureka Service registry. I do *not* recommend this configuration for production. You can configure load

Chapter 10. Service Orchestration and Composition

balancing and security yourself. Or you can let your platform - Tanzu PAS or Tanzu PKS or Azure Spring Cloud or any of a ton of other options - do the work for you.

Go to the Spring Initializr to configure a new Eureka Service registry. Generate a new project - perhaps you could name it `eureka-service`? - with the Spring Cloud BOM and the Spring Cloud Eureka Server dependency:

- `org.springframework.cloud` : `spring-cloud-starter-netflix-eureka-server`

The main class couldn't be more straightforward.

```
package rsb.orchestration;

import org.springframework.boot.SpringApplication;
import org.springframework.boot.autoconfigure.SpringBootApplication;
import org.springframework.cloud.netflix.eureka.server.EnableEurekaServer;

@SpringBootApplication
@EnableEurekaServer ①
public class EurekaApplication {

    public static void main(String args[]) {
        SpringApplication.run(EurekaApplication.class, args);
    }

}
```

① The only notable thing here is the presence of the `@EnableEurekaServer` annotation

The only complexity, if you can call it that, lives in the configuration file.

```
spring.application.name=eureka-service
①
server.port=8761
eureka.client.fetch-registry=false
eureka.client.register-with-eureka=false
```

① The most important bit is that this service registry wil be available from HTTP port 8761

Run the service registry and then leave it running and need it for most of the rest of the chapter.

10.2. Some Simple Sample Services

Now that we've got a service registry up and running, we're going to need some services with which to interact. They' all have but two dependencies:

- `org.springframework.boot` : `spring-boot-starter-webflux`
- `org.springframework.cloud` : `spring-cloud-starter-netflix-eureka-client`

The `spring-boot-starter-webflux` dependency is there so we can build reactive Spring Webflux-powered services. The next, `spring-cloud-starter-netflix-eureka-client`, connects our application to the Eureka service registry. The client autoconfiguration will connect each of the applications to the default host and port (`localhost:8761`). Each client will startup, register itself with the service registry, and then resolve other services in the registry.

We'll look at the Java code in turn, but each of the services has at a minimum the following configuration in their respective `application.properties` file.

```
①
spring.application.name=profile-service
server.port=0
eureka.instance.instance-id=${spring.application.name}:${spring.application.instance_id:${random.value}}
```

① Here, I'm showing the configuration for the `profile-service`. Each service will vary their `spring.application.name`. This property determines how the service will advertise itself to other services in the cluster through Eureka.

I'll assume that you've created a similar file for each service as a baseline, and only revisit service configuration to prescribe each service's specific value for `spring.application.name` and add any additional configuration needed.

All services are also standalone Spring Boot applications, and so have a typical `main` class. I won't reprint each of these or revisit them unless there's something novel to investigate.

There are five (trivial) services.

- `customer-service`: provides information about `Customer` entities. A customer has person-specific information like a name.
- `profile-service`: provides information related to `Profile` entities attached to the `Customer`. This is a one-to-one relationship with the `Customer` data. Each customer will have only one profile. The profile specifies things like the account username and password.
- `order-service`: provides all the orders that belong to a given `Customer`. This is a one-to-many relationship, with each `Customer` able to have many `Order` instances.
- `slow-service`: this service provides slow responses to demonstrate what to do given a slow response
- `error-service`: this service offers endpoints that fail in particular ways, also for demonstration

10.2.1. Customer Service

The `customer-service` surfaces information about `Customer` entities, whose definition looks like this.

```java
package rsb.orchestration;

import lombok.AllArgsConstructor;
import lombok.Data;
import lombok.NoArgsConstructor;

@Data
@AllArgsConstructor
@NoArgsConstructor
class Customer {

    private Integer id;

    private String name;

}
```

The service itself boils down to a single endpoint, /customers. Most of the controller's complexity arises because, to avoid involving a database, I've built up an in-memory repository of Customer records.

```java
package rsb.orchestration;

import org.springframework.beans.factory.annotation.Value;
import org.springframework.web.bind.annotation.GetMapping;
import org.springframework.web.bind.annotation.RequestParam;
import org.springframework.web.bind.annotation.RestController;
import reactor.core.publisher.Flux;

import java.time.Duration;
import java.util.Arrays;
import java.util.Map;
import java.util.Optional;
import java.util.stream.Collectors;
import java.util.stream.Stream;

@RestController
class CustomerRestController {

    private final int delayInMillis;

    private final Map<Integer, Customer> customers = Map
            .of(1, "Jane", 2, "Mia", 3, "Leroy", 4, "Badhr", 5, "Zhen", 6, "Juliette", 7,
```

```java
                    "Artem", 8, "Michelle", 9, "Eva", 10, "Richard")//
            .entrySet()//
            .stream()//
            .collect(Collectors.toConcurrentMap(Map.Entry::getKey,
                    e -> new Customer(e.getKey(), e.getValue())));

    CustomerRestController(@Value("${rsb.delay:2000}") int delayInMillis) {
        this.delayInMillis = delayInMillis;
    }

    private Flux<Customer> from(Stream<Customer> customerStream,
            boolean delaySubscription) {

        return (delaySubscription)
                ? Flux.fromStream(customerStream)
                        .delaySubscription(Duration.ofMillis(this
    .delayInMillis))
                : Flux.fromStream(customerStream);
    }

    @GetMapping("/customers")
    Flux<Customer> customers(@RequestParam(required = false) Integer[] ids,
            @RequestParam(required = false) boolean delay) {
        var customerStream = this.customers.values().stream();
        return (Optional//
                .ofNullable(ids)//
                .map(Arrays::asList)//
                .map(listOfIds -> from(customerStream.filter(customer -> {
                    var id = customer.getId();
                    return listOfIds.contains(id);
                }), delay))//
                .orElse(from(customerStream, delay)));
    }

}
```

10.2.2. Order Service

The `order-service` surfaces information about `Order` entities, whose definition looks like this.

```java
package rsb.orchestration;

import lombok.AllArgsConstructor;
import lombok.Data;
import lombok.NoArgsConstructor;

@Data
@AllArgsConstructor
@NoArgsConstructor
class Order {

    private String id;

    private Integer customerId;

}
```

The service itself boils down to a single endpoint, /orders. Most of the complexity in the controller arises because, to avoid involving a database, I've built up an in-memory repository of Order records. Again, this is a trivial demo. The controller initializes a random list of Order instances associated with each customerId.

```java
package rsb.orchestration;

import org.springframework.web.bind.annotation.GetMapping;
import org.springframework.web.bind.annotation.RequestMapping;
import org.springframework.web.bind.annotation.RequestParam;
import org.springframework.web.bind.annotation.RestController;
import reactor.core.publisher.Flux;

import java.util.Arrays;
import java.util.List;
import java.util.Map;
import java.util.UUID;
import java.util.concurrent.CopyOnWriteArrayList;
import java.util.stream.Collectors;
import java.util.stream.IntStream;

@RequestMapping("/orders")
@RestController
class OrderRestController {
```

```
    // customerId -> orders
    private final Map<Integer, List<Order>> orders = //
            IntStream//
                    .range(0, 10)//
                    .boxed()//
                    .map(id -> Map.entry(id, new CopyOnWriteArrayList<Order>
())) 
                    .collect(Collectors.toConcurrentMap(Map.Entry::getKey, e
-> {
                        var listOfOrders = e.getValue();
                        var max = (int) (Math.random() * 10);
                        if (max < 1) {
                            max = 1;
                        }
                        for (var i = 0; i < max; i++) {
                            listOfOrders.add(
                                    new Order(UUID.randomUUID().toString(),
e.getKey()));
                        }
                        return listOfOrders;
                    }));

    @GetMapping
    Flux<Order> orders(@RequestParam(required = false) Integer[] ids) {
        var customerStream = this.orders.keySet().stream();
        var includedCustomerIds = Arrays.asList(ids);
        var orderStream = customerStream.filter(includedCustomerIds::
contains)//
                .flatMap(id -> this.orders.get(id).stream());
        return Flux.fromStream(orderStream);
    }

}
```

10.2.3. Profile Service

The `profile-service` surfaces information about `Profile` entities, whose definition looks like this.

```java
package rsb.orchestration;

import lombok.AllArgsConstructor;
import lombok.Data;
import lombok.NoArgsConstructor;

@Data
@AllArgsConstructor
@NoArgsConstructor
class Profile {

    private Integer id;

    private String username, password;

}
```

The service itself boils down to a single endpoint, /profiles. Most of the complexity in the controller arises because, to avoid involving a database, I've built up an in-memory repository of Profile records. Again, this is a trivial demo.

```
package rsb.orchestration;

import org.springframework.web.bind.annotation.GetMapping;
import org.springframework.web.bind.annotation.PathVariable;
import org.springframework.web.bind.annotation.RestController;
import reactor.core.publisher.Mono;

import java.util.Map;
import java.util.UUID;
import java.util.stream.Collectors;

@RestController
class ProfileRestController {

    private final Map<Integer, Profile> profiles = Map
            .of(1, "jane", 2, "mia", 3, "leroy", 4, "badhr", 5, "zhen", 6, "juliette", 7,
                    "artem", 8, "michelle", 9, "eva", 10, "richard")
            .entrySet().stream()
            .collect(Collectors.toConcurrentMap(Map.Entry::getKey,
                    e -> new Profile(e.getKey(), e.getValue(),
                            UUID.randomUUID().toString())));

    @GetMapping("/profiles/{id}")
    Mono<Profile> byId(@PathVariable Integer id) {
        return Mono.just(this.profiles.get(id));
    }

}
```

10.2.4. Error Service

The `error-service` is meant only to cause trouble! Not the kind of service you'd want in production, but hopefully, it'll let us simulate some real issues.

```
package rsb.orchestration;

import lombok.extern.log4j.Log4j2;
import org.springframework.boot.web.context.WebServerInitializedEvent;
import org.springframework.context.event.EventListener;
import org.springframework.web.bind.annotation.GetMapping;
import org.springframework.web.bind.annotation.RequestParam;
```

```java
import org.springframework.web.bind.annotation.RestController;
import reactor.core.publisher.Mono;

import java.util.Map;
import java.util.concurrent.ConcurrentHashMap;
import java.util.concurrent.atomic.AtomicInteger;

@Log4j2
@RestController
class ErrorRestController {

    ①
    private final AtomicInteger port = new AtomicInteger();

    ②
    private final Map<String, AtomicInteger> clientCounts = new ConcurrentHashMap<>();

    @EventListener
    public void webServerInitializedEventListener(WebServerInitializedEvent event) {
        port.set(event.getWebServer().getPort());
    }

    private int registerClient(String uid) {
        if (null != uid) {
            this.clientCounts.putIfAbsent(uid, new AtomicInteger(0));
            return this.clientCounts.get(uid).incrementAndGet();
        }
        return 1;
    }

    ③
    @GetMapping("/ok")
    Mono<Map<String, String>> okEndpoint(@RequestParam(required = false) String uid) {
        var countThusFar = this.registerClient(uid);
        return Mono.just(Map.of("greeting", String.format(
                "greeting attempt # %s from port %s", countThusFar,
this.port.get())));
    }

    ④
    @GetMapping("/retry")
    Mono<Map<String, String>> retryEndpoint(@RequestParam String uid) {
        var countThusFar = this.registerClient(uid);
        return countThusFar > 2
```

```
                    ? Mono.just(Map.of("greeting",
                            String.format("greeting attempt # %s from port %s",
    countThusFar,
                                this.port.get())))
                    : Mono.error(new IllegalArgumentException());
        }

        ⑤
        @GetMapping("/cb")
        Mono<Map<String, String>> circuitBreakerEndpoint(@RequestParam String uid) {
            registerClient(uid);
            return Mono.error(new IllegalArgumentException());
        }

    }
```

① The `AtomicInteger` is to store the port of the service (which we get in the `webServerInitializedEventListener` method) to include it in the responses sent back to clients. That'll help us understand where responses are coming.

② The `clientCounts` map stores the client ID to the count of times we've seen requests from that client. It helps us preserve the notion of session state for specific demos later on.

③ The `/ok` endpoint returns a `Map<K,V>` of data. No errors. This one works well.

④ The `/retry` endpoint returns a `Map<K, V>` but only after the client has attempted the request at least two times.

⑤ The `/cb` endpoint fails every time. This is ideal for demonstrating a circuit breaker.

10.2.5. Slow Service

The `slow-service` returns streams of `GreetingResponse` data.

```
package rsb.orchestration;

import lombok.AllArgsConstructor;
import lombok.Data;
import lombok.NoArgsConstructor;

@Data
@AllArgsConstructor
@NoArgsConstructor
class GreetingResponse {

    private String message;

}
```

It does so after a configurable delay. This is ideal when trying to demonstrate latency and ways to deal with it.

```
package rsb.orchestration;

import lombok.extern.log4j.Log4j2;
import org.springframework.beans.factory.annotation.Value;
import org.springframework.boot.web.context.WebServerInitializedEvent;
import org.springframework.context.event.EventListener;
import org.springframework.web.bind.annotation.GetMapping;
import org.springframework.web.bind.annotation.RequestParam;
import org.springframework.web.bind.annotation.RestController;
import reactor.core.publisher.Mono;

import java.time.Duration;
import java.time.Instant;
import java.util.concurrent.atomic.AtomicInteger;

@Log4j2
@RestController
class SlowRestController {

    private final long dtim;

    private final AtomicInteger port = new AtomicInteger();

    ①
    SlowRestController(@Value("${rsb.slow-service.delay}") long dtim) {
        this.dtim = dtim;
```

```java
    }

    ②
    @EventListener
    public void web(WebServerInitializedEvent event) {
        port.set(event.getWebServer().getPort());
        if (log.isInfoEnabled()) {
            log.info("configured rsb.slow-service.delay=" + dtim + " on port "
                    + port.get());
        }
    }

    ③
    @GetMapping("/greetings")
    Mono<GreetingResponse> greet(
            @RequestParam(required = false, defaultValue = "world") String name) {
        var now = Instant.now().toString();
        var message = "Hello, %s! (from %s started at %s and finished at %s)";
        return Mono
                .just(new GreetingResponse(String.format(message, port, name, now,
                        Instant.now().toString())))
                .doOnNext(r -> log.info(r.toString()))
                .delaySubscription(Duration.ofSeconds(dtim));
    }

}
```

① Note the delay. You can start multiple instances of this service and override the delay by specifying --rsb.slow-service.delay=10, for example, on the command line. This would delay the response sent by the client by ten seconds.

② Here, we record the services' port to include it in our responses. This is useful when trying to understand which service produced which response when everything's running on the same machine.

③ The /greetings endpoint uses the very convenient delaySubscription operator to delay when the framework can start subscribing (and thus serving) to the response.

10.2.6. The Client

Most of the examples that we'll look at will live in a module I've unimaginatively named `client`. I also set the `spring.application.name` to `client`. I'll demonstrate a bunch of concerns in different applications in different packages in this one application. It has dependencies on at a minimum the following dependencies:

- `org.springframework.boot` : `spring-boot-starter-webflux`
- `org.springframework.cloud` : `spring-cloud-starter-netflix-eureka-client`.

We'll introduce the new dependencies as we use them. The client has a `spring.application.name` value of `client` and uses `server.port=0` to obtain a random, unused port. I've also copied the Java DTOs from each of the respective services - `Order` from `order-service`, `Profile` from `profile-service`, `Customer` from `customer-service` and `GreetingResponse` from `slow-service` - into a root package (`rsb.orchestration`) of the `client` module.

Throughout this section, we'll also rely on some utility methods that I've extracted into a class, `TimerUtils`.

```java
package rsb.orchestration;

import lombok.extern.log4j.Log4j2;
import reactor.core.publisher.Flux;
import reactor.core.publisher.Mono;

import java.util.concurrent.atomic.AtomicLong;

@Log4j2
public abstract class TimerUtils {

    ①
    public static <T> Mono<T> cache(Mono<T> cache) {
        return cache.doOnNext(c -> log.debug("receiving " + c.toString())) .cache();
    }

    public static <T> Flux<T> cache(Flux<T> cache) {
        return cache.doOnNext(c -> log.debug("receiving " + c.toString())) .cache();
    }

    ②
    public static <T> Mono<T> monitor(Mono<T> configMono) {
        var start = new AtomicLong();
        return configMono//
                .doOnError(exception -> log.error("oops!", exception))//
                .doOnSubscribe((subscription) -> start.set(System.currentTimeMillis())) //
                .doOnNext((greeting) -> log.info("total time: {}",
                        System.currentTimeMillis() - start.get()));
    }

    public static <T> Flux<T> monitor(Flux<T> configMono) {
        var start = new AtomicLong();
        return configMono//
                .doOnError(exception -> log.error("oops!", exception))//
                .doOnSubscribe((subscription) -> start.set(System.currentTimeMillis())) //
                .doOnNext((greeting) -> log.info("total time: {}",
                        System.currentTimeMillis() - start.get()));
    }

}
```

① The `cache` methods force a `Publisher<T>` to remember their contents. This is great if you're going to iterate (via subscribe) over the same stream multiple times as the values won't be recomputed each time. This method also installs a bit of logging to announce when a new value has been produced, which is just as interesting when it *doesn't* announce anything when values are cached.

② The `monitor` captures the start of a reactive stream and the end of a reactive stream, computes the delta, and then logs it out. Great for very simple, high level benchmarking.

10.3. Client Side Loadbalancing in the `WebClient`

It doesn't all that much matter whence the `Publisher<T>` that we use in the demonstration in this chapter originate. We can source them from HTTP, or RSocket, or anything else. To keep things familiar, we're using HTTP, so we'll need to use the `WebClient` in several places. The first thing we can do to make our services just that much more reliable is to use load balancing. The act of picking a particular instance, given many choices, is called load balancing. There are two common kinds of load balancing available to us. DNS load balancing and client-side load balancing.

DNS load balancing has all the well understood benefits of being infrastructure-level, and so it works for all DNS clients. It's a great choice when you want to introduce smarter load balancing to clients that don't otherwise have those smarts.

Client-side load balancing is a bit different. In a client-side load balancing scenario, the client - our Spring Cloud-powered JVM code - will choose to which node it should send the request. Client-side load balancing typically goes hand in hand with a service registry like Netflix's Eureka, at which we've already looked.

We want to use the information available to us about the state of each application to make smarter load balancing decisions. There are a lot of reasons we might use the client-side load balancer instead of DNS. First, Java DNS clients tend to cache the resolved IP information, which means that subsequent calls to the same resolved IP would end up subsequently dogpiling on top of one service. You can disable that, but you're working against the grain of DNS, a caching-centric system. DNS only tells you *where* something is, not *if* it is. Put another way; you don't know if there is going to be anything waiting for your request on the other side of that DNS based load balancer. Wouldn't you like to be able to know before making the call, sparing your client the tedious timeout period before the call fails? Service registries and client-side load balancing are excellent implements, and they make some patterns like hedging (which we're going to look at shortly) possible.

The power of client-side loadbalancing lives in the imminent flexibility and customizability. You can configure your load balancing algorithms to do interesting things. Perhaps you want to pin all requests given a particular JWT token to a specific service in the service registry. Maybe you want to route the request to a region-specific service. Perhaps you want to take advantage of edge-caching to handle resolution. The client-side load balancer is where you'd encode that logic. By default, Spring Cloud Load Balancer uses an algorithm to identify the least recently used (LRU) instance.

Almost all of the sample applications will use a load-balancing `WebClient`, so I've extracted that into some auto-configuration that will run *unless* some other bean is provided to override the default one, which we'll occasionally need to do. Behind the scenes, this `ReactorLoadBalancerExchangeFilterFunction` delegates to a `ReactiveLoadBalancer` instance, a part of the Spring Cloud LoadBalancer project. Here's the autoconfiguration itself.

```java
package rsb.orchestration;

import lombok.extern.log4j.Log4j2;
import org.springframework.boot.autoconfigure.condition.ConditionalOnMissingBean;
import org.springframework.cloud.client.loadbalancer.reactive.ReactorLoadBalancerExchangeFilterFunction;
import org.springframework.context.annotation.Bean;
import org.springframework.context.annotation.Configuration;
import org.springframework.web.reactive.function.client.WebClient;

@Log4j2
@Configuration
class WebClientAutoConfiguration {

    @Bean
    @ConditionalOnMissingBean
    WebClient loadBalancingWebClient(WebClient.Builder builder,
            ReactorLoadBalancerExchangeFilterFunction lbFunction) { ①
        log.info(
                "registering a default load-balanced " + WebClient.class.getName() + '.');
        return builder.filter(lbFunction).build();
    }

}
```

① The `ReactorLoadBalancerExchangeFilterFunction` is an autoconfigured `ExchangeFilterFunction` that handles load balancing HTTP requests for us.

The `ReactorLoadBalancerExchangeFilterFunction` resolves the host in a URI with a lookup in the service registry, not DNS. So, given a URI of the form, `http://error-service/ok`, the `ReactorLoadBalancerExchangeFilterFunction` would attempt to resolve all the `error-service` service instances in the Eureka service registry and then pick from among the returned instances just one to use in completing this request. We'll assume the client-side load balancing throughout most of this chapter.

10.4. Resilient Streams with Reactor Operators

A considerable part of efficient service orchestration and composition is knowing that you'll get a response in the first place. We've already seen that we can very easily leverage load balancing to reduce the possibility of dogpiling on one particular service unnecessarily. Loadbalancing lets us divide the work across several running instances in the system.

But things can still go wrong. There's nothing to guarantee, given a load-balanced service instance, that something won't go wrong between when you resolve the service instance and when you make the request. Indeed, there's nothing to guarantee that the service won't suddenly die, or garbage collect, or whatever. In this section and the next few, we'll look at some patterns for raising the likelihood of requests returning successfully.

The first thing we can do is take advantage of the operators provided in Reactor out of the box. There are a few worth knowing, and who knows - they might be enough to let you sleep at night.

All the examples in this section will leverage the same `Flux<Order>` data, so I've extracted that out to a separate class, `OrderClient`.

```java
package rsb.orchestration.reactor;

import lombok.RequiredArgsConstructor;
import org.springframework.stereotype.Component;
import org.springframework.util.StringUtils;
import org.springframework.web.reactive.function.client.WebClient;
import reactor.core.publisher.Flux;
import rsb.orchestration.Order;

@Component
@RequiredArgsConstructor
class OrderClient {

    private final WebClient http;

    Flux<Order> getOrders(Integer... ids) {
        var ordersRoot = "http://order-service/orders?ids="
                + StringUtils.arrayToDelimitedString(ids, ",");
        return http.get().uri(ordersRoot).retrieve().bodyToFlux(Order.class);
    }

}
```

You should timebox any request that may fail. You can specify that a request that goes to a downstream service should timeout after a certain period using the `timeout` operator.

```java
package rsb.orchestration.reactor;

import lombok.RequiredArgsConstructor;
import org.springframework.boot.context.event.ApplicationReadyEvent;
import org.springframework.context.ApplicationListener;
import org.springframework.stereotype.Component;

import java.time.Duration;

@Component
@RequiredArgsConstructor
class TimeoutClient implements ApplicationListener<ApplicationReadyEvent> {

    private final OrderClient client;

    @Override
    public void onApplicationEvent(ApplicationReadyEvent event) {
        this.client.getOrders(1, 2)//
                .timeout(Duration.ofSeconds(10))//
                .subscribe(System.out::println);
    }

}
```

A timeout doesn't guarantee that the downstream service won't fail, but it does mean we won't wait too long for it to do that. In a situation where we have an SLA, we must have predictability around the timeframe for a given exchange. If the request is still ongoing after that timeout, it'll throw an exception which we can then trap and use as an opportunity to either degrade gracefully or retry the request.

Graceful degradation is critical in building reliable user services. It's also effortless to do so using the various operators in Reactor.

```java
package rsb.orchestration.reactor;

import lombok.RequiredArgsConstructor;
import org.springframework.boot.context.event.ApplicationReadyEvent;
import org.springframework.context.ApplicationListener;
import org.springframework.stereotype.Component;
import reactor.core.publisher.Flux;

@Component
@RequiredArgsConstructor
class DegradingClient implements ApplicationListener<ApplicationReadyEvent> {

    private final OrderClient client;

    @Override
    public void onApplicationEvent(ApplicationReadyEvent event) {
        this.client.getOrders(1, 2)//
                .onErrorResume(exception -> Flux.empty()) ①
                .subscribe(System.out::println);
    }

}
```

① In this example, the `DegradingClient` returns an empty `Flux<T>` when an exception is encountered. You could use this callback to either start another request or return a useful, albeit unsuccessful, response.

Retrying the request is a widespread strategy. You could retry the request against the same service instance or - more usefully - against another service instance. Reactor provides some convenient operators for that, too: `retry` and `retryWhen`.

Chapter 10. Service Orchestration and Composition

```java
package rsb.orchestration.reactor;

import lombok.RequiredArgsConstructor;
import org.springframework.boot.context.event.ApplicationReadyEvent;
import org.springframework.context.ApplicationListener;
import org.springframework.stereotype.Component;

@Component
@RequiredArgsConstructor
class RetryClient implements ApplicationListener<ApplicationReadyEvent> {

    private final OrderClient client;

    @Override
    public void onApplicationEvent(ApplicationReadyEvent event) {
        this.client.getOrders(1, 2)//
                .retry(10)①
                .subscribe(System.out::println);

    }

}
```

① This will retry the same request ten times until it succeeds or the ten tries have elapsed, at which point it'll return an error.

Blindly retrying the request might cause a stampede on the downstream services, which are just trying to get out from under some load. A slightly more indulgent approach might be to wait for the first retry to fail, and if it fails, to wait just a little longer, then retry. And wait some more time still and then retry again. And so on. This delay between retries is a backoff, and you can specify that Reactor *backoff* the requests a bit more with the retryWhen operator.

```
package rsb.orchestration.reactor;

import lombok.RequiredArgsConstructor;
import org.springframework.boot.context.event.ApplicationReadyEvent;
import org.springframework.context.ApplicationListener;
import org.springframework.stereotype.Component;
import reactor.util.retry.Retry;

import java.time.Duration;

@Component
@RequiredArgsConstructor
class RetryWhenClient implements ApplicationListener<ApplicationReadyEvent> {

    private final OrderClient client;

    @Override
    public void onApplicationEvent(ApplicationReadyEvent event) {
        this.client.getOrders(1, 2)//
                .retryWhen(Retry.backoff(10, Duration.ofSeconds(1)))①
                .subscribe(System.out::println);
    }

}
```

① This will retry the same request ten times until it succeeds or the ten tries have elapsed, at which point it'll return an error.

10.5. Resilient Streams with Resilience4J

Resilience4J is a third party project that endeavors to make building robust clients as easy as possible, and it ships with support for four patterns that you can use in a reactive and non-reactive context. To use Resilience4J, you'll need to add a few dependencies to the build. I defined a property, resilience4j.version, and set it to the version of Resilience4J that I want to use. See the source code of the book for the particular version. Then, I added the following dependencies to the build:

- io.github.resilience4j : resilience4j-ratelimiter : ${resilience4j.version}
- io.github.resilience4j : resilience4j-circuitbreaker :

- `io.github.resilience4j:resilience4j-retry:${resilience4j.version}`
- `io.github.resilience4j:resilience4j-bulkhead:${resilience4j.version}`
- `io.github.resilience4j:resilience4j-reactor:${resilience4j.version}`

These modules all follow the same basic arrangement. There is a thing - let's call it a `T` - that we can use to configure the application of a given feature. Usually, we say `T t=T.of(···)`. We'll need a `TConfig` to pass into that `T.of(···)` call. We can then use that `T` to conjure up a Reactor `UnaryOperator<Publisher<T>>` implementation (of the form `TOperator`), which we can then apply to our reactive pipeline using the `transformDeferred` operator. It's confusing when I write it all out, but trust me you'll notice the pattern quickly. Let's take a look.

10.5.1. Retries

Resilience4J supports retrying a request, just like we did with the Reactor `retry` operator. The Resilience4J operator supports a combination of retrying, backoff, and timeouts. So, in that sense, it obviates the need for a lot of the basic Reactor operators we looked at earlier. The endpoint our client is invoking is configured to fail for the first two times, and return a value the third time. Accordingly, I've configured this Resilience4J client to give up after three attempts. So it *should* get a result just in the nick of time. You can try lowering the threshold to see what happens if you don't get a result.

```java
package rsb.orchestration.resilience4j;

import io.github.resilience4j.core.IntervalFunction;
import io.github.resilience4j.reactor.retry.RetryOperator;
import io.github.resilience4j.retry.Retry;
import io.github.resilience4j.retry.RetryConfig;
import lombok.RequiredArgsConstructor;
import lombok.extern.log4j.Log4j2;
import org.springframework.boot.context.event.ApplicationReadyEvent;
import org.springframework.context.ApplicationListener;
import org.springframework.context.annotation.Profile;
import org.springframework.stereotype.Component;
import org.springframework.web.reactive.function.client.WebClient;
import reactor.core.publisher.Mono;

import java.time.Duration;
import java.util.UUID;

@Log4j2
@Component
@Profile("retry")
@RequiredArgsConstructor
class RetryClient implements ApplicationListener<ApplicationReadyEvent> {

    private final Retry retry = Retry.of("greetings-retry", RetryConfig//
            .custom() //
            .waitDuration(Duration.ofMillis(1000)) ①
            .intervalFunction(
                    IntervalFunction.ofExponentialBackoff(Duration.ofMillis(500L), 2d))②
            .maxAttempts(3) ③
            .build());

    private final String uid = UUID.randomUUID().toString();

    private final WebClient http;

    @Override
    public void onApplicationEvent(ApplicationReadyEvent event) {
        Mono<String> retry = GreetingClientUtils
                .getGreetingFor(this.http, this.uid, "retry")
                .transformDeferred(RetryOperator.of(this.retry));④
        retry.subscribe(log::info);
    }

}
```

① This example will wait a second before retrying

② It'll back off half a second first, then multiply the backoff period for each successive wait before retrying

③ and it'll attempt to retry the request a maximum of three times

④ It's trivial to apply the `RetryOperator` to our reactive stream given the `Retry` configuration

If you want to see this in action, you'll need to enable the `retry` profile when running the `ResilientClientApplication`.

10.5.2. Circuit Breakers

The circuit breaker starts rejecting requests destined to a failing endpoint after some configurable percentage of those requests in a moving window have failed. So, suppose we've tried to make a request three times, and we've now given up any hope that that request will ever return successfully. We want to prevent any further requests from failing, so we disable the request immediately. If the request had succeeded, we'd say the circuit is *closed*. As the request failed, the circuit breaker moved to the *open* state, stopping any subsequent requests from even being attempted. They fail immediately. We demonstrate this effect in the following demo by having the client attempt to call a downstream service and, after enough failed attempts, have those calls rejected with `CallNotPermittedException`.

```java
package rsb.orchestration.resilience4j;

import io.github.resilience4j.circuitbreaker.CallNotPermittedException;
import io.github.resilience4j.circuitbreaker.CircuitBreaker;
import io.github.resilience4j.circuitbreaker.CircuitBreakerConfig;
import io.github.resilience4j.reactor.circuitbreaker.operator.CircuitBreakerOperator;
import lombok.RequiredArgsConstructor;
import lombok.extern.log4j.Log4j2;
import org.springframework.boot.context.event.ApplicationReadyEvent;
import org.springframework.context.ApplicationListener;
import org.springframework.context.annotation.Profile;
import org.springframework.stereotype.Component;
import org.springframework.web.reactive.function.client.WebClient;
```

```java
import org.springframework.web.reactive.function.client.WebClientResponseException;
import reactor.core.publisher.Mono;

import java.time.Duration;
import java.util.UUID;

@Log4j2
@Profile("cb")
@Component
@RequiredArgsConstructor
class CircuitBreakerClient implements ApplicationListener<ApplicationReadyEvent> {

    private final CircuitBreaker circuitBreaker = CircuitBreaker.of("greetings-cb",
            CircuitBreakerConfig.custom()//
                    .failureRateThreshold(50)①
                    .recordExceptions(
                            WebClientResponseException.InternalServerError.class)②
                    .slidingWindowSize(5)③
                    .waitDurationInOpenState(Duration.ofMillis(1000))//
                    .permittedNumberOfCallsInHalfOpenState(2) //
                    .build());

    private final WebClient http;

    private final String uid = UUID.randomUUID().toString();

    @Override
    public void onApplicationEvent(ApplicationReadyEvent event) {

        buildRequest() //
                .doOnError(ex -> {
                    if (ex instanceof WebClientResponseException.InternalServerError) {
                        log.error("oops! We got a " + ex.getClass().getSimpleName()
                                + " from our network call. "
                                + "This will probably be a problem but we might try again...");
                    }
                    if (ex instanceof CallNotPermittedException) {
                        log.error(
                                "no more requests are permitted, now would be a good time to fail fast");
                    }
```

```
                    }
                }) //
                .retry(5).subscribe();
    }

    private Mono<String> buildRequest() {
        return GreetingClientUtils.getGreetingFor(this.http, this.uid, "cb")
                .transformDeferred(CircuitBreakerOperator.of(this
.circuitBreaker));
    }

}
```

① The circuit breaker will move to the *open* state if 50% of the attempted requests fail…

② where failure is defined as a `InternalServerError`…

③ within any given five requests

If you want to see this in action, you'll need to enable the `cb` profile when running the `ResilientClientApplication`.

10.5.3. Rate Limiters

Rate limiters measure how many requests we can make in a given interval of time. I've configured the Resilience4J `RateLimiter` to have a *very* low threshold below. It'll allow no more than ten requests for any given second. I want to test this, so I've fired off 20 requests which should — all things being equal - have more than enough time to begin and even return a response. If, for whatever reason, that's not the case, you can ramp down the `limitForPeriod` value below or ramp up the `limitRefreshPeriod` value from 1 second to 5 seconds. I've then configured two atomic numbers to track both valid responses and `RequestNotPermitted` responses. If we observe an accurate value, then we'll increment the results counter. Otherwise, we'll increment the `errors` counter.

```
package rsb.orchestration.resilience4j;

import io.github.resilience4j.ratelimiter.RateLimiter;
```

```java
import io.github.resilience4j.ratelimiter.RateLimiterConfig;
import io.github.resilience4j.reactor.ratelimiter.operator.RateLimiterOperator;
import lombok.RequiredArgsConstructor;
import lombok.SneakyThrows;
import lombok.extern.log4j.Log4j2;
import org.springframework.boot.context.event.ApplicationReadyEvent;
import org.springframework.context.ApplicationListener;
import org.springframework.context.annotation.Profile;
import org.springframework.stereotype.Component;
import org.springframework.web.reactive.function.client.WebClient;
import reactor.core.publisher.Mono;

import java.time.Duration;
import java.time.Instant;
import java.util.UUID;
import java.util.concurrent.CountDownLatch;
import java.util.concurrent.atomic.AtomicInteger;

@Log4j2
@Component
@Profile("rl")
@RequiredArgsConstructor
class RateLimiterClient implements ApplicationListener<ApplicationReadyEvent> {

    private final String uid = UUID.randomUUID().toString();

    private final WebClient http;

    private final RateLimiter rateLimiter = RateLimiter.of("greetings-rl",
            RateLimiterConfig//
                    .custom() //
                    .limitForPeriod(10)①
                    .limitRefreshPeriod(Duration.ofSeconds(1))②
                    .timeoutDuration(Duration.ofMillis(25))//
                    .build());

    @SneakyThrows
    @Override
    public void onApplicationEvent(ApplicationReadyEvent event) {

        var max = 20;
        var cdl = new CountDownLatch(max);
        var result = new AtomicInteger();
        var errors = new AtomicInteger();
        for (var i = 0; i < max; i++)
```

Chapter 10. Service Orchestration and Composition

```java
                this.buildRequest(cdl, result, errors, rateLimiter, i).subscribe();

        cdl.await();

        log.info("there were " + errors.get() + " errors");
        log.info("there were " + result.get() + " results");

    }

    private Mono<String> buildRequest(CountDownLatch cdl, AtomicInteger results,
            AtomicInteger errors, RateLimiter rateLimiter, int count) {
        return GreetingClientUtils//
                .getGreetingFor(this.http, this.uid, "ok")//
                .transformDeferred(RateLimiterOperator.of(rateLimiter))//
                .doOnError(ex -> {
                    errors.incrementAndGet();
                    log.info("oops! got an error of type " + ex.getClass().getName());
                })///
                .doOnNext(reply -> {
                    results.incrementAndGet();
                    log.info("count is " + count + " @ " + Instant.now() + " (" + reply
                            + ")");
                })//
                .doOnTerminate(cdl::countDown);

    }
}
```

① The rate limiter kicks in, stopping any further requests, if the requests exceed ten requests...

② over anyone second

If you want to see this in action, you'll need to enable the `rl` profile when running the `ResilientClientApplication`.

10.5.4. Bulkheads

The idea behind a bulkhead is to ensure that we constrain the number of threads involved. We don't want to spawn too many threads and risk oversubscription of our limited resources. Obviously, in a genuinely reactive application, having too many threads is *really* hard to do! There are very few ways to get too many threads involved, so I've had to fairly artificially constrain this example by running everything on the same thread. I'm not even sure if you're going to need this! You'll see that roughly half of the requests are launched before the bulkhead kicks in. You may need to fiddle with the `maxWaitDuration` value on your machine. Too high a value and the in-flight requests will finish right up and free up a thread. Too low a value, and maybe nothing gets done.

```java
package rsb.orchestration.resilience4j;

import io.github.resilience4j.bulkhead.Bulkhead;
import io.github.resilience4j.bulkhead.BulkheadConfig;
import io.github.resilience4j.reactor.bulkhead.operator.BulkheadOperator;
import lombok.RequiredArgsConstructor;
import lombok.extern.log4j.Log4j2;
import org.springframework.boot.context.event.ApplicationReadyEvent;
import org.springframework.context.ApplicationListener;
import org.springframework.context.annotation.Profile;
import org.springframework.stereotype.Component;
import org.springframework.web.reactive.function.client.WebClient;
import reactor.core.publisher.Mono;
import reactor.core.scheduler.Scheduler;
import reactor.core.scheduler.Schedulers;

import java.time.Duration;
import java.util.UUID;

@Log4j2
@Component
@Profile("bulkhead")
@RequiredArgsConstructor
class BulkheadClient implements ApplicationListener<ApplicationReadyEvent> {

    private final String uid = UUID.randomUUID().toString();

    private final int availableProcessors = Runtime.getRuntime()
        .availableProcessors();

    private final int maxCalls = availableProcessors / 2;

    private final WebClient http;
```

Chapter 10. Service Orchestration and Composition

```java
    private final Bulkhead bulkhead = Bulkhead.of("greetings-bulkhead",
BulkheadConfig //
            .custom() //
            .writableStackTraceEnabled(true) //
            .maxConcurrentCalls(this.maxCalls)①
            .maxWaitDuration(Duration.ofMillis(5)) //
            .build());

    @Override
    public void onApplicationEvent(ApplicationReadyEvent event) {
        log.info("there are " + availableProcessors
                + " available, therefore there should be " +
availableProcessors
                + " in the default thread pool");
        var immediate = Schedulers.immediate();
        for (var i = 0; i < availableProcessors; i++) {
            buildRequest(immediate, i).subscribe();
        }
    }

    private Mono<String> buildRequest(Scheduler scheduler, int i) {
        log.info("bulkhead attempt #" + i);
        return GreetingClientUtils //
                .getGreetingFor(this.http, this.uid, "ok") //
                .transform(BulkheadOperator.of(this.bulkhead)) //
                .subscribeOn(scheduler)//
                .publishOn(scheduler) //
                .onErrorResume(throwable -> {
                    log.info("the bulkhead kicked in for request #" + i
                            + ". Received the following exception "
                            + throwable.getClass().getName() + '.');
                    return Mono.empty();
                }) //
                .onErrorStop();
    }

}
```

① The Bulkhead kicks in if we have more than `maxCalls` concurrent calls at the same time to a downstream stream

If you want to see this in action, you'll need to enable the `bulkhead` profile when running the `ResilientClientApplication`.

10.6. Hedging

Timeouts give us a way to upper bound how much time we spend on any one call, and in this way, they're a useful feature. Timeouts are a beneficial quality when trying to work within a service level agreement (SLA). Broadly, SLAs define how long a given service can take before exceeding some understood, agreed upon, or even legally enforced agreement. Timeouts give us a natural way to attempt a request, timebox it, and abandon it and either retry the request or return an error in a timely fashion. They're a convenient addition to our toolbox, but they're not always the only or even the best, way to try to guarantee timely responses.

Let's suppose that our service, A, has an insanely indulgent SLA of a whole second. That's an eternity for most APIs! Suppose our service A depends on another service, B. In that case, that means that the B service has an SLA of only half a second because we need to be able to attempt that call, abandon it if it fails, and - hopefully - try it again while still meeting the SLA for service A. Suppose service B has a dependency on yet another service, C. The problem is even worse here: service C needs to produce a response in a quarter of a second (0.25) if service B is to have any hope of abandoning the first failed request and retrying it. And so on. This dynamic creates an unfair situation: services downstream have ever more demanding SLAs only by virtue of their proximity or distance from the request's origin. Worse, all of this time budgeting and gymnastics only buys us two bites at the apple; if one request fails, we get to retry it but one more time. These outcomes are hardly ideal.

It's a familiar aphorism: don't put all your eggs in one basket. Don't invest in only one stock. Don't bet the farm on one gambit. We want to hedge our bet by diversifying the risks. In concrete terms, we want to launch concurrent requests to otherwise identically configured service instances of the same service in the hopes that one of them will return in time. Perhaps a service instance is garbage collecting or inundated. Surely they can't *all* be down! And if they are, then that's an entirely different problem and a perfect example of why you should pair hedging with other patterns like a circuit breaker.

The hedging pattern isn't ideal for every interaction. First, it's potentially wasteful. By definition, you're going to launch the same request more than once. Any (or all) of the repetitive requests may succeed! In this case, you've done the same work more than once.

It assumes that you're making idempotent calls to a downstream service. A request is said to be idempotent if it may be repeated multiple times without any undue observable side effects. So, charging the customer's credit card? You can only do that *once*. Or not at all. But most customers will *not* appreciate it if you charge them twice! Are you reading the profile information for a given customer? That can be repeated as many times as you need. Most database reads are idempotent. Some writes are also idempotent. Suppose you want to update a user's username from josh to Joshua. Neither your user nor the database schema will care if you set it to be Joshua one or more times, so long as you do. Many databases support a concept of versioning where the write-only succeeds if the write is against a record whose version matches what's specified in the write. The record's version increments every time it's updated in any way. The write has no effect, but it doesn't matter because the write has already succeeded at least once, and the result is precisely what was intended by the client.

If your request is idempotent, then hedging is a great pattern to employ, above and beyond the necessary timeout. It's also a pattern that's *very* easy to implement in a reactive context. Here's the basic approach:

- use the `ReactiveDiscoveryClient` to load all the unique instances (hosts and ports) for a given service. Ideally, this will return more than one instance of the service.

- Choose a randomized set of service instances. You won't benefit from the pattern if you don't use more than one instance. The precise number, of course, is up to you. You might only have three instances and so decided to launch all requests to all three instances. You might prefer a percentage of the total number of instances. It depends on how many service instances you have and how much tolerance for duplicative network traffic. If you want the same odds as you'd get with timeouts, then use two instances. Any number of instances above that favors your getting a result in time.

- Fashion a request destined for each of the chosen service instances
- Use the `Flux.first(Publisher<T>…)` operator to ask Reactor to launch all N requests and retain only the fastest reactive stream. `Flux.first` is a bit like `select()` in the POSIX APIs in that it'll return the first thing to produce a value. `Flux.first()` goes one step further and applies backpressure to the remaining instances so that, if they haven't already finished their work, they will have the chance to abandon their work and avoid any further waste.

The algorithm is relatively straightforward, so I've put it all in an `ExchangeFilterFunction` that we can apply to any `WebClient`, and it'll handle it transparently for us. Given a URL of the form `http://error-service/ok`, the filter will select `maxNodes` instances as a subset of the total number of available instances and attempt to invoke all of them.

```
package rsb.orchestration.hedging;

import lombok.RequiredArgsConstructor;
import lombok.extern.log4j.Log4j2;
import org.springframework.cloud.client.ServiceInstance;
import org.springframework.cloud.client.discovery.ReactiveDiscoveryClient;
import org.springframework.web.reactive.function.client.ClientRequest;
import org.springframework.web.reactive.function.client.ClientResponse;
import org.springframework.web.reactive.function.client.ExchangeFilterFunction;
import org.springframework.web.reactive.function.client.ExchangeFunction;
import reactor.core.publisher.Flux;
import reactor.core.publisher.Mono;

import java.net.URI;
import java.time.Duration;
import java.util.ArrayList;
import java.util.Collections;
import java.util.List;

@Log4j2
@RequiredArgsConstructor
class HedgingExchangeFilterFunction implements ExchangeFilterFunction {

    private final ReactiveDiscoveryClient reactiveDiscoveryClient;

    private final int timeoutInSeconds = 10;
```

Chapter 10. Service Orchestration and Composition

```java
    private final int maxNodes;

    @Override
    public Mono<ClientResponse> filter(ClientRequest clientRequest,
            ExchangeFunction exchangeFunction) {
        var requestUrl = clientRequest.url();
        var apiName = requestUrl.getHost();
        return this.reactiveDiscoveryClient //
                .getInstances(apiName) ①
                .collectList()②
                .map(HedgingExchangeFilterFunction::shuffle)③
                .flatMapMany(Flux::fromIterable)④
                .take(maxNodes)⑤
                .map(si -> buildUriFromServiceInstance(si, requestUrl)) ⑥
                .map(uri -> invoke(uri, clientRequest, exchangeFunction)) ⑦
                .collectList() ⑧
                .flatMap(list -> Flux.first(list)
                        .timeout(Duration.ofSeconds(timeoutInSeconds))
.singleOrEmpty());⑨
    }

    private static Mono<ClientResponse> invoke(URI uri, ClientRequest request,
            ExchangeFunction next) {
        var newRequest = ClientRequest//
                .create(request.method(), uri) //
                .headers(h -> h.addAll(request.headers()))//
                .cookies(c -> c.addAll(request.cookies()))//
                .attributes(a -> a.putAll(request.attributes()))//
                .body(request.body())//
                .build();
        return next//
                .exchange(newRequest)//
                .doOnNext(cr -> log.info("launching " + newRequest.url()));
    }

    private static <T> List<T> shuffle(List<T> tList) {
        var newArrayList = new ArrayList<T>(tList);
        Collections.shuffle(newArrayList);
        return newArrayList;
    }

    private static URI buildUriFromServiceInstance(ServiceInstance server,
            URI originalRequestUrl) {
        return URI.create(originalRequestUrl.getScheme() + "://" + server
.getHost() + ':'
```

```
                    + server.getPort() + originalRequestUrl.getPath());
   }
}
```

① Find all the service instances using the `ReactiveDiscoveryClient` abstraction implementation that talks to the Eureka service registry

② Assemble all the `ServiceInstance`'s into a `List<ServiceInstance>`...

③ which we can then randomly shuffle to avoid dogpiling on to any one particular instance...

④ Turn the list of service instances back into a reactive stream of `ServiceInstances`...

⑤ Preserving only the first `maxNodes` of the total instances...

⑥ `buildUriFromServiceInstance` turns a ServiceInstance and the original URI into a resolved URI, with an actual hostname or IP for the host.

⑦ And with that resolved URI, we're able to transform the `ClientRequest` in the filter chain into a new `ClientRequest` that has the resolved host and then continue the reactive chain of execution until all the filters have completed, ultimately returning a `Mono<ClientResponse>`.

⑧ By this point, we have a `Flux<Mono<ClientResponse>>`, where what we want is a `List<Mono<ClientResponse>>`, so we use `collectList()` to obtain a list.

⑨ We can then give the list to the `Flux.first` The operator will launch all of the reactive streams and apply backpressure to all but the fastest to respond.

To demonstrate this hedging feature in action, you should launch a few instances of the `slow-service`. I like to launch two instances of the `slow-service` configured to run with a delay so that they don't produce a response for ten seconds. I then launch one with the default delay of zero seconds. You can use the following shell script to launch a slow instance of the service on a UNIX-like environment with Bash. Change the environment variable `RSB_SLOW_SERVICE_DELAY` to be 0 to get a fast service instance.

Chapter 10. Service Orchestration and Composition

```bash
#!/usr/bin/env bash
export RSB_SLOW_SERVICE_DELAY=10
cd `dirname $0` && mvn spring-boot:run
```

After you've launched, let's say, two slow instances and one fast instance, you can then configure a `WebClient` to use the new filter when invoking the service.

```java
package rsb.orchestration.hedging;

import lombok.extern.log4j.Log4j2;
import org.springframework.beans.factory.annotation.Value;
import org.springframework.boot.SpringApplication;
import org.springframework.boot.autoconfigure.SpringBootApplication;
import org.springframework.boot.context.event.ApplicationReadyEvent;
import org.springframework.cloud.client.discovery.ReactiveDiscoveryClient;
import org.springframework.context.ApplicationListener;
import org.springframework.context.annotation.Bean;
import org.springframework.web.reactive.function.client.WebClient;
import rsb.orchestration.GreetingResponse;

@Log4j2
@SpringBootApplication
public class HedgingApplication {

    ①
    @Bean
    HedgingExchangeFilterFunction hedgingExchangeFilterFunction(
            @Value("${rsb.lb.max-nodes:3}") int maxNodes,
ReactiveDiscoveryClient rdc) {
        return new HedgingExchangeFilterFunction(rdc, maxNodes);
    }

    ②
    @Bean
    WebClient client(WebClient.Builder builder,
            HedgingExchangeFilterFunction hedgingExchangeFilterFunction) {
        return builder.filter(hedgingExchangeFilterFunction).build();
    }

    ③
    @Bean
    ApplicationListener<ApplicationReadyEvent> hedgingApplicationListener(
            WebClient client) {
```

441

```
        return event -> client//
                .get()//
                .uri("http://slow-service/greetings")//
                .retrieve()//
                .bodyToFlux(GreetingResponse.class)//
                .doOnNext(log::info)//
                .doOnError(ex -> log.info(ex.toString()))//
                .subscribe();
    }

    public static void main(String[] args) {
        SpringApplication.run(HedgingApplication.class, args);
    }
}
```

① We'll need a configured instance of our `HedgingExchangeFilterFunction`. I've set a default value of three for the `maxNodes` property here.

② The customization here is similar to what we've been doing for most of the chapter so far using the load balancing `ExchangeFilterFunction`.

③ The use of the `WebClient` looks identical to every other use of it we've seen thus far.

In this example, we customized the sole `WebClient` in the application. Recall what we said earlier: there are some situations where you will *not* want to use hedging, such as when charging the customer credit card. Therefore, it might be useful to create your own custom Spring qualifier annotations here so that the use-cases that demand the hedging `WebClient` can use that one, and every other use case will get the load-balanced instance. I'll leave that as a (trivial) exercise for you, dear reader.

10.7. Reactive Scatter/Gather

One of the most apparent wins when using reactive APIs is when handling scatter/gather composition kinds of tasks. Scatter / gather work describes "scattering" requests (launching many concurrent requests) and "gathering" the results when they all return, usually in a way as to orchestrate lots of results. Scattering work implies concurrency, which complicates the task of gathering. In a non-reactive world, things like the

`ForkJoinPool` [https://docs.oracle.com/javase/8/docs/api/java/util/concurrent/ForkJoinPool.html], `CyclicBarrier` [https://docs.oracle.com/javase/7/docs/api/java/util/concurrent/CyclicBarrier.html] or the `CountDownLatch` [https://docs.oracle.com/javase/7/docs/api/java/util/concurrent/CountDownLatch.html] quickly become your best friends. Indeed, launching work and gathering results is such an everyday use case that there are accommodations for it all sorts of applications. If you're using Spring Integration, in an enterprise application integration context, you might use a splitter and aggregator to achieve this in an application integration flow. If you're using Spring Batch, you can achieve this with remote chunking or a thread pool configured on a `Step`. If you're using a workflow engine or business process management engine like Flowable [https://flowable.com/], then you'll find that BPMN provides explicit support for parallel gateways that eventually join up. But all of those require a lot more extra work than what we're trying to do, so let's get into it.

A long time ago, in a galaxy far away, I worked at an organization with a very sophisticated framework built on top of Spring MVC that supported this notion of "pods." Pods required their configuration. They isolated fragments of a page into little zones, each of which could have tributary dependencies. So, imagine the product search page for a typical e-commerce engine. You enter a search query, and all the results for your query show up. But alongside those results, the e-commerce engine will no doubt inundate you with related searches, and perhaps personalized information about the products, and product reviews about individual items when you mouseover, and perhaps details related to each product. It might also show you who of your friends on Facebook also purchased a given item. Some of this data is embarrassingly parallel - that is, you can quickly obtain other data at the same time; there is no dependency on one piece of data to obtain the other. Other data imply an ordering - one thing must be loaded into memory before another thing. Reactive programming gives us a natural idiom to express this exact kind of data flow logic.

Let us look at an example that loads all the `Customer` records from the `customer-service` given some customer IDs. Then, for each customer, we'll load the associated profile and the associated orders and emits a new aggregate, `CustomerOrders`, for each aggregation of a `Customer`, a `Profile`, and all the `Order`s.

```java
package rsb.orchestration.scattergather;

import lombok.Data;
import lombok.RequiredArgsConstructor;
import rsb.orchestration.Customer;
import rsb.orchestration.Order;
import rsb.orchestration.Profile;

import java.util.Collection;

@Data
@RequiredArgsConstructor
class CustomerOrders {

    private final Customer customer;

    private final Collection<Order> orders;

    private final Profile profile;

}
```

I've built a `CrmClient`, which handles the boilerplate work of issuing HTTP requests to the appropriate HTTP endpoints.

Chapter 10. Service Orchestration and Composition

```java
package rsb.orchestration.scattergather;

import lombok.RequiredArgsConstructor;
import org.springframework.stereotype.Component;
import org.springframework.util.StringUtils;
import org.springframework.web.reactive.function.client.WebClient;
import reactor.core.publisher.Flux;
import reactor.core.publisher.Mono;
import rsb.orchestration.Customer;
import rsb.orchestration.Order;
import rsb.orchestration.Profile;

@Component
@RequiredArgsConstructor
class CrmClient {

    private final WebClient http;

    ①
    Flux<Customer> getCustomers(Integer[] ids) {
        var customersRoot = "http://customer-service/customers?ids="
                + StringUtils.arrayToDelimitedString(ids, ",");
        return http.get().uri(customersRoot).retrieve().bodyToFlux(Customer
.class);
    }

    ②
    Flux<Order> getOrders(Integer[] ids) {
        var ordersRoot = "http://order-service/orders?ids="
                + StringUtils.arrayToDelimitedString(ids, ",");
        return http.get().uri(ordersRoot).retrieve().bodyToFlux(Order.class);
    }

    ③
    Mono<Profile> getProfile(Integer customerId) {
        var profilesRoot = "http://profile-service/profiles/{id}";
        return http.get().uri(profilesRoot, customerId).retrieve()
                .bodyToMono(Profile.class);
    }

}
```

① the getCustomers method returns all the Customer objects that match a given reange of ID values

② the `getOrders` method returns all the orders that belong to any of the customer IDs specified as parameters to the `getOrders` method

③ the `getProfile` method returns a `Profile` given a single customer ID.

What's interesting is that some of these methods return results for multiple aggregates. For example, the `getOrders` method returns all the `Orders` belonging to all of the `Customer` whose IDs are specified as a parameter. The `getCustomers` method return all `Customer` instances whose ID matches any of those specified as a parameter. Many datastores accommodate these kinds of queries. In SQL, it could be as simple as: `select * from orders where customer_fk IN ( ⋯ ).` Take advantage of this approach, whenever possible, to avoid needless extra queries and network roundtrips.

The `getProfile` method returns a single `Profile`, which is unfortunate because it means that we're stuck with the N+1 problem: for each of the `Customer` records, we must make a network request. We see this kind of worst-case performance characteristic in the context of ORMs where, for each aggregate, some number of dependent records need to be retrieved. This pattern is wasteful for two reasons: it takes longer, because typically the ORM serially visits each record, prolonging the response in a manner proportionate to the number of records to return. It's also wasteful of network resources because each record requires a network roundtrip to the database. In our example, we'll see that if we want to render 100 `Customer` records, we'll need to make 100 distinct calls to the `getProfile` method. This is unfortunate, but here too, reactive programming helps us out considerably. We can use the reactive `WebClient` to launch 100 requests at the same time. Yes, this is still wasteful of network resources, but it should be much faster than launching 100 network requests serially. And, of course, if the services to which you're making those 100 requests are reactive, then they should be much better prepared to withstand the deluge of demand!

Let's now turn to how we can compose the streams returned from each of those methods in a single application.

```
package rsb.orchestration.scattergather;

import lombok.RequiredArgsConstructor;
```

Chapter 10. Service Orchestration and Composition

```java
import lombok.extern.log4j.Log4j2;
import org.springframework.boot.context.event.ApplicationReadyEvent;
import org.springframework.context.ApplicationListener;
import org.springframework.stereotype.Component;
import reactor.core.publisher.Flux;
import reactor.core.publisher.Mono;
import rsb.orchestration.Customer;
import rsb.orchestration.Order;
import rsb.orchestration.Profile;
import rsb.orchestration.TimerUtils;

import java.util.List;

@Log4j2
@RequiredArgsConstructor
@Component
class ScatterGather implements ApplicationListener<ApplicationReadyEvent> {

    private final CrmClient client;

    @Override
    public void onApplicationEvent(ApplicationReadyEvent event) {
        var ids = new Integer[] { 1, 2, 7, 5 }; ①
        ②
        Flux<Customer> customerFlux = TimerUtils.cache(client.getCustomers(ids));
        Flux<Order> ordersFlux = TimerUtils.cache(client.getOrders(ids));
        Flux<CustomerOrders> customerOrdersFlux = customerFlux//
                .flatMap(customer -> { ③

                    ④
                    Mono<List<Order>> filteredOrdersFlux = ordersFlux //
                            .filter(o -> o.getCustomerId().equals(customer.getId()))//
                            .collectList();

                    ⑤
                    Mono<Profile> profileMono = client.getProfile(customer.getId());

                    ⑥
                    Mono<Customer> customerMono = Mono.just(customer);

                    ⑦
                    return Flux.zip(customerMono, filteredOrdersFlux, profileMono);
                })⑧
```

447

```
                .map(tuple -> new CustomerOrders(tuple.getT1(), tuple.getT2(
),
                        tuple.getT3()));

    for (var i = 0; i < 5; i++) ⑨
        run(customerOrdersFlux);
  }

  private void run(Flux<CustomerOrders> customerOrdersFlux) {
      TimerUtils //
              .monitor(customerOrdersFlux)//
              .subscribe(customerOrder -> {
                  log.info("--------------");
                  log.info(customerOrder.getCustomer());
                  log.info(customerOrder.getProfile());
                  customerOrder.getOrders().forEach(order -> log
                          .info(customerOrder.getCustomer().getId() + ": "
 + order));
              });
  }

}
```

① I've got a list of `Customer` records we'll want to investigate

② I'm using the `TimerUtils.cache` method to memoize the returned values from the reactive stream, so that the results are not sourced again

③ Given a `Customer`...

④ Find all the orders in the returned stream of orders whose `customerId` attribute matches this particular customer's ID and materializes them into a `Mono<List<Order>>`. The list hasn't been resolved yet, but we will expect it to be when we need it, shortly.

⑤ Load each individual `Profile`..

⑥ Let's wrap the `customer` into a reactive stream so that we then have three `Publisher<T>`: a `Mono<Customer>`, a `Mono<Profile>`, and a `Flux<Order>`. These represent three asynchronous things.

⑦ We will use the `zip` operator to await the resolution of all three asynchronous things and then produce a `Flux<Tuple3<T1,T2,T3>>`. The `zip` operator has overloaded methods for one, two, three… up to eight individual elements. You'll get a `Tuple1`, `Tuple2`, `Tuple3`, etc. You can work with more than eight reactive streams if you want, but you won't get the type of safety and parameter genericization that you see in these first eight special case classes.

⑧ This line is where it all comes together: we're given a `Tuple3<Customer, Collection<Order>, Profile>` and can then unpack each of the constituent values to create a new `CustomerOrders` record.

⑨ The program's first run will be slower than subsequent runs, which benefit from caching.

Not bad, eh? Not a single `Executor`, `Thread`, `CountDownLatch` in sight! You can use Reactor operators like `zip`, `cache`, and `flatMap` to make short work of all sorts of composition work. We also looked at some API design strategies to make this kind of scatter/gather work easier.

10.8. API Gateways with Spring Cloud Gateway

An API gateway sits between clients and services. It can act as a reverse proxy, routing requests from clients to services. It's ideally positioned to perform cross-cutting tasks like authentication, routing, payload and protocol transformation, rate limiting, and redirects. API gateways act as intermediaries between the clients and backend services. They're in a natural place to provide composed views of disparate backend services using some of the techniques we've looked at in this chapter. API gateways are also a great place to centralize things like authentication and routing. API gateways can translate backend protocols, like RSocket, and adapt them to client-friendly protocols like HTTP or WebSockets. They also reduce the surface area for attack, insulating backend services in the same way that a facade insulates private implementation details in object-oriented programming.

Spring Cloud Gateway is a purpose-built framework for building API gateways and is built on top of Spring Webflux. It's reactive at its core. The reactive nature of Spring Cloud Gateway is one of its strengths: it can consume arbitrary downstream services and stream the results back with better scalability and efficiency.

You'll need to add the following dependencies for this section:

- `org.springframework.cloud` : `spring-cloud-starter-gateway`
- `org.springframework.boot` : `spring-boot-starter-data-redis-reactive`
- `org.springframework.boot` : `spring-boot-starter-security`

Also, we'll want to disable the autoconfiguration that configures the classic Netflix Ribbon load balancer. Make sure to add the following to your `application.properties`:

```
spring.cloud.loadbalancer.ribbon.enabled=false
```

There are many ways to use Spring Cloud Gateway. It is, in my view, a unique piece of code in the Spring ecosystem. It can be used equally as infrastructure, configurable almost entirely with YAML and property files, or through the Java DSL, as a library that you consume like any other library in a Java application. We'll start with the Java DSL because I find it makes the concepts more straightforward.

As we review these examples, note the `@Profile` annotation on the respective examples as you'll need to activate that profile to run the example.

10.8.1. A Microproxy

The most straightforward use of Spring Cloud Gateway is just to set up a proxy. Simple. Nothing fancy here. A request comes in, and it is forwarded otherwise unadulterated to some other endpoint. Run this example and visit the application on localhost at whatever port appears in the logs. You'll see the Spring homepage! Everything. CSS. Images. JavaScript. It's all there. You can even start clicking around, and everything should work if the link is on the same domain. Content on subdomains will cause issues, of course.

Chapter 10. Service Orchestration and Composition

```java
package rsb.orchestration.gateway;

import org.springframework.cloud.gateway.route.RouteLocator;
import org.springframework.cloud.gateway.route.builder.RouteLocatorBuilder;
import org.springframework.context.annotation.Bean;
import org.springframework.context.annotation.Configuration;
import org.springframework.context.annotation.Profile;

@Configuration
@Profile("routes-simple")
class SimpleProxyRouteConfiguration {

    @Bean ①
    RouteLocator gateway(RouteLocatorBuilder rlb) {
        return rlb //
                .routes()//
                .route(routeSpec -> routeSpec ②
                        .alwaysTrue() ③
                        .uri("https://spring.io") ④
                ) //
                .build();
    }

}
```

① A Spring Cloud Gateway application is at its heart a bean of type `RouteLocator`. `RouteLocator` is a *very* simple interface with one method, `getRoutes()`. You'll need the `RouteLocatorBuilder` to build routes.

② In Spring Cloud Gateway, a route describes a request into the system, the optional filters that act on that request (not shown), and the destination URI. In this example, we've only got one route.

③ We're using the `alwaysTrue()` predicate to match any incoming request...

④ and forward that request to a downstream URI, `https://spring.io`.

Tada! A very simple proxy. Not bad, eh?

There are dozens of useful predicates that you can use to match incoming requests. You can match on cookies, request parameters, whether a request was before or after a specific time, hostnames, the contents of the request's path, and so much more. If none of the built-in predicates do the trick, then you can plug in your custom predicate.

This was a pretty trivial example, but it should highlight what's possible. The proxy does nothing to the request, leaving it utterly unchanged save for the host and port. The site we're proxying in a way that it uses relative URLs for images and CSS, so just about everything in the proxied version of the site comes through just fine and quickly.

10.8.2. Predicates

A Spring Cloud Gateway route matches incoming requests. There are a ton of built-in predicates that can be used to match incoming requests.

Chapter 10. Service Orchestration and Composition

```java
package rsb.orchestration.gateway;

import org.springframework.cloud.gateway.route.RouteLocator;
import org.springframework.cloud.gateway.route.builder.RouteLocatorBuilder;
import org.springframework.context.annotation.Bean;
import org.springframework.context.annotation.Configuration;
import org.springframework.context.annotation.Profile;
import reactor.core.publisher.Mono;

@Configuration
@Profile("predicates")
class PredicateConfiguration {

    @Bean
    RouteLocator predicatesGateway(RouteLocatorBuilder rlb) {
        return rlb //
                .routes() //
                .route(routeSpec -> routeSpec //
                        .path("/")①
                        .uri("http://httpbin.org/") //
                ) //
                .route(routeSpec -> routeSpec //
                        .header("X-RSB")②
                        .uri("http://httpbin.org/") //
                ) //
                .route(routeSpec -> routeSpec //
                        .query("uid")③
                        .uri("http://httpbin.org/") //
                ) //
                .route(routeSpec -> routeSpec ④
                        .asyncPredicate(
                                serverWebExchange -> Mono.just(Math.random() > .5))
                        .and().path("/test").uri("http://httpbin.org/") //
                ) //
                .build();
    }

}
```

① Match on whether the incoming request's path matches a certain pattern...

② Match on whether the incoming request has a particular header...

③ Match on whether the incoming request has a query parameter (?uid=···

) present...

④ If none of the pre-provided predicates work, you can combine them using `and()` or `or()` and you can provide your own `AsyncPredicate` instances. In this example, I match if a request has a path of `/test` and, arbitrarily, by testing whether a random number is greater than 0.5.

10.8.3. Filters

In this case, we proxied everything after the root, `/`, to `https://spring.io`, the root of the spring.io site. But suppose we wanted to proxy requests to a custom path on localhost to a custom downstream path? We would need to transform the incoming request path into one suitable for the downstream HTTP endpoint.

Here, Spring Cloud Gateway filters come into their own. Let's look at another example.

Chapter 10. Service Orchestration and Composition

```java
package rsb.orchestration.gateway;

import lombok.extern.log4j.Log4j2;
import org.springframework.cloud.gateway.route.RouteLocator;
import org.springframework.cloud.gateway.route.builder.RouteLocatorBuilder;
import org.springframework.context.annotation.Bean;
import org.springframework.context.annotation.Configuration;
import org.springframework.context.annotation.Profile;

@Log4j2
@Configuration
@Profile("routes-filter-simple")
class SimpleProxyFilterRouteConfiguration {

    @Bean
    RouteLocator gateway(RouteLocatorBuilder rlb) {
        return rlb //
                .routes()//
                .route(routeSpec -> routeSpec //
                        .path("/http") ①
                        .filters(fs -> fs.setPath("/forms/post"))
                        .uri("http://httpbin.org") //
                ) //

                .build();
    }

}
```

① This example matches all incoming requests to http://localhost:8080/http and transforms the path - everything after the port - to be /forms/post. The result is a request destined for http://httpbin.org/forms/post. The example is pretty trivial, and there was no dynamic URL. If we had some dynamic behavior to rewrite, we could've used the rewritePath operator to rewrite the URL using regular expressions.

Once you've matched an incoming request, you can process it before sending it off to a downstream destination using filters like the setPath filter we just examined. There are a ton of pre-provided filters, but you can also plugin your own.

```java
package rsb.orchestration.gateway;
```

```
import lombok.extern.log4j.Log4j2;
import org.springframework.cloud.gateway.route.RouteLocator;
import org.springframework.cloud.gateway.route.builder.RouteLocatorBuilder;
import org.springframework.context.annotation.Bean;
import org.springframework.context.annotation.Configuration;
import org.springframework.context.annotation.Profile;
import org.springframework.http.HttpHeaders;

import java.util.HashSet;
import java.util.Set;
import java.util.UUID;

@Log4j2
@Profile("routes-filters")
@Configuration
class FilterConfiguration {

    @Bean
    RouteLocator gateway(RouteLocatorBuilder rlb) {
        return rlb.routes() ///
                .route(routeSpec -> routeSpec//
                        .path("/")//
                        .filters(fs -> fs//
                                .setPath("/forms/post")①
                                .retry(10) ②
                                .addRequestParameter("uid", UUID.randomUUID().toString())③
                                .addResponseHeader(
                                        HttpHeaders.ACCESS_CONTROL_ALLOW_ORIGIN, "*")④
                                .filter((exchange, chain) -> { ⑤
                                    var uri = exchange.getRequest().getURI();//
                                    return chain.filter(exchange) //
                                            .doOnSubscribe(
                                                    sub -> log.info("before: " + uri))
                                            .doOnEach(signal -> log
                                                    .info("processing: " + uri))
                                            .doOnTerminate(() -> log.info(
                                                    "after: " + uri
                                                            + ". "
                                                            + "The response status code was "
                                                            + exchange.getResponse()
```

Chapter 10. Service Orchestration and Composition

```
                                            .getStatusCode()
                                    + '.'));
                    })//
                )//
                .uri("http://httpbin.org"))//
            .build();
    }
}
```

① the setPath filter replaces the incoming URI path with the one you specify

② Another retry! This just goes to show you that if at first, you don't succeed, retry(), retry(), retry()! And yes, I'm just as impressed as you are with the many wondrous ways to retry a request reactively.

③ The addRequestParameter operator adds a request parameter - ?uid=…. - to the outgoing request

④ The addResponseHeader operator adds a request header to the outgoing request. This is a natural thing to want to do in a security context, or even for more commonplace things like making a service accessible to JavaScript clients with cross-origin request scripting.

⑤ And if none of the pre-provided filters suit you, then it's trivial to contribute a GatewayFilter, whose signature ought to look familiar: it's identical to the WebFilter in Spring Webflux

One of my all-time favorite filters is the RateLimiter. Yes, *another* rate limiter! This rate limiter is incredibly convenient because it gives us more control over the granularity of the rate-limiting. When we looked at rate-limiting with Resilience4J, we limited how many requests a client to a downstream service could make. With Spring Cloud Gateway, we can limit how many requests ever get through to a downstream service in a single place. We can store the current count and quote in a Redis service, which means that all Spring Cloud Gateway nodes will see the same count. There is no risk that you'll overwhelm the downstream service should you choose to add more Spring Cloud Gateway nodes to the ensemble; doing so will not suddenly multiply the requests permitted downstream.

```java
package rsb.orchestration.gateway;

import org.springframework.cloud.gateway.filter.ratelimit.PrincipalNameKeyResolver;
import org.springframework.cloud.gateway.filter.ratelimit.RedisRateLimiter;
import org.springframework.cloud.gateway.route.RouteLocator;
import org.springframework.cloud.gateway.route.builder.RouteLocatorBuilder;
import org.springframework.context.annotation.Bean;
import org.springframework.context.annotation.Configuration;
import org.springframework.context.annotation.Profile;

@Profile("rl")
@Configuration
class RateLimiterConfiguration {

    @Bean
    RedisRateLimiter redisRateLimiter() {
        return new RedisRateLimiter(5, 7);
    }

    @Bean
    RouteLocator gateway(RouteLocatorBuilder rlb) {
        return rlb //
                .routes() //
                .route(routeSpec -> routeSpec //
                        .path("/") //
                        .filters(fs -> fs //
                                .setPath("/ok") //
                                .requestRateLimiter(rl -> rl //
                                        .setRateLimiter(redisRateLimiter())
                                        ① 
                                        .setKeyResolver(new PrincipalNameKeyResolver())  ②
                                )) //
                        .uri("lb://error-service")) //
                .build();
    }
}
```

① The rate limiter requires an implementation to handle the work of rate-limiting. The `RedisRateLimiter` instance is here configured to handle five requests per second, potentially bursting to seven requests as a second. These are very indulgent numbers! Bad for production, but great for a demo. Feel free to turn them way up after you've determined which numbers work best for your environment.

② Given that Redis is a key/value store, the `RateLimiter` needs a strategy to determine which key should manage the atomic number reflecting traffic into the application per second. If there's only one key, then that means that all users will share that same five requests per second. Spring Cloud Gateway will reject any requests beyond that. We're using a little more dynamic strategy: we're divining a key based on the current authenticated `Principal` object.

This example was straightforward with the only possible exception being the involvment of the `java.security.Principal` and Spring Security. But still, it's not *that* bad!

```
package rsb.orchestration.gateway;

import org.springframework.context.annotation.Bean;
import org.springframework.context.annotation.Configuration;
import org.springframework.security.config.Customizer;
import org.springframework.security.config.web.server.ServerHttpSecurity;
import
org.springframework.security.core.userdetails.MapReactiveUserDetailsService;
import org.springframework.security.core.userdetails.User;
import org.springframework.security.web.server.SecurityWebFilterChain;

@Configuration
class SecurityConfiguration {

    @Bean
    SecurityWebFilterChain authorization(ServerHttpSecurity http) {
        return http //
                .httpBasic(c -> Customizer.withDefaults()) //
                .csrf(ServerHttpSecurity.CsrfSpec::disable) //
                .authorizeExchange(ae -> ae //
                        .pathMatchers("/rl").authenticated() ①
                        .anyExchange().permitAll()) //
                .build();
    }

    @Bean
    MapReactiveUserDetailsService authentication() {
        return new MapReactiveUserDetailsService(User
.withDefaultPasswordEncoder()
                .username("jlong").password("pw").roles("USER").build());
    }

}
```

① We want to ensure that the /rl endpoint (exposed by Spring Cloud Gateway) is authenticated. Everything else is left wide open.

Now, if a client attempts a request to this endpoint that is unauthenticated or that exceeds the per-second budget the rate limiter will enforce, then the request will be rejected.

10.8.4. Discovery and Routing

Thus far, every downstream URI has been on the public internet. It's far

Chapter 10. Service Orchestration and Composition

more likely that you'll use Spring Cloud Gateway to front other microservices in your organization. Spring Cloud Gateway can proxy requests to HTTP and WebSocket endpoints. Spring Cloud Gateway also supports a custom URI scheme - `lb://`. URIs that start with this scheme are load-balanced. So, `lb://error-service` would end up as a client-side load-balanced HTTP request using the Spring Cloud Load Balancer.

```
package rsb.orchestration.gateway;

import org.springframework.cloud.gateway.route.RouteLocator;
import org.springframework.cloud.gateway.route.builder.RouteLocatorBuilder;
import org.springframework.context.annotation.Bean;
import org.springframework.context.annotation.Configuration;
import org.springframework.context.annotation.Profile;

@Configuration
@Profile("routes-lb")
class LoadbalancingProxyRouteConfiguration {

    @Bean
    RouteLocator gateway(RouteLocatorBuilder rlb) {
        return rlb //
                .routes()//
                .route(rs -> rs //
                        .alwaysTrue().uri("lb://error-service") //
                )//
                .build();
    }

}
```

Don't want to do all the work yourself? You can have Spring Cloud Gateway automatically setup routes for all services registered in the service registry. Add the following properties to your `application.properties`:

```
spring.cloud.gateway.discovery.locator.enabled=true
spring.cloud.gateway.discovery.locator.lower-case-service-id=true
```

Now, you should be able to go to `http://localhost:8080/error-service/ok`, and you should get a response, just as if you went directly to the host and port on which the `error-service` was running and then went to the `/ok` path.

10.8.5. Events

Spring Cloud Gateway pays close attention to whenever anything might cause the routes to become invalid. What if a service instance disappears from the registry? What if a route in Spring Cloud Gateway has changed? Spring Cloud Gateway will notify you of any changes to its working set of routes if you listen for the `RefreshRoutesResultEvent`.

Chapter 10. Service Orchestration and Composition

```java
package rsb.orchestration.gateway;

import lombok.extern.log4j.Log4j2;
import org.springframework.cloud.gateway.event.RefreshRoutesEvent;
import org.springframework.cloud.gateway.event.RefreshRoutesResultEvent;
import org.springframework.cloud.gateway.route.CachingRouteLocator;
import org.springframework.cloud.gateway.route.Route;
import org.springframework.cloud.gateway.route.RouteLocator;
import org.springframework.cloud.gateway.route.builder.RouteLocatorBuilder;
import org.springframework.context.annotation.Bean;
import org.springframework.context.annotation.Configuration;
import org.springframework.context.annotation.Profile;
import org.springframework.context.event.EventListener;
import org.springframework.util.Assert;
import reactor.core.publisher.Flux;

@Log4j2
@Profile("events")
@Configuration
class EventsConfiguration {

    @EventListener
    public void refreshRoutesResultEvent(RefreshRoutesResultEvent rre) {
        log.info(rre.getClass().getSimpleName());
        Assert.state(rre.getSource() instanceof CachingRouteLocator);
        CachingRouteLocator source = (CachingRouteLocator) rre.getSource();
        Flux<Route> routes = source.getRoutes();
        routes.subscribe(route -> log.info(route.getClass() + ":"
                + route.getMetadata().toString() + ":" + route.getFilters())
);
    }

    @Bean
    RouteLocator gateway(RouteLocatorBuilder rlb) {
        return rlb //
                .routes() //
                .route(routeSpec -> routeSpec //
                        .path("/")//
                        .filters(fp -> fp.setPath("/guides")) //
                        .uri("http://spring.io") //
                ) //
                .build();
    }

}
```

Significantly, Spring Cloud Gateway routes *can* change after their initial construction.

10.8.6. Alternative Configuration

Thus far, we've used the `RouteLocatorBuilder` to build up our routes using Java code. But this is not the only way forward. Recall that the heart of Spring Cloud Gateway is `RouteLocator` beans. The `RouteLocator` definition is trivial:

```
package org.springframework.cloud.gateway.route;

import reactor.core.publisher.Flux;

public interface RouteLocator {

    Flux<Route> getRoutes();

}
```

As you can imagine, there's not a lot to build an implementation of this interface ourselves. Indeed, Spring Cloud Gateway makes it trivial!

Chapter 10. Service Orchestration and Composition

```java
package rsb.orchestration.gateway;

import org.springframework.cloud.gateway.filter.OrderedGatewayFilter;
import org.springframework.cloud.gateway.filter.factory.SetPathGatewayFilterFactory;
import org.springframework.cloud.gateway.route.Route;
import org.springframework.cloud.gateway.route.RouteLocator;
import org.springframework.context.annotation.Bean;
import org.springframework.context.annotation.Configuration;
import org.springframework.context.annotation.Profile;
import reactor.core.publisher.Flux;
import reactor.core.publisher.Mono;

@Profile("custom-route-locator")
@Configuration
class CustomRouteLocatorConfiguration {

    @Bean
    RouteLocator customRouteLocator(
            SetPathGatewayFilterFactory setPathGatewayFilterFactory) {①
        var setPathGatewayFilter = setPathGatewayFilterFactory
                .apply(config -> config.setTemplate("/guides")); ②
        var orderedGatewayFilter = new OrderedGatewayFilter
(setPathGatewayFilter, 0);③
        var singleRoute = Route④
                .async() //
                .id("spring-io-guides") //
                .asyncPredicate(serverWebExchange -> Mono.just(true)) //
                .filter(orderedGatewayFilter) //
                .uri("https://spring.io/") //
                .build();

        return () -> Flux.just(singleRoute);⑤
    }

}
```

① We'll need to take care of wiring up the filters ourselves. Fortunately, that's pretty easy. You need only inject instances of the filter's associated `GatewayFilterFactory` instance. In this case, we're going to configure the `setPath` filter, so we'll need the `SetPathGatewayFilterFactory`.

② The `GatewayFilterFactory` factories new instances of a given filter with the `apply` method.

③ Importantly, you'll need to wrap `GatewayFilterFactory` instances with `OrderedGatewayFilter`. The filters will *not* work unless you do this!

④ Then we can use the handy `Route` builder class to build an instance of the particular `Route` we want.

⑤ The easiest part is satisfying the `RouteLocator` contract; it's a functional interface, so this is an absolute breeze!

Run this, and it will work just as anything you would've done with the `RouteLocatorBuilder` would've. This ability to easily create custom `RouteLocator` beans opens a lot of possibilities. Who's to say the information that drives these particular routes cant come from a database or some configuration file?

Indeed, it's widespread and sometimes expected that the configuration comes from a config file. Spring Cloud Gateway supports most filters through the property-based or YML-based configuration format, as well.

`application-gateway.yml`. *You'll need to enable the* `gateway` *profile to load these profile-specific configuration values.*

```
spring:
  application:
    name: gateway
  cloud:
    gateway:
      routes:
        - id: guides
          uri: https://spring.io
          predicates:
            - After=2020-09-02T00:00:00.000-00:00[America/Denver]
```

Another distinct and useful possibility is that you could version control that configuration and then connect our client applications to the configuration through the Spring Cloud Config Server. We could take it a step further and change that configuration in the version control system, and force the clients to *refresh* their working view of the routes. And that would, of course, trigger the `ApplicationEvent` types that we saw earlier, which would give us a dynamic, reconfigurable routing infrastructure. The possibilities are endless! I've covered the Spring Cloud Configuration Server in my earlier book *Cloud Native Java*, which looks at microservices and microservice-adjacent use cases.

10.9. Next Steps

In this chapter, we've reviewed a *ton* of useful applications of reactive programming when orchestrating other services. It's fair to say that most of this book is about building services. In this chapter, we looked at the capabilities that reactive programming brings to the table when building clients for those services.

Reactive Spring

Chapter 11. Action!

The book is done (for now) but there's still more to learn and do! In this section I'll provide a few things you want to bookmark or buy.

11.1. Websites to Bookmark

You should bookmark the following locations for your own reference and edication for later.

- the website for this book, ReactiveSpring.io [http://ReactiveSpring.io]
- the Spring blog [http://spring.io/blog]
- the Spring Initializr [http://start.Spring.io]
- If you want to follow me on my little adventures, please check out my Twitter account (@starbuxman) [http://twitter.com/starbuxman], the book's Twitter account (@ReactiveSpring) [http://twitter.com/ReactiveSpring] and my blog [http://joshlong.com].

11.2. Additional reading

Want to learn more and take the next steps? Check out the following resources.

- the Spring guides [http://spring.io/guides]
- I love Spring ninja and all around awesome guy Greg Turnquist's *Learning Spring Boot* [https://www.amazon.com/Learning-Spring-Boot-Greg-Turnquist-ebook/dp/B00QAMMHKS] (or, really, any of his books). This one in particular provides a great foundation for Spring Boot.
- Spring Boot in Action [https://www.manning.com/books/spring-boot-in-action]
- If you want a deeper dive into Spring Cloud and microservices, you might enjoy my last book, *Cloud Native Java* [http://cloudnativejava.io]

11.3. Next Steps

You've come this far. Take some time off, and then go build the next big thing.

About the Author

Josh Long (@starbuxman) [http://twitter.com/starbuxman] became the first Spring Developer Advocate when he joined the Spring team at VMware in 2010. Josh is a Kotlin Google Developer Expert, a Java Champion, author or co-author of six books (including O'Reilly's *Cloud Native Java: Designing Resilient Systems with Spring Boot, Spring Cloud, and Cloud Foundry* [http://CloudNativeJava.io]) and numerous best-selling video trainings [http://joshlong.com/livelessons.html] (including *Building Microservices with Spring Boot Livelessons* with Spring Boot co-founder Phil Webb), and an open-source contributor (Spring Boot, Spring Integration, Spring Cloud, Activiti, Vaadin, etc). He hosts the *Bootiful Podcast* [http://BootifulPodcast.fm] weekly and frequently releases *Spring Tips* videos on YouTube [http://bit.ly/spring-tips-playlist].

Josh is a contributor to the Reactive Foundation [https://www.reactive.foundation/] and a contributor to the *Reactive Principles* document.

When he's not writing books, writing code and speaking to audiences worldwide, Josh spends his days in sunny San Francisco, CA.

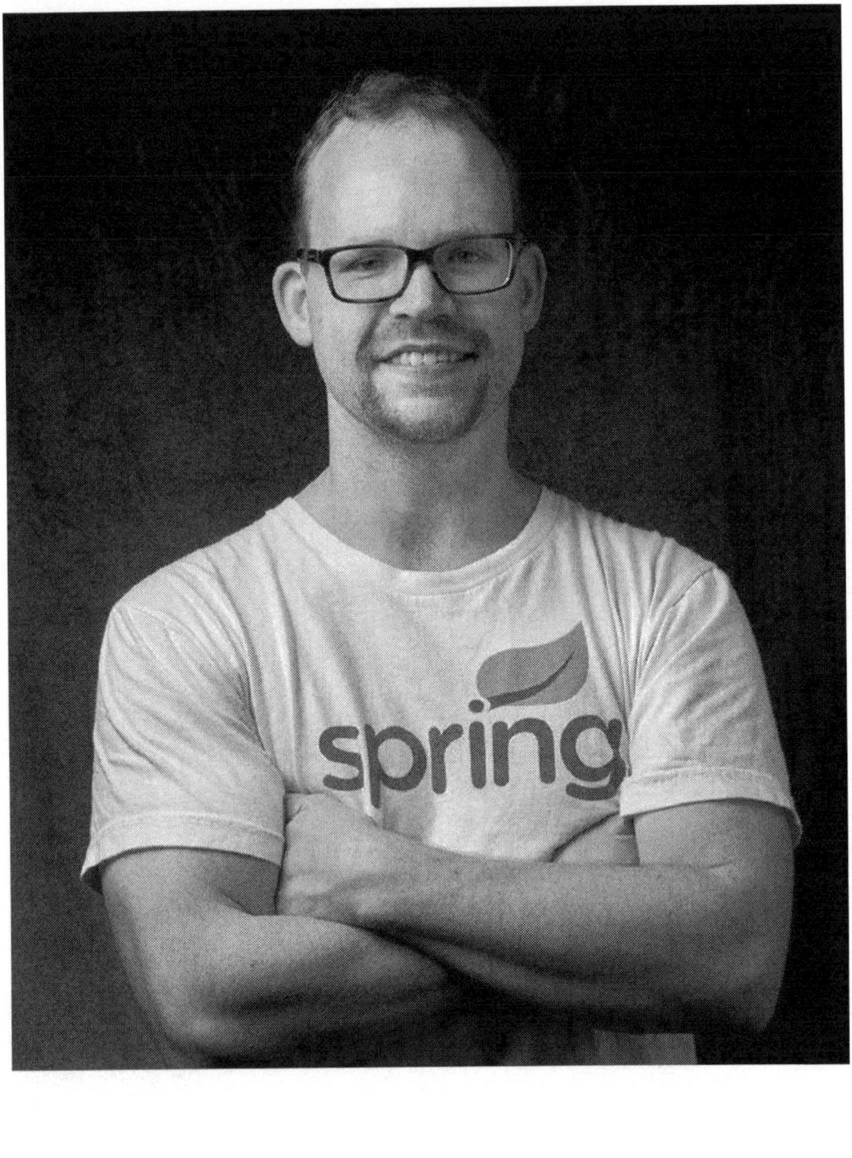
spring

Acknowledgements

Thank you, Spring team, for your constant feedback and help on various aspects of the book. Without their mentorship, I'd be lost. I joined the Spring team in 2010 and spend every waking day grateful for the opportunities they've given me.

Thank you, dear community, for the inspiration.

Thank you Dan Allen (@mojavelinux) [http://twitter.com/mojavelinux] and the Asciidoctor [https://asciidoctor.org] community for their tireless work on such an amazing technology.

Thank you, Richard Sumilang [https://www.richardsumilang.com/], for the amazing portrait photography. You did the absolute best with what you had to work with, and for that I couldn't be more grateful!

Thank you!

Reactive Spring

Colophon for *Reactive Spring*

Finally! A colophon for which I've got something to say.

When I was in school in the 1990s, I spent a lot of time at my school's computer labs using copies of a software program called Aldus PageMaker. PageMaker support "desktop publishing," the pagination and composition of text and images on the printed page. If you wanted to build magazines, newsletters, reports, small books, newspapers, etc., you'd use something like PageMaker. PageMaker was the first successful desktop publishing platform. It left an indelible mark on the publishing industry but soon gave way to QuarkXpress. QuarkXpress pioneered a frame-based layout system, where every element on a page has a bounding box. QuarkXPress eventually dominated the market. Adobe later acquired Aldus PageMaker. It stagnated as the team working on PageMaker developed what a program hailed in the press as a "Quark-killer:" Adobe InDesign.

Contemporaneously, starting in the 1980s, programs that were more geared towards long-document publishing emerged. Two pieces of software - Ventura Publisher and Frame Technology's Framemaker - most typified the day's long-document publishing tools. PageMaker, QuarkXpress, and InDesign optimized for design-heavy documents; FrameMaker and Ventura were better suited for long documents with tables of contents, indexes, tables, and formulae footnotes, etc.

Magazine? PageMaker, QuarkXpress or InDesign.

Science or mathematics textbooks? A physician's reference? Ventura Publisher or FrameMaker.

The dichotomy continued into the early 2000s when suddenly Adobe InDesign's memory and CPU requirements started paling compared to modern computers' available power. Suddenly, the most current and well-integrated of all the software started sprouting decent long-document publishing features. It had *almost* everything! Tables, table-of-contents, running footers and footnotes, inline figures, a built-in text editor, scriptability, and - through community plugins - support things like mathematical formulae.

Adobe InDesign was… *in!*

I've been using these tools, indeed even programming these tools, for *decades*! And here we are, at the end of what is my **sixth** book. Yet, I never controlled the design or pagination of the first five books. I was just an author and a member of a larger team. I wrote my first few books using Microsoft Word running inside a VMWare Virtual Machine hosted on my Ubuntu host, where I wrote code. It worked, but it was *agony*. The Word documents would occasionally become corrupt. I'd lose countless hours of work. Invariably, I would send what I wrote in Microsoft Word to the folks working on the book's layout where, once the text placed, it was, eh, *tedious* - if not impossible - to effect updates to it. This process *worked*, but it was painful. I sympathize with the folks downstream, doing the pagination, as I've been on that side of the workflow. I wasn't using Adobe InDesign.

Fast forward to 2015, when I started working on O'Reilly's *Pro Spring Boot*. I eventually added my buddy Kenny Bastani to the writing team and renamed that book to *Cloud Native Java*. We used their publishing suite based on Asciidoc (not Asciidoctor), Git, and more. It was not quite what we wanted. We had to resort to some horrific hacks to get certain things like includes and multiple git repositories, but if you lined things up *just right*, you could `git commit` and `git push` your way to an O'Reilly book! *Bravo*, O'Reilly. It's no wonder O'Reilly is a well-liked publisher among developers. The result looked great, and it worked consistently. And, I wasn't using Adobe InDesign.

I wanted something as convenient as what we used for *Cloud Native Java*, but with more flexibility to control the pipeline when writing this book. My friend Matt Raible (@mraible) [http://twitter.com/mraible] published a book with InfoQ, *The JHipster Book* [http://www.jhipster-book.com/] (which you should read!), and decided he wanted to get the book into as automated a pipeline as possible. He built an Asciidoctor-powered pipeline. Asciidoctor is an extension of Asciidoc. It's accessible to - with concise, easily version-controlled text files - author documents and books. It scales nicely. It goes far further than something like Markdown. Spring Boot co-founder and all-around fantastic person Phil Webb (@phillip_webb) does a great job enumerating some of its many features [https://twitter.com/phillip_webb/status/1282641330233962496].

Asciidoctor does not require anything more than a plain text editor. I used Git, Microsoft's Visual Studio Code, and IntelliJ IDEA for 99% of this book's production. Git all but eliminates the hassle of conflict resolution!

It's trivial to split Asciidoctor documents into multiple files. Code snippets may be included and run during the build. Macros can extend Asciidoctor's behavior. You may not need to: it already has built-in support for generating multiple output formats from one source. Asciidoctor makes it easy to centralize styling across the various projects, too. Asciidoctor is a vibrant ecosystem and integrates well with numerous build systems and languages, and it has terrific integrations for most editors and IDEs. It's so ubiquitous that you can even preview it on many different websites, like Github.

Asciidoctor is a fantastic breath of fresh air! I initially set out to use Matt's Asciidoctor build process, combined with a healthy dose of Rob Winch's Gradle-fu, and I got the basic build working for .PDF. My resulting build was fragile, a mashup of Bash scripts and Gradle. I liked the results but not the fragility and seeming irreproducibility of the whole thing. But it worked, and it was all automated. At the heart of it was Asciidoctor, an opensource set of tools for turning Asciidoctor markup into any number of output formats. The Asciidoctor ecosystem is enormous, and at the core of the community, few figure as prominently as Dan Allen (@mojavelinux) [http://twitter.com/mojavelinux]). Just search the forums and the docs, and you'll see; he is *everywhere*. He's a constant champion of Asciidoctor, having worked on it for what seems like at least a decade. He's generous with his time and runs a business dedicated to supporting the Asciidoctor community. I owe a lot to the Asciidoctor community and Dan in particular. I learned a little bit more about the Asciidoctor API (and again, thanks to Dan) and put together an open-source publication pipeline [https://github.com/reactive-spring-book/publication] based on it that powers this book's workflow. And, I am not using Adobe InDesign.

I've open-sourced it here: github.com/reactive-spring-book/publication. It's Apache 2 licensed, as all the code in this book is. Please feel free to use it, extend it, etc. A pipeline employs a sequence of `DocumentProducer`. Each `DocumentProducer` supports a different kind of output format. The pipeline supports `.PDF` (both a screen-ready and a prepress-ready version), `.EPUB`, `.MOBI`, and `.HTML`. It's all shipped as Spring Boot autoconfiguration with related configuration properties. I imagine that, once this book is out the door, I'll fork that module and turn it into something even more turnkey.

Printed in Great Britain
by Amazon